D0933912

Econometric Society Monographs No. 17

The Econometric Analysis of Transition Data

Econometric Society Monographs

Editors:

Avinash K. Dixit   *Princeton University*
Alain Monfort   *Institut National de la Statistique et des
    Etudes Economiques*

The Econometric Society is an international society for the
advancement of economic theory in relation to statistics
and mathematics. The Econometric Society Monograph
Series is designed to promote the publication of original
research contributions of high quality in mathematical
economics and theoretical and applied econometrics.

Other titles in the series:

Werner Hildenbrand, Editor   *Advances in economic theory*
Werner Hildenbrand, Editor   *Advances in econometrics*
G. S. Maddala   *Limited-dependent and qualitative
    variables in econometrics*
Gerard Debreu   *Mathematical economics*
Jean-Michel Grandmont   *Money and value*
Franklin M. Fisher   *Disequilibrium foundations of
    equilibrium economics*
Bezalel Peleg   *Game theoretic analysis of voting in
    committees*
Roger Bowden and Darrell Turkington   *Instrumental
    variables*
Andreu Mas-Colell   *The theory of general economic
    equilibrium*
James J. Heckman and Burton Singer   *Longitudinal
    analysis of labor market data*
Cheng Hsiao   *Analysis of panel data*
Truman F. Bewley, Editor   *Advances in economic theory
    – Fifth World Congress*
Truman F. Bewley, Editor   *Advances in econometrics –
    Fifth World Congress (Volume I)*
Truman F. Bewley, Editor   *Advances in econometrics –
    Fifth World Congress (Volume II)*
Hervé Moulin   *Axioms of cooperative decision making*
L. G. Godfrey   *Misspecification tests in econometrics*

The Econometric Analysis of Transition Data

TONY LANCASTER

Brown University

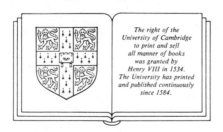

The right of the
University of Cambridge
to print and sell
all manner of books
was granted by
Henry VIII in 1534.
The University has printed
and published continuously
since 1584.

CAMBRIDGE UNIVERSITY PRESS

Cambridge
New York   Port Chester   Melbourne   Sydney

Published by the Press Syndicate of the University of Cambridge
The Pitt Building, Trumpington Street, Cambridge CB2 1RP
40 West 20th Street, New York, NY 10011, USA
10 Stamford Road, Oakleigh, Melbourne 3166, Australia

First published 1990

Printed in the United States of America

Library of Congress Cataloging-in-Publication Data
Lancaster, Tony.
The econometric analysis of transition data / Tony Lancaster.
    p.   cm. – (Econometric Society monographs)
Includes bibliographic references.
ISBN 0-521-26596-7
1. Econometrics.   I. Title.   II. Title: Transition data.
III. Series.
HB139.L35   1990
330′.01′5195–dc20   89-17386
                                                                    CIP

British Library Cataloguing in Publication Data
Lancaster, Tony
The econometric analysis of transition data.
1. Labour market. Econometric models
I. Title   II. Series
331.12′0724

ISBN 0-521-26596-7 hardback

This book is dedicated to JCTR, my *sine qua non.*

Contents

Contents

Preface

The econometric analysis of the duration of events began in the late 1970s and is now almost a decade old. It is time that the field was exposited in a systematic way and to do so is the aim of this book. The early work was mainly the analysis of the duration of single events, principally unemployment spells, and the book reflects this emphasis. I have tried, however, to provide a reasonably complete account of the analysis of data in which we observe both the duration of an event and the destination that is entered at its end. This is why the title of the book refers to transition data and not to duration data. Transition data refers not only to how long events last but also to what happens when they end. I also give an account of the situation in which we observe consecutive durations of events of different types – for example, spells of employment, unemployment and nonparticipation in the labour market. But my treatment of this latter type of data is less complete, partly for reasons of space, and partly because it reflects the state of the art in econometrics. The illustrations I give are usually drawn from applied labour economics, but this is only a reflection of my own research experience. The methods I describe are of much broader applicability in applied economics. Urban and industrial economics and economic demography are just a few of the other fields to which the econometric methods I describe should find application, and it may be that other social scientists will find sections of the book relevant to their research.

The emphasis in the book is on individual data. There is an econometric literature dealing with the analysis of data on the total numbers of people moving between states in a period of time: the macroeconomic gross-flow literature. A number of the sections of the book are relevant to this area of work, particularly Chapter 4, but I do not otherwise discuss the macroeconomic literature.

Statisticians and biometricians have produced a large literature on the analysis of duration data in the last fifteen years, and a number of excellent texts and monographs have been produced while this book was in preparation, notably Cox and Oakes (1984). But econometrics is not statistics and the problems posed by an econometric analysis are not identical to those that a statistician would see. I have tried to write a book for econometricians that draws on the contributions of economists, statistical theorists, and workers in several areas of applied statistics.

Notation and Numbering

Equations are numbered within chapters and sections so that, for example, (5.2.7) refers to the seventh equation of Section 2 of Chapter 5. Figures and examples are numbered within chapters. I have tried to denote random variables by capital letters and their realisations by lower case letters but there are places in which strict adherence to this rule would complicate the exposition rather than clarify it. The word 'variate' and the phrase 'random variable' are used synonymously. I have used the symbol ■ to indicate the ends of proofs and examples. The symbol $\sim$ means 'is distributed as'.

At the end of each chapter, apart from the first, I have included notes which give the main references on which the exposition has drawn together with some indicators of further reading.

Acknowledgments

I am grateful to a number of people who have offered comments on drafts of the book. In particular, I am in the debt of Guido Imbens; Wilbert van der Klaauw, who also assisted with the production of the figures; Tom Espenshade; Walter Freiberger; Robert Moffitt; Geert Ridder; Gerard van der Berg; two anonymous referees for the Econometric Society, who did a remarkably thorough job; the editor of the Econometric Society's monograph series, Chuck Manski; and the former editor, Angus Deaton.

I have also accumulated debts, which I am happy to acknowledge, to the Department of Statistics of the Australian National University, a visit to which enabled me to begin work on the book, to the Center for Economic Research at Tilburg University, and to the Economic and Social Research Council for their grant B00232133.

I would also like to acknowledge the help of Mrs. Margaret Parkinson, who typed several early drafts of the book.

PART I

Model Building

CHAPTER 1

Some Basic Results

1   Introduction

1.1   An Overview of the Book

This book is about the movement of individuals[1] among a set of states, and a transition is a movement from one state to another. Transition data record the sequence of states that were occupied and the times at which movements between them occurred. The states will be finite in number and may be defined in any way that the economics of the problem suggests is useful. All that is required is that they be clearly defined and that we have a rule for telling which state a person is in at each moment of time. Some simple examples of states might be

1. Unemployed,
2. Employed,
3. Out of the labour force;

or

1. Married,
2. Unmarried;

or

1. Employed,
2. Retired.

Our concern will be with the passage of people among such sets of states. We shall give an account of the building of models for such movement, of the fitting of such models to data, and of the use of models and data to test economic and statistical hypotheses. In the first part of the

---

[1] Strictly, economic agents – people, households, firms, and so on.

3

book – chapters 1 through 6 – we shall describe ways of building models for fitting to transition data. In the rest of this introductory chapter we shall give an account of the two fundamental tools for the study of duration data, the hazard function and the Exponential distribution, and we shall examine some duration data. In chapter 2 we examine the hazard function and the distribution of observable data when the model includes regressor variables, and particularly we study the case in which those variables change during the occupation of a state. This is the case of time-varying regressors or covariates. In chapters 3 and 4 we consider a sequence of parametric models for the process of movement between states. The emphasis in these chapters is on the simplest type of transition data, that in which we observe an individual's duration of stay in a single state. Econometricians usually call this *single spell data*; in biometrics the phrase is *survival data*. In chapter 5 we broaden the exposition to consider the additional tools needed for modelling when we observe both the duration of stay in a state, or sequence of states, and the states to which exit took place. These are *multiple spell* and *multiple destination* data. Finally, chapter 6 deals with a number of models for transitions which are derived explicitly from a model of optimal choice by economic agents.

The second part of the book deals with inference – the use of models to interpret data. The first consideration in inference about unknown parameters and functions is whether they are identifiable from a particular class of data. So chapter 7 deals with problems of identification that have arisen in the econometrics literature. The next two chapters are concerned with inference in models specified either – chapter 8 – up to a finite parameter vector or – chapter 9 – in models involving unspecified functions. These correspond to fully and semi-parametric inference, respectively. Finally, chapters 10 and 11 deal with questions of model misspecification; what happens to inferences when the assumed model is wrong, and how wrong models can be detected.

1.2   An Example

To introduce many of the major themes of the book let us look at a particular example, that of the movement into employment of someone who is looking for a job. One way of building a model for this transition is to suppose that as a result of his search he receives offers of jobs from time to time. Of the possible offers he could get, some he would find worth accepting and some not. Then, whether he moves into employment on any day depends upon whether he receives an offer that day and on whether, if he does, he deems it worth accepting. An economist

could then develop this approach by asking, and solving, the questions
what set of wage offers it is optimal for a given person to accept and how
much resources should optimally be devoted to search? The answers to
these questions will depend not only on the criterion of optimality chosen by the economist but also on the circumstances of the unemployed
person, in particular, of course, the resources he possesses and the constraints he faces. To be a little more specific suppose that in some such
theory the relevant circumstances of a person who has been looking for
a job for t days are assembled in a vector $\mathbf{x}(t)$. The elements of this
vector might include, for example, the level of unemployment benefit
available after t or the average wage payable in jobs that might be offered to him. For a person described at t by $\mathbf{x}(t)$ suppose his optimal
amount of search produces a probability, say, $\lambda(\mathbf{x}(t))\,dt$, that a job offer
will be made to him in the interval of time from t to $t + dt$, and there
is a probability $P(\mathbf{x}(t))$ that if such an offer is received it will be worth
accepting. Then the outcome of this model-building effort is a quantity
$\lambda(\mathbf{x}(t))P(\mathbf{x}(t))\,dt = \theta(\mathbf{x}(t))\,dt$ giving the probability of a transition out
of unemployment in the time interval $(t, t + dt)$ given, of course, that he
was still unemployed when it began. Such a function $\theta(\mathbf{x}(t))$ is called a
hazard function when, as in our example, there is only a single destination state (employment). There is an analogous set of functions when
there are multiple destinations and in that context they are called *transition intensities*. A theory which specifies the hazard function – of $\mathbf{x}$ and
t – is refutable from observation of the movement of persons between
states and thus once such a function is specified by an econometrician
the model-building phase of an analysis is complete.

Let us compare this model with a more traditional microeconometric
model, say, a model of consumer demand. In a demand model there is
as above a resource and constraint vector $\mathbf{x}$ and there is an optimality
criterion. The outcome of the modelling is an optimal quantity demanded
$q = q(\mathbf{x})$ or sequence of such quantities $q(t) = q(\mathbf{x}(t))$. Random variation
may be introduced by supposing that elements of $\mathbf{x}$, representing, for
example, 'tastes', are not observed by the econometrician and these vary
over the population to be sampled. Comparing this with the transition
model, we see that there are two main differences. The first is that
the choice variables in the transition model that correspond to q in the
demand model are the rate of search and the set of acceptable wage offers
and these are not necessarily observed. They may be, but even if they are
not we will be able to use the theory because of its implications for the
hazard function. Thus in the transition model we can often make only
indirect observations on the choice variables. The second difference is
that in the transition model even if all relevant $\mathbf{x}$ variables were known to

the investigator he still would not be able to say with certainty whether a transition will occur. Neither the econometrician nor the unemployed person can say for sure whether a transition will occur today. Thus the transition model is intrinsically stochastic. As Mortensen and Neumann (1984) have put it, both 'choice and chance' enter fundamentally into the transition model. It is indeed this combination that gives the subject its fascination to the present writer.

It may be, of course, that also, in the transition model, some elements of $\mathbf{x}(t)$ are unknown to the investigator and must be supposed to vary over the population. This gives, then, a second source of stochastic variation in the model in the form of *neglected heterogeneity*. Much of this book will be concerned with the problems that arise in such *doubly stochastic models*.

In the example we have been discussing, the fact that the unemployed person was choosing his rate of search and his acceptance set optimally is important. It is this choice component that distinguishes the econometric analysis of transition data from standard applied statistical analysis of survival and transition data and gives a richness but also an added complexity to econometric work. Of course, it is possible to ignore the choice structure underlying a hazard function model but this is not desirable in econometric work since it leads to results incapable of clear behavioural interpretation. But even though the choice element in the econometric modelling of transition data is essential, the basic mathematical tools for both modelling and inference phases of our analysis are largely common to all analyses of transition data. In this chapter and the next two we shall describe them beginning with the hazard function $\theta(\mathbf{x}(t))$ introduced informally above.

2   The Hazard Function

2.1   Continuous Time

Let us think of time to exit as a continuous random variable, T, and consider a large population of people who enter some given state at a time we shall identify as $T = 0$. The calendar time of entry need not be the same for all people and in practical cases it usually will not be. Thus, T does not refer to calendar time but rather it measures time on person-specific clocks that are each set to zero at the moment a person enters the state in question. T is the *duration of stay* in the state. The population is assumed to be homogeneous with respect to the systematic factors, regressor variables, that affect the distribution of T. This means that everyone's duration of stay will be a realisation of a random variable from the same probability distribution. In the next chapter we shall see how to modify the results of the present section to take explicit account of the way in which regressor variables might enter into the distribution of duration of stay.

We shall now define the probability that a person who has occupied a state for a time t leaves it in the short interval of length dt after t. The probability that such a person leaves the state within an interval dt at or after t is $P(t \leq T < t + dt \mid T \geq t)$, where the conditioning event that $T \geq t$ is just the event that the state is still occupied at t, that he has not left before then. If we divide this probability by dt we get the average probability of leaving per unit time period over a short time interval after t, and by considering this average over shorter and shorter intervals we formally define

$$\theta(t) = \lim_{dt \to 0} \frac{P(t \leq T < t + dt \mid T \geq t)}{dt} \tag{2.1}$$

as the hazard function. It is the instantaneous rate of leaving per unit time period at t.

The rough interpretation of the function θ is that $\theta(t)\,dt$ is the probability of exit from a state in the short interval of length dt after t, conditional on the state still being occupied at t. It is also perfectly sensible to talk about the probability of exit in the short interval of length dt after t *without* the condition $T \geq t$, but this is quite a different concept from the hazard function. The hazard function gives the probability that a forty-five-year-old person will die whereas the unconditional concept gives the probability that a person will die at forty-five. In terms of relative frequencies $\theta(45)\,dt$ gives the *proportion of forty-five-year-olds* who die within dt of their forty-fifth birthday. The unconditional concept gives the *proportion of people* (ever born) who die within dt of their forty-fifth birthday.

We can express both the hazard function and the unconditional probability of exit in terms of the distribution and probability density functions of the continuous random variable T, the duration of occupancy. Let the duration distribution function be $P(T < t) = F(t)$, $t \geq 0$, at the point[2] t, and let the probability density function be $f(t) = dF/dt$. Then, by the law of conditional probability,

$$P(t \leq T < t + dt \mid T \geq t) = \frac{P(t \leq T < t + dt, T \geq t)}{P(T \geq t)},$$

[2] This is more convenient when studying duration data than the usual definition, $F(t) = P(T \leq t)$.

$$= \frac{P\left(t \leq T < t + dt\right)}{P\left(T \geq t\right)},$$

assuming $P\left(T \geq t\right) > 0$, since the intersection of the sets $t \leq T < t + dt$ and $T \geq t$ is just $t \leq T < t + dt$. In terms of the distribution function this probability equals

$$\frac{F(t + dt) - F(t)}{1 - F(t)}.$$

Dividing by dt and letting dt go to zero, we get

$$\theta(t) = \lim_{dt \to 0} \frac{F(t + dt) - F(t)}{dt} \cdot \frac{1}{1 - F(t)}$$

$$= F'(t) \cdot \frac{1}{1 - F(t)}$$

$$= \frac{f(t)}{1 - F(t)}.$$

Thus the hazard function at t is the probability density function divided by one minus the distribution function.[3] One minus the distribution function occurs so often in mathematical expressions to do with durations and transitions that it has a special name, *the survivor function*, since it gives the probability of survival to t, or, in terms of relative frequencies, it gives the fraction of a large generation who stay at least t years. It also has a special notation, $1 - F(t) = \overline{F}(t)$, and the more compact expression for the hazard is thus

$$\theta(t) = \frac{f(t)}{\overline{F}(t)}. \tag{2.2}$$

Note that $\theta(t)$ is also equal to $-d \log \overline{F}(t)/dt$.

In contrast, the unconditional probability of exit in the short interval of length dt after t is just the area under the probability density function (p.d.f.) of T from t to $t + dt$, $f(t)dt$, which may be seen to be quite different from the conditional probability, $f(t)dt/\overline{F}(t)$, except at $t = 0$, where $\overline{F} = 1$.

---

[3] The expression (2.2) is similar to the formula for the conditional probability density function of t given that it exceeds t_0, which is $f(t)/(1 - F(t_0))$, $t \geq t_0$. In consequence, one sometimes finds the hazard function described as a conditional p.d.f. It is not. It is a function of t defined, generally, over the whole non-negative axis.

Since $f(t) = -d\overline{F}(t)/dt$, equation (2.2) is a differential equation in t whose solution, subject to the initial condition $\overline{F}(0) = 1$, is

$$\overline{F}(t) = \exp\left\{-\int_0^t \theta(s)\, ds\right\},\tag{2.3}$$

as can be verified by differentiation. Equation (2.3) shows how one can calculate the probability distribution of duration of state occupancy given the hazard function, and it is an important relation in the construction of models of transitions. Note that, from (2.2) and (2.3), the density function of T can be written

$$f(t) = \theta(t)\exp\left\{-\int_0^t \theta(s)\, ds\right\}.\tag{2.4}$$

Figure 1.1 shows some examples of hazard functions. In the hazard function of figure 1.1(c) the probability of exit from a state does not depend at all on how long it has been occupied, and this is the simplest hazard function one could have. It is also a quite fundamental form in that, as we shall shortly show, any other hazard function can be transformed into the constant hazard by a transformation of the time scale. The hazard function of figure 1.1(b) shows a model in which the probability of exit from a state decreases monotonically with the time that has been spent in it. Such decreasing hazard functions are commonly found with labour market data, for example, unemployment durations. The hazard function of figure 1.1(a) has the conditional probability of exit rising to a peak before starting to fall. Hazard functions with this shape arise in some models for the process of leaving employment.

Since $\theta(t)\, dt$ is a probability, hazard functions must be non-negative. Furthermore, if exit is certain in the sense that $\lim_{t\to\infty} \overline{F}(t) = 0$, then θ must be such that

$$\lim_{t\to\infty}\int_0^t \theta(s)\, ds = \infty.$$

That is, the integrated hazard must diverge. However, some models for transitions in economics do, as we shall see, imply that with positive probability exit never takes place, so that $\lim_{t\to\infty} \overline{F}(t) > 0$. Such a duration distribution is called *defective*. We shall describe models of this type in chapter 6.

Note that if we knew $\theta(t)$ for all t then we would know $\overline{F}(t)$, from (2.3); similarly θ could be deduced from $\overline{F}$ via (2.2). Thus θ, f, and $\overline{F}$ are alternative ways of describing the distribution of the probability of exit over the positive axis; if we know one, we can deduce the others. There are still other functions that are equivalent to F or $\overline{F}$, for example, the

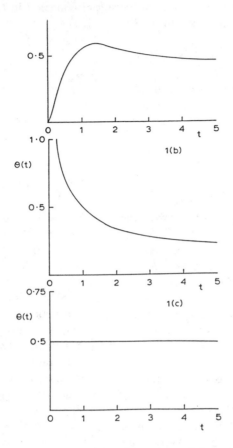

Figure 1.1.   Three hazard functions.

characteristic function, which is well known to determine a distribution uniquely. The emphasis on the particular function θ in this book arises because economists often find it most natural to construct their models of the exit process in terms of the hazard and then to deduce from that model its implications for F.

2.2   The Product Integral Representation

The derivation of the fundamental relation between hazard and survivor function by the solution of a differential equation is not particularly insightful. There is an alternative argument which we shall now give which offers more insight and which will be important when we come to study the role played by regressor variables which may be changing through time.

Consider the event that $T \geq t$ which has probability $\overline{F}(t)$. Divide the interval from zero to t into $n-1$ sub-intervals by the points $0 = s_1$, $s_2, \ldots, s_{n-1}, s_n = t$. Then, in order to survive to t a person must, of course, survive through each of the subintervals, $[s_j, s_{j+1})$, and so the event $T \geq t$ is equivalent to the event $\{T \geq s_1, T \geq s_2, \ldots, T \geq s_n\}$. Thus, by the law of conditional probability,

$$P\,(T \geq t) = \prod_{j=2}^{n} P\,(T \geq s_j \mid T \geq s_{j-1})$$

$$= \prod_{j=2}^{n} [1 - P\,(T < s_j \mid T \geq s_{j-1})]$$

$$= \prod_{j=2}^{n} [1 - P\,(s_{j-1} \leq T < s_j \mid T \geq s_{j-1})]$$

$$= \prod_{j=2}^{n} [1 - \theta(s_{j-1}^*)(s_j - s_{j-1})] + R_n, \tag{2.5}$$

where the remainder term R_n goes to zero as the largest of the interval lengths $s_j - s_{j-1}$ goes to zero. Here s_{j-1}^* is a point in the interval $[s_{j-1}, s_j)$. Since (2.4) is true for any n

$$P\,(T \geq t) = \lim_{n \to \infty} \prod_{j=2}^{n} [1 - \theta(s_{j-1}^*)(s_j - s_{j-1})]$$

$$= \wp_0^t\,[1 - \theta(s)\,ds]. \tag{2.6}$$

The second equality in (2.6) defines the *product integral*[4] of the function $\theta(s)$ from 0 to t. The limit is taken as both $n \to \infty$, and the largest of the $\{s_j - s_{j-1}\}$ goes to zero.

Product integrals have several interesting properties among which are the facts that

$$\wp_0^t = \wp_0^{t_1}\,\wp_{t_1}^t, \qquad \text{for } 0 \leq t_1 \leq t,$$

and that

$$\wp_0^t\,[1 - \theta(s)\,ds] = \exp\left\{-\int_0^t \theta(s)\,ds\right\} \tag{2.7}$$

[4] The symbol $\wp$ is a script p, for product.

when θ is a continuous function, which shows that we recover the relation (2.3) between hazard and survivor functions by this probabilistic argument. Essentially, in the product integral representation of the survivor function at t we think of survival to t as survival through a sequence of two-outcome, Bernouilli, trials in which 'success' is surviving through $[s_{j-1}, s_j)$. The probability of success, given survival to the start of the interval, is one minus the hazard for that interval times the interval length, as that length becomes small.

When the hazard function is zero except at the finite or countably infinite number of isolated points $\{t_j\}$ where it takes the values $\{\theta_j\}$ we have a discrete-time hazard model. If we return to the penultimate line of (2.5) we note that $\mathrm{P}\,(s_{j-1} \leq T < s_j \mid T \geq s_{j-1})$ is equal to θ_k if $[s_{j-1}, s_j)$ contains the point t_k and zero if it contains none of the points $\{t_j\}$, assuming the interval lengths are sufficiently short to contain at most one of the points $\{t_j\}$. Thus if we reinterpret $\theta(s_{j-1}^*)(s_{j-1} - s_j)$ in this sense the product integral representation of the survivor function, (2.6), remains valid, but instead of (2.7) we have

$$\mathrm{P}\,(T \geq t) = \wp_0^t\,[1 - \theta(s)\,ds] = \prod_{j \mid t_j < t} (1 - \theta_j). \qquad (2.8)$$

Note that the product is taken over all j such that $t_j < t$. Thus the product integral representation of the relationship between the hazard and survivor functions is more general than (2.3) because it encompasses both the discrete- and the continuous-time cases. It also includes the case in which the hazard has both continuous and discrete components.

The value of the discrete-time hazard at the time point t_j is formally defined by

$$\theta_j = \mathrm{P}\,(\text{exit at } t_j \mid \text{survival to } t_j)$$

$$= \frac{\mathrm{P}\,(\text{exit at } t_j)}{\mathrm{P}\,(\text{survival to } t_j)}$$

$$= \frac{f(t_j)}{\overline{F}(t_j)}, \qquad j = 1, 2, \ldots, N, \qquad (2.9)$$

where there are N (possibly infinite) isolated times at which exit could occur and $f(t_j)$ is the discrete probability mass function at t_j.

We shall in this book normally do our modelling work in continuous-time. There are three reasons for this. First it is often mathematically simpler and more elegant. Second, there is rarely in economics a natural discrete-time unit. And third, if different investigators each work with a continuous-time model they will report estimates of parameters that are at least dimensionally comparable even when their data may be grouped or aggregated over time in different ways. It is usually efficient to do one's theorising in continuous-time and then to consider as necessary any complications introduced by discretely recorded data.

2.3   Hazards and Remaining Durations

Another function of interest in models of duration is the expected duration conditional upon survival in the state to time s. Let us denote this by $e(s)$. A related quantity is the expected time to exit given survival to s, which is obviously $e(s) - s = r(s)$, say. The function $e(s)$ provides the expected *total* duration, and $r(s)$ is the expected *remaining* duration of people who stay at least for s. The p.d.f. of complete duration, T, conditional upon survival to s is

$$g(t \mid T \geq s) = \frac{f(t)}{\overline{F}(s)}, \qquad t \geq s.$$

Assuming a continuous-time model the expectation in this distribution is

$$e(s) = \int_s^{\infty} t f(t)\, dt / \overline{F}(s). \tag{2.10}$$

If we integrate by parts the numerator of (2.10) we get

$$\int_s^{\infty} t f(t)\, dt = \lim_{m \to \infty} \int_s^m t f(t)\, dt$$

$$= \lim_{m \to \infty} \left[mF(m) - sF(s) - \int_s^m F(t)\, dt \right],$$

$$= \lim_{m \to \infty} \left[-m\overline{F}(m) + s\overline{F}(s) + \int_s^m \overline{F}(t)\, dt \right],$$

$$= s\overline{F}(s) + \int_s^{\infty} \overline{F}(t)\, dt,$$

since $\lim_{m \to \infty} m\overline{F}(m) = 0$ is necessary for the existence of $\mathrm{E}\,(T)$. Thus

$$e(s) = s + \int_s^{\infty} \overline{F}(t)\, dt / \overline{F}(s), \tag{2.11}$$

and, in particular, the expected duration of stay, the average stay of entrants to the state, is

$$e(0) = r(0) = \mathrm{E}\,(T) = \int_0^{\infty} \overline{F}(t)\, dt, \tag{2.12}$$

a fact that we shall use repeatedly in later chapters. It states that *the mean is the integral of the survivor function.*

Differentiating $e(s)$ in (2.10) gives us

$$e'(s) = \frac{f(s)}{\overline{F}(s)} \cdot \int_s^\infty \frac{\overline{F}(t)}{\overline{F}(s)} \, dt$$

$$= \theta(s)\{e(s) - s\}. \tag{2.13}$$

It follows that $\theta(s) = e'(s)/\{e(s) - s\} = \{1 + r'(s)\}/r(s)$ and thus that

$$\overline{F}(t) = \exp\left\{-\int_0^t \frac{e'(s) \, ds}{e(s) - s}\right\},$$

$$= \frac{r(0)}{r(t)} \exp\left\{-\int_0^t \frac{ds}{r(s)}\right\}. \tag{2.14}$$

So $e(s)$ is another function of which knowledge is equivalent to knowledge of the distribution of exit probability over the positive axis.

Consideration of a special case might help in the understanding of these formulae, so let us see what happens when the expected remaining life at s is a constant, say, c, independent of s. This means that however long the state has been occupied, whether for a day or a year, the expected time to exit is always c. Then

$$e(s) = s + c,$$
$$e'(s) = 1, \qquad \text{and, from (2.13).}$$
$$\theta(s) = c^{-1}.$$

So a constant remaining duration implies a constant hazard. Since substituting $\theta(s) = c^{-1}$ in (2.11) easily gives $e(s) - s = c$, we see that a constant remaining life and a constant hazard are equivalent properties of a duration distribution – either one implies the other.

3   A Look at Some Data

Before continuing with our account of the probability algebra of transition processes let us look at some numbers which are not untypical of the type of single spell duration data that confront the econometrician and which we shall use to illustrate the methods discussed in later chapters. Table 1.1 gives information on the duration of first jobs of a sample of 703 college graduates. It is a grouped distribution and the first column gives the start of each successive group or interval of time, measured in months. The second column shows how many people were recorded as still employed at the start of each three month interval. The third column shows the numbers of people who were lost from the study in

Table 1.1.   703 Graduates in Their First Job

Interval start time in months	Number recorded as still employed at T	Number censored in interval from T	Number leaving in interval from T	Estimated hazard function	Estimated survivor function
0	703	0	3	.0014	1.000
3	700	0	17	.0081	.996
6	683	0	31	.0151	.972
9	652	1	33	.0169	.929
22	618	0	60	.0324	.883
15	558	0	22	.0131	.801
18	536	0	29	.0180	.770
21	507	2	33	.0218	.730
24	472	1	40	.0283	.684
27	431	1	17	.0132	.628
30	413	5	28	.0229	.604
33	380	4	22	.0195	.563
36	354	4	26	.0152	.531
39	334	1	10	.0100	.508
42	323	5	13	.0136	.493
45	305	10	9	.0102	.473
48	286	6	8	.0095	.459
51	272	3	8	.0099	.446
54	261	3	10	.0129	.433
57	248	1	4	.0054	.416
60	243	13	7	.0101	.410
63	223	2	1	.0015	.398
66	220	4	2	.0031	.396
69	214	11	2	.0033	.393
72	201	10	4	.0070	.389
75	187	10	1	.0019	.381
78	176	15	1	.0021	.379
81	160	30	1	.0026	.377
84	129	–	–	–	.374

the three month interval commencing at the time indicated in column 1. For these people we know only that the duration of their first job was at least the number of months shown in column 1. Their actual complete duration was *censored* at the column 1 time. Column 4 gives the number of people whose employment ended in the three months after the column 1 time. For these people we know their completed employment durations to an accuracy of three months.

These four columns constitute the data. They are typical of much economic data in the size of sample, which is much larger than those usually found in other areas where durations are studied, for example, in medical statistics. They are also typical in that many observations are right censored, partly because the longest period of observation was 84 weeks and a substantial fraction of the sample were still in employment at that time. They are untypical in that in economics we normally observe for each individual a vector of, possibly time-varying, regressor variables, for example, the age of the person when he started his job; we sometimes observe variables jointly dependent with duration, for example, the wage he earned at the time he left his job; and we sometimes observe his destination state, for example, whether he became unemployed or went to another job.

If it were reasonable to think of the people in the sample as homogeneous in the sense that each exit or censoring time was a realisation of the same stochastic transition process, then it would make sense to estimate from these data a distribution function, a survivor function, and a hazard function. The fifth column gives an estimated hazard function calculated with $\theta(t)$ constrained to be constant in each successive three month interval so that θ is a step function. The estimated hazard function is plotted in figure 1.2. The plot is quite irregular, reflecting the fact that the estimates of the value of the function in different intervals are stochastically independent. The smooth curve was drawn by eye to indicate the general shape of the hazard indicated by the estimates. Note that the probability of leaving the job rises for the first 18 months or so and then falls fairly steadily. There is some indication of leaving being bunched at years' ends.

The method of calculation is by maximum likelihood estimation of the heights of each of the steps in the hazard function. Though we shall give the method in detail in chapter 8, it is in fact a common-sense calculation. The value of the hazard function in the m'th three month interval is found by dividing the number of people who were observed to leave in that interval – column 4 – by the number who could, in principle, have been observed to leave in that interval. This latter number, often called the size of the *risk set* at $m - 1$, is equal to the numbers still recorded as employed at the start of the interval – column 2 – less those censored in the interval – column 3. The resulting ratio is then divided by three to give the rate of leaving *per unit time period*, that is, per month.

The final column is the estimated survivor function of leaving the first job. This is calculated using the estimated hazard function using the formula (2.3) with θ a piecewise-constant function. Again, the method of calculation is detailed in chapter 8.

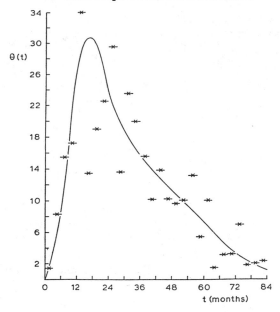

Figure 1.2.   First job durations of 703 college graduates: estimated hazard function.

4   The Exponential Distribution

In this section we shall describe the properties of the Exponential distribution, which is of fundamental importance in the modelling and analysis of transition data.

When the hazard function is independent of how long the state has been occupied, that is, of elapsed duration, as in figure 1.1(c), the integral in (2.3) becomes

$$\int_0^t \theta(s)\, ds = \theta t. \tag{4.1}$$

The survivor function is thus

$$\overline{F}(t) = \exp\{-\theta t\}, \qquad \theta > 0, \quad t \geq 0, \tag{4.2}$$

and the probability density function is

$$f(t) = \theta \exp\{-\theta t\}. \tag{4.3}$$

This is the Exponential probability density function defined for every positive value of θ. We shall write $T \sim \mathcal{E}(\theta)$, which reads '$T$ is distributed as an Exponential variate with parameter θ'. The sample space is $\{T; T \geq 0\}$, but, as this will be the sample space for every duration distribution we shall look at in this book, we shall not mention this fact from now on. The p.d.f. is sketched in figure 3.3 of chapter 3 for $\theta = 1$, the unit Exponential distribution.

The moment generating function (m.g.f.) is

$$M(s) = \mathrm{E}\,(e^{sT}) = \int_0^\infty \theta e^{-(\theta-s)t}\,dt$$

$$= \frac{\theta}{\theta - s} \int_0^\infty (\theta - s)e^{-(\theta-s)t}\,dt$$

$$= \frac{\theta}{\theta - s}$$

$$= (1 - s/\theta)^{-1}, \qquad s < \theta,$$

where the integral in the second line is the integral of an Exponential p.d.f. over its sample space and thus is equal to one. The cumulant generating function, which is often the more convenient quantity to work with in dealing with duration models, is the logarithm of the moment generating function, $K(s) = \log M(s)$. The derivative $d^j K/ds^j$ at $s = 0$ gives the kth cumulant, κ_j. The first four cumulants are related to the moments by

$$\kappa_1 = \mu,$$
$$\kappa_2 = \mu_2,$$
$$\kappa_3 = \mu_3,$$
$$\kappa_4 = \mu_4 - 3\mu_2^2, \qquad\qquad (4.4)$$

where $\mu = \mathrm{E}\,(T)$ and $\mu_j = \mathrm{E}\,[(T - \mu)^j]$, $j = 2, 3, 4, \ldots$ For the Exponential distribution $K(s) = -\log(1 - s/\theta)$ and repeated differentiation shows that $K^{(j)}(s) = \theta^{-j}(j - 1)!(1 - s/\theta)^{-j}$, so that from the first two derivatives at $s = 0$ we find the mean and variance of an Exponential variate to be

$$\mathrm{E}\,(T) = \theta^{-1}; \qquad \mathrm{var}\,(T) = \theta^{-2},$$

and in general the jth cumulant is

$$\kappa_j = \theta^{-j}(j - 1)!, \qquad j = 0, 1, 2, 3, \ldots. \qquad (4.5)$$

Note that the variance is the square of the mean, and the mean is the reciprocal of the hazard function. Also, since $\mathrm{E}\,(T)$ has the dimension of time, for example, days, θ has dimension one over time, for example, 'per day', and since dt has dimension 'time' $\theta\,dt$ is dimensionless, as a probability should be.

We remarked earlier that a distribution with any form of hazard function can be transformed into a constant hazard, that is, Exponential form, by a transformation of the time scale. This transformation is particularly important in the analysis of the goodness of fit of transition and duration models. Consider the transformation from T to $Z(T)$ defined by

$$Z = \int_0^T \theta(s)\,ds, \tag{4.6}$$

so that

$$\delta Z = \frac{dZ}{dT}\,\delta T = \theta(T)\,\delta T.$$

Thus a unit time interval on the old, T, time scale corresponds to an interval of length $\delta Z/\theta(T)$ on the new scale. If θ is independent of T this merely means a redefining of the unit time period. To find the duration probability distribution over the new time axis we note that since θ is non-negative

$$\mathrm{P}\,(T \geq t) = \mathrm{P}\,\left(\int_0^T \theta(s)\,ds \geq \int_0^t \theta(s)\,ds \right),$$

$$= \mathrm{P}\,\left(Z \geq \int_0^t \theta(s)\,ds \right). \tag{4.7}$$

But also

$$\mathrm{P}\,(T \geq t) = \exp\left\{ -\int_0^t \theta(s)\,ds \right\}, \qquad \text{from (2.3).} \tag{4.8}$$

Equating (4.7) and (4.8) we see that for every non-negative number z, $\mathrm{P}\,(Z \geq z) = e^{-z}$. Since this expression provides the survivor function for the random variable Z at the point z, we can conclude that Z has an Exponential distribution of mean one – a unit Exponential distribution – with constant hazard equal to unity. *The integrated hazard is a unit Exponential variate.*

A final property of the Exponential distribution which is of great use in the econometric analysis of transition data is the cumulant generating function (c.g.f.) not of T but, rather, of $\log T$. The m.g.f. is

$$M_{\log T}(s) = \mathrm{E}\,(e^{s \log T})$$

$$= \mathrm{E}\,(T^s)$$

$$= \int_0^\infty t^s \theta e^{-\theta t}\,dt$$

$$= \theta^{-s}\,\Gamma(1 + s), \tag{4.9}$$

where $\Gamma(\cdot)$ is the complete Gamma function described in appendix 1. Thus

$$K_{\log T}(s) = -s \log \theta + \log \Gamma(1+s), \tag{4.10}$$
$$K'(s) = -\log \theta + \psi(1+s),$$
$$K^{(j)}(s) = \psi^{(j-1)}(1+s), \qquad j = 2, 3, \ldots,$$

where $\psi^{(j-1)}$ is the j'th derivative of the logarithm of the complete Gamma function – also described in the appendix. Thus, from $K'(0)$ and $K''(0)$,

$$\mathrm{E}\,(\log T) = -\log \theta + \psi(1), \tag{4.11}$$
$$\mathrm{var}\,(\log T) = \psi'(1), \tag{4.12}$$

where $\psi(1)$ and $\psi'(1)$ are known constants approximately equal to -0.5772 and 1.6449, respectively. We can therefore write the regression-like equation

$$\log T = -\log \theta + U, \tag{4.13}$$

where the 'error term' U has known mean $\psi(1)$ and *known* variance $\psi'(1)$, not depending on θ. Thus, $\log T$ is homoscedastic. The probability density function of $U = \log \theta T = \log Z$ can be found from the unit Exponential density of Z by changing the variable from Z to U using $du = dz/z$, giving

$$f(u) = e^u \exp\{-e^u\}, \qquad -\infty < u < \infty. \tag{4.14}$$

This is the density function of the logarithm of a unit Exponential variate also known in econometrics as a Type 1 Extreme Value distribution. The cumulant generating function of U is readily found from that of $\log T$, (4.10), to be

$$K_U(s) = \log \Gamma(1+s). \tag{4.15}$$

CHAPTER 2

Covariates and the Hazard Function

1 Introduction

Economic data are rarely homogeneous; we seldom have observations that can be regarded as repeated drawings from the same probability distribution. We normally must allow for measured, and possibly for unmeasured, systematic differences between people, firms, or whatever is the unit of observation. In this chapter we shall introduce regressors or covariates[1] explicitly into the hazard function and discuss the various types of covariate that econometricians seem likely to want to consider. We shall see that some of the relations of chapter 1 can fail to hold when covariates are present.

We shall suppose in this section that all covariates are fully observed by the econometrician. In chapter 4 and subsequently in many parts of the book we shall deal with models containing unobserved covariates.

2 Time-Invariant Covariates

The simplest covariates are those which do not change over time. Two examples might be the sex or the race of a person. More generally, the relevant characteristics of an agent at the time of entry to the state under study, that is, his relevant biography to that point in time, constitute a set of duration-invariant regressor variables. Other variables can and do change as the duration of stay changes, but at a sufficiently slow pace relative to typical durations of stay that, for practical purposes, they can be treated as if they were constants. Two examples might be the age of a person, or the state of the business cycle, in the context of studies of unemployment duration.

---

[1] We use these two terms synonymously.

In the presence of time-invariant regressors assembled in a vector $\mathbf{x}$, the hazard function at t is defined as being conditional on the value of $\mathbf{x}$:

$$\theta(t; \mathbf{x}) = \lim_{dt \to 0} \frac{\mathrm{P}\left(t \leq T < t + dt \mid T \geq t, \mathbf{x}\right)}{dt}. \qquad (2.1)$$

Thus $\theta(t; \mathbf{x}) \, dt$ gives the fraction of the survivors at t who leave in the short interval from t to $t + dt$ in a large population of people who are homogeneous with respect to $\mathbf{x}$. The hazard is related to the density and survivor functions of T given $\mathbf{x}$, as in section 2 of chapter 1, by

$$\theta(t; \mathbf{x}) = \frac{f(t; \mathbf{x})}{\overline{F}(t; \mathbf{x})},$$

$$\overline{F}(t; \mathbf{x}) = \exp\left\{- \int_0^t \theta(s; \mathbf{x}) \, ds \right\}. \qquad (2.2)$$

Example 1
In the Exponential distribution of the last chapter a simple way of introducing a regressor vector $\mathbf{x}$ into the time-invariant Exponential hazard function is

$$\theta(t; \mathbf{x}) = \exp\{-\mathbf{x}'\beta\}, \qquad (2.3)$$

where $\mathbf{x}$ now includes a unit dummy variable to allow for a constant term or intercept in the log hazard. The specification (2.3) ensures the required non-negativity of θ without constraining the parameter space for β. This model allows the data to be drawn from Exponential distributions with different means given by $\mathrm{E}\,(T \mid \mathbf{x}) = \theta^{-1} = \exp\{\mathbf{x}'\beta\}$ depending upon the regressor vector.

With this specification, equation (4.13) of chapter 1 becomes

$$\log T = \mathbf{x}'\beta + U, \qquad (2.4)$$

where U has, from (4.11) of chapter 1, known mean $\psi(1)$, which would be absorbed in the constant term of $\mathbf{x}'\beta$, and, from (4.12) of chapter 1, it has the *known* variance $\psi'(1)$, not depending on the mean. Thus, with this model, $\log T$ has linear and homoscedastic regression on $\mathbf{x}$. This is, of course, a very restrictive model since the error density function involves no unknown parameters. So viewed as a model for economic data the Exponential model is unattractive. It does, however, provide a starting point for generalisations which do provide interesting and useful models, as we shall show in the next chapter. ∎

3   Time-Varying Covariates

We now consider the case in which the probability of exit is determined
by a vector of time-varying covariates $\{\mathbf{x}(s)\}$ whose value at time t is
denoted by $\mathbf{x}(t)$. Models in which there are such time-varying covariates,
which would appear to be particularly important for econometricians,
raise some rather subtle issues not all of which have been fully clarified
in the literature. The material in the rest of this chapter is therefore both
rather preliminary and relatively difficult. Since much of this book can
be read without a detailed understanding of these issues some readers
may find it helpful to note the conclusions to this section and postpone
a close reading.

We shall adopt the notation

$$\mathbf{X}(t_1, t_2) \equiv \{\text{the path of } \{\mathbf{x}(s)\} \text{ from } t_1 \text{ to } t_2\},$$
$$\mathbf{X}(t) \equiv \{\text{the path of } \{\mathbf{x}(s)\} \text{ from } 0 \text{ to } t\},$$
$$\mathbf{X} \equiv \mathbf{X}(\infty).$$

Thus a capital letter denotes a path, a small letter denotes a value at a
point in time, and $\mathbf{X}$ is the complete time path from entry to the state.
The process $\{\mathbf{x}(s)\}$ may be stochastic or it may be a purely deterministic function of time. If stochastic, its state space may be discrete or
continuous. In particular, $\{\mathbf{x}(s)\}$ might record the transitions between
discrete-states in some process other than one whose duration of stay
we are studying. We shall not distinguish in our notation between the
covariate process and its realisations – which is meant should be clear
from the context.

In order to get a feel for the issues involved let us first look at some
examples of time-varying covariates that might arise in econometric applications.

Example 2
A rather trivial example of a time-varying covariate is time itself.   ∎

Example 3
A time-varying regressor that seems likely to influence the rate of leaving
unemployment is the rate of benefits payable to an unemployed person
at each time t during his spell. This varies over time in many social
security systems.   ∎

Example 4
Again, in the context of unemployment durations it seems reasonable
that the speed of leaving should depend upon the rate or intensity of

job search, measured perhaps in hours per day, that a person undertakes. This is likely to vary over time. It is also an example of a regressor which will be hard to observe. ∎

Example 5
In models for the time interval between births one would expect that a binary indicator of contraceptive use would play a role in the hazard function. Again this may vary over time. ∎

Example 6
To return to the job search example, it is possible that the hazard rate at t depends upon an agent's views as to the rate at which job offers may arise. These in turn might depend upon the number of offers he has received to date. Thus a time-varying covariate might be the number of offers received so far. ∎

Example 7
In studies of labour force participation the propensity to leave employment may be dependent on a person's marital status so that one might wish to use a time-varying binary indicator of this status as a regressor variable. ∎

Example 8
In models for the process of leaving a job a time-varying covariate of interest is the wage paid in that job, the level of which is presumably a major determinant of a person's propensity to leave. ∎

The appropriate way to define a hazard ought to depend upon what is meaningful and interesting for the phenomenon under study. In the case of unemployment benefit in a model for unemployment duration the complete time path of this covariate is defined by law and presumably known to each agent. In this case it may be sensible to argue throughout conditionally on this complete path. If the path is defined by a series of rules, such as '\$x until time s_1 and then \$y for a further s_2 weeks' and so on, then this amounts to conditioning on the sequence of numbers x, y, ..., s_1, s_2 .... This provides a high dimensional, but time-invariant, covariate vector and leads to the hazard definition

$$\theta(t; \mathbf{X}) = \lim_{dt \to 0} \frac{\mathrm{P}\left(t \leq T < t + dt \mid T \geq t, \mathbf{X}\right)}{dt}. \tag{3.1}$$

This expression gives the fraction of those survivors at t whose complete covariate path is (would be) $\mathbf{X}$ who exit in the short interval from t to

$t + dt$, per unit time period. Knowledge of (3.1) enables an investigator to answer questions about how differences in the rules governing the stream of benefits alter the probabilities of exit at all dates.

For this type of covariate and conditioning the algebra of the last section goes through unchanged and we can define conditional hazard and survivor functions as in (2.2) with **x** replaced by **X**.

$$\theta(t; \mathbf{X}) = \frac{f(t; \mathbf{X})}{\overline{F}(t; \mathbf{X})},$$

$$\overline{F}(t; \mathbf{X}) = \exp\left\{ -\int_0^t \theta(s; \mathbf{X})\, ds \right\}. \tag{3.2}$$

Here $\overline{F}(t; \mathbf{X})$ gives the fraction of people whose complete covariate path is **X** who survive to time t. Kalbfleisch and Prentice (1980) refer to a covariate like the path of unemployment benefit as a *defined external* covariate.

We conclude that there are some time-varying covariates that we can treat essentially in the same way as time-invariant ones. We condition on their complete paths, no information is lost by doing so, and the resulting expressions enable interesting questions to be answered. But there are other types of covariate where it is not sensible to condition on the entire path. Such covariates raise essentially new issues and we discuss them next.

Consider the wage paid by an employer in a model for job tenure. This time-varying covariate is only defined until the job is left and it is therefore meaningless to attempt to argue conditionally on its path from the origin to ∞. The same is true for the rate of (unemployed) job search in a model for unemployment durations. An agent may, of course, still spend time looking for a new job once he has found one, but this is 'on the job' search, which is conceptually different. A third example is marital status in a model for, say, job tenure. This covariate is, presumably, still defined after an employee has left his job but it does not appear interesting to argue conditionally on its complete path. Conditioning on a presumably unknown future appears to have no behavioural interpretation. The appropriate conditioning for the hazard at time t in these cases would be conditioning on the covariate path to t, $\mathbf{X}(t)$. It may be that the only way in which $\mathbf{X}(t)$ affects the hazard is via its current value, $\mathbf{x}(t)$, but this can be allowed for in the detailed specification of the hazard model.

When we try to argue conditionally on the covariate path to t in a continuous-time model we run into subtle questions about the precise timing of exits and of events on the covariate path. These difficulties, which raise questions of secondary importance, can be avoided if we work with a model in which exit can occur only at a set of discrete-time points. We shall therefore work initially with such a framework and then we shall subsequently indicate how, by a suitable limiting operation, the corresponding continuous-time results can be obtained.

Suppose that exit can take place only at the isolated times $\{t_j\}$, and that the covariate path on the interval $t_{k-1} < t \leq t_k$ is $\mathbf{X}(t_{k-1}, t_k)$. The path over $0 \leq t \leq t_k$ is $\mathbf{X}(t_k)$. A reasonable definition of the hazard at t_j, conditional on $\mathbf{X}(t_j)$, would be

$$\theta(t_j; \mathbf{X}(t_j)) = \mathrm{P}\left(\text{exit at } t_j \mid \text{survival to } t_j, \mathbf{X}(t_j)\right)$$

$$= \mathrm{P}\left(T = t_j \mid T \geq t_j, \mathbf{X}(t_j)\right). \tag{3.3}$$

This is a natural extension of equation (2.9) of chapter 1. This hazard gives the probability of exit at t_j for people who had not left earlier and whose covariates had followed the path $\mathbf{X}(t_j)$ to that date. For example, $\mathbf{X}(t)$ might be the marital history to time t, or the paths followed by the rate of job search, or the wage paid. Note that (3.3) will include the case where the regressors are time-invariant, in which the covariate path is defined simply by the regressor level.

A continuous-time analogue of (3.3) would be

$$\theta(t; \mathbf{X}(t)) = \lim_{dt \to 0} \frac{\mathrm{P}\left(t \leq T < t + dt \mid T \geq t, \mathbf{X}(t + dt)\right)}{dt}, \tag{3.4}$$

although the passage to the limit will involve some continuity restrictions on these probabilities and upon the $\{\mathbf{x}(s)\}$, which we shall not discuss.

Next let us examine the probabilities of observations of both the exit time and the covariate path. Consider first the event that a person survives past time t_j and has covariate path $\mathbf{X}(t_j)$ to that point. As in section 2.2 of chapter 1 we can build up this probability by multiplying together the probabilities of events in each sub-interval from the origin to t_j. Thus

$$\mathrm{P}\left(T > t_j, \mathbf{X}(t_j)\right) = \prod_{k=1}^{j} \mathrm{P}\left(T > t_k, \mathbf{X}(t_{k-1}, t_k) \mid T > t_{k-1}, \mathbf{X}(t_{k-1})\right)$$

$$= \prod_{k=1}^{j} \mathrm{P}\left(T > t_k \mid T > t_{k-1}, \mathbf{X}(t_k)\right)$$
$$\times \mathrm{P}\left(\mathbf{X}(t_{k-1}, t_k) \mid T > t_{k-1}, \mathbf{X}(t_{k-1})\right)$$

$$= \prod_{k=1}^{j} [1 - \mathrm{P}\left(T \leq t_k \mid T > t_{k-1}, \mathbf{X}(t_k)\right)]$$

$$\times \prod_{k=1}^{j} P\left(\mathbf{X}(t_{k-1}, t_k) \mid T \geq t_k, \mathbf{X}(t_{k-1})\right)$$

$$= \prod_{k=1}^{j} [1 - P\left(T = t_k \mid T \geq t_k, \mathbf{X}(t_k)\right)]$$

$$\times \prod_{k=1}^{j} P\left(\mathbf{X}(t_{k-1}, t_k) \mid T \geq t_k, \mathbf{X}(t_{k-1})\right)$$

$$= \prod_{k=1}^{j} [1 - \theta(t_k; \mathbf{X}(t_k))]$$

$$\times \prod_{k=1}^{j} P\left(\mathbf{X}(t_{k-1}, t_k) \mid T \geq t_k, \mathbf{X}(t_{k-1})\right). \qquad (3.5)$$

Here the second line follows from the law of conditional probability if we note that $\mathbf{X}(t_k)$ is $\mathbf{X}(t_{k-1})$ together with $\mathbf{X}(t_{k-1}, t_k)$, and the last line follows from the hazard definition, (3.3).

For someone who leaves at t_j and whose covariate path is $\mathbf{X}(t_j)$ we have the probability

$$P\left(T = t_j, \mathbf{X}(t_j)\right) = P\left(T = t_j, T \geq t_j, \mathbf{X}(t_{j-1}, t_j), \mathbf{X}(t_{j-1})\right)$$

$$= P\left(T = t_j \mid T \geq t_j, \mathbf{X}(t_j)\right)$$
$$\times P\left(\mathbf{X}(t_{j-1}, t_j) \mid T \geq t_j, \mathbf{X}(t_{j-1})\right)$$
$$\times P\left(T > t_{j-1}, \mathbf{X}(t_{j-1})\right)$$

$$= \theta(t_j; \mathbf{X}(t_j)) \prod_{k=1}^{j-1} [1 - \theta(t_k; \mathbf{X}(t_k))]$$

$$\times \prod_{k=1}^{j} P\left(\mathbf{X}(t_{k-1}, t_k) \mid T \geq t_k, \mathbf{X}(t_{k-1})\right). \qquad (3.6)$$

Here the last line follows by use of (3.5).

We now turn to the interpretation of the terms in (3.5) and (3.6). Consider the second factor in (3.5), which also appears in (3.6), and which we write out for reference as

$$\prod_{k=1}^{j} P\left(\mathbf{X}(t_{k-1}, t_k) \mid T \geq t_k, \mathbf{X}(t_{k-1})\right). \qquad (3.7)$$

In the light of the list of examples that we have given above there are two possibilities. The first is the case mentioned earlier in which a covariate is meaningfully defined only until exit occurs. Examples would be the wage paid in a job tenure model and the rate of unemployed job search. In these cases the condition $T \geq t_k$ plays an essential role in (3.7) because an expression like P $(\mathbf{X}(t_{k-1}, t_k) \mid \mathbf{X}(t_{k-1}))$ is not a meaningful probability. The reason is that some of the people whose covariate path to time t_{k-1} is $\mathbf{X}(t_{k-1})$ will leave at that time and *will have no path* $\mathbf{X}(t_{k-1}, t_k)$. A similar difficulty arises in studies of human survival where typically a measurement made on a patient is only meaningful while that patient is still alive. Kalbfleisch and Prentice (1980) refer to such covariates in the context of survival models as *internal*.

The second possibility is that the $\{\mathbf{x}(s)\}$ process is still defined after exit has occurred – as, for example, marital status after a job has been left. In this case, either the terms in (3.7) do depend upon the conditions $T \geq t_k$ or they do not. The difference between these cases, in the context of models in which we argue conditionally on the covariate path to t, is the difference between covariates which are exogenous and those which are endogenous for the leaving process.

Definition 1   *A covariate process* $\{\mathbf{x}(t)\}$ *is exogenous for* T *if and only if*

$$\mathrm{P}\left(\mathbf{X}(t, t+dt) \mid T \geq t + dt, \mathbf{X}(t)\right) = \mathrm{P}\left(\mathbf{X}(t, t+dt) \mid \mathbf{X}(t)\right) \qquad (3.8)$$

for all $t \geq 0$, $dt > 0$.

A covariate that is not exogenous is endogenous, so internal covariates in the sense defined above are also endogenous, even though for them the expression on the right of (3.8) is not defined. This definition says that the information that a person has survived to $t + dt$ does not aid prediction of the path of the covariate process from t to $t + dt$ given its history to t. Definition 1 is similar in spirit to Granger's (1969) definition of non-causality for processes in discrete-time. Note that in the definition we implictly assume the existence of an appropriate probability measure for the paths of the covariate process. We shall not go into the technicalities involved in defining probabilities for stochastic processes in continuous-time and space but refer the reader to stochastic process texts, for example Karlin and Taylor (1975).

The first thing to notice about this definition is that any time-invariant regressor is necessarily exogenous. This is because the whole time path of such a covariate is determined by its path over any interval, so knowledge that $T \geq t + dt$ cannot add anything to our ability to predict its future given its past.

The second thing to note about this definition is that any covariate whose path is determined independently of whether any particular agent has or has not left the state in question is exogenous. An example of such a covariate might be the regional rate of unemployment whose evolution is presumably independent of whether any particular person has or has not found a job. Kalbfleisch and Prentice (1980) refer to this class of covariates as *external*.

A third point is that there certainly exist covariates which are not defined externally to the agent but which are not necessarily endogenous either. An example might be marital status in a model for job tenure. The path of this covariate reflects choices made by an agent, presumably, and the information that employment had not been left by $t + dt$ may, or may not, help predict the course of the covariate over $(t, t+dt)$. Thus marital status could be either endogenous or exogenous for employment tenure.

We can now exploit the definition of exogeneity given in definition 1 in our attempt to interpret the expressions (3.5) and (3.6). If the covariate process is exogenous in the sense of this definition then the elements in the second product of (3.5) do not depend upon the conditions $T \geq t_k$. Thus that second term is

$$\prod_{k=1}^{j} P\left(\mathbf{X}(t_{k-1}, t_k) \mid \mathbf{X}(t_{k-1})\right).$$

This is just the marginal probability of the path $\mathbf{X}(t_j)$. Hence the first factor in (3.5) must be the conditional probability that $T > t_j$ given the path $\mathbf{X}(t_j)$, and the first two factors in (3.6) must be the probability of exit at t_j conditional on $\mathbf{X}(t_j)$. Thus, we conclude that when the covariate process is exogenous we have the equalities

$$P\left(T > t_j \mid \mathbf{X}(t_j)\right) = \prod_{k=1}^{j} [1 - \theta(t_k; \mathbf{X}(t_k))], \qquad (3.9)$$

$$P\left(T = t_j \mid \mathbf{X}(t_j)\right) = \theta(t_j; \mathbf{X}(t_j)) \prod_{k=1}^{j-1} [1 - \theta(t_k; \mathbf{X}(t_k))]. \qquad (3.10)$$

If, however, the covariate vector is endogenous then (3.7) is not the marginal distribution of the path, and the remaining terms in (3.5) and (3.6) are not probabilities conditional on $\mathbf{X}(t_j)$. Thus we reach the important conclusion that the term

$$\theta(t_j; \mathbf{X}(t_j)) \prod_{k=1}^{j-1} [1 - \theta(t_k; \mathbf{X}(t_k))] \qquad (3.11)$$

is always a factor in the joint probability of the event $T = t$ and the covariate path to t, but this expression does not, in general, in spite of its apparent similarity to a discrete probability density function, have an interpretation as a probability conditional on the covariate path. It will have such an interpretation only when the the covariates are exogenous. This result is similar to that given by Engle, Hendry, and Richard (1983, p. 283) in their discussion of exogeneity in discrete-time series.

We conclude our interpretation of (3.5) and (3.6) by noting that even when (3.10) is interpretable as a probability of exit conditional on the covariate path to time t it is not correct to describe it as the value of the probability density function of T, given $\mathbf{X}(t)$, at the point t. This is because the conditioning event, $\mathbf{X}(t)$, is itself a function of the argument of the supposed density function and therefore changes when t changes. Similarly, where the first factor in (3.5) is a valid probability conditional on $\mathbf{X}(t)$ it is not the value of a conditional survivor function of T at t, for the same reason.

The result of our investigation does not mean that one cannot use the first factors of (3.5) and (3.6) alone to construct an appropriate likelihood function from which to make inferences about the hazard function. One can, in spite of the fact that these factors do not ever have survivor and density function interpretations, although if the second factors in these expressions involve parameters of the hazard function, inference using only the first factors may be seriously inefficient. The product of the first factors in (3.5) and (3.6) is in fact a *partial likelihood*. We shall give an account of such likelihoods in chapter 9, particularly section 2.11.

A suitable limiting argument, using the product integral algebra of chapter 1, would give

$$\mathrm{P}\left(t \le T < t + dt, \mathbf{X}(t)\right) = \theta(t; \mathbf{X}(t)) \exp\left\{-\int_0^t \theta(s; \mathbf{X}(s))\, ds\right\} dt$$

$$\times \lim_{n \to \infty} \prod_{k=2}^n \mathrm{P}\left(\mathbf{X}(s_{k-1}, s_k) \mid T \ge s_{k-1}, \mathbf{X}(s_{k-1})\right), \qquad (3.12)$$

as the continuous-time version of the joint density of the exit time and the covariate path, although to make this argument precise is not easy.

The main conclusions of this section can be summarised as follows. When we have a model involving time-varying covariates, and we write the hazard function at t conditional on the covariate path to that time, as seems natural in many econometric applications, then expressions like (3.11) appear in the likelihood based on the joint density of the exit time and the covariate path. Such expressions are valid probabilities, conditional on the covariate path, if the covariates are exogenous in the sense of definition 1, but not otherwise. And such expressions are never interpretable as the values of probability density functions, conditional on the time-varying covariate path to date. Nonetheless, inferences about the parameters of the hazard function can be based on the product over agents of terms like (3.11). These conclusions serve to emphasise how much more fundamental is the hazard function than the density function in modelling duration data. The hazard function conditional on the covariate path is always defined even where there may not exist a conditional density and survivor function to correspond to it.

The integrated hazard function in the continuous-time model

$$Z = \int_0^T \theta(s; \mathbf{X}(s))\, ds$$

is still distributed in unit Exponential form if the covariates are time-invariant or otherwise exogenous, by a simple extension of the argument of section 4 of chapter 1.

It should be emphasised that we have been assuming full observability of the covariate process. It will often be the case in econometric models that the covariate process is not observed by the econometrician or is only partially observed. For example, in studying job tenure one may observe not the entire wage path but only the wage paid at a particular time point. In these cases it will generally be necessary to write down the density function for the data that *can* be seen, which may involve an integration over the possible covariate paths that are consistent with the data. This may well lead one back to a model whose only observed covariates are either time-invariant or external. Chapter 4 deals with models involving an unobserved (but time-invariant) covariate. The study of inference with partially observed endogenous covariates, particularly when those covariates represent optimally chosen stochastic controls, appears to be an interesting research topic.

NOTE

The discussion in section 3 draws on Kalbfleisch and Prentice (1980), Cox and Oakes (1984), unpublished work by Petersen (1986), and work by the present author. Kalbfleisch and Prentice made the first attempt that I am aware of to classify the possible types of time-varying covariate. They studied the forms of data distributions in the presence of what we have referred to as endogenous covariates, though without using that phrase, and exploited the concept of a product integral, used much earlier by Arley (1943), who introduced the notation $\wp_0^t$, and others. The important work of Cox (1972), later exposited in his book with Oakes, also made extensive use of time-varying covariates in the estimation of hazard functions. Lancaster and Chesher (1984) seem to have written the first econometric paper to tackle the problem of endogenous covariates in a hazard model. However, Petersen, in a significant, as yet unpublished, paper was the first to study the connection between the problem of types of covariate and the econometrician's concepts of exogeneity and endogeneity and with discussions of 'causality' in time series.

CHAPTER 3

Parametric Families of Duration Distributions

1   Introduction and Overview

The theoretical basis for a specification of a hazard function is a model of optimal choice by the agents whose transitions are to be studied. Such a model can be specified in great detail leading to a hazard function that is determined by economic theory up to some set of unknown parameters. Or the investigator might abstain from such a detailed specification, choosing instead only to let economic theory suggest the relevant regressor variables and the probable directions of their effects. Both approaches have been used in the econometric literature. Sometimes the former is called a *structural* approach and the latter, rather disparagingly, a *reduced form* approach. There is, however, no clear distinction between them but rather only a difference of degree. In chapter 6 we shall give an account of some structural models whereas in this chapter and the next we shall be concerned with families of models whose functional form is not, precisely, dictated by economic-theoretical considerations, but which are convenient vehicles for an econometric investigation. Such families need to allow for the following facts:

1. The duration distributions of different people differ because, for example, they face different prices, have different wealth and income, and have differing stocks and types of human capital.

2. These sources of difference can be represented by a regressor vector, $\mathbf{x}$, for each person, where $\mathbf{x}$ may have components which should, according to our economic theory, have been measured, but were not.

3. The regressor vector may have elements that are functions either of calendar time, for example, regressor values changing over the business cycle, or of duration, which is time measured from the date of entry to the state. An example is the stream of unemployment benefits, which in the British system used to vary both with the duration of unemployment

and among persons. Thus we have, in general, $\mathbf{x} = \mathbf{x}(t, s)$ where, say, t is duration and s calendar time. Though in our notation we shall sometimes suppress the possible time dependence of $\mathbf{x}$, it must be borne in mind.

4. Duration data are usually partly censored, and often one is able to measure not the duration itself but only some quantity which provides partial information about it.[1]

5. Economic-theoretical interest often centres on the hazard as a function of both t and $\mathbf{x}$; it rarely, if ever, centres on the mean duration alone, although this latter will need to be studied as a function of $\mathbf{x}$ for policy application of any fitted model.

Several of these points provide the justification for constructing parametric families of duration distributions, thus allowing inference by likelihood methods as opposed to (possibly non-linear) Least Squares regression analysis of durations as a function of $\mathbf{x}$. In particular, the possible time dependence of elements of $\mathbf{x}$, the frequent presence of censoring or other partially observed data, and the theoretical interest in the hazard function all point to likelihood methods. Indeed, regression analysis cannot easily handle either time-varying regressors or censored data. It is also true that even where Least Squares regression is feasible maximum likelihood estimators are more efficient than Least Squares ones. We shall document this fact in chapter 8. Until section 6 the emphasis will be on the case in which any regressor variables are time-invariant.

In sections 2 and 3 we shall describe two broad approaches to the construction of parametric families of duration distributions. In the first of these we show how reasonably flexible parametric families of duration distributions can be derived by a process of successively generalising the form of the error distribution in a linear regression equation. In the second approach, in section 3, we give an account of parametric families that can be generated by a direct specification of the hazard function. Together these cover most of the parametric families that have been used in econometrics and many which have not. Section 4 deals with some parametric families that are of interest but do not fit into the framework provided in either of the preceding two sections.

In section 5 we digress somewhat to examine the question of how an econometrician might compare duration distributions with respect to their concentration or inequality. This is a question that will be of interest to students of economic welfare when the state under study is, for example, that of unemployment.

---

[1] As in the study by Lancaster (1979), in which it was possible only to observe whether unemployed people found a job within a fixed interval of time.

Section 6 gives some further remarks about time-varying covariates and the ways in which the hazard function might depend upon them.

2   Generalising the Error Distribution

Though we have emphasized that the specification of the hazard function is the econometrician's most natural way of writing down a model, there exists, when the regressors are time-invariant, a useful and tractable class of models that can be simply explained as generalisations of a regression equation, an entity familiar to econometricians. We therefore begin with this class.

2.1   One-Parameter Errors

Let us start from the Exponential model of chapter 1, equation (4.13), in the form

$$\log(\theta\,T) = U, \tag{2.1}$$

where $\theta = \theta(\mathbf{x})$, for example, $\theta = \exp\{\beta'\mathbf{x}\}$ in the simple model of chapter 2, equation (2.4). Since $\theta\,T$ is the integrated hazard, $\exp\{U\}$ is a unit Exponential variate. Where $\mathbf{x}$ is time-invariant, equation (2.1) provides, as we have seen, a regression model for $\log T$ with an error distribution which has no unknown parameters. Let us consider generalising the distribution of the error term, U, to a more flexible form involving unknown constants. Allowing for more general error distributions is a route to more general models that is familiar to econometricians.

A natural first generalisation is to introduce a constant of proportionality into the error term in (2.1) by writing

$$\log(\lambda\,T) = \frac{U}{\alpha}, \qquad \alpha > 0, \tag{2.2}$$

where as before $\exp\{U\} \sim \mathcal{E}(1)$. (We have written λ here instead of θ since the expression multiplying T in (2.2) is no longer the hazard function in these generalised models and we use the symbol θ exclusively to denote the hazard function.) This now allows the error variance of $\log T$ to take any positive value since var$(\log T)$ is α^{-2} times the variance of the logarithm of a unit Exponential variate and is thus, using equation (4.12) of chapter 1, equal to $\alpha^{-2}\psi'(1)$, whose value depends upon α. The model reduces to the Exponential distribution when $\alpha = 1$. The distribution of T is easily found since $\lambda\,T = \exp\{U/\alpha\}$, hence $(\lambda\,T)^{\alpha} = \exp\{U\} \sim \mathcal{E}(1)$. Thus $(\lambda\,T)^{\alpha}$ is the integrated hazard function, so from equation (2.3) of chapter 1,

$$\overline{F}(t) = \exp\{-(\lambda\,t)^{\alpha}\} \tag{2.3}$$

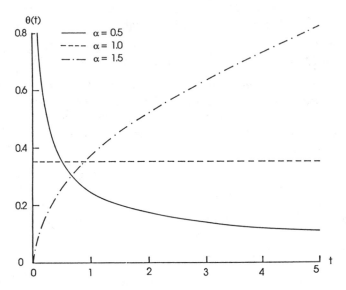

Figure 3.1. Weibull hazard functions.

and

$$f(t) = \alpha \lambda^{\alpha} t^{\alpha - 1} \exp\{-(\lambda t)^{\alpha}\}$$

(2.4)

with the hazard, $f/\overline{F}$, given by

$$\theta(t) = \alpha \lambda^{\alpha} t^{\alpha - 1}.$$

(2.5)

This is the *Weibull* family of duration distributions and has been the model most commonly used in applied econometric work to date. The hazard function (2.5) is time-dependent unless $\alpha = 1$, which is the Exponential case. The hazard increases or decreases monotonically according to whether $\alpha > 1$ or $\alpha < 1$. Note that when time-invariant regressors enter λ, for example in the form $\lambda = \exp\{-\beta' \mathbf{x}\}$, the proportionate effect of each element of $\mathbf{x}$ on the hazard is the same at all dates. For example, if being over fifty years of age lowers the probability of leaving unemployment on the first day by 2 percent it lowers the probability of leaving on the hundred and first day by just the same percentage. Some Weibull hazard functions are sketched in figure 3.1 and some density functions in figure 3.2. All three distributions pictured have a median duration of two time periods.

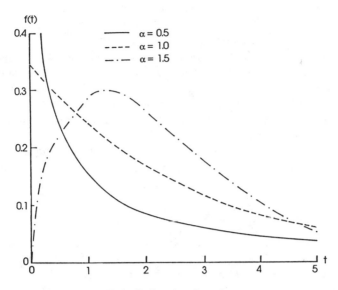

Figure 3.2.   Weibull density functions.

The moments of T are readily found from the fact that $(\lambda T)^{\alpha}$ is distributed as $\mathcal{E}(1)$, so, using equation (4.9) of chapter 1,

$$E\,(\lambda T)^{\alpha s} = \Gamma(1+s),$$

giving

$$E\,(T^j) = \lambda^{-j}\Gamma(1+j/\alpha). \qquad (2.6)$$

In particular

$$E\,(T) = \lambda^{-1}\Gamma(1+1/\alpha), \qquad (2.7)$$
$$\mathrm{var}(T) = \lambda^{-2}\{\Gamma(1+2/\alpha) - \Gamma^2(1+1/\alpha)\}. \qquad (2.8)$$

The moment generating function of $\log T$, $M(s)$, is (2.6) with $j = s$, so the c.g.f. is

$$K_{\log T}(s) = -s\log\lambda + \log\Gamma(1+s/\alpha). \qquad (2.9)$$

The j'th cumulant is thus

$$\kappa_j = \psi^{(j-1)}(1)\,\alpha^{-j}, \qquad j = 2,3,4,\ldots. \qquad (2.10)$$

We get

$$E\,(\log T) = -\log\lambda + \psi(1)/\alpha, \qquad (2.11)$$
$$\mathrm{var}(\log T) = \psi'(1)/\alpha^2. \qquad (2.12)$$

In summary, we have generalised the Exponential model by introducing a scale parameter into the error distribution. The model remains restrictive in that the hazard function is necessarily monotonic. The Weibull model could not, for example, fit the data of section 3 of chapter 1 since, as figure 1.2 of that chapter shows, the hazard function is not monotonic. The Weibull model is, however, analytically easy to handle and computationally straightforward, which doubtless accounts for its use in applied work. If a theory says that people behave in such a way as to continually increase the probability of their leaving unemployment, for example, by steadily lowering their reservation wage, the Weibull model is the simplest one which allows for this possibility and permits measurement of the rate at which the hazard falls.

2.2   Two-Parameter Errors

A natural further extension is to retain the scale parameter α but to assume that, instead of being unit Exponential, $\exp\{U\}$ is a standard Gamma variate with parameter m, a distribution denoted $\mathcal{G}(m)$. That is, if $Y = \exp\{U\}$,

$$f(y) = \frac{y^{m-1}e^{-y}}{\Gamma(m)}, \qquad y \geq 0, \quad m > 0, \tag{2.13}$$

which of course reduces to the model of the last section when $m = 1$. That is, the distribution $\mathcal{G}(1)$ is the same as the distribution $\mathcal{E}(1)$. We now have, since $\log(\lambda T) = U/\alpha$,

$$(\lambda T)^{\alpha} = \exp\{U\} = Y. \tag{2.14}$$

To find the p.d.f. of T we change the variable in (2.13) using $\alpha\lambda^{\alpha}t^{\alpha-1}\,dt = dy$ to get

$$f(t) = \frac{\alpha\lambda^{\alpha m}t^{\alpha m-1}\exp\{-(\lambda t)^{\alpha}\}}{\Gamma(m)}. \tag{2.15}$$

This is the *generalised Gamma* family of density functions. It reduces to the Weibull when $m = 1$, to the two-parameter Gamma distribution when $\alpha = 1$, and to the Exponential model from which we started when $\alpha = m = 1$.

The survivor function is an incomplete Gamma integral (after the change of variable from t to t^{α}) and cannot be written in closed form. Thus neither can the hazard function. The hazard function is not necessarily monotonic and indeed for $\alpha m > 1$ and $\alpha < 1$ it is inverted U-shaped varying from zero at $t = 0$ to zero at $t \to \infty$, and for $\alpha m < 1$ and $\alpha > 1$ it is U-shaped varying from ∞ at $t \to 0$ to ∞ at $t \to \infty$.

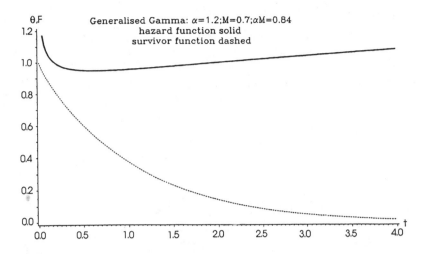

Figure 3.3a.   A generalised Gamma distribution: the hazard (—) and survivor function (--): $\alpha = 1.2, m = 0.7$.

Outside these regions the hazards vary monotonically between zero and infinity, increasing if alpha exceeds one and decreasing otherwise. If this distribution were fitted to the employment duration data of Chapter 1 we would expect to find $\alpha < 1$ and $\alpha m > 1$ implying $m > 1$. Figure 3.3 sketches some generalised Gamma hazard functions.

The moments of T and the m.g.f. of $\log T$ are readily found from that of the standard Gamma variate Y with p.d.f. given by (2.13) for

$$\mathrm{E}\,(Y^j) = \int_0^\infty \frac{y^{j+m-1}e^{-y}\,dy}{\Gamma(m)}$$

$$= \frac{\Gamma(j+m)}{\Gamma(m)}. \tag{2.16}$$

Then from the relation (2.14)

$$\mathrm{E}\,(T^j) = \frac{\lambda^{-j}\,\Gamma(m+j/\alpha)}{\Gamma(m)}, \tag{2.17}$$

and, in particular,

$$\mathrm{E}\,(T) = \lambda^{-1}\frac{\Gamma(m+1/\alpha)}{\Gamma(m)}, \tag{2.18}$$

$$\mathrm{var}(T) = \lambda^{-2}\left\{\frac{\Gamma(m+2/\alpha)}{\Gamma(m)} - \left[\frac{\Gamma(m+1/\alpha)}{\Gamma(m)}\right]^2\right\}. \tag{2.19}$$

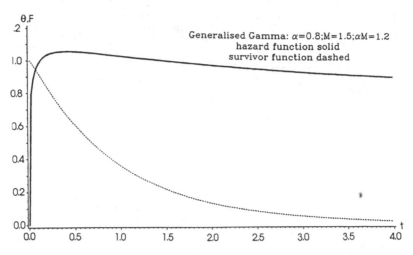

Figure 3.3b. A generalised Gamma distribution: the hazard (—) and survivor function (−−): $\alpha = 0.8, m = 1.5$.

The cumulant generating function of $\log T$ is the log of (2.17) with $j = s$,

$$K_{\log T}(s) = -s \log \lambda + \log \Gamma(m + s/\alpha) - \log \Gamma(m), \qquad (2.20)$$

from which we easily derive

$$\mathrm{E}\,(\log T) = -\log \lambda + \psi(m)/\alpha, \qquad (2.21)$$
$$\mathrm{var}(\log T) = \psi'(m)/\alpha^2, \qquad (2.22)$$

generalising (2.11) and (2.12). Of course, we still have a homoscedastic model for $\log T$, linear in $\mathbf{x}$ if $\lambda = \exp\{-\beta'\mathbf{x}\}$, by construction because we are simply generalising the error distribution in such a homoscedastic log-linear model.

2.3   Accelerated Failure-Time Models

The models of the last two sections are clearly special cases of a general family of models, which are usually called *accelerated failure-time* models. In these models the duration for a person with time-invariant regressor vector $\mathbf{x}$ can be written

$$T = T_0/\lambda(\mathbf{x}'\beta). \qquad (2.23)$$

Here T_0 is a random variable with a distribution not involving $\mathbf{x}$ or β. For example, in section 2.1 T_0 was distributed as a positive power of a unit Exponential variate, whereas in section 2.2 it was distributed as a positive power of a standard Gamma variate. The duration or failure-time of someone with regressor vector $\mathbf{x}$ is accelerated or decelerated relative to T_0 according to whether $\lambda > 1$ or $\lambda < 1$, which explains the name of the family.

On taking the logarithm of (2.23) we have

$$\log T = -\log \lambda(\mathbf{x}'\beta) + \log T_0. \tag{2.24}$$

This means that the accelerated failure-time models are those in which $\log T$ satisfies a regression model like (2.24) with an error term whose distribution is that of $\log T_0$. The regression is parametrically linear if $\lambda(.)$ is the Exponential function and non-linear otherwise. In either case the model is homoscedastic.[2]

These log-linear models for T should not be confused with the family of log-linear hazard models which we shall describe in section 3.1.2.

3   Direct Specification of the Hazard

A fact we use repeatedly in this book is that the integrated hazard is a unit Exponential variate (when the regressors are time-invariant or exogenous) implying that

$$Z = \int_0^T \theta(s, \mathbf{x})\, ds \sim \mathcal{E}(1) \tag{3.1}$$

given $\mathbf{x}$, or, equivalently,

$$\log Z(T, \mathbf{x}) = U, \tag{3.2}$$

where $\exp\{U\} \sim \mathcal{E}(1)$ given $\mathbf{x}$. In the previous section we produced a family of models for duration distributions by restricting $Z(T, \mathbf{x})$ to be of the form $\lambda(\mathbf{x})\, T$ and then generalising the distribution of U regarded as the error term in a linear model for $\log T$. In this section we retain the assumption that $\exp\{U\}$ is unit Exponential and consider more general forms for $Z(\mathbf{x}, T)$ than $\lambda(\mathbf{x})\, T$. We shall consider functional forms for the hazard, and therefore the integrated hazard, as functions of fixed and time-varying regressors and of duration. This route to more general models has been the one taken by most econometricians because economic theory can sometimes provide guidance about the choice of functional forms for θ.

---

[2] Ridder (1988) has discussed a generalisation of this class of models in which the left-hand side is replaced by $\log z(t)$, where $z(.)$ is an an arbitrary non-decreasing function defined on $[0, \infty)$. He calls these generalised accelerated failure-time, or GAFT, models.

3.1   Two General Families

3.1.1 *Proportional Hazards*

If the regressors are time-invariant a model for $\theta(\mathbf{x}, t)$ of the form

$$\theta(\mathbf{x}, t) = k_1(\mathbf{x})\, k_2(t), \tag{3.3}$$

where k_1 and k_2 are the same functions for all individuals, is called a *proportional hazard* model. This is because the hazards for two people with regressor vectors $\mathbf{x}_1$ and $\mathbf{x}_2$ are in the same ratio, $k_1(\mathbf{x}_1)/k_1(\mathbf{x}_2)$, for all t. For example, the Exponential model with $\theta(\mathbf{x}, t) = \exp\{\beta'\mathbf{x}\}$ is a proportional hazard (PH) model, with $k_2 \equiv 1$. The function $k_2(t)$ is called the *baseline hazard*.

The assumption of proportional hazards permits a great simplification of inference in duration models because, as Cox (1972) pointed out, it is possible to estimate the unknown parameters of $k_1(\mathbf{x})$ (even when the regressors are time-varying) without specifying the form of the common function k_2, thus providing a partially non-parametric estimator for these constants. We shall give an account of this approach in Chapter 9. In fact, however, economists have normally provided a fully parametrically specified model but have nonetheless often adopted a factoring assumption like (3.3) in their specification.

If the model contains time-varying covariates and takes the form $\theta(\mathbf{x}, t) = k_1(\mathbf{x}(t))k_2(t)$ then it is no longer a proportional hazard, unless the time-varying covariates are the same functions for every member of the population. Nonetheless the phrase 'proportional hazard' is commonly used to describe models of this type. This usage refers to models involving a multiplicative, common, function of time, that is, a baseline hazard, which the investigator proposes to leave parametrically unspecified.

3.1.2 *Log-Linear Hazards*

A model in which the hazard can be written

$$\log \theta(\mathbf{x}, t) = \sum_{j=1}^{K} \gamma_j k_j(\mathbf{x}(t), t), \tag{3.4}$$

where the $\{k_j\}$ are *known* functions is a log-linear hazard model. The 'linearity' is linearity in the parameters $\{\gamma_j\}$, not in $\mathbf{x}$ or t. This class of models also offers some advantages, in particular, the likelihood function in, possibly right censored, random sampling from the distribution of T can be shown to be concave which, of course, is important in the calculation of maximum likelihood estimates. We shall expand upon this point in chapter 8, which deals with fully parametric inference. The Exponential model with $\theta = \exp\{\mathbf{x}'\beta\}$ is both log-linear and PH, and the Weibull model of section 2.1, which is also PH, can be reparametrised to be log-linear when λ takes this form.

3.2   Piecewise-Constant Hazards

A model which sets

$$
\theta(t) = \left\{
\begin{array}{ll}
\theta_1, & 0 \leq t \leq c_1, \\
\theta_2, & c_1 < t \leq c_2, \\
\cdot & \\
\cdot & \\
\theta_M, & c_{M-1} < t < \infty,
\end{array}
\right. \tag{3.5}
$$

for $M - 1$ known constants $\{c_m\}$ and M unknown constants $\{\theta_m\}$ is *piecewise-constant*. The survivor function is

$$
\overline{F}(t) = \exp\left\{ -\int_0^t \theta(s)\, ds \right\}
$$

$$
= \exp\left\{ -\sum_{j=0}^{m} b_j \theta_j - (t - c_m)\theta_{m+1} \right\}; \tag{3.6}
$$

$$
c_m < t \leq c_{m+1}, \quad m = 0, 1, 2, \ldots, M - 1,
$$

where $b_j = c_j - c_{j-1}$ and using the convention that $c_0 = 0 = b_0, c_M = \infty$. The (discontinuous) density function is

$$
f(t) = \theta_{m+1} \overline{F}(t); \qquad c_m < t \leq c_{m+1}; \quad m = 0, 1, 2, \ldots, M - 1. \tag{3.7}
$$

The piecewise-constant hazard is essentially a way of letting the data tell us how the hazard behaves as a function of time. The $\{\theta_m\}$ are a set of descriptive statistics and they would not generally have any behavioural interpretation. The piecewise-constant hazard was the model fitted to the employment data of chapter 1 generating the hazard function depicted in figure 1.2. It is clearly possible to generalise the method to fit a continuous piecewise linear, or general piecewise polynomial, hazard function by the method of splines. This would give smoother fitted functions at the expense of more computation. It is also straightforward to introduce time-invariant regressors into the model in a proportional hazards form by, say, writing

$$
\theta(t) = k_1(\mathbf{x})\,\theta_m; \qquad c_{m-1} < t \leq c_m, \quad m = 1, 2, \ldots, M. \tag{3.8}
$$

One can also extend the model to allow for time-varying regressors by writing

$$
\theta(t) = k_1(\mathbf{x}(t))\theta_m; \qquad c_{m-1} < t \leq c_m, m = 1, 2, \ldots, M.
$$

This extension is relatively simple if the regressors can be assumed time-invariant *within* each interval $(c_{m-1}, c_m]$.[3] Note that if $\log k_1$ is parametrically linear the piecewise-constant model is a log-linear model if we reparametrise from the theta's to their logarithms.

3.3   Weibull Hazards

The proportional hazard model

$$\theta(t) = k_1(\mathbf{x})\,\alpha t^{\alpha-1}$$

is the Weibull model, derived by generalising the error term in section 2.1 and discussed there. In the notation of that section, $k_1 = \lambda^{\alpha}$. The choice $k_1(\mathbf{x}) = \exp\{\beta'\mathbf{x}\}$ is the most commonly used regression functional form. With this choice the Weibull model is log-linear.

3.4   Log-Logistic Hazards

The Weibull hazard is monotonic. A similarly simple hazard that permits non-monotonic behaviour is the form

$$\theta(t) = \frac{k_1(\mathbf{x})\alpha t^{\alpha-1}}{1 + k_1(\mathbf{x})t^{\alpha}} \tag{3.9}$$

with survivor function

$$\overline{F}(t) = (1 + k_1(\mathbf{x})t^{\alpha})^{-1}, \tag{3.10}$$

and density function

$$f(t) = \frac{k_1(\mathbf{x})\alpha t^{\alpha-1}}{(1 + k_1(\mathbf{x})t^{\alpha})^2}. \tag{3.11}$$

The change of variable to $y = \log t$ in (3.11) gives

$$f(y) = \frac{\alpha e^{\alpha(y-\mu)}}{(1 + e^{\alpha(y-\mu)})^2}, \qquad -\infty < y < \infty,$$

for $\mu = -\alpha^{-1}\log k_1(\mathbf{x})$.

This is recognisable as a Logistic p.d.f. of mean μ and variance $\pi^2/3\alpha^2$. Thus $\log T$ has a Logistic distribution when the hazard is of the form (3.9) and it has linear homoscedastic regression on $\mathbf{x}$ when $k_1(\mathbf{x})$ is of the form $\exp\{\mathbf{x}'\beta\}$.

The hazard function behaves in the following way:

---

[3] See Meyer (1986).

$\alpha < 1, \theta$ decreases monotonically from ∞ at the origin to zero as $t \to \infty$;

$\alpha = 1, \theta$ decreases monotonically from k_1 at the origin to zero as $t \to \infty$;

$\alpha > 1, \theta$ increases from zero at the origin to a single maximum at $t = [(\alpha - 1)/k_1]^{1/\alpha}$ and then approaches zero as $t \to \infty$.

Thus an inverted U-shape is generated if α exceeds 1. Note that the model is neither proportional hazard nor log-linear.

3.5   Box–Cox Hazards

If we write the Weibull hazard in the form

$$\theta(t) = k_1(\mathbf{x})\, \alpha \exp\{(\alpha - 1)\log t\} \tag{3.12}$$

another generalisation suggests itself from the facts, much used in econometrics, that the function $(t^\lambda - 1)/\lambda = t^{(\lambda)}$ – the Box–Cox transformation – is such that

$$t^{(1)} = t - 1$$
$$\lim_{\lambda \to 0} t^{(\lambda)} = \lim_{\lambda \to 0} (t^\lambda - 1)/\lambda$$
$$= \lim_{\lambda \to 0} t^\lambda \log t, \quad \text{by l'Hôpital's rule,}$$
$$= \log t.$$

Thus the hazard

$$\theta(t) = k_1(\mathbf{x})\alpha \exp\{\gamma t^{(\lambda)}\}, \qquad \gamma = \alpha - 1, \quad \lambda \ge 0, \tag{3.13}$$

reduces to the Weibull hazard for $\lambda = 0$ and to the *Gompertz* form

$$\theta(t) = k_1(\mathbf{x})\alpha \exp\{\gamma t - \gamma\} \tag{3.14}$$

when $\lambda = 1$. This latter form has the property that the duration distribution is defective if $\gamma < 0$, that is, $\alpha < 1$, since

$$\int_0^t \theta(s)\, ds \propto \exp\{\gamma t\},$$

which converges if $\gamma < 0$. A hazard which decreases exponentially goes to zero too fast to let everyone leave with probability one. Some fraction of a large cohort of entrants to the state will stay there forever.

Although the hazard (3.13) does generalise the Weibull, it still permits only monotonic variation since $dt^{(\lambda)}/dt = t^{\lambda-1}$, which is of constant sign. Flinn and Heckman (1982) have suggested adding a second Box–Cox transformation and writing

$$\theta(t) = k_1(\mathbf{x}) \exp\{\gamma_1 t^{(\lambda_1)} + \gamma_2 t^{(\lambda_2)}\} \tag{3.15}$$

with $\lambda_2 > \lambda_1 \geq 0$. This can generate non-monotonic hazards, for example, when $\lambda_2 = 2$ and $\lambda_1 = 1$, $\log \theta$ is of the quadratic log hazard form

$$\log \theta(t) = \text{constant} + \gamma_1 t + \gamma_2 t^2. \tag{3.16}$$

For $\gamma_2 < 0$ and $\gamma_1 > 0$ this has a maximum at $t = -\gamma_1/\gamma_2$, though like the Gompertz model the hazard goes to zero too fast as $t \to \infty$ to generate a proper duration distribution. It is defective if $\gamma_2 < 0$. If $\gamma_2 > 0$ and $\gamma_1 < 0$ the hazard is U-shaped and goes from ∞ to ∞ with a minimum at $t = -\gamma_1/\gamma_2$.

3.6   Rational Log Hazards

Another family giving a richness of possible hazard forms is that generated by letting the log hazard be a rational function of t,

$$\log \theta(t) = \log k_1(\mathbf{x}) + \gamma A(t)/B(t), \tag{3.17}$$

where A and B are polynomials of low order of the form

$$\frac{A(t)}{B(t)} = \frac{1 + \alpha_1 t + \alpha_2 t^2 + \ldots + \alpha_p t^p}{1 + \beta_1 t + \beta_2 t^2 + \ldots + \beta_q t^q}. \tag{3.18}$$

This log hazard is $\log k_1(\mathbf{x}) + \gamma$ at the origin and as t goes to ∞ it behaves like $[\alpha_p/\beta_q]t^{p-q}$, where p and q are the terms in A and B of largest order with non-zero coefficients.

An alternative possibility is to replace t by $\log(t+c)$, $t > 0$, in (3.18). The particular case where A is quadratic, B is one, and $\gamma = 1$ gives

$$\log \theta(t) = \log k_1(\mathbf{x}) + \alpha_1 \log(t + c) + \alpha_2 \log^2(t + c).$$

The reason for the constant c is that with $c > 0$ the hazard is finite at the origin, whereas with $c = 0$ the hazard is infinite at the origin and the integral

$$\lim_{u \to 0} \int_u^t \theta(s)\, ds$$

diverges. Effectively, all the probability of leaving is placed at the origin and the model is degenerate if $\alpha_2 > 0$ in (3.18). A positive c allows a greater variety of hazard shapes. With $c = 1$ week this model fits the job tenure data of chapter 1 rather well.[4] If, as with these data, $\alpha_1 > 0$ and $\alpha_2 < 0$ the hazard is inverted U-shaped and the distribution is defective since for large t the hazard behaves like $\exp\{\alpha_2 \log^2(t + 1)\}$, whose integral over the positive axis converges. An interpretation of this

---

[4] See Lancaster, Imbens, and Dolton (1987).

defectiveness would be the lifetime attachment of an employee to the same firm.

Both Box–Cox and rational hazards are not computationally simple since, in general, they do not give a closed form representation for the survivor function. This means that calculating the likelihood function for N observations requires N numerical integrations. This is feasible but lengthy.

4   Some Other Models

In this section we shall give a number of other models which do not readily fit into the framework of our exposition but which it is useful to mention.

4.1   The Lognormal Model

In this model $\log T$ is distributed Normally with mean $\mu = \mu(\mathbf{x})$ and variance σ^2. Thus, as in the models of section 2, the Lognormal model can provide a homoscedastic linear model for $\log T$. If ϕ denotes the *standard* Normal density function and Φ the corresponding distribution function with $\overline{\Phi}$ its complement, the density function for T in the Lognormal model is

$$f(t) = \frac{\phi(x)}{\sigma t}, \qquad \text{where } x = \frac{\log t - \mu}{\sigma}. \tag{4.1}$$

The survivor function is

$$\overline{F}(t) = \overline{\Phi}(x) \tag{4.2}$$

and the hazard function is

$$\theta(t) = \frac{\phi(x)}{\sigma t \overline{\Phi}(x)}$$
$$= \frac{h(x)}{\sigma t}. \tag{4.3}$$

Before giving the properties of θ let us consider the function $h(x) = \phi(x)/\overline{\Phi}(x)$ of (4.3) regarded as a function of x. This function, which may, with some abuse of language since x is not non-negative, be called the standard Normal hazard function, occurs in several areas of econometrics and it is worth noting its shape which is given in the figure 3.4.

Some particular values are given in table 3.1.

The function $h(x)$ increases monotonically from zero as x increases from $-\infty$, and as $x \to \infty$, $h(x)$ approaches x.

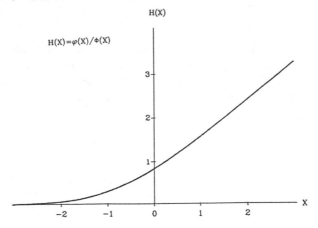

Figure 3.4. The standard Normal hazard function.

Turning now to the hazard function of the Lognormal distribution we see that since $h(x) \sim x$ for large x then $\theta(t) \sim (\log t - \mu)/t\sigma^2$ for large t so that $\theta(t)$ approaches zero as $t \to \infty$. Furthermore, since the Lognormal p.d.f. is zero at the origin then $\theta(0) = 0$. Thus the hazard first increases from zero and then, ultimately, falls to zero. It does in fact have a single maximum at a value of $x = (\log t - \mu)/\sigma$ satisfying

$$h(x) = \sigma + x,$$

an equation which can be solved using figure 3.4 for any choice of σ. Figure 3.5 sketches a Lognormal hazard function for $\mu = 0$ and $\sigma = 1$ for which $\mathrm{E}\,(T) = 1.649$ and $\mathrm{var}(T) = 4.671$.

Table 3.1. Some
Values of the
Standard Normal
Hazard Function

x	$h(x)$
-3	.0044
-2	.0553
-1	.2876
0	.7978
1	1.5249
2	2.3684
3	3.2593

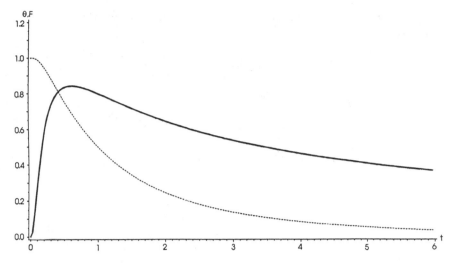

Figure 3.5. A Lognormal hazard (—) and survivor function (--):
$\mu = 0, \sigma = 1$.

The moments of T are readily deduced from the moment generating
function of the standard Normal variate $Y = (\log T - \mu)/\sigma$ given by

$$M_Y(s) = \mathrm{E}\left(e^{sY}\right) = \exp\{s^2/2\},$$

since $\mathrm{E}\left(T^j\right) = \mathrm{E}\left(\exp\{j \log T\}\right) = \mathrm{E}\left(\exp\{j(\sigma Y + \mu)\}\right)$. Thus,

$$\mathrm{E}\left(T^j\right) = \exp\{j\mu + j^2\sigma^2/2\} \tag{4.4}$$

and in particular,

$$\mathrm{E}\left(T\right) = \exp\{\mu + \sigma^2/2\},$$
$$\mathrm{var}(T) = \exp\{2\mu + \sigma^2\}(e^{\sigma^2} - 1). \tag{4.5}$$

The coefficient of variation of T is $\sqrt{\exp\{\sigma^2\} - 1}$.

4.2 The Inverse Gaussian Model

The Inverse Gaussian distribution is the distribution of the first passage
time to an absorbing barrier in a particular continuous-time random
walk, namely, Brownian motion. It arises rather naturally in a class of
structural econometric models in which an optimal decision to change
state can be represented as the event that a stochastic process crosses
a barrier. We shall discuss this class of structural models in chapter 6;
here we record the main properties of the distribution.

The distribution is a two-parameter (μ, σ) family, the density function being

$$f(t) = \frac{1}{t^{3/2}} \phi\left(\frac{\mu t - 1}{\sigma\sqrt{t}}\right), \tag{4.6}$$

and the survivor function being,

$$\overline{F}(t) = \overline{\Phi}\left(\frac{\mu t - 1}{\sigma\sqrt{t}}\right) - e^{2\mu/\sigma^2}\overline{\Phi}\left(\frac{\mu t + 1}{\sigma\sqrt{t}}\right). \tag{4.7}$$

All moments exist if $\mu > 0$ and in this case the mean and variance of T are

$$\mathrm{E}\,(T) = \frac{1}{\mu},$$

$$\mathrm{var}(T) = \frac{\sigma^2}{\mu^3}. \tag{4.8}$$

If $\mu = 0$ the distribution is proper but has no finite positive moments. If $\mu < 0$ the distribution is defective. The density function is unimodal, zero at the origin, and skewed to the right though not as much as a Lognormal distribution with the same coefficient of variation. The hazard function rises from zero at the origin to a single maximum located at t_m satisfying

$$\frac{1}{3\sigma^2} < t_m < \frac{2}{3\sigma^2}$$

and then falls to approach the value $\mu^2/2\sigma^2$ asymptotically as $t \to \infty$. Additional information about the Inverse Gaussian distribution is given in chapter 6.

5   The Concentration of Duration Distributions

In this chapter we have been examining parametric families of duration distributions and making comparisons among them primarily in terms of their hazard functions. There are, of course, many other ways of comparing families of distributions and one in particular which will be of interest to economists is to study their concentration. When economists compare distributions of income or wealth they may examine the extent to which the distributions are unequal or concentrated. This comparison may also be of interest when the variable is not wealth but time. For instance, suppose that a large number of people become unemployed and they return to work stochastically according to some duration distribution with survivor function $\overline{F}(t)$. It seems reasonable to inquire how the total burden of unemployment experienced by these people is shared

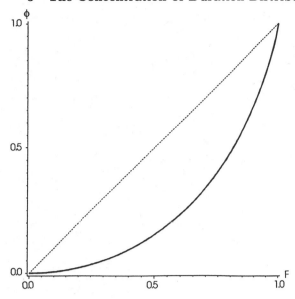

Figure 3.6.   The Lorenz curve for the Exponential distribution.

among them. Does the form of $\overline{F}$ imply that a small minority of people suffer most of the unemployment or is it that there is near equality in the length of spells?

To examine the concentration of income or wealth it is customary to study the Lorenz curve and the Gini coefficient. The same tools apply when studying the concentration of unemployment durations and are, in fact, particularly analytically tractable for many common families of duration distributions.

Let $f(t)$ be the density function of duration corresponding to the survivor function $\overline{F}$ and distribution function F and let $\mu = E(T)$. In a large population the proportion of the total months of unemployment that is undergone by those whose durations are at most t is

$$G(t) = \frac{\int_0^t s f(s)\,ds}{\mu}.$$

The Lorenz curve plots $G(t)$ against $F(t)$, and the Gini coefficient, g, is twice the area between this curve and the 45° line, $G = F$. As can be seen from figure 3.6,

$$g = 2 \int_0^1 F\,dG - 1.$$

Since $\int_0^1 F\,dG = \int_0^\infty F(s)sf(s)\,ds/\mu$, integration by parts shows that g may be written

$$g = 1 - \frac{\int_0^\infty \overline{F}^2(s)\,ds}{\mu}$$

$$= 1 - \frac{\int_0^\infty \overline{F}^2(s)\,ds}{\int_0^\infty \overline{F}(s)\,ds}. \tag{5.1}$$

Here we have used the fact – equation (2.7) of chapter 1 – that the mean is the integral of the survivor function. Similarly, the equation of the Lorenz curve may be written as

$$G(F) = \frac{\int_0^t \overline{F}(s)\,ds - t\overline{F}(t)}{\int_0^\infty \overline{F}(s)\,ds}. \tag{5.2}$$

These expressions of the Lorenz curve and Gini coefficient in terms of the survivor function, and hence in terms of the integrated hazard function, are convenient for duration distributions specified in terms of the hazard function. Let us use them to examine some particular cases and then give an interesting general theorem.

Example 1   The Exponential Distribution
When $\overline{F}(t) = e^{-\theta t}$,

$$\int_0^\infty \overline{F}^k(s)\,ds = \frac{1}{k\theta}, \qquad k > 0.$$

Thus we find that for the Exponential distribution $g = \frac{1}{2}$ independently of the value of θ. The Lorenz curve is readily found to be

$$\overline{G} = \overline{F} - \overline{F}\log\overline{F},$$

where $\overline{G} = 1 - G$. $\overline{G}$ is the fraction of all the unemployment experienced by the $100\overline{F}$ percent of people with the longest spells.

Some particular points on the curve are given in table 3.2.

From the table we see, for example, that one third of all the unemployment is experienced by 10 percent of the people, and 85 percent of it is experienced by half the people. The Gini coefficient of one half is large compared to the values we are used to seeing with income and wealth data. The Gini coefficients for income distributions in developed economies are typically of the order of 0.35. If duration distributions *were* Exponential, unemployment would be much more unequally distributed than, say, British or American incomes. ∎

Table 3.2.   The
Exponential
Lorenz Curve

$\overline{F}$	$\overline{G}$
.05	.20
.10	.33
.50	.85
.90	.995
.95	.999

Example 2   The Weibull Distribution
When $\overline{F}(t) = e^{-\theta t^\alpha}$ we find that

$$g = 1 - (1/2)^{\frac{1}{\alpha}}.$$

Note that if $\alpha < 1$, so the hazard is monotonically decreasing, then $g > 1/2$ and the distribution is more concentrated than the Exponential. ∎

Example 3   Gamma Mixture of Exponentials
To anticipate a model discussed in chapter 4, if θ in Example 1 varies over the population according to the Gamma distribution with mean $\overline{\theta}$ and variance $\sigma^2(< 1)$, we have the particular *Burr* family,

$$\overline{F}(t) = (1 + \sigma^2\overline{\theta}t)^{-1/\sigma^2},$$

and we find that

$$g = \frac{1}{2 - \sigma^2}.$$

Note again that $g > 1/2$ if $\sigma^2 > 0$. Also, as σ^2 approaches 1 – it must be less than 1 for $\mathrm{E}(T)$ to exist – g approaches 1 and the Lorenz curve approaches the edge of the 'Lorenz Box'. ∎

   The last two examples suggest that any distribution with a strictly decreasing hazard function is more concentrated than the Exponential distribution. This is in fact true and follows as a corollary of a theorem of Barlow and Proschan. Let us, for purposes of the theorem, refer to a distribution with strictly decreasing hazard function as a *Decreasing Failure Rate* (DFR) distribution.

Theorem 1   *Let F be a DFR distribution with mean μ and let $\overline{H}$ be the survivor function of an Exponential distribution of the same mean,*

$\overline{H}(t) = e^{-t/\mu}$. *Then if* $\phi(t)$ *is decreasing*

$$\int_0^\infty \phi(t)\overline{F}(t)\,dt \le \int_0^\infty \phi(t)\overline{H}(t)\,dt.$$

Proof: Since F is a DFR distribution, $\log \overline{F}(t)$ is a decreasing convex function of t and therefore the line $-t/\mu$ agrees with $\log \overline{F}(t)$ at the origin and intersects $\log \overline{F}(t)$ at most once for $t > 0$. If $-t/\mu$ does not intersect $\log \overline{F}(t)$ then $\overline{F}(t) > e^{-t/\mu}, t > 0$, and $\int_0^\infty \overline{F}(t)\,dt = \mu > \int_0^\infty e^{-t/\mu}\,dt = \mu$, which is a contradiction. Hence $\overline{F}$ intersects $e^{-t/\mu}$ only once, from below, at, say, t_0. Thus

$$\int_0^\infty \phi(t)[\overline{F}(t) - \overline{H}(t)]\,dt = \int_0^\infty [\phi(t) - \phi(t_0)][\overline{F}(t) - \overline{H}(t)]\,dt \le 0. \quad \blacksquare$$

As a corollary of this theorem we have that no DFR distribution has a smaller Gini coefficient than the Exponential distribution.

Corollary　*For any decreasing failure rate (hazard) distribution* $g \ge \frac{1}{2}$.

Proof: Two applications of the theorem with ϕ successively as $\overline{F}$ and $\overline{H}$, both decreasing, give

$$\int_0^\infty \overline{F}^2(s)\,ds \le \int_0^\infty \overline{H}^2(s)\,ds \le \int_0^\infty e^{-2s/\mu}\,ds = \frac{\mu}{2}.$$

Hence

$$g = 1 - \frac{\int_0^\infty \overline{F}^2(s)\,ds}{\mu} \ge 1 - \frac{\mu/2}{\mu} = \frac{1}{2}. \quad \blacksquare$$

The fact that no DFR distribution has a smaller Gini coefficient than the Exponential distribution does not imply that no DFR distribution has a Lorenz curve that never lies above that for the Exponential, but this is in fact true.

Theorem 2　*The Lorenz curves of DFR distributions lie below the Lorenz curve for the Exponential distribution.*

We omit the proof, which is straightforward.

Since it is empirically true that hazard functions for exit from unemployment are decreasing, the corollary to theorem 1 implies that Gini coefficients in excess of one half describe the concentration of (single spell) unemployment experience. These results must, however, be qualified by the observation that to the extent that people experience repeat spells of unemployment the effects of ill luck will average out and inequality will tend to be reduced. A comparison of the inequality of single spells will exaggerate the inequality in, say, lifetime experience of unemployment.

6   Time-Varying Regressors

We shall conclude this account of some parametric models with a few remarks about models involving a time-varying covariate $x(t)$. Consider a model in which the hazard at time t, conditional on the entire path, $\mathbf{X}$, of a defined external covariate – chapter 2, section 3 – depends upon this path only through the current level of the variate, $x(t)$, and the dependence is of the simple form

$$\theta(t; \mathbf{X}) = \exp\{\beta_0 + \beta_1 x(t)\}. \tag{6.1}$$

Note that it may be that $x(t)$ itself summarises the relevant features of the *future* path of some more fundamental process, such as where $x(t)$ is the time remaining from t until exhaustion of entitlement to unemployment benefit.

The interpretation of the coefficient β_1 is that it measures the effect on the log hazard of a unit change in the value of x at time t. In our example it would measure the effect on the probability of leaving unemployment at t of, say, a one month increase in the time to benefit exhaustion. However, in practice one is likely to want to calculate the effect of a change in the path of an exogenous covariate upon the expected duration of stay. This expectation is given by

$$\mathrm{E}\,(T|\mathbf{X}) = \int_0^\infty \exp\left\{ -\int_0^t \theta(s; x(s))\, ds \right\} dt, \tag{6.2}$$

where we have used the fact that when we condition on the entire covariate path the integrand is a valid survivor function, and the fact that the mean is the integral of the survivor function. Determination of the way in which this expectation changes when the path of $\{x(t)\}$ changes may be done analytically if, as in the case of unemployment benefits, that path is specified by a number of constants, for example, the expiration date and the various levels of payment at different times. In this case one would simply differentiate under the integrals in (6.2) with respect to, say, the expiration date. In the case where the path is not so specified it would be reasonable to compute numerically the value of (6.2) for alternative choices of the covariate path.

One interesting feature of the model (6.1) is brought out by comparing it to a model with a time-constant regressor vector

$$\theta(t; x) = \exp\{\beta_0 + \beta_1 x\} \tag{6.3}$$

and a Weibull model with no regressors

$$\theta(t) = \alpha t^{\alpha - 1}$$
$$= \exp\{\log \alpha + (\alpha - 1) \log t\}$$
$$= \exp\{\beta_0 + \beta_1 x(t)\} \tag{6.4}$$

for $x(t) = \log t$. Comparing (6.1) and (6.4) we see that the introduction of a defined external regressor is really only a more complex, and usually person-specific, form of time dependence in the hazard function. But notice that to identify β_1 in (6.3) we must observe individuals with different values of x, whereas we can identify β_1 in (6.1) and β_1 in (6.4) even when the function $x(t)$ is the same function for every individual. The information used to estimate the slope coefficients in (6.1) and (6.4) is, in this case, in the comparison of the fraction of the survivors *at different dates* who leave 'the next day', whereas the information used to estimate β_1 in (6.3) is in the comparison of groups of survivors *with different x's* at possibly the same time. In effect, variation in x over time is an alternative to variation over people in allowing us to estimate its effect.

In models in which one conditions only on the covariate path to time t, $\mathbf{X}(t)$, it will be necessary to calculate expected values of T from the joint probability of $T = t$ and $\mathbf{X}(t)$, given by equations (3.6) and (3.12) of chapter 2. This is because there is no meaningful density of T conditional on $\mathbf{X}(t)$ and therefore no meaningful conditional expectation in this case. One would calculate $P(T = t)$ by summing or integrating over the possible realisations of the path $\mathbf{X}(t)$ for each value of t, and then form $E(T)$ as $\sum t P(T = t)$. This is a rather complicated calculation, and moreover it is not clear that the result would be of much econometric interest.

There has been little study so far of parametrisations of the dependence of the hazard on time-varying covariates that might be useful to econometricians and we shall therefore leave the subject at this point. In the next chapter we move to a subject that has preoccupied econometricians, namely, the question of models with unobserved covariates.

7   Concluding Remarks about Parametric Models

This chapter has covered a great variety of models ranging from those, such as the Weibull, in which time variation in the hazard is represented by a single parameter to those, such as the piecewise-constant model, which allow as many parameters as the data will support. At the present stage of econometric work in this area it seems as though models specified in terms of a very small number of parameters are no longer necessary. The availability of sample sizes that are usually in the hundreds and often more, together with the vastly increased access to, and speed of, computer hardware and software, mean that extreme parametric economy is not required. It is true that a proliferation of parameters can make the interpretation of one's results more difficult, but this is not necessarily so. The model fitted to the job tenure data in chapter 1, the output of which is represented in figure 1.2 of that chapter, is not difficult to comprehend and that model allows the data to reveal in some detail the time path of the hazard function. I conclude that an econometric investigation ought generally to feature a parametrisation rich enough to allow the data to reveal clearly the apparent behaviour of the agents from whom it is obtained. Extremely parsimonious parametrisations seem to belong to an earlier stage in the evolution of the subject.

NOTE

There are now a number of texts that give an account of the main parametric families that might be used in modelling duration data. These include Cox and Oakes (1984) and Kalbfleisch and Prentice (1980). The proportional hazards specification was emphasised and exploited by Cox (1972) and has been used by econometricians. It is interesting to note that no econometrician, to the author's knowledge, has ever given an economic-theoretical justification of why hazards should be proportional, or even approximately so. The log-linear hazard specification is treated in Lancaster and Imbens (1986). The Inverse Gaussian model was used in Lancaster (1972). Meyer (1986) has used piecewise-constant hazard models with time-varying covariates.

CHAPTER 4

Mixture Models

1   Introduction

In this chapter we shall give an account of models for single and multiple spell duration data that are generated by supposing that the population from which we are sampling consists of a set of sub-populations in each of which the duration of stay in a state is determined by a stochastic model of the type we have been describing in the last three chapters. When these models vary between sub-populations we are sampling from a mixture of distributions and the model governing the sample data is a *mixture model.*

Suppose now that θ involves an individual specific, time-invariant, quantity v, to be regarded as a realisation of a random variable V, so we write the hazard as

$$\theta(t; \mathbf{x}, v) \tag{1.1}$$

in the presence of the time-invariant covariate vector $\mathbf{x}$.[1] The relative frequency interpretation of this expression is that $\theta(t; \mathbf{x}, v)\,dt$ gives the fraction of a large population, *homogeneous with respect to* $\mathbf{x}$ *and* v, who leave in the short interval from t to $t + dt$. We shall refer to (1.1) as the *conditional hazard.*

But suppose that in practice v is both unmeasured (unknown) and varies over the population of interest so the distribution of T which we can observe is that unconditional on V, that is, a distribution in which v is not fixed. Let the distribution function of V over this population,

---

[1] It would be possible to generalise the model by replacing v by $v(t)$ where $v(t)$ is a realisation of an unobserved stochastic process, as suggested in Lancaster (1979), and allowing the regressors to be time-varying. Such extensions do not appear to have been studied.

given $\mathbf{x}$, be denoted by $H(v; \mathbf{x})$. We find the unconditional distribution of T by forming the joint distribution of T and V (given $\mathbf{x}$) and then integrating out V to get

$$
\begin{aligned}
g(t; \mathbf{x}) &= \int g(t|\mathbf{x}, v) \, dH(v; \mathbf{x}) \\
&= \int \theta(t; \mathbf{x}, v) \exp\left\{ -\int_0^t \theta(u; \mathbf{x}, v) \, du \right\} dH(v; \mathbf{x}) \qquad (1.2) \\
&= \mathrm{E}\left[g(t; \mathbf{x}, v) \right].
\end{aligned}
$$

The survivor function is

$$
\begin{aligned}
\overline{G}(t; \mathbf{x}) &= \int \exp\left\{ -\int_0^t \theta(u; \mathbf{x}, v) \, du \right\} dH(v; \mathbf{x}) \qquad (1.3) \\
&= \mathrm{E}\left[\overline{G}(t; \mathbf{x}, v) \right].
\end{aligned}
$$

A distribution of the form (1.2) and (1.3) is a *mixture model*; the mixing is with respect to the scalar v; and $H(v; \mathbf{x})$ is the *mixing distribution*.

Note that the unconditional density and survivor functions are the conditional ones averaged with respect to the distribution of V, that is, averaged over the sub-populations within which V is the same.

A mixture model can be justified in several ways depending on the functional form of $\theta(t; \mathbf{x}, v)$, and in the next section we shall give some arguments that lead to such a model.

2   Some Arguments Leading to Mixture Models

2.1   Error in Recorded Durations

Suppose that the duration we record is a realisation of a random variable T but that there exists a true or correctly measured duration S differing from T by random multiplicative measurement error Z distributed independently of S. We write $T = S \times Z$. The true random duration S has hazard function $\overline{\theta}(s; \mathbf{x})$, given $\mathbf{x}$, which is of the Weibull form, so

$$
\overline{G}(s) = \mathrm{P}\left(S \geq s \right) = \exp\{ -s^\alpha k_1(\mathbf{x}) \}. \qquad (2.1)
$$

The survivor function of the recorded duration T is then found as

$$
\begin{aligned}
\mathrm{P}\left(T \geq t \right) &= \mathrm{E}\left[\mathrm{P}\left(T \geq t | Z = z \right) \right], \quad \text{by the law of iterated expectations,} \\
&= \mathrm{E}\left[\mathrm{P}\left(S \geq t/z | Z = z \right) \right], \quad \text{since } S = T/Z, \\
&= \mathrm{E}\left[\exp\{ -(t/z)^\alpha k_1(\mathbf{x}) \} \right],
\end{aligned}
$$

from (2.1) and independence of S and Z,

$$= \mathrm{E}\left[\exp\left\{-\int_0^t \theta(u; \mathbf{x}, v)\, du\right\}\right]$$

for $\theta(t; \mathbf{x}, v) = \alpha t^{\alpha-1} k_1(\mathbf{x}) v$ and $v = z^{-\alpha}$. This is of the mixture form (1.3). Thus when the hazard is of Weibull form and v enters it multiplicatively the variation attributable to V can be interpreted as due to multiplicative random measurement error in the 'dependent' variable, T. With a Weibull model, including the Exponential as a special case, error in the duration data generates a mixture model. This argument works because the integrated hazard for the Weibull is proportional to t^α, so multiplicative error in t becomes multiplicative error in the hazard function.

2.2   Error in Recorded Regressors

Suppose now that the hazard function is proportional and that the regressor vector enters exponentially as

$$\theta(t, \mathbf{x}_1) = e^{\mathbf{x}_1' \beta}\, k_2(t), \tag{2.2}$$

where the constant term in $\mathbf{x}_1$ is absorbed in k_2. Assume that we measure a regressor vector $\mathbf{x}$ differing from $\mathbf{x}_1$ by random additive measurement error $\mathbf{x}_2$ distributed independently of $\mathbf{x}_1$;

$$\mathbf{x} = \mathbf{x}_1 + \mathbf{x}_2.$$

Then the joint probability/probability density function of the event $T \geq t$ and $\mathbf{x}_1$ and $\mathbf{x}_2$ is

$$\mathrm{P}\,(T \geq t, \mathbf{x}_1, \mathbf{x}_2) = \mathrm{P}\,(T \geq t | \mathbf{x}_1, \mathbf{x}_2)\, f(\mathbf{x}_1, \mathbf{x}_2)$$

$$= \exp\left\{-e^{\mathbf{x}_1' \beta} \int_0^t k_2(s)\, ds\right\} f(\mathbf{x}_1, \mathbf{x}_2).$$

Changing the variables to $\mathbf{x} = \mathbf{x}_1 + \mathbf{x}_2$ and $\mathbf{x}_2$, with unit Jacobian, and dividing by the marginal density function of $\mathbf{x}$, we get

$$\mathrm{P}\,(T \geq t, \mathbf{x}_2 | \mathbf{x}) = \exp\left\{-v e^{\mathbf{x}' \beta} \int_0^t k_2(s)\, ds\right\} f(\mathbf{x}_2 | \mathbf{x}),$$

where $v = \exp\{-\mathbf{x}_2' \beta\}$. Finally, integrating out $\mathbf{x}_2$ or, equivalently, integrating out v gives

$$\mathrm{P}\,(T \geq t | \mathbf{x}) = \int \exp\left\{-v e^{\mathbf{x}' \beta} \int_0^t k_2(s)\, ds\right\} f(v | \mathbf{x})\, dv$$

$$= \int \exp\{-z(t, \mathbf{x}, v)\} f(v | \mathbf{x})\, dv, \tag{2.3}$$

which again is the mixture form (1.3), where here, in general, the distribution of V depends on $\mathbf{x}$. The expression $z(t, \mathbf{x}, v)$ denotes the integrated conditional hazard.

Thus a random scalar in the integrated hazard can be interpreted as representing the effect of additive measurement error in the regressor variables if the $\mathbf{x}$ dependence of the hazard function is multiplicative and Exponential.

In econometric textbook presentations of the linear model a justification for 'the error term' is the likely presence of errors in the variables. Indeed, in the early texts this was the principal justification. It is interesting to see that an 'errors in the variables' argument can be deployed to justify an 'error term' in a class of models for transition data, as this and the previous section demonstrate.

2.3   Mixture Models in Econometrics

Mixture models generated by mixing a specific parametric family of duration distributions with respect to a scalar heterogeneity term as in (1.4) have been the standard way econometricians have modelled duration data. People are usually assumed to make rational choices under uncertainty in a given chance environment and these choices both determine and change over time the probability of exit – the hazard function. If we could observe the hazard function of a number of people living in the same chance environment and operating the same decision making policy or, more generally, operating in environments and using policies which differ in known ways, we could confirm or refute the theory of their behaviour and determine-parameters which have an economic-theoretical interpretation. A model representing rational behaviour is a structural model and its parameters structural parameters. It is such models and parameters that have been the principal objects of the econometrician's interest. The econometrician has therefore typically written down a model for the hazard function intended to represent the (partial) outcome of rational behaviour in a given chance environment under uncertainty. He then wishes to allow for the possibility that measured sources of variation among people, typically the regressors, fail to account fully for the true differences among people in their policy or environment. Hence the error or heterogeneity term in the hazard and so in the integrated hazard.

In its simplest form the econometrician might assert that if he could know the regressor vector $\mathbf{z}$ in the hazard model $\theta = \exp\{\mathbf{z}'\gamma\}\psi_2(t)$ then that is sufficient to account for all variation in the policies or chance environments of a population under study. However, he must write $\theta = v\exp\{\mathbf{z}_1'\gamma_1\}\psi_2(t)$ if all he can measure is a subset $\mathbf{z}_1$ of the theoretically appropriate vector $\mathbf{z}$. Then $v = \exp\{\mathbf{z}_2'\gamma_2\}$ represents the total effect of unmeasured systematic differences on the hazard function. This is an argument which is closely analogous to the economist's second traditional rationalisation of the error term in the linear model – the 'errors in the equation' argument – in which a deterministic model of choice behaviour becomes a stochastic one when allowance is made for the failure to measure variable quantities that the economic theory assumes constant.

This 'omitted variables' argument is a third rationalisation for a mixture model. It is one that econometricians tend to find more persuasive than statisticians in areas of application where the connection between the statistical model and the underlying substantive theory is perhaps less close than in economics. Note that the argument that v represents the effect of omitted regressors suggests that v enters $\theta(t,\mathbf{x},v)$ in the same functional way as the time-independent $\mathbf{x}$'s. It also implies that it is the structural parameters of the conditional hazard $\theta(t,\mathbf{x},v)$ that are of interest, the distribution of the error term carrying no information of value to the economist. Much effort has been put into (a) devising tests for the presence of a heterogeneity term in the hazard – we shall give an account of these procedures in chapter 11 – and (b) devising methods of inference about the parameters of the conditional model that are insensitive to the specification of the mixing distribution. We shall give an account of these methods in chapter 9.

3   Some Algebra of Mixtures

3.1   General Results

Let us now give some results that enable us to compare the properties of the conditional distribution with integrated hazard $z(t,v)$ and the mixture distribution. These results are useful in interpreting the findings of an econometric analysis. We sometimes wish to know whether some observed phenomenon is 'real' and telling us about the behaviour of the people we are studying, or whether it is spurious and due to our having sampled from a population more heterogeneous than our model allows for. To make this decision correctly we need to know the main characteristics of data drawn from heterogeneous populations; that is, we need to know the main properties of mixture distributions.

We shall denote by $\overline{G}$, g, and θ the conditional survivor, density, and hazard functions, which depend upon v, and by these expressions with the subscript 'm' the corresponding functions for the mixture distribution. We shall confine our attention to the case in which the regressors, if any, are either time-invariant or otherwise exogenous. We suppress the regressor dependence in our notation until we wish to take account of it.

First, by (1.4),

$$\overline{G}_m(t) = \int \overline{G}(t)h(v)\, dv = \mathrm{E}\left[\overline{G}(t)\right].$$

The mixture hazard function is derived by differentiating minus the logarithm of $\overline{G}_m$ giving

$$\theta_m(t) = \frac{\int g(t)h(v)\, dv}{\int \overline{G}(t)h(v)\, dv}$$

$$= \frac{\int \theta(t)\overline{G}(t)h(v)dv}{\int \overline{G}(t)h(v)\, dv} \tag{3.1}$$

since $\theta = g/\overline{G}$. Thus $\theta_m(t)$ is the expectation of $\theta(t)$ with respect to the density function of v given by

$$f(v) = \frac{\overline{G}(t)\, h(v)}{\int \overline{G}(t)\, h(v)\, dv}. \tag{3.2}$$

To interpret this distribution consider the density function of V given $T \geq t$, that is, the distribution of V over those members of a large entry cohort who survive until t. The joint probability/probability density function of the event $T \geq t$ and v is

$$p(T \geq t, v) = \mathrm{P}\left(T \geq t|v\right)h(v) = \overline{G}(t)\, h(v).$$

Hence the density function of V given $T \geq t$ is

$$p(v|T \geq t) = \frac{\overline{G}(t)\, h(v)}{\int \overline{G}(t)\, h(v)\, dv}, \tag{3.3}$$

which is (3.2). Thus the mixture hazard function at t is an average of the conditional hazards at t, averaged with respect to the distribution of V *over the survivors to that date.*

Further interesting results can be obtained if we specialise the way in which v enters the conditional hazard. In particular, suppose that v enters $z(t,v)$ and $\theta(t,v)$ multiplicatively and let $\theta(t,v) = v\overline{\theta}(t)$ and $z(t,v) = v\overline{z}(t)$. First consider the mean value of V among the survivors at t which, after specialising (3.3), becomes

$$\mathrm{E}\left(V|T \geq t\right) = \frac{\int v e^{-v\overline{z}(t)}h(v)\, dv}{\int e^{-v\overline{z}(t)}h(v)\, dv}. \tag{3.4}$$

Differentiating with respect to t gives

$$\frac{d\mathrm{E}\,(V|T \geq t)}{dt} = \bar{\theta}(t)\left[-\frac{\int v^2 e^{-v\bar{z}(t)}h(v)\,dv}{\int e^{-v\bar{z}(t)}h(v)\,dv} + \left(\frac{\int v e^{-v\bar{z}(t)}h(v)\,dv}{\int e^{-v\bar{z}(t)}h(v)\,dv}\right)^2\right]$$

$$= \bar{\theta}(t)[-\mathrm{E}\,(V^2|T \geq t) + \mathrm{E}^2(V|T \geq t)]$$

$$= -\bar{\theta}(t)\,\mathrm{var}(V|T \geq t). \tag{3.5}$$

This expression is negative so the mean V among survivors at t decreases with t. This is a selection effect, reflecting the fact that since large v's mean large hazards and a high propensity to exit, other things being equal, the group of survivors is increasingly composed of people with relatively small v's.

Next consider the mixture hazard, which, specialising (3.1), is

$$\theta_m(t) = \bar{\theta}(t)\mathrm{E}\,(V|T \geq t). \tag{3.6}$$

Differentiating $\theta_m(t)$ gives

$$\frac{d\theta_m(t)}{dt} = \frac{d\bar{\theta}(t)}{dt}\mathrm{E}\,(V|T \geq t) - \bar{\theta}^2(t)\,\mathrm{var}(V|T \geq t).$$

Dividing by θ_m gives the proportionate rate of time variation of θ_m,

$$\frac{d\log\theta_m(t)}{dt} = \frac{d\log\bar{\theta}(t)}{dt} - \bar{\theta}(t)\frac{\mathrm{var}(V|T \geq t)}{\mathrm{E}\,(V|T \geq t)}. \tag{3.7}$$

Since the last term on the right is negative, in general, we see that

$$\frac{d\log\theta_m(t)}{dt} < \frac{d\log\theta(t)}{dt} \tag{3.8}$$

because $\log\theta(t) = \log v + \log\bar{\theta}(t)$. Thus the mixture hazard falls everywhere proportionately faster than the conditional hazard function.

These results relate to the properties of the mixture hazard as a function of time, but what of its behaviour as a function of regressor variables? Let us make the assumption that time-invariant regressors, $\mathbf{x}$, enter the hazard multiplicatively as well as continuing to assume that v does, so we let

$$\theta(t, \mathbf{x}, v) = v e^{\mathbf{x}'\beta}\bar{\theta}(t), \qquad z(t, \mathbf{x}, v) = v e^{\mathbf{x}'\beta}\bar{z}(t)$$

be the forms taken by the conditional hazard and its integral. Notice that in this specification the derivative of the logarithm of the conditional hazard with respect to each x_j is β_j, which does not depend on either $\mathbf{x}$ or t. Now consider the behaviour of the mixture hazard as a function of **x**. If we take the logarithm of $\theta_m(t)$ using the above model and the relation (3.6) we have

$$\log\theta_m(t) = \mathbf{x}'\beta + \log\overline{\theta}(t) + \log\mathrm{E}\,(V|T \geq t).$$

Now even though $\mathrm{E}\,(V)$ is independent of **x**, $\mathrm{E}\,(V|T \geq t)$ is not, because of the presence of $\overline{G}(t)$ in $f(v|T \geq t)$. Indeed, if we take the logarithm of (3.4) and differentiate with respect to x_j we find

$$\frac{\partial\log\mathrm{E}\,(V|T \geq t)}{\partial x_j} = -\beta_j e^{\mathbf{x}'\beta}\overline{z}(t)\frac{\mathrm{var}(V|T \geq t)}{\mathrm{E}\,(V|T \geq t)}.$$

Thus

$$\frac{\partial\log\theta_m(t)}{\partial x_j} = \beta_j\left[1 - e^{\mathbf{x}'\beta}\overline{z}(t)\frac{\mathrm{var}(V|T \geq t)}{\mathrm{E}\,(V|T \geq t)}\right]. \tag{3.9}$$

Since the term in square brackets in (3.9) depends upon both **x** and t we see that the derivative of the log mixture hazard at any t depends upon both **x** and t: it is both time-dependent and non-constant with respect to **x**. Furthermore, because the term in square brackets in (3.9) is less than one, $\partial\log\theta_m(t)/\partial x_j < \beta_j$. This mixture derivative is smaller than the conditional one. Note that this result does *not* require that the distribution of V among entrants, $h(v|\mathbf{x})$, be dependent upon **x**.

This result tells us that any theory that implies that the proportionate effect of a regressor variable upon the hazard is independent of its level and the same however long the state has been occupied will be refuted if the data are disturbed by unmeasured heterogeneity. In particular, referring back to our earlier rationalisations of V in sections 2.1 and 2.2, the presence of unrecognised measurement error in the duration data (in a Weibull model) or in the regressors will cause a constant derivative model to be rejected even though it is correct for the hazard of the true durations as a function of the true regressors.

3.2   The Gamma Mixing Distribution

Some elegant explicit results for mixture distributions can be obtained when V, multiplying the hazard function, has a Gamma distribution.[2] Specifically, let V be a Gamma variate of unit mean and variance σ^2, $V \sim \mathcal{G}(1,\eta)$, $\eta = \sigma^{-2}$. The unit mean is no restriction, as long as the mean is finite, since we can always absorb a departure from unit mean

[2] Appendix 1 gives details of this distribution.

into the rest of the conditional hazard function. Then we have for the density function corresponding to $H(v)$,

$$h(v) = \eta^\eta v^{\eta-1} e^{-\eta v} / \Gamma(\eta). \tag{3.10}$$

Using (3.10) in (1.4) we find the mixture survivor function is then

$$\overline{G}_m(t) = \eta^\eta \int e^{-v\overline{z}} e^{-\eta v} v^{\eta-1} \, dv / \Gamma(\eta)$$

$$= (1 + \sigma^2 \overline{z})^{-\eta}. \tag{3.11}$$

Note that if we let $\sigma^2 \to 0$ in (3.11) we have that

$$\lim_{\sigma^2 \to 0} \overline{G}_m(t) = e^{-\overline{z}(t)},$$

which is the conditional survivor function when V is at its (unit) mean. The mixture hazard got by differentiating $-\log \overline{G}_m(t)$ is

$$\theta_m(t) = \frac{\overline{\theta}(t)}{1 + \sigma^2 \overline{z}(t)}. \tag{3.12}$$

This is the conditional hazard at the mean of the marginal distribution $H(v)$ divided by an increasing function, since $\overline{z}(t)$ is increasing. The probability density function of V over the survivors at t, (3.3), becomes

$$h(v|T \geq t) \propto v^{\eta-1} e^{-v(\eta + \overline{z}(t))}. \tag{3.13}$$

This is also a Gamma distribution but with moments

$$\mathrm{E}\,(V|T \geq t) = \frac{\eta}{\eta + \overline{z}(t)} = \frac{1}{1 + \sigma^2 \overline{z}(t)}, \tag{3.14}$$

$$\mathrm{var}(V|T \geq t) = \frac{\eta}{[\eta + \overline{z}(t)]^2} = \frac{\sigma^2}{[1 + \sigma^2 \overline{z}(t)]^2}. \tag{3.15}$$

Since $\overline{z}$ is proportional to the integrated conditional hazard it varies monotonically from zero to infinity (for a proper conditional distribution). Thus the mean and variance of V over the survivors at t decrease monotonically, though the relative dispersion as measured by the coefficient of variation remains constant at σ. If the conditional distribution is defective so that $\lim_{t \to \infty} \overline{z}(t)$ is finite the distribution of V over the survivors at t approaches a Gamma distribution with mean and variance given by (3.14) and (3.15) with $\overline{z}$ replaced by its limiting value.

A particularly interesting form is that taken by the derivative of the logarithm of the mixture hazard with respect to x_j when some or all fixed regressors multiply the hazard in the form $\exp\{\mathbf{x}'\beta\}$. Using (3.14) and (3.15) the expression (3.9) becomes

$$\frac{\partial \log \theta_m(t)}{\partial x_j} = \beta_j \left(1 - \frac{\sigma^2 \bar{z}(t)}{1 + \sigma^2 \bar{z}(t)}\right)$$

$$= \beta_j \frac{1}{1 + \sigma^2 \bar{z}(t)}$$

$$= \beta_j [\bar{G}_m(t)]^{\sigma^2}, \qquad \text{using (3.11).} \qquad (3.16)$$

The derivative of the logarithm of the mixture hazard decreases monotonically over time since $\bar{G}_m$ does and, moreover, it is always closer to zero than the derivative of the log conditional hazard, since $|\bar{G}_m(t)| < 1$ for $t \geq 0$. Thus multiplicative unmeasured heterogeneity attenuates the proportionate response of the hazard to variation in x at any date; indeed, the response vanishes in the limit if the conditional duration distribution is proper. People who have been in the state a long time will have a hazard independent of each x even though conditionally on v the response of the hazard to x is the same at all dates.

The moments of a Gamma mixture can be derived from those of $Z(t, \mathbf{x})$, for any assumed form for the function $\bar{z}(t)$. Regarding (3.11) as the survivor function of $\bar{Z}$, the j'th moment of $\bar{Z}$ is

$$E\left(\bar{Z}^j\right) = \int_0^\infty s^j (1 + \sigma^2 s)^{-\eta - 1} \, ds.$$

After changing the variable to $y = \sigma^2 s/(1+\sigma^2 s)$ this becomes a complete Beta integral

$$E\left(\bar{Z}^j\right) = \int_0^1 s^j (1 - s)^{\eta - j - 1} \sigma^{-2(j+1)} \, ds,$$

which converges for $j > -1$ and $\eta > j$, that is, the j'th moment exists for

$$-1 < j < \frac{1}{\sigma^2},$$

where σ^2 is the variance of the mixing distribution. For such values of j we then have

$$E\left(\bar{Z}^j\right) = \frac{\Gamma(j+1)\Gamma(\eta - j)}{\sigma^{2(j+1)}\Gamma(\eta + 1)}. \qquad (3.17)$$

Given that $\bar{z}(t, \mathbf{x})$ can be expressed in terms of t (given $\mathbf{x}$), (3.17) sometimes enables one to solve for the finite moments of the mixture distribution of T.

If we adopt specific functional form assumptions for $\bar{\theta}$ and $\bar{z}$ we generate mixture distributions specified up to a set of unknown parameters which can therefore be fitted to data. In particular, the choice

$$\bar{z} = k_1(\mathbf{x})\, t^\alpha, \qquad \alpha \geq 0, \tag{3.18}$$

gives a Gamma mixture of Weibull distributions which is called the *Burr distribution*. The survivor function is

$$\bar{G}_m(t) = (1 + \sigma^2 k_1(\mathbf{x})\, t^\alpha)^{-\eta}. \tag{3.19}$$

If we refer back to equation (2.3.10) we see that the Burr family contains the Log-Logistic as the special case $\sigma^2 = 1 = \eta$, so the Log-Logistic is a mixture distribution. From (3.17) the j'th moment of T is

$$\mathrm{E}\,(T^j) = k_1(\mathbf{x})^{-j/\alpha} \frac{\Gamma(1 + \frac{j}{\alpha})\Gamma(\eta - \frac{j}{\alpha})}{\sigma^{2(1+\frac{j}{\alpha})}\Gamma(\eta + 1)}, \tag{3.20}$$

which exists for $-\alpha < j < \alpha/\sigma^2$.

Since $\mathrm{E}\,(\bar{Z}^j)$ exists for j in an interval covering zero the expression (3.17) gives the moment generating function of $\log \bar{Z}$. Hence the cumulant generating function of $\log \bar{Z}$, replacing j by s, is

$$K_{\log \bar{Z}}(s) = \log \Gamma(1+s) + \log \Gamma(\eta-s) + (s+1)\log \eta - \log \Gamma(\eta+1), \tag{3.21}$$

so for the Burr distribution the c.g.f. of $\log T$ is given by (3.21) with s replaced by s/α and with $-(s/\alpha)\log k_1(\mathbf{x})$ added. Thus, in particular,

$$\mathrm{E}\,(\log T) = -\alpha^{-1}\log k_1(\mathbf{x}) + \alpha^{-1}[\psi(1) - \psi(\eta) + \log \eta], \tag{3.22}$$
$$\mathrm{var}(\log T) = \alpha^{-2}[\psi'(1) + \psi'(\eta)]. \tag{3.23}$$

Notice that the regression of $\log T$ on $\mathbf{x}$ is homoscedastic and, if $k_1(\mathbf{x})$ is $e^{\mathbf{x}'\beta}$, linear, just as in the Weibull case.

Differentiating minus $\log \bar{G}_m(t)$ given by (3.19) gives the hazard of the Burr distribution as

$$\theta_m(t) = \frac{k_1(\mathbf{x})\alpha t^{\alpha-1}}{1 + \sigma^2 k_1(\mathbf{x})t^\alpha}. \tag{3.24}$$

Figure 4.1 sketches this hazard function for several values of α and σ^2. The case $\sigma^2 = 0$ corresponds to the Weibull model, of course.

The sequence of expected remaining times to exit given survival to s for the Burr family is also instructive. From (1.2.6) and equation (3.19) we find for the expected remaining life given survival to s,

$$e(s) - s = (1 + \sigma^2 k_1 s^\alpha)^\eta \int_0^\infty (1 + \sigma^2 k_1 [s + t]^\alpha)^{-\eta}\, dt.$$

This integral exists for $\eta \geq 1$, that is, for $\sigma^2 < \alpha$, and may be given in closed form for $\alpha = 1$, a Gamma mixture of Exponential distributions.

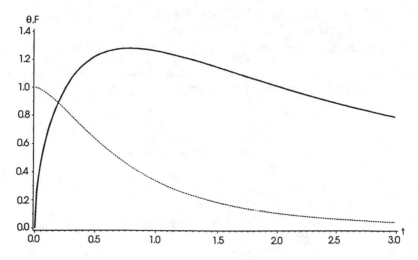

Figure 4.1a.   Burr hazard (—) and survivor function (--): $\alpha = 1, \sigma = 0.707$.

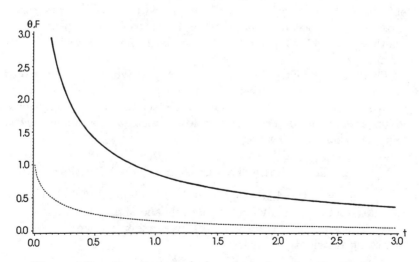

Figure 4.1b.   Burr hazard (—) and survivor function (--): $\alpha = 0.7, \sigma = 0.707$.

Table 4.1.   Expected Time to Exit for
Occupants of s Months Standing

s	Expected Remaining duration	Expected Total duration
0	4	4
4	8	12
8	12	20
12	16	28

In this case it simplifies to

$$e(s) - s = \int_0^\infty (1 + \lambda t)^{-\eta}\, dt, \qquad \text{where} \quad \lambda = \frac{\sigma^2 k_1(\mathbf{x})}{1 + \sigma^2 k_1(\mathbf{x})\, s},$$

$$= \frac{1 + \sigma^2 k_1(\mathbf{x})\, s}{(1 - \sigma^2) k_1(\mathbf{x})}. \tag{3.25}$$

Notice that this is increasing in s if $\sigma^2 > 0$; the longer a person has
occupied a state the longer we can expect him to wait until leaving it.
For example, if $1/k_1 = 2$ months and $\sigma^2 = 0.5$ a randomly selected
entrant to the state $(s = 0)$ can be expected to leave in 4 months. But
those who have occupied the state for 4 months can be expected to stay
another $4 \times (1 + 0.5 \times 0.5 \times 4) = 8$ months. Table 4.1 gives some further
calculations.

There is apparently an alarming – or gratifying, depending on the
nature of the state – deterioration in people's chances of exit which is
quite illusory and only a reflection of the fact that increasingly the survivors are composed of people with lower and lower but *time-invariant*,
$[v\, k_1(\mathbf{x})]$, chances of leaving.

3.3   The Exponential Family Mixing Distribution

When the unmeasured heterogeneity, V, is Gamma distributed the mixture distribution is analytically tractable and simple results can be derived. This simplicity is largely preserved under a more general family
of mixing distributions. Let

$$h(v) = \frac{v^\delta e^{-\lambda v} m(v)}{\phi(\delta, \lambda)} = \mathcal{P}(\delta, \lambda), \qquad v \geq 0, \tag{3.26}$$

be called the *Exponential family* of mixing distributions. It includes the
$\mathcal{G}(1, \eta)$ density as the particular case $\delta = \eta - 1$, $\lambda = \eta$, $m(v) \equiv 1$,
$\phi(\delta, \lambda) = \Gamma(\delta + 1)\lambda^{-\lambda}$, but includes other densities such as the Inverse

Gaussian (chapter 3, section 4.2), the generalised Inverse Gaussian,[3] the Poisson (possibly without the zero), truncated Normal, two-point, and non-central chi-squared. The family is not necessarily a two-parameter family since $m(v)$ may contain additional parameters not indicated in the notation.

Note first that

$$\phi(\delta, \lambda) = \int_0^\infty v^\delta e^{-\lambda v} m(v)\, dv \qquad (3.27)$$

since (3.26) integrates to one. Furthermore, differentiating both sides of (3.27) with respect to λ we see that

$$-\frac{\partial \phi(\delta, \lambda)}{\partial \lambda} = \phi(\delta + 1, \lambda). \qquad (3.28)$$

With these results we may derive the following properties of the mixture distribution. As in the last section the conditional survivor function at t is

$$\overline{G}(t) = e^{-v\bar{z}(t)}.$$

Taking expectations with respect to V the mixture survivor function is

$$\overline{G}_m(t) = \int v^\delta \exp\{-v(\lambda + \bar{z})\} m(v)\, dv / \phi(\delta, \lambda)$$

$$= \frac{\phi(\delta, \lambda + \bar{z})}{\phi(\delta, \lambda)}, \qquad (3.29)$$

which is tractable if ϕ can be easily computed. (This is not necessarily the case; for example, in the generalised Inverse Gaussian distribution ϕ involves modified Bessel functions.)

The density of V among survivors at t is

$$h(v | T \geq t) = \frac{h(v)\, P(T \geq t | v)}{\overline{G}_m(t)}$$

$$= \frac{v^\delta e^{-v(\lambda + \bar{z})}}{\phi(\delta, \lambda)} \frac{\phi(\delta, \lambda)}{\phi(\delta, \lambda + \bar{z})}$$

$$= \mathcal{P}(\delta, \lambda + \bar{z}). \qquad (3.30)$$

Hence, as we saw with the Gamma mixing distribution in (3.13), the density of V preserves its functional form as we consider the groups of survivors at successively later dates. Equation (3.30) generalises (3.13).

---

[3] See Jørgensen (1982).

We can also consider the density of V among those who leave at t, which is

$$h(v|t) = h(v,t)/g_m(t)$$

$$= \frac{\theta v e^{-v\bar{z}} v^\delta e^{-v\lambda} m(v)}{\phi(\delta, \lambda)} \frac{\phi(\delta, \lambda)}{-\theta \phi'(\delta, \lambda + \bar{z})},$$

where $g_m(t)$ is minus the derivative of $\overline{G}_m(t)$,(3.29). Using (3.28) this is

$$h(v|t) = \mathcal{P}(\delta + 1, \lambda + \bar{z}), \tag{3.31}$$

so again, the functional form of the distribution of V is preserved among successive groups of leavers.

4   Local Mixtures

When the model is a mixture with survivor function of the form

$$\overline{G}_m(t) = \int \overline{G}(t)\, dH(v) \tag{4.1}$$

the properties of $\overline{G}_m$ obviously depend upon those of the mixing distribution $H(v)$. Since the economist is not usually provided by his theorising with a family of models for H this is a source of difficulty in econometric modelling. One possible route is to consider the form taken by the mixture distribution when V has little dispersion so that the departure from homogeneity of the data (given $\mathbf{x}$) is small. We can arrive at this by noting that (4.1) is the expected value of $\overline{G}(t)$ with respect to V. Let us formally expand $\overline{G}(t)$ as a function of v about the mean of V which, as we noted earlier, can be taken to be unity with no loss of generality as long as the mean exists, to get

$$\exp\{-v\bar{z}\} = e^{-\bar{z}}\left(1 + (v-1)(-\bar{z}) + \frac{(v-1)^2}{2}\bar{z}^2 + \cdots\right).$$

Taking expectations of this series and neglecting terms of higher order than the quadratic gives

$$\mathrm{E}\,(e^{-V\bar{z}}) = \overline{G}_m(t) \sim e^{-\bar{z}}(1 + \eta\bar{z}^2), \qquad \eta = \sigma^2/2.$$

The right-hand expression is the local mixture approximate 'survivor function', which we shall denote by

$$\overline{F}_m(t) = e^{-\bar{z}}(1 + \eta\bar{z}^2). \tag{4.2}$$

Note that $\overline{F}_m(0) = 1$ since $\bar{z}(0) = 0$ and $\lim_{t\to\infty} \overline{F}_m(t) = 0$, as required by a proper survivor function, and it is also non-negative. Differentiating

$\overline{F}_m$ with respect to t gives

$$f_m(t) = \theta e^{-\overline{z}}\{1 + \eta(\overline{z}^2 - 2\overline{z})\}. \qquad (4.3)$$

The term $(\overline{z}^2 - 2\overline{z})$ multiplying η has a minimum at $\overline{z} = 1$ at which the value of the term in braces is $1 - \eta$. Thus $f_m(t)$ is everywhere non-negative for $\eta \leq 1$, that is, $\sigma^2 < 2$, and $\overline{F}_m(t)$ is, therefore, a valid survivor function for these values of σ^2. We shall call it the *local mixture distribution*.

Note that since $\mathrm{E}(V) = 1$, σ^2 is the squared coefficient of variation of V, so $\overline{F}_m$ is a valid survivor function for values of σ^2 which seem empirically reasonable, though it would only be a good approximation to any given mixture distribution for much smaller values of σ^2. When $\sigma^2 = 0$ and $H(v)$ is concentrated at $v = 1$ then $\overline{Z}$ is the integrated hazard function and thus is distributed as $\mathcal{E}(1)$ with $\mathrm{E}(\overline{Z}^j) = j!$ implying $\mathrm{E}(\overline{Z}^2 - 2\overline{Z}) = 0$. Thus the term multiplying η in f_m has zero mean when $\eta = 0$.

The principal use for the local mixture distribution is not as a model for fitting to data, though this could be done if one were convinced that σ^2 was small, but as the basis for score tests for the presence of heterogeneous V in the hazard function. In this connection we shall meet the local mixture probability density function (4.3) again in chapters 10 and 11.

5   Generalised F

A mixture model that has been advocated for duration data can be found by returning to chapter 3, section 2, where we considered generalising the error distribution in a linear model for $\log T$. Then we wrote

$$\log(\lambda T) = U, \qquad (5.1)$$

where in turn we took

$U \sim \log$ of an $\mathcal{E}(1)$ variate,

$U \sim W/\alpha$, where W is the *log* of an $\mathcal{E}(1)$ variate,

$U \sim W/\alpha$, where W is the *log* of a $\mathcal{G}(m)$ variate.

The last model yielded the generalised Gamma p.d.f. for T,

$$f(t) = \frac{\alpha \lambda^{\alpha m} t^{\alpha m - 1} \exp\{-(\lambda t)^\alpha\}}{\Gamma(m)}. \qquad (5.2)$$

In the following section we retained the assumption that $e^U \sim \mathcal{E}(1)$ but generalised the functional form for the left-hand side in (5.1), the log integrated hazard, and in this chapter we have been considering mixture models got by multiplying the integrated hazard by a random heterogeneity term, V. Let us combine the first and last of these approaches to the construction of duration models by supposing that $\lambda = \lambda_0 V^{1/\alpha}$ and that (5.2) is the density of T given the value of V, which in fact varies randomly over the population as a Gamma variate of mean 1 and variance $\sigma^2 = \eta^{-1}$. Thus $V \sim \mathcal{G}(1, \eta)$. Then the marginal density function of T is the mixture

$$f(t) = \frac{\alpha \lambda_0^{\alpha m} t^{\alpha m - 1}}{\Gamma(m)} \int_0^\infty \frac{v^{m+\eta-1} \exp\{-v(\eta + (\lambda_0 t)^\alpha)\}\, dv}{\Gamma(\eta)\eta^{-\eta}}$$

$$= \frac{\alpha \lambda_0^{\alpha m} t^{\alpha m - 1}\{\eta + (\lambda_0 t)^\alpha\}^{-\eta - m}}{B(m, \eta)}, \qquad (5.3)$$

where

$$B(m, n) = \frac{\Gamma(m)\Gamma(\eta)}{\Gamma(m + \eta)},$$

the complete Beta function. To identify the distribution (5.3) we change the variable to $x = (\lambda_0 t)^\alpha / \eta$, giving

$$g(x) = \frac{x^{m-1}(1 + x)^{-m-\eta}}{B(m, \eta)}. \qquad (5.4)$$

This distribution may be recognised as that of (m/η) times that of a variate distributed as Fisher's F with degrees of freedom $2m$ and 2η. That is, $(\lambda_0 T)^\alpha / m \sim F(2m, 2\eta)$ and hence the name generalised F for the distribution (5.3).

From standard properties of the F distribution we may deduce that

$$\mathrm{E}\,(T^s) = \lambda_0^{-s} \eta^{s/\alpha} \frac{\Gamma(m + s/\alpha)\Gamma(\eta - s/\alpha)}{\Gamma(m)\Gamma(\eta)}, \qquad s < \alpha\eta, \qquad (5.5)$$

and, in particular,

$$\mathrm{E}\,(T) = \lambda_0^{-1} \eta^{1/\alpha} \frac{\Gamma(m + 1/\alpha)\Gamma(\eta - 1/\alpha)}{\Gamma(m)\Gamma(\eta)} \qquad (5.6)$$

if it exists, which requires $\sigma^2 < \alpha$. Regarding (5.5) as giving the m.g.f. of $\log T$, the c.g.f. is then

$$K_{\log T}(s) = -s \log \lambda_0 + (s/\alpha) \log \eta + \log \Gamma(m + s/\alpha) + \log \Gamma(\eta - s/\alpha) \quad (5.7)$$

apart from a constant. The mean and variance may then be deduced to be, assuming $\lambda_0 = \exp\{-\mathbf{x}'\beta\}$,

$$\mathrm{E}\,(\log T) = \mathbf{x}'\beta + \alpha^{-1}\{\psi(m) - \psi(\eta) + \log \eta\} \qquad (5.8)$$

and $\qquad \text{var}(\log T) = \alpha^{-2}\{\psi'(m) + \psi'(\eta)\}.$ $\qquad\qquad$ (5.9)

We still have a homoscedastic linear model for $\log T$ with now a three-parameter (α, m, η) error distribution.

$\qquad$ Since the error term multiplies λ in (4.1) it also multiplies t, and so v can be thought of as an error of measurement in the dependent variable t. Specifically, if we think of a true duration s as having density (5.2) (with $\lambda = \lambda_0$) and a measured duration $t = sv^{-1/\alpha}$ with v independent of s then t has the mixture density (5.3).

$\qquad$ The model (5.3) includes as special cases the generalised Gamma ($\eta \to \infty$), the Weibull ($m = 1, \eta \to \infty$), and the Log-Logistic ($m = \eta = 1$) and can thus generate a wide variety of shapes for the hazard function.

6 $\qquad$ Joint Duration Distributions Generated by Mixing

Consider two durations, T_1 and T_2, for the same person and suppose the integrated conditional hazard for spell j is of the form

$$v\bar{z}_j(t_j), \qquad j = 1, 2,$$ $\qquad\qquad$ (6.1)

where $\bar{z}_j$ may depend upon observed regressors $\mathbf{x}_j$ and involve parameters β_j. The expression (6.1) defines the integrated hazard of T_j conditional on v, $\mathbf{x}_j$, and β_j. Suppose that, given v and $(\mathbf{x}_j, \beta_j)$, $j = 1, 2, T_1$ and T_2 are stochastically independent, so that if one knows v, together with the $\mathbf{x}$'s and the β's, then also knowing T_1 will be of no help in predicting T_2. If one doesn't know v then knowledge of T_1 will tell one something about v and therefore be helpful in predicting T_2. Thus the unconditional – mixture – distribution of T_1 and T_2 can be expected to show stochastic dependence. We shall derive this joint distribution and study its properties in this section.

$\qquad$ Let us consider the distributions of $\bar{z}_j(t_j)$, $j = 1, 2$, from which we can then deduce the distributions of the T_j themselves for any particular choices of functional form for the way in which the $\{\bar{z}_j\}$ depend upon the $\{t_j\}$. To simplify the notation we shall, for this section, drop the bars from the $\bar{z}_j$ and we shall also take the conditioning on $\{\beta_j, \mathbf{x}_j\}$ for granted. The $\{vz_j\}$, which are the integrated conditional hazards, are independently unit Exponential variate, given v, or, equivalently, Z_1 and Z_2 are independent $\mathcal{E}(v)$ variates given v. We shall first give some general results on the joint and conditional mixture distributions of the $\{Z_j\}$ and then exemplify them using two families of mixing distributions.

6.1   General Results

The joint survivor function of Z_1 and Z_2 is

$$\overline{F}(z_1, z_2) = P(Z_1 \geq z_1 \cap Z_2 \geq z_2). \qquad (6.2)$$

In the present case this is

$$\overline{F}(z_1, z_2) = e^{-(z_2 + z_2)v}$$

$$= e^{-vz}, \qquad \text{given } v, \text{ with } z = z_1 + z_2, \text{ and} \qquad (6.3)$$

$$\overline{F}(z_1, z_2) = \int e^{-vz} h(v) \, dv \qquad (6.4)$$

unconditionally. The negative first partial derivative of $\overline{F}$ is

$$-\frac{\partial \overline{F}(z_1, z_2)}{\partial z_1} = P(z_1 \cap Z_2 \geq z_2). \qquad (6.5)$$

(Since the z's appear symmetrically in these formulae we just give the results for z_1.) In the present application this is

$$P(Z_1 \cap Z_2 \geq z_2) = ve^{-vz}, \qquad \text{given } v, \text{ and} \qquad (6.6)$$

$$P_m(z_1 \cap Z_2 \geq z_2) = \int ve^{-vz} h(v) \, dv \qquad (6.7)$$

unconditionally. The cross partial derivative of $\overline{F}$ is the joint probability density function of Z_1 and Z_2. Conditionally on v it is just the product of two $\mathcal{E}(v)$ densities,

$$f(z_1, z_2) = v^2 e^{-vz}, \qquad (6.8)$$

and unconditionally it is

$$f_m(z_1, z_2) = \int v^2 e^{-vz} h(v) \, dv. \qquad (6.9)$$

It is useful to note that these mixture results can be written compactly if we write

$$L(s) = \int_0^\infty e^{-vs} h(v) \, dv, \qquad (6.10)$$

which is the Laplace transform of the mixing distribution h.[4] Then equations (6.4), (6.7), and (6.9) become

$$\overline{F}_m(z_1, z_2) = L(z), \qquad (6.11)$$

---

[4] Appendix 2 summarises some of the relevant properties of the Laplace transform.

$$P_m(z_1 \cap Z_2 \geq z_2) = -L'(z) = P_m(Z_1 \geq z_1 \cap z_2), \quad (6.12)$$

$$f_m(z_1, z_2) = L''(z). \quad (6.13)$$

We can now define some interesting conditional probabilities which are useful in modelling and understanding the dependence between variates representing durations of stay. There seem to be two types of conditioning event that are important. The first is conditioning on the event that $Z_j \geq z_j$, and the second is conditioning on the event that $Z_j = z_j$; conditioning on survivial to z_j and departure at z_j, respectively. In the first case we are looking at the distribution of the second spell duration given that the first lasted at least six weeks, say, and in the second case we are looking at this distribution given that the first lasted exactly six weeks.

For the first case consider the survivor function of Z_1 given that $Z_2 \geq z_2$, which is

$$\begin{aligned}
\overline{F}_m(z_1|Z_2 \geq z_2) &= P\left(Z_1 \geq z_1 | Z_2 \geq z_2\right) \\
&= \frac{P\left(Z_1 \geq z_1 \cap Z_2 \geq z_2\right)}{P\left(Z_2 \geq z_2\right)} \\
&= \frac{\overline{F}_m(z_1, z_2)}{\overline{F}_m(0, z_2)} \\
&= \frac{L(z)}{L(z_2)}, \quad \text{from (6.11).} \quad (6.14)
\end{aligned}$$

The density function is found by differentiation to be

$$f_m(z_1|Z_2 \geq z_2) = -\frac{L'(z)}{L(z_2)}, \quad (6.15)$$

and the mixture hazard is the ratio of these,

$$\theta_m(z_1|Z_2 \geq z_2) = -\frac{L'(z)}{L(z)}. \quad (6.16)$$

Now conditionally on v the z's are independent and so the hazard for Z_1 given $Z_2 \geq z_2$ is just v. Written out explicitly this hazard, (6.16), is

$$\theta_m(z_1|Z_2 \geq z_2) = \frac{\int v e^{-vz} h(v) \, dv}{\int e^{-vz} h(v) \, dv}. \quad (6.17)$$

Thus (6.17) is the expected value of the conditional hazard, V, with respect to the density function which is proportional to $e^{-vz} h(v)$. It is easy to show that this density function is $h(v|Z_1 \geq z_1 \cap Z_2 \geq z_2)$. It follows that θ_m given by (6.17) is the average value of V among people who have survived to z_1 and whose first spell lasted at least

z_2. This generalises our earlier result, (3.1). Furthermore, differentiation with respect to z_1 gives

$$\frac{d\mathrm{E}\,(V|Z_1 \geq z_1 \cap Z_2 \geq z_2)}{dz_1} = -\,\mathrm{var}(V|Z_1 \geq z_1 \cap Z_2 \geq z_2), \qquad (6.18)$$

which essentially generalises (3.5). The average value of V is smaller the longer the current spell has lasted *and* the longer the previous spell lasted.

For the second type of conditioning the mixture survivor function is

$$\mathrm{P}\,(Z_1 \geq z_1|Z_2 = z_2) = \frac{P_m(Z_1 \geq z_1 \cap z_2)}{f_m(z_2)}.$$

The numerator is $-L'(z)$ from (6.12) and the denominator is the marginal mixture density function of Z_2,

$$f_m(z_2) = \int v e^{-vz_2} h(v)\,dv = -L'(z_2). \qquad (6.19)$$

Thus

$$\overline{F}(z_1|Z_2 = z_2) = \frac{L'(z)}{L'(z_2)}, \qquad (6.20)$$

from which we readily derive the density and hazard function,

$$f_m(z_1|Z_2 = z_2) = -\frac{L''(z)}{L'(z_2)}, \qquad (6.21)$$

$$\theta_m(z_1|Z_2 = z_2) = -\frac{L''(z)}{L'(z)}. \qquad (6.22)$$

These may be compared with (6.15) and (6.16). Note that they are of the same form throughout except that the order of differentiation is one higher.

If we write out (6.22) explicitly we find that it is equal to the expected value of the conditional hazard, V, with respect to $h(v|Z_1 \geq z_1 \cap Z_2 = z_2)$ analogous to (6.17) and there is a corresponding version of (6.18).

Before going on to give results for specific families of mixing distributions we record two further properties of joint distributions generated by mixing. The first relates to the distribution of the smallest – the minimum. The smallest of the two Z's has survivor function, at the point z, given by

$$\overline{F}(z) = P(Z_1 \geq z \cap Z_2 \geq z)$$
$$= \overline{F}_m(z, z)$$
$$= L(2z), \qquad \text{from (6.11).} \qquad (6.23)$$

This is of the same functional form as the marginal mixture survivor function of any one Z. In practice one would be interested in the smallest, not of the Z's but of the T's, and this has the same simplicity as (6.23) when the hazards, and therefore the integrated hazards, are proportional in the sense that

$$z_j(t) = \mu_j z_0(t), \qquad j = 1, 2. \tag{6.24}$$

For in this case the survivor function of the minimum of the T's at the point t is

$$
\begin{aligned}
\overline{G}(t) &= \mathrm{P}\,(T_1 \geq t \cap T_2 \geq t) \\
&= \mathrm{P}\,(\mu_1 z_0(T_1) \geq \mu_1 z_0(t) \cap \mu_2 z_0(T_2) \geq \mu_2 z_0(t)) \\
&= \mathrm{P}\,(Z_1 \geq \mu_1 z_0(t) \cap Z_2 \geq \mu_2 z_0(t)) \\
&= \overline{F}_m(\mu_1 z_0(t), \mu_2 z_0(t)) \\
&= L([\mu_1 + \mu_2] z_0(t)), \qquad \text{from (6.11).} \tag{6.25}
\end{aligned}
$$

Thus when hazards are proportional the distribution of the minimum has the same form as that of each T taken separately but with a factor of proportionality in the hazard which is the sum of those for each T_j.

A final result is the joint moment generating function of the logarithms of the Z's. Given v the Z's are independently $\mathcal{E}(v)$ variates whose logarithms have moment generating function, from the appendix, of the form $\Gamma(1+s)v^{-s}$. Thus the mixture joint moment generating function is

$$
\begin{aligned}
\mathrm{E}\,(Z_1^{s_1} Z_2^{s_2}) &= \mathrm{E}\,(\mathrm{E}\,\{Z_1^{s_1} Z_2^{s_2} | v\}) \\
&= \Gamma(1 + s_1)\Gamma(1 + s_2)\mathrm{E}\,(v^{-(s_1 + s_2)}) \\
&= \Gamma(1 + s_1)\Gamma(1 + s_2)\, M_{\log v}(-s_1 - s_2). \tag{6.26}
\end{aligned}
$$

Differentiation then gives the moments and in particular we find that

$$
\begin{aligned}
\mathrm{var}(\log Z_j) &= \psi'(1) + \mathrm{var}(\log V), \qquad j = 1, 2 \\
\mathrm{cov}(\log Z_1 \log Z_2) &= \mathrm{var}(\log V), \qquad \text{and} \\
\rho_{\log Z_1 \log Z_2} &= \frac{\mathrm{var}(\log V)}{\psi'(1) + \mathrm{var}(\log V)}. \tag{6.27}
\end{aligned}
$$

Since $\psi'(1) = 1.645$ and the variance of the logarithm of a variate would normally be expected to be less than one, the correlation of the logs of the integrated hazards induced by mixing is likely to be significantly less than one half. Note that if the T's are Weibull variates then $\log Z_j$ is a linear function of $\log T_j$ and (6.27) gives the (observable) correlation of the $\log T$'s induced by mixing.

We now consider two particular forms of mixing distribution.

Table 4.2.	Some Probabilities for Gamma and Stable Mixing

	Gamma mixing	Stable mixing
$\overline{F}_m(z_1, z_2)$	$(1 + z\sigma^2)^{-\eta}$	e^{-z^α}
$\overline{F}_m(z_j)$	$(1 + z_j\sigma^2)^{-\eta}$	$e^{-z_j^\alpha}$
$\theta_m(z_1)$	$(1 + z_1\sigma^2)^{-1}$	$\alpha z_1^{\alpha-1}$
$\theta_m(z_1 \mid Z_2 \geq z_2)$	$(1 + z\sigma^2)^{-1}$	$\alpha z^{\alpha-1}$
$\theta_m(z_1 \mid Z_2 = z_2)$	$(1 + \sigma^2)(1 + z\sigma^2)^{-1}$	$\alpha z^{\alpha-1} - (\alpha - 1)z^{-1}$
$\overline{G}_m(t)$	$(1 + \mu z_0\sigma^2)^{-\eta}$	$e^{-\mu^\alpha z_0^\alpha}$

$z = z_1 + z_2$; $\overline{G}_m$ is the survivor function of min (Z_1, Z_2); $\eta = \sigma^{-2}$; $\mu = \mu_1 + \mu_2$; $z_0 = z_0(t)$; and the last row applies when the T's have proportional hazards of the form (6.24).

## 6.2	Gamma and Stable Mixing Distributions

If we take the Gamma distribution of unit mean and variance σ^2 to be the distribution of V the Laplace transform is, say,

$$L_G(s) = (1 + s\sigma^2)^{-\eta}, \qquad (6.28)$$

from equations (12) and (14) of appendix 1, where $\eta = \sigma^{-2}$.

The family of Positive Stable distributions are characterised by the Laplace transform

$$L_S(s) = e^{-s^\alpha}, \qquad \alpha \in (0, 1]. \qquad (6.29)$$

For $\alpha = 1$ this distribution is degenerate at $V = 1$, and for $\alpha < 1$ it has no finite (positive) moments. For $\alpha < 1$ the density function cannot be written in closed form, except for the particular case $\alpha = 0.5$ when the distribution is a particular case of the Inverse Gaussian family.[5]

The Positive Stable is an interesting family of mixing distributions for reasons we shall explain shortly. Let us first apply (6.28) and (6.29) to the results of section 6.1 to examine the forms taken by some of those general results. The comparisons are conveniently made by setting out the various formulae in the following table.

The mixture hazards are decreasing even though the conditional hazards (of the Z's) are time-independent. The hazards conditional on information about the other duration decrease slower than the hazards

[5] The Positive Stable distribution with $\alpha = 0.5$ is called the Lévy distribution.

without this information – this is because the other duration contains information about V and the more information about V we condition on the closer we approach to the hazard conditional on V itself. Z_2 is a proxy for V in econometric jargon. The hazard conditional on $Z_2 = z_2$ is larger than that conditional on $Z_2 \geq z_2$. This is because people who left at z_2 have larger V's on average than those who left later.

The final row of the table shows that when hazards are proportional this proportionality is preserved when the mixing distribution is Stable but not when it is Gamma. To verify this, just differentiate minus $\log \overline{G}_m$ with respect to t and see whether the result is a PH model or not. This preservation of the proportional hazards form is an interesting property of the Positive Stable family and it will prove to be important when we discuss identifiability of mixed proportional hazards models in chapter 7.

The study of joint distributions in which the dependence is induced wholly, or partly, through mixing is a new area of work and rather few results are yet available. The growing availability of longitudinal data in econometrics makes it seem probable that this is a subject that will form a major research area in the near future. The purpose of this section has been to describe what seem to be some of the fundamentals of the subject.

NOTE

The interpretations of unmeasured heterogeneity in the hazard given in section 2 were published in Lancaster (1985), and much of the material of sections 3.1 and 3.2 is from Lancaster and Nickell (1980), drawing in part on Lancaster (1979). Statisticians often describe models with an additional source of variation as 'doubly stochastic'. Demographic statisticians have long been interested in duration models with unmeasured heterogeneity. Vaupel, Manton, and Stallard (1979) and Sheps and Menken (1973) are important references. A very early use of this class of model was the study of labor mobility by Blumen, Kogan, and McCarthy (1955). Demographers often refer to an unmeasured random term in the hazard function – our V – by the evocative term 'frailty'. Interesting recent papers in this area are by Hougaard (1984, 1986), and sections 3.3 and 6.2 draw heavily on his work. His papers give many more results than we have mentioned. A useful recent survey paper on multivariate survival models is Hougaard (1987). Aalen (1987) has recently begun the study of mixtures of continuous-time Markov chains where the mixing is with respect to multiplicative factors in the transition intensities of the chain – see chapter 5. Section 4 was influenced by Cox (1984) and also Chesher (1984). A clear and full account of the generalised F distribution of section 5 is in Prentice (1975). An important subject which we have not considered in this chapter, and which would repay study, is the properties of models in which there are both neglected heterogeneity and endogenous measured covariates.

CHAPTER 5

Some Important Processes

1   Introduction and Overview

The process of movement from state to state generates a sequence of points on the time axis – the times at which transitions are made. Since movements are probabilistic the passage of a person over time is a realisation of a stochastic, point process. There is a very large literature dealing with the mathematical properties of such processes. Much of this literature deals with the long-run or equilibrium properties when the transition probabilities are constant over time and the process is stationary. In econometrics we usually have to model processes observed over rather short periods of time and which are not stationary, so results from the theory of point processes are not directly relevant. Nevertheless some knowledge of the basic stochastic processes is helpful in thinking about the properties of econometric data as is illustrated by the following example.

Many government statistical services collect and publish information about the duration of unemployment. They obtain this by sampling the population of registered unemployed people and asking them how long they have been unemployed and then they collect the answers in a grouped frequency distribution. Table 5.1 below gives such a distribution for the UK in 1984.

In spite of the fact that the title of the table refers to 'unemployment duration' the quantity whose frequency distribution is tabulated is not the same quantity as that for which we have been constructing models in previous chapters. There a duration was a time from entry to a state to exit from it, and yet here the nearly two and a quarter million people whose misfortune is catalogued above have not yet left the state of unemployment. What we have in the table are durations of uncompleted spells of unemployment. The question then arises as to what is the connection between these incomplete spells and the completed durations

83

84   5   **Some Important Processes**

Table 5.1.   U.K. Male Unemployment Duration
in January 1984

Duration	Number(1000's)	Percentage
≤ 2 weeks	118.5	5.3
2–4 weeks	75.5	3.4
4–8 weeks	168.2	7.5
8–13 weeks	183.0	8.2
13–26 weeks	378.8	16.9
26–52 weeks	392.2	17.5
≥ 52 weeks	929.1	41.4
Total	2245.4	

Source: *Employment Gazette*, vol. 92, No. 11, November 1984.

they may eventually become. To think about this is easier if one has some acquaintance with the particular class of point processes known as renewal processes, for the theory of such processes considers precisely this question. In particular, that literature allows us to imagine sampling a point process at a fixed point of time, for example January 1984, and enables us to deduce, under simplifying assumptions, the distribution of the time from the sampling date to the previous point – entry to unemployment – to the next subsequent point – exit from unemployment – and the whole time between the two-points which contain the sampling date within them. Thus the theory of renewal processes provides us with a basis for modelling the relation between data such as that in the table and a theory which specifies how long an entrant to unemployment will take to leave that state.

It should be emphasised that basic renewal theory by itself will not provide an adequate model both because it is quite unreasonable to suppose that the data above constitute observations on two and a quarter million identical renewal processes and because it is clear from a glance at tables for other years that the process is non-stationary. Nonetheless an acquaintance with the theory of the simplest case is helpful in formulating more reasonable models. In this chapter we shall therefore outline[1] some basic results about stochastic processes with particular emphasis on those that are used in the econometric literature. All of the processes

[1] In the note at the end of this chapter we list some texts on discrete-state stochastic processes which the reader should consult for a more complete and more rigorous treatment of this area.

we shall describe have found econometric application either in the construction of models or in the building of likelihood functions for data.

We shall begin in section 2 with the simplest model, the Poisson process, which has been used in many econometric applications, including that of modelling the process of job search. In sections 3 and 4 we outline the basic results on renewal processes, the theory of which is fundamental to the correct interpretation of data such as that on unemployment durations given in table 5.1.

In section 5 we give a rather detailed account of the probability algebra of models in which we can observe both the duration of an event *and* the state which is entered at its end. An example of this might be where we can observe both the duration of a spell of unemployment and whether it was ended by recall to the previous job or by the finding of a new one. Section 6 contains some of the main results on models in which we can observe an individual passing, at random times, through a sequence of discrete-states.

Section 7 concludes the chapter with an account of the way in which a Wiener process can generate an econometric duration model by its first passage time to an absorbing barrier. This is a model which has found application in the study both of the duration of strikes and of job tenures.

2   Poisson Processes

Consider events, for example, the occurrence of job offers, arising, in a certain sense, randomly in time. Think of each event as a point on the positive (time) axis $0 \leq t < \infty$. Suppose that the process generating a sequence of such events satisfies the following conditions. For any t and positive dt let $N(t, t + dt)$ be the number of events occurring in the time interval from t to $t + dt$. Then the events occur in a Poisson process if, for $\lambda > 0$,

$$P\{N(t, t + dt) = 0\} = 1 - \lambda dt + \circ(dt), \tag{2.1}$$

$$P\{N(t, t + dt) = 1\} = \lambda dt + \circ(dt), \tag{2.2}$$

and $N(t, t + dt)$ is stochastically independent of the number of events occurring before t. In (2.1) and (2.2) the expression $\circ(dt)$ means any function of dt, for example, $(dt)^2$, such that

$$\lim_{dt \to 0} \frac{\circ(dt)}{dt} = 0.$$

Note that (2.1) and (2.2) together imply that

$$P\{N(t, t + dt) > 1\} = \circ(dt), \tag{2.3}$$

which means that in a sufficiently short time interval only one or no events occur – there is no bunching. A process satisfying these assumptions is a Poisson process of rate λ. Strictly, if $N(t), t \geq 0$, is the number of events that have occurred by time t, it is $N(t)$ itself which *is* the Poisson process.

Of particular interest are the probability distribution of the number of events that occur in any fixed, not necessarily small, time interval and the distribution of the times between the occurrence of events. To find these let

$$p_j(t) = P(j \text{ events before time } t), \qquad j = 0, 1, 2, \ldots,$$

Now j events occur before $t + dt$ if

$$j \text{ events occur before } t \text{ and } N(t, t + dt) = 0$$
$$\text{or } j - 1 \text{ events occur before } t \text{ and } N(t, t + dt) = 1$$
$$\text{or } j - 2 \text{ events occur before } t \text{ and } N(t, t + dt) = 2$$
$$\vdots \qquad\qquad \vdots = \vdots$$
$$\text{or } 0 \text{ events occur before } t \text{ and } N(t, t + dt) = j.$$

Since these outcomes are mutually exclusive their probabilities add and thus

$$p_j(t + dt) = p_j(t)(1 - \lambda dt) + p_{j-1}(t)\lambda dt + \circ(dt).$$

Rearranging we get

$$p_j(t + dt) - p_j(t) = -\lambda p_j(t)dt + \lambda p_{j-1}(t)dt + \circ(dt).$$

Dividing by dt and letting $dt \to 0$ we then have

$$p_j'(t) = -\lambda p_j(t) + \lambda p_{j-1}(t), \qquad j = 0, 1, 2, \ldots, \tag{2.4}$$

except that $p_{j-1} = 0$ for $j = 0$. For $j = 0$, (2.4) becomes

$$p_0'(t) = -\lambda p_0(t) \tag{2.5}$$

with solution, subject to the initial condition $p_0(0) = 1$,

$$p_0(t) = e^{-\lambda t}. \tag{2.6}$$

Equation (2.6) tells us that the waiting time until the first event in a Poisson (λ) process has an $\mathcal{E}(\lambda)$ distribution since (2.6) is just the survivor function of such a waiting time (duration). Equation (2.6) gives the probability of a wait of more than t before the first event, and, in fact, it may be shown that (2.6) is the probability that no events occur in an interval of length t starting at any point on the time axis, not

only the origin. In particular, it is correct when the start of the interval
is the time of occurrence of an event. This implies that *times between
events in a Poisson (λ) process are distributed as* $\mathcal{E}(\lambda)$. One can think
of a realisation of a Poisson (λ) process as a sequence of realisations of
independent $\mathcal{E}(\lambda)$ variates whose lengths mark the occurrence of events
in the process.

Given the solution of (2.4) for $j = 0$ the equations for $j = 1, 2, \ldots$
can be solved successively and it may be verified by differentiation that
they have the solution

$$p_j(t) = \frac{e^{-\lambda t}(\lambda t)^j}{j!}, \qquad j = 0, 1, 2, \ldots. \tag{2.7}$$

Again this is true not merely for an interval of length t starting at
the origin but in fact for any such interval. Since (2.7) is a Poisson
distribution we see that the numbers of events occurring in a Poisson
(λ) process during an interval of length t is a Poisson (λt) variate.

A generalisation of the Poisson process is to allow the rate λ to depend
on time. Replacing λ by $\lambda(t)$ in (2.1) and (2.2), these equations together
with (2.3) define the *time-dependent Poisson process* with rate function
$\lambda(t)$. The differential equation (2.5) now becomes

$$p_0'(t) = -\lambda(t)p_0(t), \tag{2.8}$$

whose solution subject to the initial condition $p_0(0) = 1$ is

$$p_0(t) = \exp\left\{-\int_0^t \lambda(u)\, du\right\}. \tag{2.9}$$

Again this is true for any interval of length t in the sense that

$$P\left[\text{no events in } (s, s+t)\right] = \exp\left\{-\int_s^{s+t} \lambda(u)\, du\right\}. \tag{2.10}$$

In particular, if s is the time of occurrence of an event, (2.10) is the survivor function of the waiting time, t, to the next event, so $\lambda(u), u \geq s$,
is the hazard function for the inter-event duration. The p.d.f. of this duration is, as usual, minus the derivative of the survivor function, (2.10),
namely,

$$p(t) = \lambda(s+t)\exp\left\{-\int_s^{s+t} \lambda(u)\, du\right\}, \qquad t \geq 0. \tag{2.11}$$

Returning to equations (2.4) with $\lambda = \lambda(t)$, since we have the solution
(2.9) for $j = 0$ we may solve for $j = 1, 2, \ldots$ recursively to find the

general expression

$$p_j(t) = \frac{\exp\{-\int_0^t \lambda(u)\,du\}[\int_0^t \lambda(u)\,du]^j}{j!}, \qquad j = 0, 1, 2, \ldots . \quad (2.12)$$

Again this applies for any interval of length t when we label the start of the interval as time zero, so we see that the number of events in an interval of length t in the time-dependent Poisson $(\lambda(u))$ process is a Poisson variate of mean $\int_0^t \lambda(u)\,du$.

In the next section we describe a generalisation of the time-homogeneous Poisson process.

3   Renewal Processes

Imagine a large population, say, of unemployed people, being formed at some time $t = 0$. The members of this population remain for a random duration which has survivor function $\overline{G}(x)$ and probability density function $g(x)$ independently of each other. When they leave they are instantly replaced in order to maintain the constancy of the population size. If we focus on a particular individual selected at random from the population at some subsequent point of time t_0 we can think of the period of unemployment he is experiencing as merely the latest in a sequence of such periods experienced by the man he replaced and by the man he replaced and so on back to time zero when the population came into being. Figure 5.1 depicts the situation with the origin at time zero and the sampling date at t_0. The sampled individual is experiencing the fifth spell in the sequence of such spells since the population was created, and the numbers x_1, x_2, x_3, and x_4 are independent realisations of a random variable with survivor function $\overline{G}(x)$.

The time labelled u in figure 5.1 is the time since our sampled person entered the stock of unemployed, v is the time until he leaves it, and $s = u + v$ is the total time he spends in it. We would like to deduce the distributions of the three random variables U, V, and S, of which u, v, and s are realisations, and, in particular, to see how these distributions are related to $\overline{G}$ and g. An answer to this question will be at least the beginning of an answer to the question posed in section 1 of how the numbers given there are connected to an econometric model for the duration of a spell of unemployment. In order to make this deduction we need to describe the key properties of *renewal processes*.

If we now abstract from the example of a physical population we define an ordinary renewal process as a sequence of independent, positive, identically distributed random variables $\{T_i\}$. The T's can be thought of as lifetimes and the start of each new life, apart from the first, is a re-

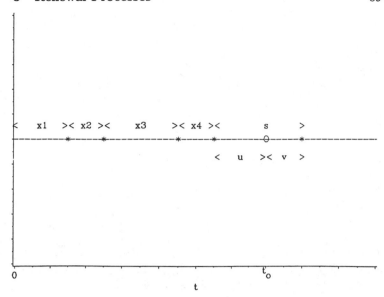

Figure 5.1.   A realisation of a renewal process.

newal. In our story about a real population, which provides the relative
frequency interpretation of the probability theory, a renewal corresponds
to a replacement of one person by his successor. Let $N(t)$ be the number
of renewals between 0 and t, $(0, t]$, and let

$$N(t_1, t_2) = N(t_2) - N(t_1).$$

The function $H(t) = \mathrm{E}\left(N(t)\right)$ is the expected number of renewals in the
interval from 0 to t and is called *the renewal function*. At any fixed time t

$$h(t) = \lim_{dt \to 0} \frac{\mathrm{E}\left(N(t, t + dt)\right)}{dt}$$
$$= H'(t)$$

is called the *renewal density* at t and is such that if lifetimes are strictly
positive $h(t)\,dt$ gives the probability of a renewal in the short interval of
length dt after t. The reason for this interpretation is that since lifetimes
are strictly positive, in a sufficiently short interval there is at most one
renewal, and the expected number of renewals is just the probability of
a renewal occurring.

The distributions we require can now be deduced easily once we establish the behaviour of the renewal density, $h(t)$, as $t \to \infty$. To this

end we give a theorem about the behaviour of $N(t), H(t)$, and $h(t)$ as t becomes large.[2]

Theorem 1

1. *If the lifetimes $\{T_j\}$ have mean μ and finite variance σ^2 then the random variable*

$$Z = \frac{N(t) - t/\mu}{\sigma\sqrt{t/\mu^3}}$$

is asymptotically Normally distributed as $t \to \infty$;
2. *$H(t) = \mathrm{E}\,(N(t)) = t/\mu + O(1)$ as $t \to \infty$;*
3. *$h(t) = H'(t) = 1/\mu + o(1)$ as $t \to \infty$.*

We give the proof of (1) only.

Proof: Let $S_n = T_1 + T_2 + \cdots + T_n$, which is the time until the end of the n'th lifetime or the time until the n'th renewal. Consider the distribution function of $N(t)$ at the point n and let

$$n = t/\mu + y\sigma\sqrt{t/\mu^3}. \tag{3.1}$$

Now $\mathrm{P}\,(N(t) < n) = \mathrm{P}\,(S_n > t)$ since there are fewer than n renewals in $(0, t]$ if and only if the time to the n'th renewal exceeds t. Furthermore S_n has mean $n\mu$ and variance $n\sigma^2$ and

$$\frac{S_n - n\mu}{\sigma\sqrt{n}} \sim N(0, 1) \qquad \text{as } n \to \infty$$

by the central limit theorem for sums of independent random variables with finite variance. Thus

$$\mathrm{P}\,(N(t) < n) = \mathrm{P}\,(S_n > t)$$
$$= \mathrm{P}\,\left(\frac{S_n - n\mu}{\sigma\sqrt{n}} > \frac{t - n\mu}{\sigma\sqrt{n}}\right)$$
$$= \mathrm{P}\,\left(\frac{S_n - n\mu}{\sigma\sqrt{n}} > -y\left[1 + \frac{y\sigma}{\sqrt{t\mu}}\right]^{-1/2}\right),$$

after using (3.1). We now fix y and let t (and therefore n) become large, which leads to

$$\mathrm{P}\,(N(t) < n) \to \Phi(y)$$

---

[2] Rigorous study of renewal theory and proofs of the theorems that we quote requires Laplace transform methods. We refer the reader with these tools, or willing to acquire them, to the monograph by Cox (1962).

$$= \Phi \left(\frac{n - t/\mu}{\sigma \sqrt{t/\mu^3}} \right), \qquad t \to \infty.$$

For part (2), in view of (1), $H(t) = t/\mu + o(t)$, but in fact it may be shown that the remainder term is $O(1)$ and takes the form $(\sigma^2 - \mu^2)/2\mu^2 + o(1)$ as $t \to \infty$. Part (3) is reasonable in view of (2) but a rigorous proof is not easy. ∎

The intuition behind (2) is that doubling the average length of spells halves the number that occur, on average, before time t. Part (3) says that a long time after the start of the process, if people are unemployed on average for μ days, so they are replaced in the stock on average every μ days, a replacement (renewal) occurs on any particular day with probability $1/\mu$.

Example 1
The Poisson (λ) process is a renewal process in which the times between events are independent Exponential variates, that is, G is Exponential. The random variable $N(t, t + dt)$ is Poisson distributed with mean λdt, and $h(t) = \lambda = 1/\mathrm{E}\,(T)$ exactly for all t and not merely as $t \to \infty$. ∎

3.1   Backwards Recurrence Times

Let us consider two ways of sampling the population described at the beginning of this section. One way is to randomly sample the members of the population at a fixed point of time, t_0. We shall refer to this as *stock sampling* since it is sampling the stock of people who occupy the state at t_0. The other way is to sample the set of people who enter the state during an interval of time. We shall call this *flow sampling*. It is sampling the entrants to the state. Now the distribution of completed durations of stay of entrants is just $G(t)$, with density function $g(t)$. But the distributions of durations measured from stock samples are, in general, quite different from G. Let us begin by using theorem 1 to deduce the distribution of U, which is the time *since entry* of a person randomly sampled from the occupants of the state at t_0. This is the time since the last renewal – usually called the *backwards recurrence time* – but which we shall sometimes refer to as his *elapsed duration*. For example, in sampling the stock of people unemployed at t_0, U is the time since the sampled person became unemployed. Reference to figure 5.1 should help the reader to follow the argument. Now, clearly, U can be at most t_0, and U equals t_0 if and only if the lifetime of the individual who was in the original population, at time zero, lasts at least for t_0, which has probability $\overline{G}(t_0)$. Where U is less than t_0 it lies in the short interval from u to $u + du$ if and only if there was a renewal in the short interval of length du between time $t_0 - u - du$ and $t_0 - u$, which has probability $h(t_0 - u)\,du$, and the lifetime that began then lasted at least for u, which has probability $\overline{G}(u)$. Thus the probability density function of U is

$$f(u = t_0) = \overline{G}(t_0)$$
$$f(u) = h(t_0 - u)\overline{G}(u), \qquad 0 < u < t_0,$$

which has a discrete lump of probability at the point t_0 together with a continuous p.d.f. over the interval from 0 to t_0.

If we now consider the form of this p.d.f. as $t_0 \to \infty$ we see that the discrete component of the distribution vanishes because $\overline{G}(t_0) \to 0$; the sample space extends to the whole positive axis, and since $h(t_0 - u) \to 1/\mu$ by theorem 1 for every fixed u we see that the p.d.f. of U approaches

$$f(u) = \frac{\overline{G}(u)}{\mu}, \qquad 0 < u < \infty. \tag{3.2}$$

Note that this density function is written in terms of the *distribution function* of completed durations and note also that (3.2) is a proper p.d.f. since it is both non-negative and integrates to one because the mean is the integral of the survivor function. The expression (3.2) gives the probability density function of the elapsed unemployment duration of an individual randomly sampled from the stock of unemployed people in a model which assumes a constant population (pool of unemployed) size. It could be regarded as a rough first approximation to the distribution of the durations given in table 5.1. It shows, approximately, how the numbers of that table are connected to the distribution, $g(u)$, of completed unemployment durations of a sample of newly unemployed people.

Let us consider the moments of the distribution (3.2). Denote the k'th moment of U round the origin by m'_k and denote the k'th moment of completed durations of entrants, that is, the distribution G, by μ'_k except for the mean, which we continue to call μ.

$$m'_k = E(U^k) = \int_0^\infty \frac{s^k \overline{G}(s)\,ds}{\mu}.$$

Integrating by parts we get

$$m'_k = \frac{1}{k+1}\left[\frac{s^{k+1}\overline{G}(s)}{\mu}\right]_0^\infty + \int_0^\infty \frac{s^{k+1}g(s)\,ds}{(k+1)\mu}$$

$$= \frac{\mu'_{k+1}}{(k+1)\mu}. \tag{3.3}$$

Thus, in particular, the expected elapsed duration, m'_1, is

$$\mathrm{E}\,(U) = \frac{\mu'_2}{2\mu} = \frac{\sigma^2 + \mu^2}{2\mu} = \frac{1}{2}\left(\mu + \frac{\sigma^2}{\mu}\right), \tag{3.4}$$

where σ^2 is the variance of the completed durations of entrants.

Example 2
If all durations have the same length so G is degenerate at – concentrated upon – μ then the expected elapsed duration of an individual sampled at the fixed point t_0 is $\mu/2$, and, indeed, reference to (3.2) shows that in this case

$$f(u) = \frac{1}{\mu}, \qquad 0 < u < \mu;$$

that is, U is uniformly distributed over the interval 0 to μ.   ∎

Example 3
Another special case is found by asking when U has the same expected value as the lifetime distribution G so that $\{\mu + \sigma^2/\mu\} = 2\mu$, which has solution $\sigma^2 = \mu^2$. We know that for the Exponential distribution the variance equals the square of the mean, so we have the surprising result that when the duration of entrants are Exponentially distributed, the completed durations of entrants and the elapsed durations of current members have the same expectation. If newly unemployed people will be, on average, out of work for six months, a randomly selected unemployed person will have been out of work, on average, for six months! Indeed, if G is Exponential with mean μ so that $\overline{G}(x) = e^{-x/\mu}$ we see from (3.2) that $f(u) = e^{-x/\mu}/\mu$, which is an Exponential distribution of mean μ. Thus when completed durations are Exponentially distributed, that is, we are observing a Poisson process at a fixed point on the time axis, then elapsed durations and the completed durations of entrants are identically distributed and it may be shown that the Exponential is the only duration distribution for which this identity holds.   ∎

3.2   Backwards and Forwards Times

Next let us consider the joint distribution of the elapsed duration, U, and the remaining duration, V. We proceed by considering the distribution of V conditional on $U = u$ and then, multiplying by $f(u)$, deduce the joint p.d.f. Now, given $U = u$ a remaining life of v occurs if and only if the total life is $u + v$, which has probability

$$f(v \mid u) = \frac{g(u+v)}{\overline{G}(u)}, \qquad v > 0, \qquad (3.5)$$

which is the probability of a total duration of $u+v$ given that it exceeds u. Thus the joint p.d.f. of U and V is

$$f(v,u) = f(v \mid u)f(u) = \frac{g(u+v)}{\overline{G}(u)}\frac{\overline{G}(u)}{\mu}$$

$$= \frac{g(u+v)}{\mu}, \qquad u,v > 0. \qquad (3.6)$$

Note that from the form of (3.6) elapsed and remaining durations are, in general, stochastically dependent. The exception is the Exponential case where $g(x) = e^{-x/\mu}/\mu$ whence $f(u,v) \propto e^{-u/\mu}e^{-v/\mu}$ so that when completed durations are Exponentially distributed, remaining and elapsed durations are stochastically independent and, indeed, this is the only distribution for which this independence holds.

To find the marginal distribution of the remaining duration we integrate u out of (3.6), giving

$$f(v) = \int_0^\infty \frac{g(u+v)\,du}{\mu} = \int_v^\infty \frac{g(s)\,ds}{\mu}$$

$$= \frac{\overline{G}(v)}{\mu}, \qquad v > 0,$$

which is identical to the p.d.f. of elapsed durations. Thus, at least for observations at times remote from the origin, elapsed and remaining durations are identically distributed.

3.3   Complete Durations of Stock Samples

Finally, let us deduce the distribution of the total duration, $U + V = S$, of an individual sampled from the stock in a constant population model. In the joint p.d.f. (3.6) change the variables to $s = u + v$ and v and integrate out v noting that $v < s$, thus

$$f(s) = \int_0^s \frac{g(s)\,dv}{\mu} = \frac{sg(s)}{\mu}, \qquad s > 0. \qquad (3.7)$$

This distribution is called the *first moment distribution*[3] corresponding to $g(s)$. The moments of the distribution are simply related to those of g because

$$E\left(S^k\right) = \int_0^\infty \frac{s^{k+1}g(s)\,ds}{\mu} = \frac{\mu'_{k+1}}{\mu}. \tag{3.8}$$

In particular,

$$E\left(S\right) = \frac{\mu'_2}{\mu} = \frac{\sigma^2 + \mu^2}{\mu} = \mu + \frac{\sigma^2}{\mu} > \mu. \tag{3.9}$$

Thus the expected durations of unemployment of individuals randomly sampled from the stock are always greater than those of new entrants.

Example 4
As a particular case, when completed durations are Exponentially distributed, implying that $\sigma^2 = \mu^2$, we see that $E\left(S\right) = 2E\left(T\right)$; stock sampled completed durations are on average twice those of entrant ones.   ■

This paradoxical sounding result – and (3.7) in general – can be explained as follows. Picking an individual from the unemployed stock and observing his subsequently completed duration is non-randomly sampling the durations of entrants. Indeed if one thinks in terms of figure 5.1 the fixed observation point t_0 is more likely to be straddled by a long duration than by a short one and, in particular, a spell twice as long as another is twice as likely to straddle t_0, which explains the factor s multiplying $g(s)$ in (3.7). We have in fact what is often called *length-biased sampling* of complete durations in which the probability that a spell will be sampled is proportional to its length, thus the probability of observing a duration of length s is, as in (3.7), proportional to $sg(s)$.

In figure 5.2 we have plotted $g(s)$ and $sg(s)/\mu$, where g is a Weibull density function of mean $\mu = 1$ and parameter $\alpha = 0.7$. Note that $g(s)$ has an infinite ordinate at the origin, because $\alpha < 1$, but $sg(s)/\mu$ is zero at the origin, which shows rather dramatically the effect of length biased sampling.

It is of some interest to look at the relation between the hazard functions corresponding to the distributions f and g. The survivor function

---

[3] First moment distributions also arise in econometrics in the study of the concentration of income and wealth; see, for example, Aitchison and Brown (1957). See also section 5 of chapter 3.

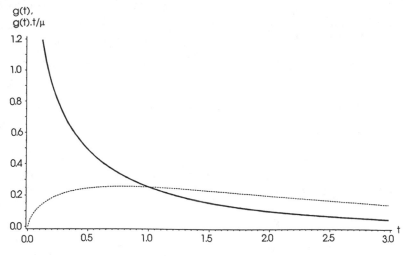

Figure 5.2. The density (—) and first moment density (−−) of a Weibull distribution: $\alpha = 0.7, \mathrm{E}\,(T) = 1$.

of S is

$$\overline{F}(s) = \int_s^\infty ug(u)\,du/\mu = -\int_s^\infty u\overline{G}'(u)\,du/\mu.$$

Integration by parts gives

$$\overline{F}(s) = \overline{G}(s)\left[s + \frac{\int_s^\infty \overline{G}(u)\,du}{\overline{G}(s)}\right]/\mu. \tag{3.10}$$

But the term in square brackets is, from chapter 1, equation (2.11), the expected total duration of an entrant given that it exceeds s, namely, $e(s)$. Hence, taking the ratio of (3.7) to (3.10) the hazard for the completed durations of stock samples is

$$\lambda(s) = \theta(s)\frac{s}{e(s)} \leq \theta(s),$$

where θ is the hazard corresponding to g, the entrant density function, and the inequality follows from $e(s) \geq s$. We conclude that the stock sampled duration hazard is everywhere below the entrant sampled duration hazard except at the origin and at the right-hand end of the sample space.

Example 5
When the entrant distribution is $\mathcal{E}(\theta)$, with time-invariant hazard θ, then

$$\lambda(s) = \theta . \frac{s}{s + 1/\theta},$$

which is an increasing concave function of s.   ∎

4   Alternating Renewal Processes

An easy generalisation of the renewal process is to suppose that there are two-states, for example, employment (state 1), and unemployment (state 2) which are occupied alternately. Durations in state j are denoted by T_j with survivor functions $\overline{G}_j$ and means μ_j. A realisation of the process is a realisation of T_1, followed by a realisation of T_2, followed by a realisation of T_1, and so on. We have a sequence of draws alternately from $\overline{G}_1$ and $\overline{G}_2$. All realisations of T_1 and T_2 are stochastically independent and the distributions are constant over time. Let $p_j(t)$ be the probability that state j is occupied at time t, that is, the probability that at t we are 'in' a realisation of T_j. The key result here is

Theorem 2   *State Occupancy Probabilities in an Alternating Renewal Process*

$$\lim_{t \to \infty} p_j(t) = \pi_j = \frac{\mu_j}{\mu_1 + \mu_2}, \qquad j = 1, 2.$$

We omit the proof but the theorem is surely plausible. For example, if state 1 durations average 4 times as long as state 2 ones then the process has probability 4/5 of being in state 1 when observed.

A number of useful properties of the alternating renewal process can be got from those of the ordinary renewal process. In particular, consider the sequence of events consisting of entries to state 1. The times between such events have a distribution which is that of the sum of the duration in state 1 and a subsequent duration in state 2; that is, their distribution is the convolution of G_1 and G_2 and it obviously has mean $\mu_1 + \mu_2$. These inter-event times are positive and independent and thus they form a renewal process. In particular the renewal theorem applies and the renewal density approaches $1/(\mu_1 + \mu_2)$; that is, the probability of an entry to state 1 in dt approaches $dt/(\mu_1 + \mu_2)$ at times remote from the origin. If state 1 is occupied on average for 4 days and state 2 for 1 day then entries to state 1 occur on average every 5 days and the probability of observing such an entry on any one day will be 1/5.

Now consider figure 5.3, depicting a possible realisation of an alternating renewal process. In this realisation the process enters state 1 at

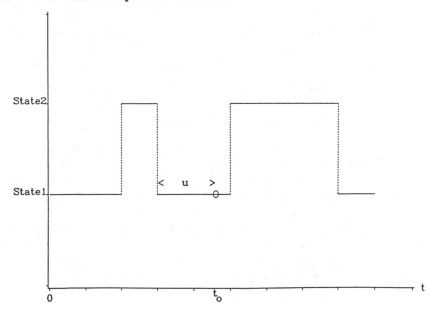

Figure 5.3.   A realisation of an alternating renewal process.

the origin, stays there for a random time, then enters state 2, and so on. Time t_0 is a fixed observation point remote from the start of the process. When observed the process happened to be in state 1 and had been there for u days. By an argument parallel to that of the last section the probability of this event, as $t_0 \to \infty$, is the probability of an entry to state 1 at $t_0 - u$ and survival in that state for at least u and this is

$$\frac{\overline{G}_1(u)}{\mu_1 + \mu_2} = P(\text{when observed the process is in state 1}$$
$$\text{and has been there for } u \text{ days}), \qquad (4.1)$$

and similarly for state 2. The conditional distribution of the elapsed duration, U, given that the process is in state 1 is got by dividing (4.1) by the probability of state 1, and is thus, for large t_0,

$$\frac{\overline{G}_1(u)}{\mu_1 + \mu_2} \div \frac{\mu_1}{\mu_1 + \mu_2} = \frac{\overline{G}_1(u)}{\mu_1}, \qquad (4.2)$$

exactly as for the backwards recurrence time in an ordinary renewal process. One can show that the distributions of V and $S = U + V$ are as in the previous section.

5   Multiple Destinations

We have until now in this and previous chapters been considering either single states or processes which alternate between two-states. In neither case is there any question of *alternative* destination states. For the models of the first four chapters the destination was unspecified – as it was for the Poisson and Renewal processes of the early part of this chapter. And even with an alternating process there is no question of choice of destination; unemployment is invariably followed by employment, and employment by unemployment. But much of the interest and richness of the subject comes in the analysis of data in which people successively occupy different states. We can introduce multiple-states into the modelling by considering separately the state biography of an individual – what states he has occupied previously and for how long   and the state future – what state he will go to. The former subject involves the study of autocorrelation and in general of dependence in the state biography. The study of multiple destinations is simpler and we tackle that first. We shall study a single duration which is terminated by exit to one of several possible destinations. An example of a multiple destination model from the econometri literature is where an unemployed person can leave that state either by recall to his old job or by finding a new one.

When one can leave a state for one of several destinations we need first of all to identify those states in our notation and we shall suppose that there are K possible destination states and label them with the subscript k, $k = 1, 2, \ldots, K$. These destinations are mutually exclusive and exhaust the possible destinations. As before we shall denote the hazard function at t by $\theta(t)$ and the duration density and survivor functions by f and $\overline{F}$. Now that we have identified several possible destination states we can formulate probability questions both *conditionally* on the name of the destination state and *jointly* with that name. We have in fact $K + 1$ random variables associated with the occupancy of a state, the duration of stay, T, and a set of K dummy variables, $\{D_k\}$, taking the value 1 if state k is entered and zero otherwise. Let us set up the notation with which to answer questions about T and the $\{D_k\}$.

Let

$$\theta_k(t) = \lim_{dt \to 0} \frac{\mathrm{P}\left(t \leq T < t + dt, D_k = 1 \mid T \geq t\right)}{dt}, \qquad (5.1)$$

so that for small dt

$$\theta_k(t)\, dt = \mathrm{P}\left(\text{departure to state } k \text{ in the short interval } (t, t + dt),\right.$$
$$\left.\text{given survival to } t\right).$$

The $\{\theta_k\}$, $k = 1, 2, \ldots, K$, are called the *transition intensities* to state k. The empirical counterpart of $\theta_k(t)$ is the fraction of the survivors at t who leave for state k on the following 'day'. The $\{\theta_k\}$ are sometimes called state specific hazard functions but this is rather misleading, as it suggests they bear a relation, such as (2.3) of chapter 1, to a survivor function, but this is not in general true, except in a purely formal sense.

The total of the survivors at t who leave on the following day is the sum over k of those who leave for destination k, which provides the relation between the hazard function $\theta(t)$ and the transition intensities $\theta_k(t)$

$$\theta(t) = \sum_{k=1}^{K} \theta_k(t). \tag{5.2}$$

The hazard function is the sum of the transition intensities over the destination states.

Next let us define the marginal probabilities of the destinations; specifically, let

$$\pi_k = P(\text{when departure occurs it is to destination } k) \quad k = 1, 2, \ldots, K.$$

We can now connect the $\{\pi_k\}$ and the $\{\theta_k\}$ by noting that

$$\begin{aligned}
\overline{F}(t)\theta_k(t)\,dt &= P(\text{survival to } t) \\
&\quad \times P(\text{departure to } k \text{ in } (t, t+dt) \mid \text{survival to } t) \\
&= P(\text{departure to } k \text{ in } t, t+dt), \tag{5.3}
\end{aligned}$$

the empirical counterpart of which is the fraction of an entering cohort who leave for state k in $(t, t+dt)$. Integrating this over t then gives the fraction of them who, ever, leave for k, which is just the required relation,

$$\pi_k = \int_0^\infty \overline{F}(s)\theta_k(s)\,ds. \tag{5.4}$$

Note that $\sum \pi_k = 1$ because $\sum \theta_k(t) = \theta(t) = f(t)/\overline{F}(t)$ from the definition of a hazard function, so

$$\sum_{k=1}^{K} \pi_k = \int_0^\infty \overline{F}(s)\frac{f(s)}{\overline{F}(s)}\,ds = \int_0^\infty f(s)\,ds = 1.$$

A final bit of notation is to introduce the conditional duration distribution, the condition being that departure, when it occurs, is to destination k. In particular, let

$$\begin{aligned}
\overline{F}_k(t) = P\,(&\text{survival to } t, \text{ given that when} \\
&\text{departure occurs it is to } k), \quad k = 1, 2, \ldots, K, \tag{5.5}
\end{aligned}$$

Table 5.2. Key Events and Their Probabilities in
Models with Multiple Destinations

Probability	Event	Conditioning event
$\theta_k(t)\,dt$	Departure to k at t	Survival to t
$\theta(t)\,dt$	Departure at t	Survival to t
π_k	Departure to k	...
$\overline{F}_k(t)$	Survival to t	Departure to k
$\overline{F}(t)$	Survival to t	...
$f_k(t)\,dt$	Departure at t	Departure to k
$f(t)$	Departure at t	...
$\theta_k(t)/\theta(t)$	Departure to k	Departure at t

with $F_k(t)$ and $f_k(t)$ being the corresponding distribution and density functions. The empirical counterpart of F_k is the sample distribution function of duration over all people who left for k. Now $\pi_k \overline{F}_k(t)$ is the probability of survival to t *and* eventual departure to k so the sum of these quantities over k just gives the survivor function at t, that is,

$$\overline{F}(t) = \sum_{k=1}^{K} \pi_k \overline{F}_k(t). \qquad (5.6)$$

Such a duration distribution is a *finite mixture distribution*. A distribution such as F_k which is conditional on the destination state is sometimes called a *holding time* distribution in contrast to the unconditional distribution, F, sometimes called a *waiting time* distribution.

Similarly $\pi_k f_k(t)\,dt$ is the probability of departure to k in $(t, t+dt)$. Thus we have the equality

$$\overline{F}(t)\theta_k(t)\,dt = \pi_k f_k(t)\,dt \qquad (5.7)$$

since both sides give the probability of departure to k in $(t, t+dt)$.

Note that the intensity of transition to k, $\theta_k(t)$, is equal to $f_k(t)\pi_k/\overline{F}(t)$ and not to $f_k(t)/\overline{F}_k(t)$ as it would be if $\theta_k(t)$ were a hazard function conditional on departure being to state k. *The conditioning event for θ_k is survival to t, not survival to t and departure to k.*

Since we have just defined a confusingly large number of events and their probabilities it may be helpful to set these out in the form of table 5.2, to which the reader can refer.

The key relations among these probabilities are

$$\theta(t) = \sum_{k=1}^{K} \theta_k(t), \tag{5.8}$$

$$\pi_k = \int_0^\infty \overline{F}(s)\theta_k(s)\,ds, \tag{5.9}$$

$$\overline{F}(t) = \sum_{k=1}^{K} \pi_k \overline{F}_k(t), \tag{5.10}$$

$$\overline{F}(t)\theta_k(t) = \pi_k f_k(t). \tag{5.11}$$

Consider now the probability density function of the $\{D_k\}$ and T. If we merely observe the event that a person exited after t days then the probability of that event is just $f(t)\,dt$ of course. If, however, we know that he left on day t and went to state k the probability of this event is $f_k(t)\pi_k$ or, equivalently, in view of (5.11), it is $\overline{F}(t)\theta_k(t)$. So the probability of our data can be written

P (left for k at time t) = $\theta_k(t)\overline{F}(t)\,dt$

$$= \theta_k(t)\exp\left\{-\int_0^t \sum_{k=1}^{K} \theta_k(u)\,du\right\}dt \tag{5.12}$$

where the latter follows from (5.8) and the fundamental relation between survivor and hazard functions. In terms of the dummy variates $\{D_k\}$ and the duration variate T the joint p.d.f. of the $\{D_k\}$ and T is

$$p(d_1, d_2, \ldots, d_K, t) = \exp\left\{-\int_0^t \theta_k(u)\,du\right\}\prod_{k=1}^{K}\theta_k(t)^{d_k},$$

or, more compactly,

$$p(\mathbf{d}, t) = \exp\left\{\sum_{k=1}^{K}\left[d_k \log\theta_k(t) - \int_0^t \theta_k(u)\,du\right]\right\}. \tag{5.13}$$

Equation (5.12) is the case of (5.13) in which $d_k = 1$ and the remaining d's are zero. Notice how simply the transition intensities enter the data distribution so that a theory that specifies the form taken by the transition intensities leads immediately to the likelihood function, (5.13).

Let us now describe some models for transition intensities with multiple destinations.

Example 6   Time-Invariant Transition Intensities
Suppose that the $\{\theta_k(t)\}$ are independent of t

$$\theta_k(t) = \theta_k, \qquad k = 1, 2, \ldots, K.$$

Then the hazard function is $\theta(t) = \sum_{k=1}^{K} \theta_k = \theta$, and from the relation
between hazard and survivor functions $\overline{F}(t) = \exp\{-\theta t\}$. Consequently
the probability of departure to k is, from (5.9),

$$\pi_k = \int_0^\infty \theta_k e^{-\theta s}\, ds = \frac{\theta_k}{\theta}.$$

Since this is the same as the probability of departure to k given departure at t the probability that a person will leave for k does not depend
on when he leaves. Moreover from (5.11) $f_k(t) = \theta \exp\{-\theta t\}$, so the
distributions of duration of people classified by their destination will
all be identical. This feature holds for a much wider class of transition
intensities as is illustrated in the next example.   ∎

Example 7   Proportional Intensity Models
An interesting restriction on the θ_k's is the proportional intensities model
in which

$$\frac{\theta_k(t)}{\theta(t)} = m_k, \qquad k = 1, 2, \ldots, K, \qquad (5.14)$$

which means that at all times the intensities of transition to any pair
of destination states are in the same ratio. This implies that, given that
departure occurs at t, the probability that it is to state k does not depend
upon t. Example 6 provides a proportional intensity model but it is not
necessary for the $\{\theta_k(t)\}$ to be independent of t for (5.14) to hold. The
probability that exit, when it occurs, will be to k is, from (5.9),

$$\pi_k = \int_0^\infty \overline{F}(s) m_k \theta(s)\, ds$$

$$= m_k \int_0^\infty \overline{F}(s) \frac{f(s)}{\overline{F}(s)}\, ds$$

$$= m_k.$$

The conditional distribution of duration given exit to k is from (5.11)

$$f_k(t) = \overline{F}(t)\theta_k(t)/\pi_k$$
$$= \overline{F}(t)\theta(t)$$
$$= f(t). \qquad (5.15)$$

Thus an implication of the proportional intensity model is that the duration distributions conditional on destination are identical and equal to

the unconditional distribution. This is a very strong implication of the proportional intensity specification and, incidentally, suggests a way of testing it. To illustrate the point numerically suppose there are two destination states labelled, say, U and E, and let the transitions intensities be specified as

$$\theta_U = 0.05 \qquad \theta_E = 0.15$$

so $\theta = 0.20$. If the unit of time is a month the results above tell us that people exit at the constant rate 0.20 per month with a mean time to exit of 5 months. Of those who exit on any day about a quarter $(0.05/0.20)$ go to U and the rest to E and the times to exit have the same distribution (and therefore the same mean of 5 months) whether they are classified by destination, U or E, or not classified at all. In an entry cohort of 1000 about 200 leave in the first month, 50 for U and 150 for E. Of the 800 survivors about 160 leave in the next month 40 for U and 120 for E, and so on. Clearly the numbers leaving for E are a constant multiple of those leaving for U and time to exit must have the same p.d.f. regardless of destination. In effect the transition intensities θ_U and θ_E tell us only about the way the leavers divide between U and E and not at all about the speed of leaving.   ∎

Example 8   Weibull Proportional Intensities
Suppose the transition intensities are

$$\theta_k(t) = \alpha \exp\{\mathbf{x}_k'\beta_k\}t^{\alpha-1}, \qquad k = 1, 2, \ldots, K,$$

where $\mathbf{x}_k$ is a vector of time-independent covariates, β_k is a parameter vector, and the parameter α is the same for all destinations. Then

$$\pi_k = \frac{\exp\{\mathbf{x}_k'\beta_k\}}{\sum_{j=1}^{K} \exp\{\mathbf{x}_j'\beta_j\}},$$

which is the familiar Logit model used in static discrete (state) choice modelling. The unconditional and destination-specific survivor functions are all given by

$$\overline{F}(t) = \exp\left\{-t^\alpha \sum_{k=1}^{K} \exp\{\mathbf{x}_k'\beta_k\}\right\},$$

which is a Weibull distribution. A particular case of this model is where the transition intensities are independent of time, $\alpha = 1$, in which case the duration distribution is Exponential.   ∎

To emphasise the simplications brought about by the proportional intensity model consider the non-proportional model with Weibull transition intensities with different α's.   ∎

Example 9   Weibull Non-Proportional Intensities
Let

$$\theta_k(t) = \alpha_k \mu_k t^{\alpha_k - 1}$$

so $$\theta(t) = \sum_{k=1}^{K} \alpha_k \mu_k t^{\alpha_k - 1} \quad \text{and} \quad \overline{F}(t) = \exp\{-\sum_{k=1}^{K} \mu_k t^{\alpha_k}\}.$$

Then the probability of departure to k given survival to t is

$$\frac{\theta_k(t)}{\theta(t)} = \frac{\alpha_k \mu_k t^{\alpha_k - 1}}{\sum_{j=1}^{K} \alpha_j \mu_j t^{\alpha_j - 1}},$$

which is a function of t. The unconditional probability of departure to k is

$$\pi_k = \alpha_k \mu_k \int_0^\infty s^{\alpha_k - 1} \exp\left\{-\sum_{j=1}^{K} \mu_j s^{\alpha_j}\right\} ds,$$

which must be calculated by numerical integration.

Example 10   Right Censoring as a Destination
Consider a model with a single destination and hazard function θ but where the duration T may be right censored by a censoring variate S with, possibly unknown, hazard θ_c. Assume T and S are independent. Then the probability that a person is both uncensored and exits in $(t, t + dt)$ is

$\mathrm{P}\,(\text{observed to exit in } t, t + dt)$
$$= \mathrm{P}\,(t \le T < t + dt, S \ge t + dt)$$
$$= \mathrm{P}\,(t \le T < t + dt) \times \mathrm{P}\,(S \ge t + dt)$$
$$= \theta(t) \exp\left\{-\int_0^t \theta(u)\,du - \int_0^t \theta_c(u)\,du\right\} dt$$

for small dt. Similarly,

$\mathrm{P}\,(\text{observed to be censored in } t, t + dt)$
$$= \mathrm{P}\,(t \le S < t + dt, T \ge t + dt)$$
$$= \mathrm{P}\,(t \le S < t + dt) \times \mathrm{P}\,(T \ge t + dt)$$
$$= \theta_c(t) \exp\left\{-\int_0^t \theta_c(u)\,du - \int_0^t \theta(u)\,du\right\} dt.$$

Comparing these with (5.12) we see that 'exit' and 'censored' are formally equivalent to two distinct destinations with transition intensities $\theta(t)$ and $\theta_c(t)$. From the mathematical, though not the substantive, point of view independent censoring just creates an additional dummy destination state 'censored'. This clearly generalises to a model with K 'real' destinations plus censoring as long as the (latent) random variables – see the next example – corresponding to the K transition intensities are independent of the censoring variate.[4]   ■

Example 11   Competing Risks
One way of formulating models with multiple destinations is to postulate the existence of K independent random variables, $T_1, \ldots, T_K$, one for each destination, which we may call latent durations or latent survival times, and to suppose that the actual destination entered is determined by whichever of the $\{T_k\}$ is the least and that this minimum is the duration we actually observe. Let T_k have hazard function $\theta_k(t)$, $k = 1$, $2, \ldots, K$. Then the probability of exit to destination k in $(t, t + dt)$ is

$$\text{P (exit to } k \text{ in } t, t + dt) = P(t \leq T_k < t + dt, \text{all other } \{T_j\} \geq t + dt)$$

$$= \theta_k(t) \exp\left\{ -\int_0^t \theta_k(u)\,du - \sum_{\substack{j=1 \\ j \neq k}} \int_0^t \theta_j(u)\,du \right\} dt,$$

by independence of the $\{T_k\}$,

$$= \theta_k(t) \exp\left\{ -\sum_{j=1}^K \int_0^t \theta_j(u)\,du \right\} dt.$$

Comparing this with (5.12) we see that a model with multiple destinations is formally equivalent to a model in which the transition intensities to each destination are the hazard functions of K independent destination-specific latent survival times. The actual exit time and destination state are determined by whichever of these latent times is the smallest. Example 10 shows that right censoring is a competing risk.

   This aproach to modelling with multiple destinations is called the *competing risks model* when used in a medical context in which the destinations are different modes of death, T_k being time to death from cause

---

[4] Consistent estimation from right censored survival data does not require independence of survival and censoring times. It is possible under a much weaker assumption about the censoring process, cf. chapter 8.

k if death from other causes was precluded. Though it may or may not be meaningful in medical statistics to discuss the distribution of time to death from cancer given that death from heart failure is precluded, in social science applications the latent failure-times do not appear generally to be meaningful. For example, consider a model in which a person may be employed, unemployed and looking for work, or out of the labour force. The notion of a time it would take an unemployed person to drop out of the labour force given that he is precluded from taking employment is clearly nonsense. Eliminating a possible destination will generally alter people's behaviour. These latent durations should be seen as mathematical fictions that may help one in thinking about the construction of models rather than as entities of real economic interest.   ∎

Example 12   Mixed Competing Risks
One can pursue the competing risks approach to the construction of multiple destination models by supposing that there exist K latent survival times $\{T_k\}$ with hazard functions $v_k \theta_k(t)$ and the $\{T_k\}$ are independent conditional on the K heterogeneity terms $\{v_k\}$. The V's are themselves jointly distributed over entrants in a K variate generalisation of the Exponential family used in section 3 of chapter 4. That is,

$$p(\mathbf{v}) = \left[\prod_{k=1}^{K} v_k^{\delta_k}\right] \exp\{-\lambda' \mathbf{v}\} M(\mathbf{v})/\phi(\delta, \lambda), \qquad (5.16)$$

a distribution denoted by $P(\delta, \lambda)$. Then since the conditional (on $\mathbf{v}$) survivor function is

$$\overline{F}(t \mid \mathbf{v}) = \exp\left\{-\sum_{k=1}^{K} \int_0^t v_k \theta_k(s)\, ds\right\},$$

the unconditional survivor function is

$$\overline{F}(t) = \int \left[\prod_{k=1}^{K} v_k^{\delta_k}\right] \exp\left\{-\mathbf{v}'\lambda - \int_0^t \mathbf{v}'\theta(s)\, ds\right\} M(\mathbf{v})/\phi(\delta, \lambda)\, d\mathbf{v}$$

$$= \int \left[\prod_{k=1}^{K} v_k^{\delta_k}\right] \exp\{-\mathbf{v}'(\lambda + \mathbf{I}(t))\} M(\mathbf{v})/\phi(\delta, \lambda)\, d\mathbf{v}$$

$$= \frac{\phi(\delta, \lambda + \mathbf{I}(t))}{\phi(\delta, \lambda)}. \qquad (5.17)$$

Here $\mathbf{I}(t)$ has k'th element $I_k(t) = \int_0^t \theta_k(s)\, ds$, and the last line follows from the observation that (5.16) integrates to unity over the K dimensional sample space of $\mathbf{v}$. The density of $\mathbf{v}$ among survivors at t is

$$
\begin{aligned}
p(\mathbf{v} \mid T > t) &= p(\mathbf{v}, T > t)/\overline{F}(t) \\
&= \overline{F}(t \mid \mathbf{v})p(\mathbf{v})/\overline{F}(t) \\
&= P(\delta, \lambda + \mathbf{I}(t)).
\end{aligned}
\tag{5.18}
$$

The density of $\mathbf{v}$ among those who leave for destination k at time t is

$$
p(\mathbf{v} \mid T = t, d_k = 1) = \frac{p(T = t, d_k = 1 \mid \mathbf{v})p(\mathbf{v})}{p(T = t, d_k = 1)}
$$

$$
\propto v_k^{\delta_k+1} \prod_{\substack{j=1 \\ j \neq k}}^{K} \exp\{-\mathbf{v}'(\lambda + \mathbf{I}(t))\} M(\mathbf{v}),
$$

which gives $p(\mathbf{v} \mid T = t, d_k = 1) = P(\delta + \mathbf{d}, \lambda + \mathbf{I}(t))$, where $\mathbf{d}$ has 1 in position k and zeros everywhere else. Thus the elegant properties of the Exponential family mixing distribution carry over to the multiple destinations case.

It should be noted that the joint density (5.16) can exhibit stochastic dependence of the V's, which in turn induces stochastic dependence of the K latent failure-times.

6   Multiple Cycles and Multiple Destinations

To consider a person moving probabilistically through a sequence of states we need to extend our definition of the transition intensities to recognise both the identity of the origin state, hitherto suppressed in our notation, and the precise role of time. At any time a person must occupy exactly one of K possible states. We suppose that the process begins at calendar time $t = 0$ with entry to a state and imagine that at some subsequent time he occupies state k. The calendar time when he entered the state is denoted by t. On entry a clock whose time is denoted s is set to zero, and started, so that s measures time from entry to a state. We define, for small ds,

$$
\begin{aligned}
\theta_{kl}(t, s)\, ds =\ & P(\text{departure from } k \text{ to } l \text{ in } s, s + ds \text{ given that it was} \\
& \text{entered at } t \text{ and has remained for } s \text{ and given the} \\
& \text{history of the process to } t + s), \\
& k, l = 1, 2, \ldots, K. \quad k \neq l
\end{aligned}
\tag{6.1}
$$

By the history of the process we mean the list of states previously occupied, the calendar times at which they were entered and left, and the values and paths of any, possibly time-dependent, regressor variables.

These thetas are just the transition intensities of the previous section with the origin state (k) and the origin calendar time (t) brought explicitly into the notation. We refer to the passage of a person from entry to a state to exit from it as a cycle. Hence we are now dealing with a process in which people in general experience multiple-cycles with alternative destinations – the last section dealt with a single-cycle and earlier sections of this chapter with multiple-cycles and single destinations.

We let $\{X(t), t \geq 0\}$ be the stochastic process identifying the state occupied at each time t. We can also identify a discrete-time process $\{X_n, n = 0, 1, 2, \ldots\}$ where X_n is the state entered at the n'th transition. $\{X_n\}$ is the discrete-time process *imbedded* in the process $\{X(t)\}$.

We now give a sequence of particular cases got by restricting the rather general formula (6.1) for transition intensities.

6.1   Continuous-Time Markov Chain

Let there be K states and suppose the $\{\theta_{kl}(t, s)\}$ depend neither on t nor on s, nor on the prior history, so we just denote them $\{\theta_{kl}\}$. Once a state, k, is entered the leaving process is, in effect, determined by $K - 1$ latent survival times which are distributed as $\mathcal{E}(\theta_{kl})$, $l = 1, 2, \ldots, K$, $l \neq k$. Or, equivalently, one could say that once state k is entered the duration of stay in it is determined by the hazard function $\theta_k = \sum \theta_{kl}, l \neq k$ and the destination l is chosen with probability equal to θ_{kl}/θ_k.

The process $\{X(t)\}$ is such that

$$P\left(X(t + s) = l \mid X(s) = k, X(u) = x(u), 0 \leq u < s\right)$$
$$= P\left(X(t + s) = l \mid X(s) = k\right) \qquad (6.2)$$

for all $s, t \geq 0$ and $l, k, x(u) = 1, 2, \ldots K$. The probabilities of the states that may be occupied at $t + s$ depend only upon the state occupied at s and not at all upon the prior state history. If $P\left(X(t + s) \mid X(s)\right)$ is independent of s the process is stationary or time-homogeneous. This formal definition of the continuous-time Markov chain – CTMC – implies that the transition intensities $\theta_{kl}(t, s)$ are independent of t, s and the state history. The transition intensities are formally defined as

$$\theta_{kl} = \lim_{dt \downarrow 0} \frac{P\left(X(t + dt) = l \mid X(t) = k\right)}{dt},$$

for $k, l = 1, 2, \ldots K$, $k \neq l$.

The process $\{X_n\}$ giving the states entered at each transition is a discrete-time *Markov chain* with transition probabilities given by

$$\pi_{kl} = \begin{cases} \theta_{kl}/\theta_k & k, l = 1, 2, \ldots, k \neq l \\ 0 & k = l. \end{cases} \qquad (6.3)$$

A property of interest in the continuous-time Markov chain is the long-run probability that when a person is observed he is found to be occupying state k, $k = 1, 2, \ldots, K$. Suppose that the state entered at $t = 0$ was state k. Let

$$p_{kl}(t) = P(X(t) = l \mid X(0) = k).$$

This is the probability of going from k to l, possibly via other states, in a period of length t. Then

$$p_{kl}(t + dt) = p_{kl}(t)(1 + \theta_{ll}\, dt) + \sum_{\substack{j=1 \\ j \neq l}}^{K} p_{kj}(t)\theta_{jl}\, dt + \mathrm{o}(dt), \tag{6.4}$$

where θ_{ll} is defined by

$$\theta_{ll} = - \sum_{\substack{j=1 \\ j \neq l}}^{K} \theta_{lj}. \tag{6.5}$$

Equation (6.4) says that one can go from k to l in a period of length $t + dt$ either by going from k to l in t and staying in l for dt, the latter having probability $1 - \sum_{\substack{j=1 \\ j \neq l}}^{K} \theta_{lj}\, dt = 1 + \theta_{ll}\, dt$; or by going from k to some state j in t and moving from j to l in a period of length dt, which has probability $\theta_{jl}\, dt$. All other possibilities involve more than one transition in a period of length dt and therefore have probabilities of smaller order than dt. Rearranging (6.4) we get

$$p_{kl}(t + dt) - p_{kl}(t) = \sum_{j=1}^{K} p_{kj}(t)\theta_{jl}\, dt.$$

Dividing by dt and taking limits gives

$$\frac{dp_{kl}(t)}{dt} = \sum_{j=1}^{K} p_{kj}(t)\theta_{jl}.$$

We now assemble the transition intensities in a matrix $\mathbf{Q}$ in which the diagonal elements are the negatives of the sums of the off-diagonal elements in the same row, so that, for example, for $K = 3$ we have

$$\mathbf{Q} = \begin{bmatrix} -(\theta_{12} + \theta_{13}) & \theta_{12} & \theta_{13} \\ \theta_{21} & -(\theta_{21} + \theta_{23}) & \theta_{23} \\ \theta_{31} & \theta_{32} & -(\theta_{31} + \theta_{32}) \end{bmatrix}. \tag{6.6}$$

If we also define $\mathbf{p}_k(t)$ as a *row* vector with l'th element $p_{kl}(t)$ this system may be written

$$\mathbf{p}'_k(t) = \mathbf{p}_k(t)\mathbf{Q}, \qquad (6.7)$$

where the prime denotes differentiation, not transposition. The elements of $\mathbf{p}_k(t)$ give the probabilities with which the K states will be occupied at time t by a person who began at $t = 0$ in state k.

If, as we have been assuming, the number of states is finite and if the transition intensities are such that it is possible to get from any state to any other – possibly via other states – then there exists a unique row vector of probabilities, $\mathbf{p}$, satisfying

$$\mathbf{p}\mathbf{Q} = 0 \qquad (6.8)$$

such that $p_l = \lim p_{kl}(t);\ l = 1,\ 2,\ \dots K$ as $t \to \infty$. This vector $\mathbf{p}$ gives the probabilities of the process being in each of the K states at an arbitrary time remote from the origin. These probabilities do not depend upon which state was occupied at time 0.

An alternative way of writing the equation (6.8) for the long-run state occupancy probabilities is as follows. For a finite Markov chain whose states inter-communicate there exists a vector of long-run state occupancy probabilities, $\bar{\pi}$, satisfying the equation

$$\bar{\pi} = \bar{\pi}\mathbf{\Pi}, \qquad (6.9)$$

where the $\mathbf{\Pi}$ matrix was defined in (6.3). The elements of $\bar{\pi}$ give the probabilities of the various states, i.e., the probability distribution of X_n, for large n. They are also called equilibrium probabilities since if the initial state is chosen according to the vector of probabilities $\bar{\pi}$ then $\bar{\pi}$ gives the probability distribution of X_n for every n. But for the continuous-time Markov chain

$$\mathbf{\Pi} = \mathbf{D}^{-1}\mathbf{Q} + I \qquad (6.10)$$

for $\mathbf{D} = \operatorname{diag}\{\theta_k\}$. Thus (6.9) implies that

$$\bar{\pi}\mathbf{D}^{-1}\mathbf{Q} = 0.$$

Comparison with (6.8) shows that

$$p_k = \frac{\bar{\pi}_k/\theta_k}{\sum_{j=1}^{K} \bar{\pi}_j/\theta_j} \qquad k = 1, 2, \dots K,$$

or equivalently, since the mean duration of stays in state k is $\mu_k = 1/\theta_k$,

$$p_k = \frac{\bar{\pi}_k\mu_k}{\sum_{j=1}^{K} \bar{\pi}_j\mu_j}. \qquad (6.11)$$

Here π_j is the j'th element of the vector π. Equation (6.11) says that the probability that the process is in state k at any arbitrary time t remote from the origin is proportional to the product of the mean duration of stays in k and the long-run probability that state k is entered at any transition.

Example 13   State Occupancy Probabilities for the Alternating Poisson Process

The alternating Poisson process is a continuous-time Markov chain with $\mathbf{Q}$ matrix given by

$$\mathbf{Q} = \begin{bmatrix} -\theta_{12} & \theta_{12} \\ \theta_{21} & -\theta_{21} \end{bmatrix} \tag{6.12}$$

and the equations (6.7) are, when the process starts in state 1,

$$p'_{11}(t) = -\theta_{12}p_{11}(t) + \theta_{21}p_{12}(t)$$
$$p'_{12}(t) = +\theta_{12}p_{11}(t) - \theta_{21}p_{12}(t). \tag{6.13}$$

The solutions, subject to the conditions $p_{11}(0) = 1, p_{12}(0) = 0$, $p_{11}(t) + p_{12}(t) = 1$, are

$$p_{11}(t) = \frac{\theta_{21}}{\theta} + \frac{\theta_{12}}{\theta}e^{-\theta t}$$

$$p_{12}(t) = \frac{\theta_{12}}{\theta} - \frac{\theta_{12}}{\theta}e^{-\theta t}$$

$$\theta = \theta_{12} + \theta_{21}, \tag{6.14}$$

as may be verified by differentiation. Similarly the probabilities of being in states 1 and 2 at t starting from state 2 at $t = 0$ are found to be

$$p_{21}(t) = \frac{\theta_{21}}{\theta} - \frac{\theta_{21}}{\theta}e^{-\theta t}$$

$$p_{22}(t) = \frac{\theta_{12}}{\theta} + \frac{\theta_{21}}{\theta}e^{-\theta t}. \tag{6.15}$$

Equations (6.14) and (6.15) may be combined if we define

$$p_j(t) = \mathrm{P}\,(\text{state } j \text{ occupied at time } t),$$

and note that

$$p_j(t) = p_1(0)p_{1j}(t) + p_2(0)p_{2j}(t). \tag{6.16}$$

Then

$$p_1(t) = \frac{\theta_{21}}{\theta} + [p_1(0) - \frac{\theta_{21}}{\theta}]e^{-\theta t}$$

$$p_2(t) = \frac{\theta_{12}}{\theta} + [p_2(0) - \frac{\theta_{12}}{\theta}]e^{-\theta t}. \tag{6.17}$$

Equation (6.17) gives the complete time path of the probabilities that state 1 or state 2 will be occupied at any time. For large t the Exponential terms in (6.17) vanish and we have the long-run, or equilibrium state occupancy, probabilities

$$p_1 = \frac{\theta_{21}}{\theta}; \qquad p_2 = \frac{\theta_{12}}{\theta}.$$

Note that since the duration of a visit to state 1 is distributed as $\mathcal{E}(\theta_{12})$ with mean $\mu_1 = 1/\theta_{12}$ and likewise visits to 2 are $\mathcal{E}(\theta_{21})$ with mean $\mu_2 = 1/\theta_{21}$ we may write

$$p_1 = \frac{\mu_1}{\mu_1 + \mu_2}$$

$$p_2 = \frac{\mu_2}{\mu_1 + \mu_2},$$

which is the same as the result stated earlier – section 4 – for the long-run probabilities of state occupancy in an alternating renewal process of which the alternating Poisson process is the particular case in which durations of stay in each state are Exponentially distributed.

The matrix $\mathbf{\Pi}$ for the imbedded discrete-time Markov chain is just

$$\mathbf{\Pi} = \begin{pmatrix} 0 & 1 \\ 1 & 0 \end{pmatrix}$$

since the states alternate. The vector π of equation (6.9) is just $(0.5, 0.5)$ since a half of all transitions are from state 1 and the rest from state 2.   ∎

Example 14   Long-Run State Occupancy Probabilities for the Three-State Markov Process

The solution for the $\{p_k\}$ is a fairly simple expression for a process with just three-states in which the $\mathbf{Q}$ matrix is given by (6.6). If we solve the equations (6.9) for the equilibrium probabilities in the imbedded Markov chain we find

$$\overline{\pi}_1 = \frac{\theta_2\theta_3 - \theta_{23}\theta_{32}}{k_1\,\theta_2\theta_3}$$

$$\overline{\pi}_2 = \frac{\theta_1\theta_3 - \theta_{13}\theta_{31}}{k_1\,\theta_1\theta_3}$$

$$\overline{\pi}_3 = \frac{\theta_1\theta_2 - \theta_{12}\theta_{21}}{k_1\,\theta_1\theta_2},$$

where

$$k_1 = \frac{2\theta_1\theta_2\theta_3 + \theta_{12}\theta_{23}\theta_{31} + \theta_{13}\theta_{21}\theta_{32}}{\theta_1\theta_2\theta_3}.$$

These give the long-run or equilibrium proportion of transitions in which entry is to state j, $j = 1, 2, 3$. To get the long-run fraction of time in which state j is occupied we must weight these entry probabilities by the average length of time spent in each state once it is entered, according to the formula (6.11). This then gives for the long-run state occupancy probabilities

$$p_1 = \frac{\theta_2\theta_3 - \theta_{23}\theta_{32}}{k_2}$$

$$p_2 = \frac{\theta_1\theta_3 - \theta_{13}\theta_{31}}{k_2}$$

$$p_3 = \frac{\theta_1\theta_2 - \theta_{12}\theta_{21}}{k_2},$$

where

$$k_2 = \theta_2\theta_3 - \theta_{23}\theta_{32} + \theta_1\theta_3 - \theta_{13}\theta_{31} + \theta_1\theta_2 - \theta_{12}\theta_{21}. \qquad \blacksquare$$

Example 15   Job to Job and Similar Transitions

In the formulation we have used transitions from one state to the same state are precluded – the model is written in terms of transition intensities out of each state. But in an application to movement of people between unemployment (U) and employment (E) it may be natural to allow people to move from one job the next without an intervening spell of unemployment. That is, one would want to allow for E to E transitions. A simple way to do this while preserving the convention that all transitions must be changes of state is to invent a second employment state and call the employment states E_1 and E_2. We would then allow movement from U to E_1 and from both E_1 and E_2 to U so that for the CTMC the transition intensity matrix would look like

$$\mathbf{Q} = \begin{array}{c} \\ U \\ E_1 \\ E_2 \end{array} \begin{array}{ccc} U & E_1 & E_2 \\ -\theta_{UE} & \theta_{UE} & 0 \\ \theta_{EU} & -\theta & \theta_{EE} \\ \theta_{EU} & \theta_{EE} & -\theta \end{array}$$

for $\theta = \theta_{EU} + \theta_{EE}$. The transition probability matrix of the imbedded Markov chain would

$$\mathbf{\Pi} = \begin{array}{c} \\ U \\ E_1 \\ E_2 \end{array} \begin{array}{ccc} U & E_1 & E_2 \\ 0 & 1 & 0 \\ \pi & 0 & 1-\pi \\ \pi & 1-\pi & 0 \end{array}$$

for

$$\pi = \frac{\theta_{EU}}{\theta_{EU} + \theta_{EE}},$$

the probability that a job is followed by a period of unemployment. The solution of the equation (6.9) for the equilibrium state occupancy probabilities in the imbedded Markov chain is

$$\overline{\pi}_U = \frac{\pi}{1+\pi}; \quad \overline{\pi}_{E_1} = \frac{1}{(2-\pi)(1+\pi)}; \quad \overline{\pi}_{E_2} = \frac{1-\pi}{(2-\pi)(1+\pi)}.$$

Note that the probability for employment is $\overline{\pi}_{E_1} + \overline{\pi}_{E_2} = (1+\pi)^{-1}$. Then if spells of unemployment last for μ_U days and jobs last for μ_E days on average the probability that a person is unemployed when observed at an arbitrary time remote from the origin is, from equation (6.11),

$$p_U = \frac{\overline{\pi}_U \mu_U}{\overline{\pi}_U \mu_U + \overline{\pi}_E \mu_E}, \qquad \overline{\pi}_E = \overline{\pi}_{E_1} + \overline{\pi}_{E_2},$$

$$= \frac{\pi \mu_U}{\pi \mu_U + \mu_E}. \qquad \blacksquare$$

The likelihood function for continuous observation of a continuous-time Markov chain is straightforward. Suppose, for example, that observation begins at any time t at which a person occupies state k. After a time interval s_1 he leaves for state l, in which he remains for at least s_2 days. The probability of these data, given the initial state k, is

$$\theta_k e^{-s_1 \theta_k} \times \frac{\theta_{kl}}{\theta_k} \times e^{-s_2 \theta_l}.$$

Notice that we do not need to know how long the initial state had been occupied prior to the start of observation. This is because of the Markov property that the probability that he remains in state k for a further s_1 days does not depend upon the previous state history and in particular it does not depend upon how long he had already been in k. To put it another way, we do not need to know how long he had been in k because of the lack of memory of the Exponential distribution. If we are willing to assume that the process is in equilibrium when first observed we could remove the conditioning on the initial state and multiply the above expression by p_k given by (6.11).

We shall give a general expression for the likelihood in chapter 8 where we shall also consider likelihoods for observational schemes other than continuous observation.

6.2   Time Inhomogeneous CTMC

A variant on the continuous-time Markov chain arises when the transition intensities depend upon calendar time t but not on elapsed duration s nor on the previous state history. In this case the matrix of transition intensities is a matrix of positive functions of t, $\mathbf{Q}(t)$. This is a multistate generalisation of the time-inhomogeneous Poisson process discussed in section 2. The state occupancy probabilities satisfy the matrix differential equation

$$\mathbf{p}'(t) = \mathbf{p}(t)\mathbf{Q}(t)$$

where $\mathbf{Q}(t) = \{\theta_{kl}(t)\}$. This is the model which is likely to be descriptively important in econometrics where time-varying regressors such as age or the state of the business cycle will cause time variation in the transition intensities. We shall give likelihoods for this model in chapter 8.

6.3   Continuous Time Semi-Markov Process

Another specialisation of the model (6.1) is to let the transition intensities depend upon s, the elapsed duration but not upon calendar time t nor upon the history of the process. The probability of a transition at any time depends upon how long the current state has been occupied. If $X(t)$ denotes the state occupied at t then $p(X(t) \mid X(s_1), X(s_2)) \neq p(X(t) \mid X(s_1))$ for distinct times s_1, s_2 prior to t because in general both $X(s_1)$ and $X(s_2)$ provide information about how long the current state has been occupied. Thus when the transition intensities depend upon the elapsed duration we no longer have a Markov process. But, as with the CTMC, there is a discrete-time Markov chain imbedded in the process and this is provided by the states occupied at the instant before each transition occurs. This chain has transition probability matrix $\mathbf{\Pi} = \{\pi_{kl}\}$ where π_{kl} is the probability that, when state k is left, it is for state l. The $\{\pi_{kl}\}$ were defined in section 5 – with the identity of the origin state there suppressed in the notation – as

$$\pi_{kl} = \int_0^\infty \overline{F}_k(s)\theta_{kl}(s)\,ds$$
$$= \mathrm{P}\,(\text{when departure from } k \text{ occurs it is to } l).$$

Here $\overline{F}_k(s)$ is the survivor function for visits to state k;

$$\overline{F}_k(s) = \exp\{-\int_0^s \theta_k(s)\,ds\}$$

for

$$\theta_k(s) = \sum_{\substack{l=1 \\ l \neq k}}^{K} \theta_{kl}(s).$$

Thus to construct a semi-Markov process we choose the sequence of states according to the transition probability matrix $\mathbf{\Pi}$ and let visits to state k have survivor function $\overline{F}_k(s)$ independently of previous durations and of the destination state, $k = 1, 2, \ldots K$. A CTMC is a special case of the semi-Markov process in which durations of stay are Exponential and so $\overline{F}_k(s) = \exp\{-\theta_k s\}$.

We shall give two important long-run results about the semi-Markov process. The first gives the probability that the process is in state k when observed at an arbitrary point of time remote from the origin. Let μ_k, $k = 1, 2, \ldots K$ be the mean duration of stay in vists to state k, and let $\overline{\pi}_k$, $k = 1, 2 \ldots K$ be the equilibrium probabilities in the imbedded Markov chain whose transition probability matrix is $\mathbf{\Pi}$. Thus

$$\mu_k = \int_0^\infty \overline{F}_k(s)\,ds, \qquad , k = 1, 2, \ldots K;$$

and the $\overline{\pi}_k$ satisfy

$$\overline{\pi} = \overline{\pi}\mathbf{\Pi}.$$

Then for large t the probability that the process is in state k is

$$p_k = \frac{\overline{\pi}_k \mu_k}{\sum_{j=1}^{K} \overline{\pi}_j \mu_j}, \qquad k = 1, 2, \ldots K. \qquad (6.18)$$

Note that this is exactly the same expression as we gave earlier, (6.11), for the continuous-time Markov process and it is valid under the same conditions on the matrix $\mathbf{\Pi}$ of the imbedded Markov chain.

Example 16
The alternating renewal process is a semi-Markov process with $\overline{\pi}_1 = \overline{\pi}_2 = 1/2$ so that (6.16) reduces to

$$p_k = \frac{\mu_k}{\mu_1 + \mu_2} \qquad k = 1, 2$$

as in section 4 of this chapter.   ∎

The second result concerns the joint probability that a semi-Markov process is in state k when observed and it will remain so for at least x more days. The survivor function for stays in k is $\overline{F}_k(s)$ with mean μ_k.

The associated forward recurrence-time density function is $\overline{F}_k(s)/\mu_k$. The result is

P(process is in state k at t and remains at least until $t + x$)

$$= p_k \int_x^\infty \overline{F}_k(u)\,du/\mu_k$$

for times t remote from the origin.

7   The Wiener Process as a Duration Model

In this section we shall give the main distributional results for the behaviour of a continuous-time random walk, or Wiener process, in the presenc of an absorbing barrier. In the next chapter we shall show how these results are useful in analysing a structural model of job tenure.

Consider a sequence of random variables generated according to the random walk

$$z_{t+1} = z_t + u_t\sigma \qquad t = 1, 2, \ldots T, \tag{7.1}$$

where the $\{u_t\}$ are independently and identically distributed as $N(0,1)$ variables independent of current and preceding values of z. The changes in z are independent $N(0, \sigma^2)$ variates. A continuous-time version of (7.1) can be obtained by writing

$$z(t + dt) = z(t) + u(t)\sigma\sqrt{dt}$$

or

$$dz(t) = u(t)\sigma\sqrt{dt} \tag{7.2}$$

where $u(t) \sim N(0,1)$ and $u(t), u(s)$ are independent for $t \neq s$. Formally, from (7.2) we see that

$$\mathrm{E}\left(dz(t)\right) = 0$$
$$\mathrm{var}(dz(t)) = \sigma^2 dt$$
$$\mathrm{cov}(dz(t)dz(s)) = 0 \tag{7.3}$$

and $dz(t)$ is Normally distributed. Thus increments of z are independently Normally distributed with mean zero and variance proportional to the length of the interval. We can give increments of z a non-zero mean by writing

$$dz(t) = \mu dt + u(t)\sigma\sqrt{dt} \tag{7.4}$$

so that the mean change in $z(t)$ in a unit time period is $\mu \neq 0$. The parameter μ is the rate of drift of the process, and the equation (7.4) with the assumptions about $u(t)$ define the Wiener process with drift μ and variance σ^2. The standard Wiener process has $\mu = 0$ and $\sigma = 1$.

We take the origin of the process as zero $z(0) = 0$. Since increments in z in unit time intervals are independent $N(\mu, \sigma^2)$ variates it follows that the distribution of $z(t)$ at a fixed time t is $N(\mu t, \sigma^2 t)$. That is,

$$f(z(t) \mid z(0) = 0) = N(\mu t, \sigma^2 t). \tag{7.5}$$

We can obtain an interesting duration model by introducing a linear barrier

$$b(t) = \alpha + \beta t, \qquad \alpha > 0 \tag{7.6}$$

and studying the time at which the process $\{z(t)\}$ first touches the barrier $b(t)$ – the first passage time – if it ever does.

First of all we note that it suffices to study the case of a constant barrier $b(t) = \alpha$. This is because

$$P\left(z(t) \geq \alpha + \beta t \mid z(s) < \alpha + \beta s; 0 \leq s < t\right) =$$
$$P\left(z(t) - \beta t \geq \alpha \mid z(s) - \beta s < \alpha; 0 \leq s < t\right). \tag{7.7}$$

But if $y(t) = z(t) - \beta t$ then

$$dy(t) = dz(t) - \beta dt$$
$$= (\mu - \beta)dt + u(t)\sigma\sqrt{dt},$$

which is a Wiener process of drift $\mu - \beta$ and variance σ^2. Thus the first passage time of $z(t)$ with drift μ from zero to a linear barrier $\alpha + \beta t$ has the same distribution as that of a Wiener process with drift $\mu - \beta$ from zero to a constant barrier at α. Let us therefore consider a Wiener process with drift μ and variance σ^2 in the face of a constant barrier at $\alpha > 0$.

If T is the first passage time the main result is that

$$f(t) = \frac{\alpha}{\sigma\sqrt{2\pi t^3}} \exp\left\{-\frac{(\alpha - \mu t)^2}{2\sigma^2 t}\right\},$$
$$= \frac{\alpha}{\sigma t^{3/2}} \phi\left(\frac{\alpha - \mu t}{\sigma\sqrt{t}}\right); \qquad t \geq 0, \tag{7.8}$$

with survivor function

$$\overline{F}(t) = \Phi\left(\frac{\alpha - \mu t}{\sigma\sqrt{t}}\right) - \exp\left\{\frac{2\mu\alpha}{\sigma^2}\right\}\Phi\left(\frac{-\alpha - \mu t}{\sigma\sqrt{t}}\right). \tag{7.9}$$

This distribution is known as the Inverse Gaussian and it was briefly discussed in chapter 3, section 4.2. If $\mu \geq 0$ then drift is not away from the barrier and $\lim_{t \to \infty} \overline{F}(t) = 0$ and the distribution is proper. On the other hand if $\mu < 0$ then drift is away from the barrier and we find that

$$\lim_{t \to \infty} \overline{F}(t) = 1 - \exp\left\{\frac{2\mu\alpha}{\sigma^2}\right\} > 0 \qquad (7.10)$$

and the distribution is defective. With probability given by (7.10) the barrier will never be reached.

When $\mu > 0$ the moment generating function is

$$M_T(s) = \exp\left\{\frac{\alpha}{\sigma^2}(\mu - [\mu^2 - 2s\sigma^2]^{1/2})\right\}. \qquad (7.11)$$

If $\mu \le 0$ no positive moments of T exist while for $\mu > 0$ we have from (7.11)

$$E(T) = \frac{\alpha}{\mu}; \qquad \text{var } T = \frac{\alpha\sigma^2}{\mu^3}. \qquad (7.12)$$

The hazard function $\theta(t) = f(t)/\overline{F}(t)$ rises from zero at the origin to a single maximum at t_m satisfying

$$\frac{\alpha^2}{3\sigma^2} \le t_m \le \frac{2\alpha^2}{3\sigma^2}$$

and then falls, approaching the limit

$$\lim_{t \to \infty} \theta(t) = \frac{\mu^2}{2\sigma^2}. \qquad (7.13)$$

Another quantity of interest in a Wiener process model with an absorbing barrier is the distribution of z at any fixed time t given that the barrier has not yet been reached. If the barrier were not present the distribution of $z(t)$ would be $N(\mu t, \sigma^2 t)$ as we remarked earlier. The condition that the barrier has not been reached constrains $z(t)$ to be less than α and also means that all previous values of z must be less than α. This latter constraint means that the distribution of z is not simply a Normal distribution truncated on the right at α but is a more complicated expression given by

$$g(z(t) \mid z(s) < \alpha; 0 \le s \le t) = g(z)$$

$$= \frac{\phi(\frac{z-\mu t}{\sigma\sqrt{t}}) - \exp\{2\mu\alpha/\sigma^2\}\phi(\frac{z-2\alpha-\mu t}{\sigma\sqrt{t}})}{\sigma\sqrt{t}\overline{F}(t)}, \qquad z \le \alpha. \quad (7.14)$$

Unlike a right truncated Normal distribution this density function has a zero ordinate at α. It is unimodal with mean given by

$$E[z(t)] = \mu t - 2\alpha \exp\left\{\frac{2\mu\alpha}{\sigma^2}\right\} \frac{\Phi(\frac{-\alpha-\mu t}{\sigma\sqrt{t}})}{\overline{F}(t)} \qquad (7.15)$$

The first component, μt, is the mean of the unconstrained Wiener process, while the second component reflects the effect of the barrier. Differentiation with respect to t shows that

$$\frac{d\mathrm{E}\left[z(t)\right]}{dt} = \mu - \theta(t)\{\alpha - \mathrm{E}\left[z(t)\right]\}. \tag{7.16}$$

This derivative is positive for $\mu > 0$, and $\mathrm{E}\left[z(t)\right]$ approaches α as $t \to \infty$.

NOTE

Texts which provide material useful for the econometrician wishing to fill out the sketch we have given in this chapter of some of the basic results concerning discrete-state, continuous-time, stochastic processes include Cox and Miller (1965), Karlin and Taylor (1975), and, particularly, Ross (1983). Monographs on special topics that are valuable include Cox (1962) on renewal theory and David and Moeschberger (1978) on competing risks. Hoem and Funck Jensen (1982) give a useful account of models for multiple-state transitions directed towards demographers, with extensive references to the demographic literature. A survey of the Inverse Gaussian distribution is provided by Folks and Chikara (1978). This chapter has also drawn on work by Jorgensen (1982), Ridder(1987), Jovanovic (1984), and Lancaster (1978).

CHAPTER 6

Some Structural Transition Models

1   Introduction

The models of chapters 1 through 5 emphasised the construction of the hazard function as the basis of model-building and thus implicitly stressed the chance character of movement between states. In economic applications as compared to applications in technology or medical science the element of choice cannot be ignored. It may be luck that an unemployed man is offered a job today, but he must choose whether or not to take it. Both choice and chance enter into the the transition process. In this chapter we shall give an account of an approach to modelling in which the choice element in each transition is emphasised. In this approach people at all times are assumed to occupy the state that they prefer, given the opportunity set that they currently face. The element of chance enters into the transition process because both the desirability of different states and the opportunities open to the economic agent vary in a partly probabilistic way over time.

When econometricians model static discrete choice among K states they find it helpful to associate with each state a utility, u_j, $j = 1$, 2, ..., K, depending upon the characteristics both of the state and of the choosing individual such that he chooses that state affording the greatest utility. In modelling choice among two-states then, state 2 is chosen if $u_2 - u_1 > 0$ and state 1 otherwise. In modelling the stochastic process of movement between states it is natural to adapt this approach to a dynamic context in which a sequence of choices is to be made. Thus we associate with each state and each time point an instantaneous utility flow, $u_j(t)$. The objective of the agent is no longer to choose the state with the greatest current utility flow. The problem in a dynamic context is to formulate a rule which tells the agent, given any vector of utility flows at time t, $\mathbf{u}(t)$, which state to occupy. The rule chosen should be that which maximises the expected present value of the stream of utilities over some horizon when states are occupied according to that decision rule. Thus a rule is a plan which says for every vector **u** and time t which state to choose. The optimal rule may or may not be of the form 'occupy the state currently affording the highest utility flow'. It may, and typically will, be optimal to occupy a state not affording the largest current utility flow in the interests of maximising the present value of the future utility stream. On the other hand, we can usually write down, for each state, an index $V_j(\mathbf{u}(t))$ which gives the expected present value of the utility stream that arises from occupying state j now, when the current utility flow is $\mathbf{u}(t)$, and when future states will be occupied according to the optimal rule. The optimal choice of state at any time is then to occupy the state whose utility index is largest.

The determination of the utility indices is a problem in dynamic programming, and they are not easy to obtain even under rather drastic simplifying assumptions. This creates a problem for the econometrician who finds himself supposing that agents solve mathematical and computational problems that he himself finds hard. It gives a slight air of unreality to such structural dynamic econometric models. On the other hand there is a great gain in ease of interpretation from fitting a structural model whose parameters correspond to constants in a clearly formulated, rational, behavioural model. When one fits a structural model one knows what the estimated parameters mean in terms of the behaviour of people and the environment they are assumed to face.

In this chapter we shall describe a selection of the structural models that have been used by econometricians and work out the distributions of potentially observable data to which they give rise.

2   A Two-State Model of Optimal Job Search

This model will illustrate the dynamic programming approach to the development of the utility indices. The two-states are employed (e) and unemployed (u). Agents start out unemployed and eventually transit to employment where they permanently reside. Thus transitions cease after a job has been obtained. The horizon is infinite and all parameters and distributions are constant over time and known to the agent. There is no learning and the model is completely stationary. The instantaneous utility flows in the two-states are

$$u_e(t) = w(t), \qquad u_u(t) = -c,$$

where the wage, w, is a realisation of a random variable, W, with distribution function F. The wage at time t is the most recent realisation of W and such realisations occur in a Poisson process at the rate λ per unit time period. The parameter c is the cost of search per unit time period – it is constant over time. The discount rate applied to future utility streams is ρ.

Since transitions cease when employment is entered the present value of the utility stream when state e is occupied now, when the current utility flow is $\{w, -c\}$, is just the present value of the wage over the infinite horizon;

$$V_e(w, -c) = \frac{w}{\rho}. \tag{2.1}$$

The utility index for the unemployed state can be deduced in the following way. We denote $V_u(w, -c)$ by V_u for short and consider an agent at time t looking ahead for the short interval of time of length h and evaluating the expected present value of his utility stream from being currently in u and moving optimally between states in the future. That is, he is calculating V_u. In that time interval of length h he receives the utility flow from being unemployed, which is $-c\,h$, and he either receives a new wage offer (a new realisation of W), an event of probability λh, or he does not, an event of probability $1 - \lambda h$. If he receives a wage offer of W he either moves to the employed state and enjoys an expected present value of utility equal to $V_e(W, -c)$ or declines it and continues to possess an expected present value of utility equal to $V_u(w, -c)$ depending on which of these two indices is the larger. Thus viewed from the present time his expectation if he receives a new wage offer is

$$E_W\left(\max\{V_e(W, -c), V_u(w, -c)\}\right) \tag{2.2}$$

where the expectation is with respect to the distribution F of W.[1] Assembling these outcomes together and applying to each the discount factor $(1 + \rho h)^{-1}$ we have the equation

$$V_u = -\frac{ch}{(1 + \rho h)} + \frac{(1 - \lambda h)V_u}{(1 + \rho h)} + \frac{\lambda h E_W\left(\max\{V_e(W), V_u\}\right)}{(1 + \rho h)} + \circ(h). \tag{2.3}$$

Here the neglected terms of $\circ(h)$ refer to the possibility of more than one new wage offer arriving in h which may be neglected as $h \to 0$. Multiplying both sides by $(1 + \rho h)$, dividing by h, and letting $h \to 0$ we find

$$(\rho + \lambda)V_u = -c + \lambda E_W\left(\max\{V_e(W), V_u\}\right). \tag{2.4}$$

---

[1] Which we assume, for simplicity, to have everywhere positive density function over $w \geq 0$.

We may simplify this expression by use of the following equality:

$$E_W\left(\max\left\{\frac{W}{\rho}, V_u\right\}\right) = V_u + E_W\left\{\frac{W}{\rho} - V_u \mid \frac{W}{\rho} > V_u\right\}\mathrm{P}\left(\frac{W}{\rho} > V_u\right)$$

$$= V_u + \rho^{-1}E\{W - \xi \mid W > \xi\}\mathrm{P}\,(W > \xi),$$

$$= V_u + \rho^{-1}\int_\xi^\infty (w - \xi)dF(w), \tag{2.5}$$

for $\xi = \rho V_u$. Here ξ is the wage that equates $V_e(W)$ to V_u – the reservation wage – and the decision rule is to move to employment on the first occasion that a wage arrives that is greater than ξ. The optimal policy is determined once ξ is calculated and this may be done by solving the equation that results from substituting (2.5) into (2.4), namely,

$$\xi = -c + \frac{\lambda}{\rho}\int_\xi^\infty (w - \xi)\, dF(w). \tag{2.6}$$

Since the left-hand side of (2.6) is increasing in ξ and the right-hand side decreasing, (2.6) has a unique solution.

It is possible that $V_u < 0$, in which case the optimal policy would be not to search at all, to allow for which would require a third state – non-participation. It is also interesting to note that from the mathematical point of view the time that an unemployed job searcher accepts employment is the first passage time of the stochastic process formed by $V_e(w(t))$ through an absorbing barrier at $V_e(\xi)$. Most structural models for the duration of events are first passage time models.

If we assume that a person actually follows this decision rule, what are the distributions of potentially observable quantities and how do these depend upon the parameters of the model? Such a person leaves unemployment in the short interval $(t, t + h)$ if and only if he receives a new wage offer in the interval, an event of probability λh, and that wage exceeds the reservation wage, an event of probability $\overline{F}(\xi)$. Thus the hazard function for leaving unemployment is

$$\theta(t) = \lambda\overline{F}(\xi), \tag{2.7}$$

which is independent of time, and thus the duration of unemployment is Exponentially distributed,

$$f(t) = \lambda\overline{F}(\xi)\exp\{-\lambda\overline{F}(\xi)t\}, \qquad t \ge 0. \tag{2.8}$$

A likelihood function based on a random sample of newly unemployed people observed until they find a job would be the product of terms like (2.8).

If one also observes the wage accepted by each person when he leaves unemployment then it is clear that this wage has distribution

$$g(w) = \frac{f(w)}{\overline{F}(\xi)}, \qquad w > \xi \geq 0. \tag{2.9}$$

Moreover, as a consequence of stationarity the accepted wage and the duration of unemployment are stochastically independent. Thus the joint distribution of T and W is the product of (2.8) and (2.9),

$$g(w,t) = \lambda f(w) \exp\{-\lambda \overline{F}(\xi)t\}, \qquad w > \xi \geq 0. \tag{2.10}$$

Again, if we observe a random sample of newly unemployed people until they gain employment the likelihood function would be the product of terms like (2.10). This likelihood function poses a non-standard problem of inference since the sample space (for W) depends upon the unknown parameter ξ if this quantity is taken to be the same for everyone. In this case the likelihood function will have to be maximised subject to the constraints

$$\xi \leq \min\{w_i\}. \tag{2.11}$$

If, on the other hand, ξ is parametrised as, say, $\xi_i = \beta_0 + \beta' \mathbf{x}_i$ then the likelihood function must be maximised subject to the constraint

$$\beta_0 + \beta' \mathbf{x}_i \leq w_i, \qquad i = 1, 2, \dots, n. \tag{2.12}$$

A third possibility is a fully structural approach in which a likelihood based on (2.10) is maximised subject to the constraint (2.6) in which ξ is represented as an implicit function of c, λ, ρ, and F. Repeated solution of (2.6) will be required in the maximisation. In each of these cases the asymptotic distribution theory for the maximum likelihood estimators will be non-standard. We shall return to this point in chapter 8.

Central to this model is the idea of the arrival of wage offers which the agent must accept or reject. There may be cases in which we can observe the number of offers which have been rejected, if any, before employment is entered. It is of interest therefore to deduce the distribution of the number of such rejected offers, a random variable which we shall denote by N.

Let us establish the short notation

$$q = F(\xi), \quad p = \overline{F}(\xi)$$

for the probabilities that an offer will be rejected or accepted, respectively. Then since offers arrive in a Poisson process of rate λ, unacceptable and acceptable offers arrive as events in independent Poisson processes of rate functions λq and λp, respectively. Suppose that the first acceptable offer arrives at time t. Then since the two types of offer arrive in independent Poisson streams the number of unacceptable offers that arrive before t has a Poisson distribution, conditional on $T = t$,

$$g(n \mid t) = e^{-\lambda qt}[\lambda qt]^n/n!, \qquad n = 0, 1, 2, \dots. \qquad (2.13)$$

Then because the density function of T itself is $g(t) = e^{-\lambda pt}\lambda p$ the joint density function of the number of offers rejected and the duration of search is

$$\begin{aligned} g(n,t) &= \lambda^{n+1} pq^n t^n e^{-\lambda t(p+q)}/n! \\ &= \lambda^{n+1} pq^n t^n e^{-\lambda t}/n!, \qquad n = 0, 1, 2, \dots, \quad t \geq 0. \quad (2.14) \end{aligned}$$

The marginal distribution of the number of rejected offers reported by someone who has returned to work is

$$\begin{aligned} g(n) &= \int_0^\infty g(n,t)\,dt \\ &= \lambda^{n+1} pq^n \int_0^\infty t^n e^{-\lambda t}\,dt/n! \\ &= \lambda^{n+1} pq^n n! \lambda^{-n-1}/n! \\ &= pq^n, \qquad n = 0, 1, 2 \dots. \qquad (2.15) \end{aligned}$$

This is a Geometric distribution with mean and variance

$$\mathrm{E}\,(N) = \frac{q}{p}, \qquad \mathrm{var}(N) = \frac{q}{p^2}. \qquad (2.16)$$

It is interesting to note that the distribution of the number of rejected offers does not involve the parameter λ, which measures the availability of job offers. Curiously enough the distribution (2.15) is precisely that which would arise in a *discrete-time model* in which one job offer arrives each time period. It does, however, indirectly depend upon λ because, from equation (2.6), ξ is a function of λ. Indeed, since ξ and therefore $F(\xi)$ are increasing functions of λ then $\mathrm{E}\,(N)$ is an increasing function of λ and one would find that the more offers were available the more, on average, would have been rejected before a job was finally taken.

To continue the study of the joint distribution of N and T we may calculate the joint moment generating function to be

$$\begin{aligned} \mathrm{E}\,(e^{s_1 N + s_2 T}) &= \lambda p \sum_{n=0}^\infty (\lambda q e^{s_1})^n \int_0^\infty t^n e^{-(\lambda - s_2)t}\,dt/n! \\ &= \lambda p \sum_{n=0}^\infty (\lambda q e^{s_1})^n (\lambda - s_2)^{-n-1}, \qquad s_2 < \lambda, \end{aligned}$$

$$= \frac{\lambda p}{\lambda - s_2 - \lambda q e^{s_1}}, \qquad \frac{\lambda q e^{s_1}}{\lambda - s_2} < 1. \qquad (2.17)$$

By differentiating the logarithm of this we find cov $(N, T) = q/\lambda p^2$, and using (2.16) and var $(T) = (\lambda p)^{-2}$ we can calculate the correlation of N and T to be

$$\rho_{N,T} = \sqrt{q} = \sqrt{F(\xi)}. \qquad (2.18)$$

This is a strong implication of the model so that observation of the numbers of rejected offers adds greatly to the econometrician's ability to test this structural model.

3   A Three-State Model of Optimal Participation and Search

In this section we shall look at a structural model that permits the study of people moving through more than one cycle and with alternative destinations at each transition. This is a three-state model of labour supply in which the states are employed (e), unemployed (u), and out of the labour market (n). The instantaneous utility flows are

$$u_e(t) = w(t); \quad u_u(t) = -c; \quad u_n(t) = n(t), \qquad (3.1)$$

where the wage w and the utility of non-market activity, n, are realisations of random variables W and N, measured in the same units, with distribution functions F and G, respectively. (Note that we are using n as a realisation of the random variable N and also as a subscript to indicate the state of non-participation.) The cost, c, is a constant known, as are F and G, to the agent. Realisations of W arrive in a Poisson stream at rates λ_e, λ_u, and λ_n, which depend upon the state currently occupied. The state u, unemployed (and looking for work), is defined to be that state in which new realisations of W arrive most frequently. Thus $\lambda_u > \lambda_e, \lambda_n$. Realisations of N appear in a Poisson stream at the rate λ regardless of the state currently occupied. The discount rate is ρ; the horizon is infinite; and all parameters are known to the agent. Thus the model is fully stationary just like the two-state model of the last section, of which the present model is a natural extension.

The model is solved by setting up the dynamic programming equations determining the expected present value of the utility stream from occupying each state and moving optimally between states thereafter. We denote the vector of current utility flows, (3.1), by $\mathbf{u}(t)$. It is the changes in these flows that trigger movements from state to state. The expected present value of occupying each state now, at t, and moving optimally between states in the future is denoted by $V(\mathbf{u}(t))$ with the appropriate subscript. We shall usually drop the dependence on $\mathbf{u}$ in our notation to enhance readability.

The equation for V_e is

$$
\begin{aligned}
V_e(\mathbf{u}(t)) = \frac{wh}{(1+\rho h)} &+ \frac{[1 - (\lambda_e + \lambda)h]V_e(w)}{(1+\rho h)} \\
&+ \frac{\lambda_e h E_W(\max\{V_e(W), V_e(w)\})}{(1+\rho h)} \\
&+ \frac{\lambda h E_N(\max\{V_e(w), V_n(N)\})}{(1+\rho h)} + \mathrm{o}(h).
\end{aligned} \tag{3.2}
$$

(Note the distinction between W, the variate whose realisation is unknown now, at t, and w the known wage at t.) The explanation for the right-hand side of this equation is that in a short interval of time of length h the utility flow wh accrues and either one new realisation of W or one new realisation of N or neither occurs. If a new realisation of W occurs – a new job – it is accepted if the value of V_e to which it gives rise exceeds the currently available $V_e(w)$. Whether it is accepted or not the agent continues in state e. If a new realisation of N occurs it is accepted and a move to state n occurs if the new value of V_n to which it gives rise exceeds the currently available $V_e(w)$.

The equation for V_u is

$$
\begin{aligned}
V_u(\mathbf{u}(t)) = \frac{-ch}{(1+\rho h)} &+ \frac{[1 - (\lambda_u + \lambda)h]V_u}{(1+\rho h)} \\
&+ \frac{\lambda_u h E_W(\max\{V_e(W), V_u\})}{(1+\rho h)} \\
&+ \frac{\lambda h E_N(\max\{V_n(N), V_u\})}{(1+\rho h)} + \mathrm{o}(h).
\end{aligned} \tag{3.3}
$$

The explanation here is analogous to that for (3.2) except that new realisations of W or N can trigger moves to employment or non-participation, respectively. The equation for V_n is

$$
\begin{aligned}
V_n(\mathbf{u}(t)) = \frac{nh}{(1+\rho h)} &+ \frac{[1 - (\lambda_n + \lambda)h]V_n(n)}{(1+\rho h)} \\
&+ \frac{\lambda_n h E_W(\max\{V_e(W), V_n(n)\})}{(1+\rho h)} \\
&+ \frac{\lambda h E_N(\max\{V_n(N), V_u\})}{(1+\rho h)} + \mathrm{o}(h).
\end{aligned} \tag{3.4}
$$

It will be noted that all movements out of jobs are quits, though it would not be difficult to allow for exogenous firings or lay-offs.[2]

If we now multiply each equation through by $(1+\rho h)/h$, allow $h \to 0$, and simplify by the use of relations analogous to (2.5) we find three equations whose solution provides numerically the optimal transition policy. They are

$$V_e(w) = \frac{w}{\rho} + \frac{\lambda_e}{\rho} \int_w^\infty \{V_e(x) - V_e(w)\}\, dF(x)$$

$$+ \frac{\lambda}{\rho} \int_{\xi_{en}}^\infty \{V_n(n) - V_e(w)\}\, dG(n), \tag{3.5}$$

$$V_u = \frac{-c}{\rho} + \frac{\lambda_u}{\rho} \int_{\xi_{ue}}^\infty \{V_e(w) - V_u\}\, dF(w)$$

$$+ \frac{\lambda}{\rho} \int_{\xi_{un}}^\infty \{V_n(n) - V_u\}\, dG(n), \tag{3.6}$$

$$V_n(n) = \frac{n}{\rho + \lambda} + \frac{\lambda}{\rho + \lambda} \int_{\xi_{nu}}^\infty \{V_n(n) - V_u\}\, dG(n) \tag{3.7}$$

$$+ \frac{\lambda}{\rho + \lambda} \int_{\xi_{ne}}^\infty \{V_e(w) - V_n(n)\}\, dF(w) + \frac{V_u}{\rho + \lambda}.$$

In these equations the ξ's are reservation values of W and N defined by

$$V_e(w) = V_n(\xi_{en}(w)), \tag{3.8}$$

$$V_u = V_e(\xi_{ue}), \tag{3.9}$$

$$V_u = V_n(\xi_{un}), \tag{3.10}$$

$$V_u = V_n(\xi_{nu}), \tag{3.11}$$

$$V_n(n) = V_e(\xi_{ne}(n)). \tag{3.12}$$

The equations (3.5) to (3.7) are functional equations whose solution provides the functions $V_e(w)$, $V_n(n)$, and $V_u(c)$ whence (3.8) to (3.12) may be solved for the reservation values. The optimal policy is simple to describe, though not easy to calculate. Someone in employment earning wage w moves to another job if he gets a new wage offer larger than w or drops out of the labour force if he gets a realisation of N larger than $\xi_{en}(w)$. An unemployed person accepts a new job if the wage exceeds ξ_{ue} or drops out if he receives an N larger than ξ_{un}. A non-participant experiencing a value of non-market time n takes employment if he receives a wage offer in excess of $\xi_{ne}(n)$ or becomes an unemployed job seeker if he receives a new value of N – he cannot retain the old one – less than ξ_{nu}.

---

[2] cf. Burdett and Mortensen (1978).

The transition intensities are also straightforward to write down. An unemployed person has the two possible destination states, e and n, and receives wage offers at the rate λ_u and new values of N at the rate λ. So the probability of a move to employment in a time interval of length dt given survival to the start of it is $\lambda_u \overline{F}(\xi_{ue})\, dt$; and the probability of a move to non-participation is $\lambda \overline{G}(\xi_{un})\, dt$. These are the transition intensities to e and n, respectively, and their sum is the hazard function for the unemployed state. Note the time constancy of the transition intensities implying Exponential unemployment durations.

A person employed at wage w has only one destination state – non-participation – to which he moves with transition intensity, and hazard function, $\lambda \overline{G}(\xi_{en}(w))$ given w. He moves within the employed state to another job with transition intensity $\lambda_e \overline{F}(w)$ given w. These transition intensities are constant over time given w but since the wage earned by someone continuously employed will change from time to time the transition intensities are not constant unconditionally. Stays in the employed state are therefore not Exponentially distributed and the whole process of movement between states does not follow a continuous-time Markov chain. On the other hand, a Markov process can be defined by enlarging the definition of a state. The transition intensities generally depend on the state occupied and on the current values of w and n. If we take the sample spaces of W and N to be discrete and finite with, say, m_w and m_n points in them, respectively, then we can define new states as e, w_i, n_j; $i = 1, 2, \ldots, m_w$; $j = 1, 2, \ldots, m_n$ and similarly for u and the non-participation state, giving a new process with a total of $3 \times m_w \times m_n$ states. In this new process the transition intensities depend only upon the identity of the current state and they are time-constant. With the new definition of states the process is a continuous-time Markov chain and its long-run properties can be studied using the results of chapter 5, section 6. This idea has not been pursued in the literature.

It is not difficult to build up the likelihood function for an entrant to any of the states e, u or non-participation and observed over a period of time, at least as long as we observe both the state he occupies and the values of w and n. To illustrate this construction suppose we observe someone take a job paying w_0, move to a new job paying w_1 after t_1 days, and stay in the new job for at least t_2 days. His contribution to the likelihood function is

$$\lambda_e \overline{F}(w_0) \exp\{-[\lambda_e \overline{F}(w_0) + \lambda \overline{G}(\xi_{en}(w_0))]t_1\} \times \frac{f(w_1)}{\overline{F}(w_0)}$$

$$\times \exp\{-[\lambda_e \overline{F}(w_1) + \lambda \overline{G}(\xi_{en}(w_1))]t_2\}. \qquad (3.13)$$

The first component in this product is the joint probability of exit at t_1 and exit to a new job; the second component is the density of the wage in the new job; and the third component is the probability of survival in the new job for t_2. The expression (3.13) is conditional on the initial wage w_0.

A major difficulty with this model lies in the value of non-market time, n, which will be hard to measure. If it is unobservable it will have to be treated as a heterogeneity term and integrated out of the likelihood function. At the time of writing no applications of this model have been reported in the literature.

4　　A Non-Stationary Model

A major interest in the labour supply literature has been in the time variation in transition intensities, yet both of the structural models of the previous two sections are stationary. In this section we shall describe a structural model of the behaviour of an unemployed person in a two-state model in which the environment changes over time causing the optimal policy of an agent itself to be time-dependent.

There are several reasons why the optimal transition policy should be time-dependent. For example, the effects of learning – on which we shall have more to say in section 5 – and of changes in the availability of job offers will both induce a time-dependent transition policy. Here we shall examine a different source of time variation, namely, a change in the costs of search. The framework will be that of the two-state search model of section 2 except that we suppose that at time t_1 there is a once-for-all increase in the cost of search from c_0 to c_1, a fact known to the agent in advance. An example of such an increase might be a fall in the level of unemployment benefits payable. Such a fall used to take place in the British system after twenty-six weeks of unemployment. In many U.S. states benefits expire after a period of the order of six to nine months. We continue to suppose that wage offers arrive in a Poisson stream at the constant rate λ and the wage offer distribution is unchanging and given by $F(w)$.

From t_1 the environment is constant so the optimal policy is as described in section 2 with $c = c_1$. This policy is to accept the first offer paying more than ξ_1, where ξ_1 satisfies the equation

$$\xi_1 = -c_1 + \frac{\lambda}{\rho} \int_{\xi_1}^{\infty} (w - \xi_1) dF(w), \qquad (4.1)$$

and $\xi_1 = \rho V_1$. V_1 is the expected present value of the utility (income) stream when unemployed at any time at or after t_1 and intending to follow an optimal policy with regard to switching into employment thereafter.

Before t_1 the optimal policy is determined by a dynamic programming equation which is the generalisation of (2.3) to a changing environment. Let $V(t)$ be the expected present value of the utility stream from being unemployed at any time t prior to t_1 and following an optimal policy thereafter. Then for $t \leq t_1$ the generalisation of (2.3) is

$$V(t) = \frac{-c_0 h}{(1 + \rho h)} + \frac{(1 - \lambda h)V(t + h)}{(1 + \rho h)}$$
$$+ \frac{\lambda h E_W \left(\max\{(W/\rho), V(t + h)\} \right)}{(1 + \rho h)} + \circ(h). \tag{4.2}$$

Multiplying through by $(1 + \rho h)/h$ we get

$$\frac{V(t) - V(t + h)}{h} + \rho V(t) = -c_0 + \frac{\lambda}{\rho} \int_{\rho V(t+h)}^{\infty} (w - \rho V(t+h)) dF(w) + \circ(1), \tag{4.3}$$

and letting $h \to 0$ gives

$$-\dot{V}(t) + \rho V(t) = -c_0 + \frac{\lambda}{\rho} \int_{\rho V(t)}^{\infty} (w - \rho V(t)) dF(w),$$

or, with $\xi(t) = \rho V(t)$,

$$\frac{\dot{\xi}(t)}{\rho} = \xi(t) + c_0 - \frac{\lambda}{\rho} \int_{\xi(t)}^{\infty} (w - \xi(t)) dF(w). \tag{4.4}$$

The reservation wage, $\xi(t)$, satisfies this non-linear differential equation for $0 \leq t \leq t_1$ with terminal condition

$$\xi(t_1) + c_1 - \frac{\lambda}{\rho} \int_{\xi(t_1)}^{\infty} (w - \xi(t_1)) dF(w) = 0. \tag{4.5}$$

Differentiating (4.4) with respect to t we get

$$\frac{\ddot{\xi}(t)}{\rho} = \dot{\xi}(t) \left[1 + \frac{\lambda}{\rho} \int_{\xi(t)}^{\infty} dF(w) \right]$$
$$= \dot{\xi}(t) \left[1 + \frac{\lambda}{\rho} \overline{F}(\xi(t)) \right]$$
$$= \dot{\xi}(t) \left[1 + \frac{\theta(t)}{\rho} \right], \qquad t \leq t_1. \tag{4.6}$$

$\xi(t)$

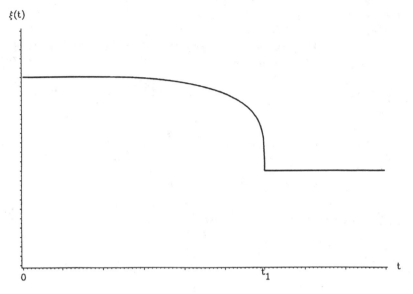

Figure 6.1.   The reservation wage with a step in the benefit stream.

So if $\xi(t)$ is ever decreasing it is always decreasing for $t \leq t_1$. But consider a time t close to t_1. Subtracting (4.5) from (4.4), with $\xi(t_1) = \xi_1$, gives

$$\frac{\dot{\xi}(t)}{\rho} = \xi(t) - \xi_1 + (c_0 - c_1)$$

$$- \frac{\lambda}{\rho} \left[\int_{\xi(t)}^{\infty} (w - \xi(t))dF(w) - \int_{\xi_1}^{\infty} (w - \xi_1)dF(w) \right]. \quad (4.7)$$

Suppose that $\dot{\xi}(t) > 0$. Then $\xi(t) < \xi_1$ and since, as we remarked earlier, $\int_{\xi}^{\infty}(w-\xi)dF(w)$ is a decreasing function of ξ the term in square brackets is > 0. Since $c_0 < c_1$ by assumption, the right-hand side of (4.7) is negative, which is a contradiction. Similarly, $\dot{\xi}(t) = 0$ can be ruled out, and, in view of (4.6), ξ is always decreasing on $0 \leq t \leq t_1$. The function $\xi(t)$ has the general shape given in figure 6.1. The reservation wage falls as the benefit change date approaches, the rate of fall increasing sharply close to t_1. The hazard function $\theta(t) = \lambda\overline{F}(\xi(t))$ in consequence looks like figure 6.2. There is some empirical evidence supporting figure 6.2 – see Meyer (1986).

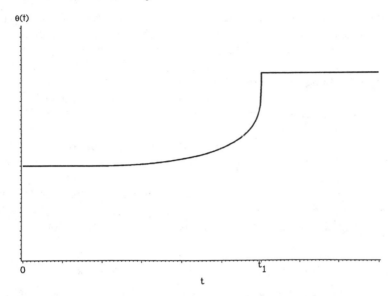

Figure 6.2.   The hazard function with a step in the benefit stream.

Since the hazard function is $\lambda \overline{F}(\xi(t))$ the duration density function is given by

$$g(t) = \lambda \overline{F}(\xi(t)) \exp\left\{-\lambda \int_0^t \overline{F}(\xi(s))\,ds\right\}. \qquad (4.8)$$

The density function of the wage accepted at t is

$$g(w \mid t) = \frac{f(w)}{\overline{F}(\xi(t))}, \qquad w > \xi(t), \qquad (4.9)$$

so the joint density function of wage and duration is

$$g(w,t) = \lambda f(w) \exp\left\{-\lambda \int_0^t \overline{F}(\xi(s))\,ds\right\}, \qquad w > \xi(t), t \geq 0. \quad (4.10)$$

In spite of the fact that this density function factors into a product of functions of w alone and t alone, W and T are dependent in this model due to the sample space condition $w > \xi(t)$. This dependence is obvious from (4.9) anyway.

In a strictly structural approach to inference one would take as the likelihood function for people observed from entry to unemployment until they find jobs the product of terms like (4.8) or (4.10) depending on whether one observes only t or both t and w. To compute the likelihood contribution of any person who leaves at t_i one must calculate $\xi(t_i)$ as a function of c_0, c_1, λ, ρ and $F(.)$. Calculation of the likelihood thus involves repeated solution of the differential equation (4.4) for different parameter values. This is computationally quite feasible. One way to proceed would be to calculate ξ_1 and then approximate (4.4) by a difference equation which may be solved recursively backwards in time from t_1.

In practice most researchers who have applied a non-stationary search model have taken the view that there is likely to be more than one reason why searchers adopt such a policy. They have thus avoided a strictly structural approach and worked with a density function in which either ξ or possibly $\theta(t)$ itself is written as a function of t and other, possibly time-varying, regressors.[3] This, as we remarked before, gives a more flexible model at the expense of losing a clear correspondence between the estimated coefficients and the parameters of a behavioural model.

5   A Non-Stationary Model with Learning

One of the most interesting transition models that has been published depends for its non-stationarity on a learning process, and this is Jovanovic's model for job tenure. In this model an employer and an employee constitute a match. The flow of output produced in a unit time period by such a match, $\delta y(t)$, has the representation

$$\delta y(t) = g(x(t)) + \mu + \epsilon(t). \tag{5.1}$$

Here $x(t)$ is a vector of exogenous characteristics of the worker as measured at time t such that g is known at time t and $g(x(t))$ is common to all matches; $\epsilon(t)$ is a sequence of independent $N(0, \sigma_\epsilon^2)$ error terms; and μ is a *match-specific* constant which is unknown (to both employer and employee) at the time when the match is formed, but about which they can learn by (and only by) observing the output produced by the match. The constant μ is a measure of the (output-producing) quality of the match. The value of μ for any particular match can be regarded as a realisation, occurring when the match is formed, of an $N(0, \sigma_\mu^2)$ variate which is the distribution of μ's over matches.

The way the model works is that a match is formed; the parties accumulate information about its quality, μ, by observing the output it

---

[3] An exception is Wolpin (1987), who estimated a discrete-time non-stationary structural model of optimal job search by young people. The source of the non-stationarity was an assumed finite time horizon. The likelihood maximisation involved repeated solution of a discrete-time analogue of (4.4).

produces; and if, and when, it becomes clear that the match is poor – μ is probably too small – the match is terminated. The time of termination is the completed job tenure so that we have a model for the duration of jobs. Moreover, Jovanovic shows that an optimal implicit contract for risk-neutral workers and firms is for the employee to be paid his expected marginal product per unit time period which is given by $g(x(t))$ plus the expected value of μ at time t. Thus we also obtain a model for the evolution of the wage with job tenure.

To develop the mathematics of the model let us work out the parties' posterior distribution of μ at time t, the key function which determines both the wage paid and the probability that the match will end. Note that both employer and employee have identical information and thus identical beliefs at all times. The prior distribution of μ is the known distribution of μ over matches, which is $N(0, \sigma_\mu^2)$. The data bearing on μ are the accumulated excess or shortfall of output y over its known component $g(x)$, from (5.1). Let us define this excess as

$$z(t) = y(t) - g(x(t)). \qquad (5.2)$$

Now if z is the total of $z(t)$ up to time t it follows from the model (5.1) that $z \sim N(\mu t, t\sigma_\epsilon^2)$ given μ. Moreover, z is a sufficient statistic for μ at time t. Hence the posterior distribution of μ given $\{z, t\}$, being proportional to the product of the prior distribution and the likelihood, is

$$g(\mu \mid z, t) \propto \phi\left(\frac{z - \mu t}{\sigma_\epsilon \sqrt{t}}\right) \times \phi\left(\frac{\mu}{\sigma_\mu}\right),$$

which is a Normal distribution of mean and variance

$$\mathrm{E}\left(\mu \mid z, t\right) = \frac{p_\epsilon z}{t p_\epsilon + p_\mu} = m(z, t),$$

$$\mathrm{var}(\mu \mid z, t) = \frac{1}{t p_\epsilon + p_\mu}. \qquad (5.3)$$

Here p_ϵ and p_μ are the precisions, the reciprocals of the variances σ_ϵ^2 and σ_μ^2, respectively.

The quantity $m(z, t)$ represents the expectation of the value of μ held by the parties to a match that has produced z by the time t. Now let us consider the variation of $m(t, z)$ at time t over the whole population of matches that are formed, a population over which μ varies Normally with mean zero and precision p_μ. The expected value of m in this distribution is

$$\mathrm{E}\, m = \mathrm{E}\left\{\mathrm{E}\left(m \mid \mu\right)\right\}$$

$$= E \left\{ \frac{p_\epsilon \mu}{t p_\epsilon + p_\mu} \right\}$$

$$= 0. \tag{5.4}$$

The variance of m in this distribution is

$$\mathrm{var}(m) = E\left\{\mathrm{var}(m \mid \mu)\right\} + \mathrm{var}\{E\left(m \mid \mu\right)\}$$

$$= \frac{p_\epsilon^2 t/p_\epsilon}{(t p_\epsilon + p_\mu)^2} + \frac{p_\epsilon^2 t^2/p_\mu}{(t p_\epsilon + p_\mu)^2}$$

$$= \frac{t p_\epsilon}{p_\mu (t p_\epsilon + p_\mu)}. \tag{5.5}$$

Furthermore, since m is proportional to z, which is Normally distributed both conditional on μ and unconditionally, m is Normally distributed with the mean and variance given by (5.4) and (5.5) over the population of matches that are ever formed.

Now consider a monotonic transformation of the time scale from t to

$$s = \frac{t p_\epsilon}{p_\mu (t p_\epsilon + p_\mu)}.$$

In the time scale of s, $m(s)$ is Normally distributed with

$$E\left(m(s)\right) = 0; \qquad \mathrm{var}(m(s)) = s$$

from (5.4) and (5.5). But, from chapter 5, section 7, this is the distribution of a standard Wiener process at time s, so let us approximate the path of $m(s)$ as a continuous-time Wiener process with zero drift and unit variance in the time scale of s. Note that as $t \to \infty$, $s \to \sigma_\mu^2$, so the whole positive axis is mapped into a finite interval by this transformation of the time scale. Jovanovic shows that an optimal rule for terminating the match is to do so if, and when, m falls below a barrier function $b(t)$ that is a monotonic increasing function of t. Let us, for tractability, write this barrier as an increasing *linear* function of s, namely,

$$b(s) = -a + \alpha s, \qquad a > 0, \alpha \geq 0. \tag{5.6}$$

(Note this will be a non-linear function of t.) The barrier is the same for all matches. Then we can determine analytically the distribution of the time to separation – it is the time for a standard Wiener process, in the time scale of s, to reach the barrier (5.6). If we write

$$n(s) = \alpha s - m(s)$$

then since

$$m > -a + \alpha s \Rightarrow \alpha s - m = n(s) < a$$

and

$$dn(s) = \alpha ds - dm(s),$$

the behaviour of $m(s)$ in the face of the barrier (5.6) is equivalent to the behaviour of $n(s)$, a Wiener process with drift α and unit variance, in the face of a constant barrier placed at a. Noting that $n(0) = m(0) = 0$ we may apply directly all the results of chapter 5, section 7. In particular, the first passage time has survivor function

$$P(T > t) = P(S > s(t))$$
$$= \Phi\left(\frac{a - \alpha s}{\sqrt{s}}\right) - e^{2a\alpha}\Phi\left(\frac{-a - \alpha s}{\sqrt{s}}\right). \tag{5.7}$$

Noting that $t \to \infty \Rightarrow s \to \sigma_\mu^2$, equation (5.7) immediately gives the result that the job tenure distribution is defective; a fraction of all matches equal to

$$\Phi\left(\frac{a - \alpha\sigma_\mu^2}{\sigma_\mu}\right) - e^{2a\alpha}\Phi\left(\frac{-a - \alpha\sigma_\mu^2}{\sigma_\mu}\right)$$

never end.

Furthermore, the density function of T is found by differentiating the negative of (5.7) with respect to s and multiplying by

$$\frac{ds}{dt} = \frac{p_\epsilon}{(tp_\epsilon + p_\mu)^2}, \tag{5.8}$$

which goes to 0 as $t \to \infty$. Thus the hazard function for T, the ratio of density and survivor functions, is the product of (5.8) and an Inverse Gaussian hazard. Since the latter rises from zero to a single maximum and then falls to a positive constant, the hazard in this model rises from zero to a single maximum and then falls to zero. Empirically this means that very few leave a job right away, there is a peak time for leaving, and some people never leave. This form of hazard is consistent with the shape of the hazard function taken by the empirical data on job tenures given in chapter 1.

Next let us consider the distribution of m among matches still in existence at time s. The distribution of $n(s)$ is given in (5.7.14) with $z = n$, $\mu = \alpha$, $\alpha = a$, and $\sigma = 1$. Changing the variable to $m = \alpha s - n(s)$ we find the density function of m among survivors at s to be

$$g(m \mid T > t) = \frac{e^{-m^2/2s} - e^{2a\alpha}e^{-(m+2a)^2/2s}}{\overline{G}(t)\sqrt{2\pi s}}, \qquad m \leq a, \tag{5.9}$$

for $s = s(t)$ and $\overline{G}(t)$ the survivor function at t given by (5.7). This distribution has mean given by

$$E\left(m(t)\right) = \frac{2ae^{2a\alpha}\Phi(\frac{-a-\alpha s}{\sqrt{s}})}{\overline{G}(t)}. \tag{5.10}$$

The mean varies over time according to

$$\frac{dE\left(m(t)\right)}{dt} = \theta(t)[E\left\{m(t)\right\} + a - \alpha s(t)]$$

$$= \theta(t)[E\left\{m(t)\right\} - b(t)] > 0, \tag{5.11}$$

where θ is the hazard function at t and $b(t)$ is the barrier at t. The mean wage paid to those still in employment at t is given by (5.10) plus $g(x(t))$ and so if x is independent of time (5.11) gives the rate of growth of the mean wages of those still in the same employment at time t. This growth is due solely to the departure of the poorly paid – who are by assumption those perceived to be ill matched – and this selection effect is greater the greater the hazard function $\theta(t)$, the first term in (5.11), and the closer the mean is to the barrier, the second term in (5.11). In figure 6.3 we have drawn some density functions of $m(t)$ – which differ from the distribution of the wages of survivors only by a location shift of $g(x)$ – for different dates; and in figure 6.4 we have drawn the mean value of m as a function of time together with the survivor function to indicate how many people are left to collect that mean wage.

It is of interest to relate the data distributions of this model to the formulation adopted in chapter 2. Departure from a job in this model is being driven by the path of the time-varying covariate which is the wage, and exit occurs when that wage falls below a barrier. But in fact the probability of exit conditional on the wage path to time t is a trivial quantity here, and not of behavioural interest. An interesting quantity is the probability of exit at t marginal on the wage, and the survivor function corresponding to this distribution is given by (5.7). Note that this probability no longer depends upon time-varying covariates. And the other interesting quantity is the distribution of the wage conditional upon survival. So in terms of the algebra of chapter 2 we are looking at the decomposition $P\left(T > t, \mathbf{X}(t)\right) = P\left(\mathbf{X}(t) \mid T > t\right)P\left(T > t\right)$ and not $P\left(T > t, \mathbf{X}(t)\right) = P\left(T > t \mid \mathbf{X}(t)\right)P\left(\mathbf{X}(t)\right)$.

This model has not been the basis of serious structural econometric modelling as yet apart from the preliminary exploration by Lancaster, Imbens, and Dolton (1987). It suffers from the weakness that it depends for tractability on some functional form assumptions – Normality and linearity of the barrier in the scale of s – that are not warranted by the economic theory.

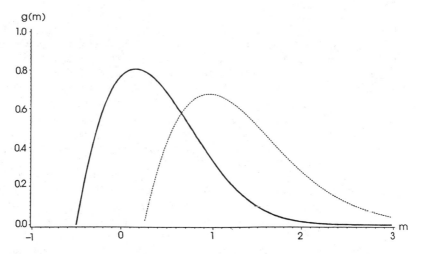

Figure 6.3. Two density functions of m among survivors at small (—) and large (--) tenures.

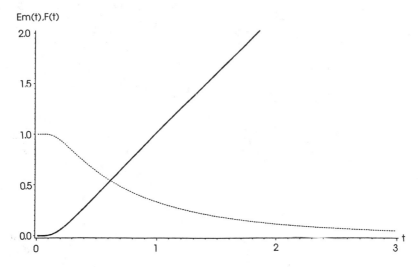

Figure 6.4. The growth of mean m with tenure: mean (—), survivor function (--).

NOTE

The optimal search model of section 2 dates back at least to Karlin (1962) and was exposited in Lippman and McCall (1976). It was the basis of applied work by Lancaster (1979), Kiefer and Neumann (1979), Nickell (1979), and Lancaster and Chesher (1984). The present exposition was suggested by Flinn and Heckman (1982) and is designed to be consistent with the exposition of the three-state model in section 3, which is due to Heckman and Coleman and was published in the Flinn and Heckman paper. The material on the distribution of the number of offers in section 2 and the later remarks of section 3 are new so far as I am aware. The non-stationary model of section 4 has been worked out by several writers independently including the present author and van der Berg (1986). Kiefer and Neumann (1979) attempted estimation of a non-stationary structural model and Narendranathan and Nickell (1985) applied a reduced form non-stationary model. Wolpin (1987) has estimated a non-stationary structural model of youth job search. Rust (1987) has estimated a non-stationary structural model of time to replacement (lifetime) of bus engines. Pakes (1986) formulated a non-stationary structural model of the lifetime of a patent, the 'exit' event being failure to renew it. The non-stationarity arose, in part, because of a legal maximum on the time a patent may be held. The model was estimated from aggregate data on the total numbers of renewals of patents of different ages. This application provides a case in which there is a natural discrete-time unit since patent renewal is an annual event. The model of section 5 is due to Jovanovic (1979, 1984).

PART II

Inference

CHAPTER 7

Identifiability Issues

1   Introduction

Before one can talk about estimation of parameters and functions it
is necessary to establish that they are identifiable. If they are not, the
question of estimation is superfluous. A number of questions of identifiability have arisen in the econometric literature on duration and transition
data, and in this chapter we shall give an account of these and of what
is known about their solution.

The main context in which these questions have arisen is that of
models with unmeasured heterogeneity leading to data distributions that
are mixtures and it is on such mixture models that we shall concentrate.
Let us return to the family of models discussed in chapter 4 in which
the hazard function takes the form

$$\theta = v\bar{\theta}(\mathbf{x}, t), \qquad (1.1)$$

where $\mathbf{x}$ is a known regressor vector and v a scalar representing unmeasured heterogeneity and regarded as a realisation of a random variable V
with distribution function $H(v)$. Equation (1.1) is the hazard conditional
on v and $\mathbf{x}$. The conditional survivor function is

$$\overline{G}(t) = \exp\{-vz(\mathbf{x}, t)\}, \qquad (1.2)$$

where

$$z(\mathbf{x}, t) = \int_0^t \bar{\theta}(\mathbf{x}, s)\, ds. \qquad (1.3)$$

(In previous chapters we have used the notation $\bar{z}$ instead of z.) But the
survivor function given the observable $\mathbf{x}$ alone is

$$\overline{G}_m(t) = \int_0^\infty \exp\{-vz(\mathbf{x}, t)\}\, dH(v). \qquad (1.4)$$

145

The survivor function $\overline{G}_m$ is observable by taking a large number of observations on T for a population homogeneous with respect to $\mathbf{x}$. Questions of identifiability with such models take the following form. Given knowledge of the function $\overline{G}_m$ together with some – usually a priori – information about the functions z and H, can we deduce z and H uniquely? Or are there several functions, z and H, even infinitely many, that are all consistent with what we know? These questions are important to econometricians if the conditional hazard $v\overline{\theta}(\mathbf{x}, t)$ has an interpretation in terms of the behaviour of agents in an environment in which both v and $\mathbf{x}$ are held constant. If this is so then in order to test a theory about such behaviour it will be necessary to determine the conditional hazard. If this is not possible then that is a severe, possibly insuperable, obstacle to the testing of that theory, and a theory that cannot be tested is of doubtful scientific value. Notice that it is knowledge of the function $\overline{\theta}$ and its integral z that is important; the distribution H is of no interest in itself to the econometrician, as it is not usually the object of economic theorising.

We should first point out that one-parameter is necessarily unidentifiable in the model (1.4) or, to put it another way, one normalisation is always required. If we change the variable of integration in (1.4) from v to w by $v = wc, c > 0$, we get

$$\int_0^\infty e^{-vz}\,dH(v) = \int_0^\infty e^{-wcz}\,dH(wc) = \int_0^\infty e^{-wcz}\,dG(w), \qquad (1.5)$$

where both H and G are proper distribution functions. Thus we could never distinguish between a model with integrated conditional hazard vz mixed with respect to v and one with integrated conditional hazard wcz mixed with respect to w where $w = v/c$. Thus a normalisation of the scale of $z(\mathbf{x}, t)$ or of v is required. We shall call this the *basic normalisation*. It is essentially the same normalisation as that by which the error term in a linear regression model is taken to have mean zero. In models in which the mean of the mixing distribution is assumed finite this normalisation can be done by assuming that all admissible mixing distributions have unit mean.

That the question of identifiability is non-trivial can be shown by the following example. Suppose that – presumably after taking an unlimited number of observations – the function $\overline{G}_m$ is *known* to be

$$\overline{G}_m(t) = (1 + \beta t)^{-\alpha}, \qquad t \geq 0, \qquad (1.6)$$

for some pair of known positive numbers α and β. Let us show that there exist at least two distinct pairs of functions z, H that are consistent with (1.6) and that in consequence the information embodied in (1.6) is inadequate to identify z and H. One choice of z and H is

Theory A $z(t) = \alpha \log(1 + \beta t)$, $H(v)$ concentrated at $v = 1$.

A second choice of z and H is

Theory B $z(t) = \alpha \beta t$, $H(v) = \alpha^\alpha \int_0^v u^{\alpha-1} e^{-\alpha u} \, du / \Gamma(\alpha)$, $v \geq 0$.

The basic normalisation here is that both mixing distributions have unit mean. Using either of these models in (1.4) yields (1.6), so both are consistent with the only knowledge we have and z and H are not identified. Theories A and B have quite different conditional hazards and quite different mixing distributions. To achieve identification more information is required.

Work on the identification problem has proceeded in two directions. One is to examine what *can* be said about z knowing only $\overline{G}_m$. The other is to find restrictions on z and H which suffice to identify them from a knowledge of $\overline{G}_m$. We shall look at each of these directions.

2   The Information in the Mixture Distribution

Some deductions about the conditional hazard can be made without any prior information other than that embodied in the expression (1.4). This representation of the problem does, of course, embody a restriction, namely that the mixing is with respect to a quantity that *multiplies* the conditional hazard.

Theorem 1   *If $\overline{G}_m(t)$ is increasing at some point t then $\overline{\theta}(t)$ is increasing at that point.*

Proof: We recall from equation (3.6) of chapter 3 that

$$\theta_m(t) = \overline{\theta}(t) \mathrm{E}\,(V \mid T > t) \qquad \text{and}$$

$$\frac{d\theta_m(t)}{dt} = \frac{d\overline{\theta}(t)}{dt} \mathrm{E}\,(V \mid T > t) - \overline{\theta}^2 \,\mathrm{var}(V \mid T > t).$$

If we observe the left-hand side to be positive then it must be that $d\overline{\theta}/dt > 0$ at that point since the mean and variance of V are non-negative.   ■

This is a useful consequence of the fact that mixing causes hazards to fall faster or rise slower than conditional hazards.

A second result of this type exploits the fact that the mixture survivor function is the Laplace transform,[1] with argument $z(\mathbf{x}, t)$, of the mixing distribution.

Theorem 2   *If $\overline{G}_m(z)$, regarded as a function of z, is not completely monotone then it cannot be a mixture of the form (1.4).*

Proof: $\overline{G}_m(z)$ is the Laplace transform of $H(v)$ so, from appendix 2, it is completely monotone, that is,

$$(-1)^n \frac{\partial^n \overline{G}_m(z)}{\partial z^n} \geq 0, \qquad n \geq 1, z \geq 0. \tag{2.1}$$

■

This theorem gives a necessary condition for a distribution to be a mixture of the form (1.4). If we see that $\overline{G}_m(z)$ is not completely monotone, then it cannot be a mixture of the form (1.4). As a particular case suppose we see that $\overline{G}_m(t)$ is not a completely monotone function of t, then $\overline{G}_m(t)$ cannot be a mixture of Exponential distributions with constant conditional hazards. This implies that not every distribution with decreasing hazard can have arisen as a mixture of distributions with constant hazards. Chamberlain (1980) has suggested a test procedure, based on this observation, for deciding whether an observed survivor function is completely monotone in t and so could have arisen as a mixture of Exponential distributions.

3   Identifiability with Proportional Hazards

Suppose that in addition to knowing $\overline{G}_m(t)$ we also know that $z(\mathbf{x}, t)$ factors into the product of a function of $\mathbf{x}$ alone and a function of t alone, so that we have a proportional hazards model – with time-invariant regressors. And suppose we also know that the mean of the mixing distribution is finite. Elbers and Ridder (1982) have shown that this extra bit of information suffices to identify z and H if we can know the survivor functions for at least two distinct regressor vectors $\mathbf{x}$. We shall now give their theorem and its proof.

---

[1] See appendix 2.

Theorem 3   *Let $\{\phi(\mathbf{x}), z(t), H(v)\}$ define a mixed proportional hazard model with mixture distributions*

$$\overline{G}_m{}^i(t) = \int_0^\infty \exp\{-v\phi_i z(t)\}\, dH(v) = \mathcal{L}_v(\phi_i z), \qquad t \geq 0, \quad i = 1, 2,$$

where $\phi_i = \phi(\mathbf{x}_i) > 0$, $i = 1$, 2, $\phi_1 \neq \phi_2$. The integrated baseline hazard function $z(t)$ is a continuous non-decreasing function with $z(0) = 0$, $z(\infty) = \infty$, and $H(v)$ is a mixing distribution function not depending on $\mathbf{x}$. All admissible mixing distributions have a finite, positive, mean. Then if the mixed proportional hazard model defined by $\{\psi(\mathbf{x}), r(t), F(v)\}$ is observationally equivalent to the model $\{\phi(\mathbf{x}), z(t), H(v)\}$,

$$\phi_1/\psi_1 = \phi_2/\psi_2 = d, \quad r(t) = cdz(t), \quad F(v) = H(cv), \qquad (3.1)$$

for some c, $d > 0$ and t, $v \geq 0$.

Proof: The proof proceeds by supposing there exists another mixed proportional hazards model defined by the triplet $\{\psi(x), r(t), F(w)\}$, implying the same set of mixture distributions as that implied by the model $\{\phi(\mathbf{x}), z(t), H(v)\}$, and deducing that, if so, (3.1) follows. Thus $z(t)$ and $H(v)$ are identified up to a scale normalisation, and the regression component up to a multiplicative constant.

On the hypothesis that both triplets imply the same mixture distributions,

$$\mathcal{L}_v(\phi_1 z(t)) = \mathcal{L}_w(\psi_1 r(t)), \qquad t \geq 0, \qquad (3.2a)$$
$$\mathcal{L}_v(\phi_2 z(t)) = \mathcal{L}_w(\psi_2 r(t)), \qquad t \geq 0. \qquad (3.2b)$$

Since Laplace transforms have inverse functions, denoted $\mathcal{L}^{-1}$ (see appendix 2), we have, using first (3.2b) and then (3.2a),

$$\psi_2 r(t) = \mathcal{L}_w^{-1}(\mathcal{L}_v(\phi_2 z(t))) = (\psi_2/\psi_1)\mathcal{L}_w^{-1}(\mathcal{L}_v(\phi_1 z(t))), \quad t \geq 0. \quad (3.3)$$

We define

$$f(s) = \mathcal{L}_w^{-1}(\mathcal{L}_v(s)). \qquad (3.4)$$

Since $\mathcal{L}(0) = 1$, $\mathcal{L}^{-1}(1) = 0$, $\mathcal{L}(\infty) = 0$, and $\mathcal{L}^{-1}(0) = \infty$ (appendix 2)

$$f(0) = 0, \quad \lim_{s \to \infty} f(s) = \infty, \qquad (3.5)$$

and (3.3) implies

$$f(\phi s) = \psi f(s), \qquad s \geq 0, \qquad (3.6)$$

where $\phi = \phi_1/\phi_2, \psi = \psi_1/\psi_2$. From (3.4), $f'(s) = \mathcal{L}'_v(s)/\mathcal{L}'_w(f(s))$ so that

$$f'(0+) = \lim_{s\downarrow 0} f'(s) = \frac{\mathcal{L}'_v(0)}{\mathcal{L}'_w(0)} = \frac{\mathrm{E}(V)}{\mathrm{E}(W)} = c,$$

where c is finite and positive by assumption.

Take $s = \phi_2 s'$. Then in (3.6)

$$f(\phi^2 s') = \psi^2 f(s'), \qquad \text{for all } s' \geq 0.$$

Repeating this procedure implies

$$f(\phi^n s) = \psi^n f(s), \qquad \text{for all } s \geq 0 \text{ and all } n.$$

Differentiating with respect to s and rearranging terms gives

$$f'(s) = \left(\frac{\phi}{\psi}\right)^n f'(\phi^n s), \qquad \text{for all } n. \tag{3.7}$$

Now assume that $\phi = \phi_1/\phi_2 < 1$ – if not, reverse the labels. We may therefore take the limit as $n \to \infty$ in (3.7),

$$f'(s) = f'(0+) \lim_{n\to\infty} \left(\frac{\phi}{\psi}\right)^n = c \lim_{n\to\infty} \left(\frac{\phi}{\psi}\right)^n, \qquad \text{for all } s \geq 0.$$

But the right-hand side does not depend on s and $f'(0+) = c$, which implies that

$$\phi = \psi, \qquad \text{and } f'(s) = c \qquad \text{for all } s \geq 0. \tag{3.8}$$

Together with $f(0) = 0$ this implies that

$$\mathcal{L}_w^{-1}(\mathcal{L}_v(s)) = f(s) = cs, \qquad \text{for all } s \geq 0. \tag{3.9}$$

This, and the uniqueness of Laplace transforms, imply that, if H is the distribution function of V and F that of W, $F(v) = H(cv)$. Finally, using (3.9) in (3.2) gives $r(t) = cdz(t)$ for all $t \geq 0$, and $d = \phi_1/\psi_1 = \phi_2/\psi_2$. ∎

The theorem says that if the model is mixed proportional hazard and we know the mixture distribution for at least two distinct values of the regression component $\phi(\mathbf{x})$, we can determine ϕ uniquely up to a multiplicative constant and we can determine the integrated base-line hazard and the mixing distribution up to a scale factor. Thus the whole conditional hazard can be determined up to two normalisations. In particular, and most importantly, since all observationally equivalent integrated baseline hazards are proportional to each other, the direction of the time variation in the baseline hazard is identifiable. The scale factor c may be set by supposing that all admissible mixing distributions have the same mean. This implies that $c = 1$.

To illustrate the force of theorem 3 consider again the example which introduced this chapter. Theories A and B are indistinguishable if all we can observe is $\overline{G}_m$ of (1.5). But the Elbers and Ridder theorem supposes that the integrated conditional hazard is multiplied by a factor ϕ and that we know $\overline{G}_m$ for at least two distinct values of ϕ. Then multiply $\alpha \log(1 + \beta t)$ in theory A, and then $\alpha \beta t$ in theory B, by such a ϕ. If $\phi = 1$ we just get $\overline{G}_m(t) = (1 + \beta t)^{-\alpha}$ from both theories. Then theory A implies

$$\overline{G}_m(t) = (1 + \beta t)^{-\phi\alpha}, \qquad (3.10)$$

whereas theory B leads to

$$\overline{G}_m(t) = \frac{\alpha^\alpha \int_0^\infty v^{\alpha-1} e^{-\alpha v} e^{-v\phi\beta\alpha t} \, dv}{\Gamma(\alpha)}$$

$$= (1 + \beta\phi t)^{-\alpha}. \qquad (3.11)$$

The expressions (3.10) and (3.11) are distinct functions (of $\mathbf{x}$ and t) and the two theories have distinguishable implications.

This is a remarkable theorem but its practical force is unclear. It does not lead to an obvious way of estimating z and H from a sample where we usually do not have enough information to estimate $\overline{G}_m$ for a set of distinct values of $\mathbf{x}$. So far there has been no method of estimation developed which enables us to exploit the theorem to calculate z and H. Note the contrast between this theorem which refers to identification of *functions*, that is, infinite parameter models, and classical identification results in econometrics which refer to identification of finite parameter vectors. These standard results on identification in simultaneous equations systems, which turn on the existence of a unique solution to a system of equations, lead directly to estimation methods.

Theorem 3 assumes that the distribution H has a finite mean. Heckman and Singer (1984) have given another identifiability theorem in proportional hazard models which relaxes this assumption but which instead requires (a) a condition, involving a parameter known a priori, on the rate of decrease of the right tail of the distribution H, (b) there exists a point $t > 0$ such that $z(t)$ has a known value at that point, and (c) we observe $\overline{G}_m$ as ϕ varies continuously over an interval.

4   A Functional Form for the Conditional Hazard

If we are prepared to adopt a more specific hypothesis about the conditional hazard then we can not only prove identifiability but also devise methods of estimation. As an extreme example suppose that we *knew* the function $z(\mathbf{x}, t)$ – as well as $\overline{G}_m$ – then we would know the Laplace transform of $H(v)$ and identifiability follows immediately. But this is to assume away the interesting problem. Suppose therefore that we know $z(\mathbf{x}, t)$ up to some finite set of unknown parameters. Then we can often prove identifiability of those parameters and of H. We shall always assume the mixture is of the form (1.4). Let us look at some examples.

Example 1 Identification of Weibull Conditional Hazards

Theorem 4   *Suppose that H has a finite mean and that the conditional hazard function is $v\alpha t^{\alpha-1}$. Then α and H are identifiable.*

Proof:

$$\overline{G}_m(t) = \int_0^\infty \exp\{-vt^\alpha\}\, dH(v) = \mathcal{L}_v(t^\alpha),$$

$$g_m(t) = \alpha t^{\alpha-1} \int_0^\infty v \exp\{-vt^\alpha\}\, dH(v) = -\alpha t^{\alpha-1} \mathcal{L}_v'(t^\alpha).$$

Consider

$$k(t) = \frac{\log(tg_m(t)/\overline{G}_m(t))}{\log t}$$

$$= \alpha + \frac{\log \alpha}{\log t} + \frac{\log(-\mathcal{L}_v'(t^\alpha)/\mathcal{L}_v(t^\alpha))}{\log t}. \tag{4.1}$$

Letting $t \to 0$ we find

$$\lim_{t\to 0} k(t) = \alpha, \tag{4.2}$$

since the right-hand member of (4.1) approaches $\mathrm{E}(V)/\log t \to 0$ because the mean of V is finite. Equation (4.2) determines α from $\overline{G}_m$, and identification of H follows from the uniqueness of the Laplace transform.[2]   ∎

If there are regressors in the model multiplying the conditional hazard by the function $\phi(\mathbf{x}'\beta)$ then these unknown parameters are identifiable

---

[2] Honoré (1987) has based an estimation method on (4.2).

up to a scale factor since

$$\lim_{t \to 0} \frac{g_m(t; \phi(\mathbf{x}_1))}{g_m(t; \phi(\mathbf{x}_2))} = \frac{\phi(\mathbf{x}_1)}{\phi(\mathbf{x}_2)}.$$

Observation of these ratios for a suitably large set of points $\mathbf{x}_j$ will determine β. The scale factor may be recovered by the normalisation $E(V) = 1$. It is worth noting that the mixed Weibull is identifiable even without regressors whereas, in the absence of a parametric assumption about the conditional hazard, regressors are essential to identification as we saw in the last section.

Proofs of identifiability for several other choices of functional form for the conditional hazard have been published although general theorems are lacking. To exemplify the method consider the Log-Logistic hazard model of chapter 3, section 3.4.

Example 2 Identification of Log-Logistic Conditional Hazards

Theorem 5   *In the mixture model in which*

$$\overline{\theta}(t) = \frac{\psi \alpha t^{\alpha-1}}{1 + \psi t^{\alpha}},$$

$\alpha, \psi,$ *and* H *are identifiable if all mixture distributions* H *have a common finite mean.*

Proof: We consider two triplets $\{\psi_0, \alpha_0, H_0\}, \{\psi_1, \alpha_1, H_1\}$ assumed to generate the same data distribution and show that, if so, $\psi_0 = \psi_1$, $\alpha_0 = \alpha_1$, $H_0 = H_1$. Then by hypothesis the density functions generated by the two triplets are the same. Thus, taking their ratio at any point t,

$$1 = \frac{\overline{\theta}_1(t) \int_0^\infty v \exp\{-v z_1(t)\} \, dH_1(v)}{\overline{\theta}_0(t) \int_0^\infty v \exp\{-v z_0(t)\} \, dH_0(v)}.$$

Taking the limit of this ratio as $t \to 0$ and using the Log-Logistic form for $\overline{\theta}$ and the assumption that the mean of V is finite and the same under the two mixing distributions gives

$$1 = \lim_{t \to 0} \overline{\theta}_1(t) / \overline{\theta}_0(t)$$

$$= \lim_{t \to 0} \frac{\psi_1 \alpha_1 t^{\alpha_1-1} (1 + \psi_0 t^{\alpha_0})}{\psi_0 \alpha_0 t^{\alpha_0-1} (1 + \psi_1 t^{\alpha_1})}. \tag{4.3}$$

Equation (4.3) implies that we must have $\alpha_0 = \alpha_1$ since otherwise the right-hand side tends to zero or infinity. The condition $\alpha_0 = \alpha_1$ together with (4.3) then imply that $\psi_0 = \psi_1$. Then, finally, since α and ψ are identifiable the Laplace transform of $H(v)$ is identifiable and the uniqueness of the Laplace transform implies identifiability of H.   ∎

The above proof is due to Heckman and Singer (1984). They have also proved identifiability of the Box–Cox hazard family of chapter 3, section 3.5, by a basically similar approach.

5   Identification with Multiple Destinations

In this section we shall consider models with K possible destinations. What we can observe, in principle, are the transition intensities $\{\theta_k(t)\}$ to these destinations, or, equivalently, the functions

$$Q_k(t) = \mathrm{P}\,(\text{survival to } t \text{ and exit to } k)$$

$$= \int_t^\infty \overline{F}(s)\theta_k(s), \qquad\qquad k = 1, 2, \ldots, K, \quad (5.1)$$

$$\text{where} \qquad \overline{F}(t) = \exp\left\{ -\int_0^t \sum_{k=1}^K \theta_k(u)\,du \right\},$$

from section 5 of chapter 5. Note that

$$-Q_k'(t) = \theta_k(t)\overline{F}(t) \propto \mathrm{P}\,[\text{exit to } k \text{ in } (t, t + dt)]. \qquad (5.2)$$

The main identification questions with multiple destinations centre on competing risks models – chapter 5, section 5 – in which the exit time and destination is determined by the minimum of K jointly distributed latent exit times $T_1, T_2, \ldots T_K$. Let the joint survivor function of these latent times be

$$\mathrm{P}\,(T_1 > t_1, T_2 > t_2, \ldots, T_K > t_K) = S(t_1, t_2, \ldots, t_K) = S(\mathbf{t}). \quad (5.3)$$

If the $\{T_k\}$ are independently distributed we say we have an independent competing risks model. The following questions have been studied. Can we identify S from knowledge of the $\{Q_k\}$ together, possibly, with some additional information? We shall outline what is known of the answers to these questions.

Theorem 6   *If all we know are the functions $\{Q_k(t)\}$ then no dependent competing risks model is identifiable.*

Proof: Knowledge of the $\{Q_k(t)\}$ is equivalent to knowledge of the transition intensities $\{\theta_k(t)\}$. Each transition intensity can be regarded as the hazard function of one of a set of K independent latent exit times whose

distributions they determine uniquely. Hence any dependent competing risks model is always observationally equivalent to one independent
competing risks model and lack of identifiability follows.   ■

If we are willing to add some a priori information then we can sometimes prove identifiability. Identifiability has been proved when $S(\mathbf{t})$ is
a member of some parametric family, for example, the bivariate Normal or various types of multivariate Exponential distribution. We shall
look at the case in which $S(\mathbf{t})$ is obtained by mixing an independent
competing risks model with respect to a scalar heterogeneity term of
the following form:

$$S(t_1, t_2, \ldots t_K) = \int_0^\infty \exp\left\{-v \sum_{k=1}^K \phi_k z_k(t)\right\} dH(v). \qquad (5.4)$$

The conditional transition intensities are of the form

$$\theta_k(t) = v\phi_k \bar{\theta}_k(t), \quad \text{with } z_k(t) = \int_0^t \bar{\theta}_k(s)\, ds.$$

It may be shown that if the functions $\{\bar{\theta}_k(t)\}$ are known then the $\{\phi_k\}$
and H are identifiable – Arnold and Brockett (1983). A more interesting
situation is where the $\{\bar{\theta}_k(t)\}$ are not known, and the following theorem
may be proved – Arnold and Brockett (1983).

Theorem 7   *With the model (5.4) and $\bar{\theta}_k(t) = \alpha_k t^{\alpha_k - 1}$, if H has finite
mean then $\{\alpha_k\}, \{\phi_k\}$, and H are identifiable.*

Proof: The proof is a generalisation of that of theorem, and we shall
leave it to the reader.   ■

6   The Finite Mean Assumption

It is important to observe that *all* the identification theorems we have
described use the hypothesis that the mean of the mixing distribution is
finite. This raises the question of whether this finiteness is essential to
identifiability. To provide an answer first consider the following example.

Example 3 Non-Identification of Weibull Conditional Hazards
Suppose that the conditional hazard is known to be Weibull and of
the form

$$\theta = v\alpha t^{\alpha-1} e^{\mathbf{x}'\beta}.$$

The investigator therefore knows the conditional hazard up to a finite parameter set. As regards the mixing distribution the investigator knows that it is some member of the Positive Stable family, indexed by an (unknown) parameter λ, $0 < \lambda \leq 1$, that we described earlier in chapter 4, section 6.2. Recall that $\lambda = 1$ gives a distribution with all its mass concentrated at the point $v = 1$; that for $\lambda < 1$ the distribution has no positive moments; and that the Laplace transform of the family is $\mathcal{L}(s) = e^{-s^{\lambda}}$. In particular, since the investigator does not know the value of λ, we do *not* assume that the investigator is sure that the mixing distribution has a finite mean.

This prior information is, in a sense, much stronger than that assumed in the identification theorems we have described in previous sections. In this example both the conditional hazard and the mixing distribution are known up to a finite set of parameters. Nevertheless we can now show that this prior information does not permit the identification of α, β, or λ.

Under this hypothesis we see from (1.4) that the observable (mixture) distribution is

$$\overline{G}_m(t; \mathbf{x}) = \exp\{-t^{\alpha\lambda} e^{\mathbf{x}'\beta\lambda}\}.$$

It follows from this that all the investigator could *ever* know is the number $\alpha\lambda$ and the vector $\beta\lambda$. For example, the models

Theory A $\alpha = 0.6$; $\beta = \{1\,1\,1\}$; $\lambda = 1$:

Theory B $\alpha = 1.2$; $\beta = \{2\,2\,2\}$; $\lambda = 0.5$:

will give identical observable data distributions. Both theories are consistent with both the data and with the prior information.[3] Theory A has a baseline hazard which is decreasing, while in theory B it is increasing. The two integrated baseline hazards, $z(t) = t^{0.6}$ and $r(t) = t^{1.2}$, are not proportional as they would be if the conditions of theorem 3 were met. Similarly, the regression components, $\phi(\mathbf{x}) = \exp\{1 + x_1 + x_2\}$ and $\psi(\mathbf{x}) = \exp\{2 + 2x_1 + 2x_2\}$ are not proportional either, nor do the mixing distributions differ only in scale. The reason why the conclusions of theorem 3 do not apply in this example is that one of the mixing distributions has a non-finite mean. Of course if the investigator *knew* the mixing distribution had a finite mean then he would know that $\lambda = 1$ and all parameters are identified. Indeed knowledge of any one-parameter suffices to identify the remaining ones.   ■

[3] The basic normalisation here sets the scale parameter of the Positive Stable family equal to one.

This example shows that by allowing infinite mean mixing distributions Weibull models lose identifiability in the sense that we can no longer identify the sign of the time variation in the conditional hazard. Since there seems to be no good reason to rule out infinite mean mixing distributions on a priori grounds this is a most important conclusion.[4]

Example 3 raises the question of precisely what are the sets of observationally equivalent mixed proportional hazard models when mixing distributions can have infinite means. Recent work by Ridder (1988) suggests that all observationally equivalent mixed proportional hazard models have integrated baseline hazards related by a transformation of the form $z(t) = ar(t)^b$ for positive constants a, b, as they are in example 3. But the precise theorem on this question remains unclear at the time of writing. If this were so it would be an encouraging result since it would indicate that non-identifiability would be confined to Weibull models. The reason for this is that it is only Weibull models which are such that both $r(t)$ and $ar(t)^b$ are integrated baseline hazards within the same family.

7   Concluding Remarks on Identification

The main thrust of the results of preceding sections has been that identification can be achieved when certain functional form restrictions can be assumed. Unfortunately these functional form restrictions generally have little or no economic-theoretical justification. There is no known economic principle that implies that hazard functions should be proportional, and the few non-stationary structural transition models that have been derived do not generally lead to proportional hazard models. Still less does economic theory imply Weibull models. Nor does economic theory imply that mixing distributions have finite means. It would seem that what is needed are theorems about identifiability in heterogeneous structural models where that identifiability is based on restrictions with economic justification. Research to this end would be useful.

Questions of identifiability also arise when we can be assumed to know the joint distribution of several durations for the same person, that is, with the same value of v. They also arise when we can know the joint distribution of several different variates for the same person, e.g. search duration and new wages. Remarkably little has been published on these questions. Multiple spell data naturally lead to identifiability

[4] It is also rather ironic in view of the predominant importance of Weibull models in applied econometric work.

under weaker conditions than for single spell data. In chapter 8 we offer some comments on identifiability with wage and duration data.

NOTE

The main paper on identifiability is Elbers and Ridder (1982), which was prompted by Lancaster and Nickell (1980). Heckman and Singer have contributed a number of important theorems in their papers of (1984) and (1985). The most general study of identifiability available is the paper of Ridder (1988). This paper deals with the (non-parametric) identification of the class of generalised accelerated failure-time (GAFT) models which we mentioned in section 2.3 of chapter 3. The mixed proportional hazards models with which the present chapter has dealt constitute a sub-class of these GAFT models. Arnold and Brockett (1983) have discussed identifiability in models with multiple destinations which are called multiple decrement models in the demographic and actuarial literature. Their paper contains references to the statistical literature on identifiability in multiple destination models, notably Tsiatis (1975). Basu (1981) provides a useful survey of the identifiability problem in competing risks models. Recently Heckman and Honoré (1989) have given a theorem on the identifiability of mixed competing risks models. This is an analogue of theorem 3 for a model with multiple destinations. Most identifiability theorems depend on properties of the Laplace transform, for which a good reference is Feller (1966), volume 2.

CHAPTER 8

Fully Parametric Inference

1 Introduction and Overview

1.1 Introduction

Fully parametric inference is where the investigator specifies the joint distribution of the data completely apart from a fixed, finite number of unknown parameters. This distribution provides the likelihood function whose study is the basis of inference both about the unknown parameters and about the adequacy of that distribution as a model for the process generating the data. The joint distribution depends upon two factors. The first is the specification of the probability law governing the passage of individuals from state to state. For a Markov or semi-Markov process this amounts to specifying the transition intensities – how they depend upon the date, upon the elapsed duration, upon both constant and time-varying regressors, possibly including unmeasured person-specific heterogeneity. The second is the sampling scheme, in particular whether we have sampled, for example, the population of entrants to a state, the population of people regardless of their state, or the population of members of a particular state. Thus we can identify four stages in fully parametric inference.

1. Specify the transition intensities, conditional on the covariates and unmeasured heterogeneity terms, if any, up to a fixed number of unknown parameters, for example,

$$\theta_{lm} = \exp\{\mathbf{x}'\beta_{lm}\}\alpha_{lm}s^{\alpha_{lm}-1}; \qquad l,m = 1,2,\dots,M; \quad l \neq m, \quad (1.1)$$

which gives Weibull transition intensities independent of the calendar date but depending upon an observed regressor vector $\mathbf{x}$, and not involving unmeasured heterogeneity.

2. Specify the distribution of the unmeasured heterogeneity factors, conditional on the covariates, up to a finite parameter vector. This distribution will generally depend upon the sampling scheme.

159

3. By consideration of the sampling scheme deduce the joint distribution of the data – the likelihood – implied by the specification of the transition intensities, by the heterogeneity distribution, and by that sampling scheme.[1]

4. Compute maximum likelihood estimates and standard errors and examine residuals and other aspects of the fit to test the model specification.

The first six chapters of this book have been primarily concerned with the first stage and aspects of the second. This chapter and the next three will be concerned with the remaining stages of inference.

So far as the sampling scheme is concerned the basic setup we have in mind is as follows. There exists a population of people[2] – for example, the members of the labour force, the set of women of child bearing age, or the set of people over 65 years old on June 1 1987. At any calendar date these people must occupy exactly one of M states – for example, employed or unemployed, having borne 1, 2, 3, ..., M children; or working or retired. The people are assumed to move from state to state according to the transition intensities specified in stage 1. The data available to the investigator are provided by a sample from such a population.

There is an infinity of possible ways of sampling a population, but there are three in particular which must be distinguished.

1. We may randomly sample the *whole population* regardless of the state they currently occupy. In our first example this would be randomly sampling the whole labour force.

2. We may randomly sample the population of people entering or leaving a given state or set of states over an interval of time. In our first example this might be sampling the set of people who become unemployed during a given month. We shall refer to this as *flow sampling*.

3. We may randomly sample the set of people who occupy a particular state at a particular time. In our first example we might sample the people registered as unemployed on June first 1987. We shall refer to this as *stock sampling*.

---

[1] The phrase 'the likelihood' does not imply that only one correct likelihood can be constructed for a given set of data and sampling scheme. One can base inferences on marginal, conditional, or partial likelihoods, as we shall explain in the next chapter. These other likelihoods are, however, derivable from the full joint distribution of the data, and it is this latter that we shall mean when we refer in this chapter to the likelihood function.

[2] The unit of observation is not necessarily a person but may be a household or firm, for example.

There are many other ways even of random sampling and we shall allude to some of them in this chapter, but the distinctions between stock, flow, and whole population sampling seem to be the most fundamental for the econometrician.

Given a mode of sampling individuals a variety of different types of data bearing on the parameters of our transition intensity model may be obtained. We may, for example, have complete observation of the movement of each person forward through time or we might collect historical or retrospective information about the states through which he has passed and the times of the transitions he made. In either case observation may cease after a fixed number of transitions have been made or after a fixed time interval. Or the observations may be incomplete and we may know only the states occupied by our sampled person at a number of isolated time points. Again there are many possible variants on these forms of data.

1.2   Overview of the Chapter

In this chapter we shall largely be concerned with the deduction of the likelihood function appropriate to the type of data collected, to the specification of the transition intensities, and to the sampling scheme. The critical point here is that *the sampling scheme modifies the data distribution* and hence the likelihood function. When we sample an individual and obtain from him some numerical data we also obtain a second, implicit, piece of information about him, namely, that he was a member of the population from which we have sampled. This extra information sounds trivial but is not, and the distribution postulated for the data must take it into account. We have already seen an example of this in chapter 5, where we showed that the distribution of completed unemployment spells collected by sampling the people unemployed at a moment of time was generally quite different from that obtained from a random sample of entrants to unemployment. The former is, under some simplifying assumptions, the first moment distribution corresponding to the latter.

An analogous point arises in the econometric literature on the analysis of discrete choices. There it is possible to sample a whole population, regardless of the choices they make; but it is also possible to sample from the sub-populations of people who make particular choices, for example, the population of those who choose to travel by train. The distributions of data are quite different in the two cases.

We have organised this chapter to try to display clearly the way in which both the type of data collected and the sampling scheme combine to produce the correct likelihood. In sections 2, 3, and 4 we discuss one type of data, single-cycles of information. In section 2 we give an account of inference when such data are obtained by sampling the flow of people entering or leaving a state. In section 3 we turn to inference when such data have been collected, as it often is in practice, in other ways. In section 4 we elaborate on the important point that the sampling scheme modifies not only the distribution of observable data but also the distribution of unobserved random terms in the model. That is, the appropriate distribution for unobserved person-specific heterogeneity terms depends, in part, upon the way in which the people in the sample were obtained.

In sections 5, 6, and 7 we repeat this sequence for the case in which the data collected consist of multiple-cycles of information for each person. Our treatment is briefer here, partly because many of the points made about single-cycle likelihoods also apply to multiple-cycles and it would be tedious to repeat them, and partly because the econometric study of multiple-cycle data is still in its infancy, and there is little published literature to exposit.

Our emphasis throughout the book is on likelihood based methods of inference, but in section 8 we take a brief look at the properties of some Least Squares estimators. We conclude the chapter in section 9 by studying some methods of inference in models derived as close representations of supposed optimising behaviour by individual agents.

Our discussion of the distribution of parameter estimators will rely heavily on asymptotic or large sample theory, and the relevant asymptotes will be those arising as the numbers of sampled individuals become large. Observations from different individuals will always be assumed to be stochastically independent. We use the notation $\mathcal{L}$ for the likelihood function and L for its logarithm.

2   Single-Cycle/Flow Data

A single-cycle[3] is a duration of stay in a state together with the label of the state to which exit occurred. Probably the simplest sampling and data situation is that in which we take a sample of people from the flow of entrants to, or leavers from, a state and observe one complete cycle. The data consist of a duration t and a vector $\mathbf{d}$ of $M - 1$ binary destination indicators of which exactly one is unity and the rest are zero. Since

---

[3] We use the word cycle rather than 'spell' because we also include the destination information in the definition of a cycle.

the sampling scheme is uninformative about t and $\mathbf{d}$, the log likelihood contribution for a single person is given, from (5.13) of chapter 5, by

$$L_i = \sum_{m=1}^{M} \left[d_{im} \log \theta_{im}(t_i) - \int_0^{t_i} \theta_{im}(u)\, du \right] \qquad (2.1)$$

where $\theta_{im}(t)$ is the transition intensity of person i out of the origin state, whose identity is suppressed in the notation, to state m, and the summation is over all possible destination states, that is, it excludes the label of the origin state. We shall avoid repeated use of the subscript $m \neq l$ and in summation over destinations it will be taken for granted that the origin state is excluded. d_{im} is the m'th element of the vector $\mathbf{d}_i$. We shall, in general, follow a policy of avoiding writing out explicitly all the conditioning events, when no ambiguity will result, in the interests of legibility. We assume that the $\{\theta_{im}\}$ are specified as functions of measured regressor variables, possibly time-varying, and of the state biography of the individual up to the date of entry, but do not involve unmeasured person-specific heterogeneity, which will be considered in section 4.

If random right censoring occurs this will, by the argument of chapter 5, section 5, be treated as entry to a dummy destination state, the corresponding transition intensity being the hazard function of the censoring variate.

The full log likelihood is the sum of terms like (2.1) over $i = 1, 2,$ ..., N and is thus[4]

$$L = \sum_{i=1}^{N} \sum_{m=1}^{M} \left[d_{im} \log \theta_{im}(t_i) - \int_0^{t_i} \theta_{im}(u)\, du \right]. \qquad (2.2)$$

We may interchange the order of summation and write

$$L = \sum_{m=1}^{M} L_m, \qquad (2.3)$$

---

[4] This likelihood is correct under a more general hypothesis than random right censoring. In particular it can be justified under the assumption of independent censoring – see Kalbfleisch and Prentice (1980). It is also correct even when there are endogenous time-varying covariates in the model, in which case it is interpretable as a partial likelihood. Section 2 of chapter 9 explains partial likelihoods.

where

$$L_m = \sum_{i=1}^{N} \left[d_{im} \log \theta_{im}(t_i) - \int_0^{t_i} \theta_{im}(u)\, du \right]. \tag{2.4}$$

We now suppose that some or all of the transition intensities are specified as parametric functions of the elapsed duration and of regressor variables which may include the origin calendar date and the lengths or frequencies of stays in previous states and which may be time-varying. The total set of parameters entering into all such transition intensities is denoted γ. Thus $L = L(\gamma)$. We now note that by (2.3) and (2.4) L is the sum of contributions from each of the $M - 1$ destinations. It follows that it is unnecessary for the investigator to specify parametrically all the transition intensities. Suppose, for example, that M^* of them are specified parametrically and the remainder are not, perhaps because the investigator has no theory about them. Then as long as the unspecified transition intensities are functionally independent of γ their contribution to L given by (2.3) becomes an additive constant in the log likelihood so far as variation in γ is concerned. Since additive constants may be deleted from log likelihoods without changing inferences in any way we may write our log likelihood as

$$L = \sum_{m \in M^*} L_m. \tag{2.5}$$

Terms in the log likelihood involving unspecified transition intensities have been dropped from (2.3) in writing (2.5).

Furthermore, if distinct destinations depend upon disjoint subsets of parameters which are functionally independent, so that θ_m depends only upon γ_m, $m = 1, 2, \ldots, M^*$, then, so far as inference about γ_m is concerned, the log likelihood may be taken simply as L_m given by (2.4). L_m may then be recognised as the log likelihood for a model with a single real destination and right censoring in which an observation is treated as uncensored if destination m is entered and censored otherwise. This is a great simplification of inference because the problem effectively is decomposed into a set of M^* sub-problems each involving a parameter space of dimensionality much smaller than that of γ. Moreover, since the log likelihood is additive, estimators of γ_m will be distributed independently of those of γ_l, $l \neq m$. However, if the specification of the transition intensities is derived from a structural model it is likely that there will be parameters common to distinct intensities. It is possible to ignore these cross-intensity constraints if the parameters are otherwise identifiable but at a cost in efficiency of estimation.

From now on in this section we take the log likelihood as given by (2.2) where the m summation is now only over the transition intensities specified parametrically, that is, involving γ, the remaining terms having been discarded as irrelevant constants so far as inference about γ is concerned. We shall simplify the notation by writing

$$z_{im} = \int_0^{t_i} \theta_{im}(u)\, du. \tag{2.6}$$

The likelihood equations are

$$\frac{\partial L}{\partial \gamma_j} = \sum_{i=1}^{N} \sum_{m \in M^*} \left[d_{im} \frac{\theta_{im}^j(t_i)}{\theta_{im}} - z_{im}^j \right] = 0, \qquad j = 1, 2, \ldots, K, \tag{2.7}$$

where

$$\theta^j = \frac{\partial \theta}{\partial \gamma_j}, \quad z^j = \frac{\partial z}{\partial \gamma_j},$$

and K is the dimensionality of γ. It may be noted that if, as would normally be the case, each log transition intensity involves a destination-specific intercept, then since the expected values of the scores – log likelihood derivatives – are always zero (in regular problems) we have, from the elements of (2.7) corresponding to these intercepts,

$$\mathrm{E}\,(d_{im} - z_{im}) = 0, \qquad m \in M^*. \tag{2.8}$$

These terms $d_{im} - z_{im}$ are in this respect like disturbance or error terms in a linear model and, as we show in chapter 11, they play a similar role in testing the model specification.

The Hessian or second derivative matrix is

$$\frac{\partial^2 L}{\partial \gamma_j \partial \gamma_k} = \sum_{i=1}^{N} \sum_{m \in M^*} \left[d_{im} \left\{ \frac{\theta_{im}^{jk}}{\theta_{im}} - \frac{\theta_{im}^j \theta_{im}^k}{(\theta_{im})^2} \right\} - z_{im}^{jk} \right], \quad j, k = 1, 2 \ldots, K. \tag{2.9}$$

This matrix is block diagonal if distinct transition intensities depend upon disjoint and functionally independent subsets of γ.

The information matrix is

$$\mathcal{I}_{jk} = -\mathrm{E} \left[\frac{\partial^2 L}{\partial \gamma_j \partial \gamma_k} \right]$$

$$= -\mathrm{E} \left[\mathbf{H}_{jk}(\gamma) \right] \tag{2.10}$$

where $\mathbf{H}$ is the Hessian (2.9). The expectation in (2.10) is taken with respect to t and $\mathbf{d}$, given the regressor vector. The expectation of d_{im} is the probability that person i enters destination m. This depends upon all the transition intensities in the model. If some of these, for example, the transition intensity corresponding to the dummy censoring destination, are unspecified then this expectation cannot be calculated. This would also be the case, in general, if the likelihood (2.2) must be read as a partial likelihood. It is usual in this case to take as an estimate of the asymptotic covariance matrix of $\hat{\gamma}$ the inverse of the negative Hessian evaluated at $\hat{\gamma}$,

$$\hat{V}(\hat{\gamma}) = -\mathbf{H}(\hat{\gamma})^{-1}. \tag{2.11}$$

The information matrix can be calculated for some simple models, in the absence of censoring, though these calculations are more of theoretical than practical interest.

Let us now examine some examples in which there is a single real destination together with some right censoring, so the log likelihood takes the form (2.4). As we remarked above this also covers the case in which there are multiple real destinations whose transition intensities depend upon disjoint and functionally independent sets of parameters.

Example 1 The Exponential Model
We let $\theta_i = \exp\{\mathbf{x}_i'\gamma\}$ so that $z_i = t_i \exp\{\mathbf{x}_i'\gamma\}$. Thus

$$L = \sum_{i=1}^{N}[d_i\mathbf{x}_i\gamma - t_i\exp\{\mathbf{x}_i\gamma\}], \tag{2.12}$$

$$\frac{\partial L}{\partial \gamma_j} = \sum_{i=1}^{N} x_{ij}[d_i - z_i] = 0, \qquad j = 1, 2\ldots, K, \tag{2.13}$$

$$\frac{\partial^2 L}{\partial \gamma_j \partial \gamma_k} = -\sum_{i=1}^{N} x_{ij}x_{ik}z_i, \qquad j, k = 1, 2, \ldots, K. \tag{2.14}$$

If we let the vector $\epsilon = \{\epsilon_i\} = \{d_i - z_i\}$, which, as we remarked above, is analogous to the error vector in a linear model, and if we write $\mathbf{\Omega} = \text{diag}\{z_i\}$, with $\mathbf{X}$ the familiar $N \times K$ regressor matrix, then equations (2.13) and (2.14) may be written

$$\frac{\partial L}{\partial \gamma} = \mathbf{X}'\epsilon = 0, \tag{2.15}$$

$$\frac{\partial^2 L}{\partial \gamma^2} = -\mathbf{X}'\mathbf{\Omega}\mathbf{X}. \tag{2.16}$$

If the $\{t_i\}$ are all positive then so are the diagonal elements of $\mathbf{\Omega}$ and (2.16) is negative definite if the regressor matrix is of full column rank. In this case the log likelihood function is strictly concave and the maximum likelihood estimator is unique. It may be found by Newton's method, for example, in which the iteration is

$$\gamma_{n+1} = \gamma_n + (\mathbf{X}'\mathbf{\Omega}_n\mathbf{X})^{-1}\mathbf{X}'\epsilon_n, \qquad (2.17)$$

where the n subscripts to $\mathbf{\Omega}$ and to ϵ indicate that they should be evaluated at $\gamma = \gamma_n$. In practice this iteration may be simplified to

$$\gamma_{n+1} = \gamma_n + (\mathbf{X}'\mathbf{X})^{-1}\mathbf{X}'\epsilon_n \qquad (2.18)$$

so that only one matrix inversion is required, although a second one will be needed to estimate the covariance matrix of $\hat{\gamma}$ from

$$\hat{V}(\hat{\gamma}) = (\mathbf{X}'\hat{\mathbf{\Omega}}\mathbf{X})^{-1}. \qquad (2.19)$$

An alternative estimate of the covariance matrix exploits the fact that $E(z_i) = E(d_i)$, from (2.8), and replaces $\hat{\mathbf{\Omega}}$ in (2.19) by $\mathbf{D} = \text{diag}\{d_i\}$, giving

$$\hat{V}(\hat{\gamma}) = (\mathbf{X}'\mathbf{D}\mathbf{X})^{-1}. \qquad (2.20)$$

This is the inverse matrix of sums of squares and products of the regressors taken only over the uncensored observations.

If there are no regressors and $\mathbf{X}$ contains only the dummy constant no iteration is required since the likelihood equation is

$$\sum_{i=1}^{N}[d_i - t_ie^\gamma] = 0 \qquad (2.21)$$

with solution

$$e^{\hat{\gamma}} = \frac{N_u}{\sum_{i=1}^{N} t_i} = \frac{\hat{\pi}}{\bar{t}}. \qquad (2.22)$$

Here, $\hat{\pi}$ is the number of uncensored observations, N_u, divided by the total number of observations, N, which is an estimate of the probability that an observation will be uncensored. In this no regressor case the variance estimates (2.19) and (2.20) both reduce to

$$\hat{V}(\hat{\gamma}) = \frac{1}{N_u}, \qquad (2.23)$$

using (2.22).

The information matrix is easily evaluated in the absence of censoring. From (2.10) and (2.16)

$$\mathcal{I} = \mathbf{X}'E(\mathbf{\Omega})\mathbf{X} = \mathbf{X}'\mathbf{X} \qquad (2.24)$$

since, in the absence of censoring, the elements of $\mathbf{\Omega}$ are unit Exponential integrated hazards of mean one. Their unit mean can also be seen from

(2.8) since with no censoring all the $\{d_i\}$ are ones. Without censoring, an alternative estimator of the asymptotic covariance matrix of $\hat{\gamma}$ would therefore be

$$\hat{V}(\hat{\gamma}) = (\mathbf{X}'\mathbf{X})^{-1}. \tag{2.25}$$

In the presence of censoring this argument fails since the elements of $\mathbf{\Omega}$ are then integrals of a hazard function, θ, up to a time which is the minimum of two quantities, a random variable with hazard θ and a censoring time. Such a quantity does not have a unit Exponential distribution and its mean depends on the distribution of the censoring time.   ∎

Example 2 The Information Matrix with Fixed Time Censoring
To show the issues that arise in evaluating the information matrix with censoring consider the Exponential model of example 1 with fixed time censoring. The censoring rule is that a study ends after c days – anyone who has not left by then is censored. The distribution of the censoring time is degenerate at the point c. In order to evaluate the expectation of the Hessian (2.16), we need to find $\mathrm{E}\,(z_i)$. This is

$$\begin{aligned} \mathrm{E}\,(z_i) &= \mathrm{E}\,(d_i) \\ &= \mathrm{P}\,(T_i < c) \\ &= 1 - e^{-\theta_i c}, \end{aligned} \tag{2.26}$$

where the first line is a consequence of (2.8).

Thus the expected negative Hessian is

$$-\mathrm{E}\left[\frac{\partial^2 L}{\partial \gamma_j \partial \gamma_k}\right] = \sum_{i=1}^{N} x_{ij} x_{ik}[1 - e^{-\theta_i c}]. \tag{2.27}$$

In matrix notation this is

$$\mathcal{I} = \mathbf{X}'\mathbf{X} - \mathbf{X}'\mathbf{C}\mathbf{X} \tag{2.28}$$

where $\mathbf{C} = \mathrm{diag}\{e^{-\theta_i c}\}$. Comparison with (2.24) shows that the right-hand matrix in (2.28) gives the loss of information due to censoring. Of course, as $c \to \infty$, $\mathbf{C} \to \mathbf{0}$. In the no-regressor case the ratio of the information in the censored sample to that in the uncensored one is given by $(1 - \exp\{-\theta c\})$. The product θc is the ratio of the censoring time to the mean completed duration, θ^{-1}, and the larger this ratio the smaller the loss of information. If the censoring time is the mean duration then a fraction $e^{-1} = 0.37$ of the information in the uncensored sample is lost.   ∎

Example 3 The Weibull Model

The Weibull model, which is a one-parameter generalisation of the Exponential, has been much applied and it is analytically tractable so it forms our next example. The transition intensity and its integral are

$$\theta_i = \alpha t^{\alpha-1} e^{\mathbf{x}_i' \gamma}, \quad z_i = t^{\alpha} e^{\mathbf{x}_i' \gamma}. \tag{2.29}$$

Then, the log likelihood is

$$L = \sum_{i=1}^{N} [d_i \log \alpha + d_i(\alpha - 1) \log t_i + d_i \mathbf{x}_i' \gamma - z_i] \tag{2.30}$$

with first and second derivatives given by

$$\frac{\partial L}{\partial \gamma_j} = \sum_{i=1}^{N} x_{ij}[d_i - z_i], \tag{2.31}$$

$$\frac{\partial L}{\partial \alpha} = \sum_{i=1}^{N} \left[\frac{d_i}{\alpha} + \log t_i (d_i - z_i) \right], \tag{2.32}$$

$$\frac{\partial^2 L}{\partial \gamma_j \partial \gamma_k} = -\sum_{i=1}^{N} x_{ij} x_{ik} z_i, \tag{2.33}$$

$$\frac{\partial^2 L}{\partial \alpha^2} = -\sum_{i=1}^{N} \left[\frac{d_i}{\alpha^2} + z_i \log^2 t_i \right], \tag{2.34}$$

$$\frac{\partial^2 L}{\partial \alpha \partial \gamma_j} = -\sum_{i=1}^{N} x_{ij} z_i \log t_i. \tag{2.35}$$

The solution of the likelihood equation is unique. To show this define $\mathbf{s}$ to be the vector with i'th element equal to $\log t_i$ and, as before, let $\Omega = \text{diag}\{I_i\}$. Then the Hessian, (2.33–2.35), is

$$\mathbf{H} = -\begin{pmatrix} \mathbf{X}'\Omega\mathbf{X} & \mathbf{X}'\Omega\mathbf{s} \\ \mathbf{s}'\Omega\mathbf{X} & \mathbf{s}'\Omega\mathbf{s} \end{pmatrix} - \begin{pmatrix} 0 & 0 \\ 0 & N_u/\alpha^2 \end{pmatrix}, \tag{2.36}$$

which is negative definite if all t_i are positive, $N_u > 0$, and $\mathbf{X}$ is of full column rank.

In the absence of censoring the information matrix can be evaluated. To do this we need to evaluate expressions of the form E $z(\log z)^k$ for $k = 0, 1, 2$. But these are the derivatives with respect to s of E (z^s) at $s = k$ which, since $z \sim \mathcal{E}(1)$ in the absence of censoring, is equal to $\Gamma(1 + s)$ from (4.7) of chapter 1. Using this fact we readily deduce the information matrix (unconditionally on $\mathbf{X}$),

$$
\mathcal{I} = N \begin{pmatrix} 1 & \mathbf{0} & m/\alpha \\ \mathbf{0} & \Sigma & -\Sigma\gamma_1/\alpha \\ m/\alpha & -\gamma_1'\Sigma/\alpha & [\psi'(1) + m^2 + Q]/\alpha^2 \end{pmatrix}, \qquad (2.37)
$$

where

$$
m = \psi(2) - \gamma_0, \quad \gamma = (\gamma_0 \, \gamma_1), \quad Q = \gamma_1'\Sigma\gamma_1,
$$

and Σ is the covariance matrix of the columns of $\mathbf{X}$ apart from the constant vector. The parameters are in the order $\gamma_0, \gamma_1, \alpha$. Inversion of (2.37) gives

$$
\mathcal{I}^{-1} = N^{-1} \begin{pmatrix} 1 + m^2 p & -m\gamma_1 p & -\alpha m p \\ -m\gamma_1' p & \Sigma^{-1} + \gamma_1\gamma_1' p & \alpha\gamma_1 p \\ -\alpha m p & \alpha\gamma_1' p & \alpha^2 p \end{pmatrix}, \qquad (2.38)
$$

where $p = 1/\psi'(1)$.

If we had instead worked with the parametrisation $\beta = \gamma/\alpha$, $\phi = 1/\alpha$, then the asymptotic covariance matrix of the maximum likelihood estimators of β and ϕ takes the rather simpler form,

$$
V(\hat{\beta}, \hat{\phi}) = N^{-1}\phi^2 \begin{pmatrix} 1 + p\psi(2)^2 & 0 & p\psi(2) \\ 0 & \Sigma^{-1} & 0 \\ p\psi(2) & 0 & p \end{pmatrix}.
$$

This may be proved either by inverting the information matrix for β and ϕ or, more directly, by the delta method. This covariance matrix is block diagonal if we reorder the parameters to β_0, ϕ, β_1. ∎

Example 4 Log Linear Hazards

In examples 1 and 3 we were able to show the strict concavity of the log likelihood and hence the uniqueness of the maximum likelihood estimates. These two examples – the Exponential and the Weibull – are particular cases of the family of models with log-linear hazard functions defined in chapter 3, section 3.1.2 by

$$
\log \theta(\mathbf{x}, t) = \sum_{j=1}^{J} \gamma_j k_j(\mathbf{x}(t), t) = \mathbf{k}'\gamma. \qquad (2.39)
$$

Here the $\{k_j\}$ are a set of *known* functions of regressors and time, and the word 'linearity' means linearity in the unknown parameters $\{\gamma_j\}$. For the Exponential model the k functions are just the $\{x_j\}$, as they are for the Weibull, except for one of the $\{k_j\}$ which is equal to $\log t$, after redefining the constant term as $\gamma_0 + \log\alpha$ and taking $\alpha - 1$ as a parameter. Other members of this family include hazards whose logarithms are polynomial in t or $\log t$, piecewise-constant hazard models – to be discussed in the next section – and the Box–Cox hazards of (3.15) of chapter 2 for given values of the parameters λ_1 and λ_2.

To see the concavity of the log likelihood note that

$$L(\gamma) = \sum_{i=1}^{N} [d_i \mathbf{k}'_i \gamma - z_i] \qquad (2.40)$$

for

$$z_i = \int_0^{t_i} \exp\{\mathbf{k}'_i(s)\gamma\} \, ds. \qquad (2.41)$$

Then two differentiations show that the Hessian is

$$\mathbf{H}(\gamma) = -\sum_{i=1}^{N} \int_0^{t_i} \mathbf{k}_i(s)\mathbf{k}'_i(s)\theta_i(s) \, ds.$$

If we define

$$\delta_i(s) = \begin{cases} 1 & \text{for } s \le t_i, \\ 0 & \text{for } s > t_i, \end{cases}$$

then

$$\mathbf{H}(\gamma) = -\sum_{i=1}^{N} \int_0^{\infty} \mathbf{k}_i(s)\mathbf{k}'_i(s)\theta_i(s)\delta_i(s) \, ds$$

$$= -\int_0^{\infty} \sum_{i=1}^{N} \mathbf{k}_i(s)\mathbf{k}'_i(s)\theta_i(s)\delta_i(s) \, ds$$

$$= -\int_0^{\infty} \mathbf{K}'(s)\mathbf{D}(s)\mathbf{K}(s) \, ds. \qquad (2.42)$$

Here, $\mathbf{K}$ is the $N \times J$ matrix whose i'th row is $\mathbf{k}_i(s)$, $\mathbf{D} = \text{diag}\{\theta_i(s)\delta_i(s)\}$ and the integral of a matrix is the matrix of integrals. To show that (2.42) is negative semi-definite we need only consider

$$\mathbf{y}'\mathbf{H}\mathbf{y} = -\int_0^{\infty} \mathbf{y}'\mathbf{K}'(s)\mathbf{D}(s)\mathbf{K}(s)\mathbf{y} \, ds \le 0$$

for every non-null vector $\mathbf{y}$ since the integrand is a positive semi-definite quadratic form for every s. Thus $\mathbf{H}$ is negative semi-definite. Under weak conditions on the data $\mathbf{H}$ may be shown to be negative definite and the log-likelihood strictly concave.

The likelihoods for log-linear hazard models are thus easy to maximise and they contain within the class a wide variety of forms of hazard function. Their drawback is that in general – the Exponential, Weibull, and piecewise-constant models are exceptions – numerical integration will be required in order to calculate L and its derivatives. ■

In the special case in which the time-varying components of the vector $\mathbf{k}_i(s)$ are common to all people, as they are, for example, in the Weibull model, the integrated hazard for person i is

$$z_i = \mu_i \int_0^{t_i} \exp\{\mathbf{k}'(s)\gamma_2\}\,ds, \qquad \mu_i = \mu_i(\mathbf{x}_i;\gamma_1).$$

If the integral needs to be calculated numerically we can exploit the commonness of the $\mathbf{k}(s)$ in the following way. The log likelihood is

$$L(\gamma) = \sum_{i=1}^{N}\left[d_i \log \mu_i + d_i\mathbf{k}'(t_i)\gamma_2 - \mu_i\int_0^{t_i}\exp\{\mathbf{k}'(s)\gamma_2\}\,ds\right].$$

The integral component of this expression may be written

$$\sum_{i=1}^{N}\mu_i\int_0^{t_i}\exp\{\mathbf{k}'(s)\gamma_2\}\,ds = \sum_{i=1}^{N}\left(\sum_{j=i}^{N}\mu_j\right)\int_{t_{i-1}}^{t_i}\exp\{\mathbf{k}'(s)\gamma_2\}\,ds,$$

after relabelling the observations in order of magnitude of t and letting $t_0 = 0$. Generally, the integrals on the right of this expression may be well approximated by the trapezoidal formula

$$\int_{t_{i-1}}^{t_i} e^{\mathbf{k}'(s)\gamma_2}\,ds \approx (t_i - t_{i-1})(e^{\mathbf{k}'(t_{i-1})\gamma_2} + e^{\mathbf{k}'(t_i)\gamma_2})/2.$$

The reason for this is that in a reasonably large sample almost all the intervals between successive observations will be small. Clayton (1983), to whom the idea is due, points out that this approximation allows the use of the statistical software GLIM to estimate this class of models.

Example 5 Piecewise-Constant Hazards – Raw Data
In this family of models the hazard for each person is a piecewise-constant function of time as in figure 8.1.
    We divide the time axis into M intervals by the points $c_1, c_2, \ldots$ c_{M-1} and write the hazard function for the i'th person in section m as

$$\theta_i(t) = \mu_i e^{\lambda_m}, \qquad c_{m-1} \le t < c_m, m = 1, 2, \ldots, M, \qquad (2.43)$$

with $c_0 = 0$ and $c_M = \infty$. The parameter μ_i is some positive function of time-invariant regressor variables. When we come to work out likelihood

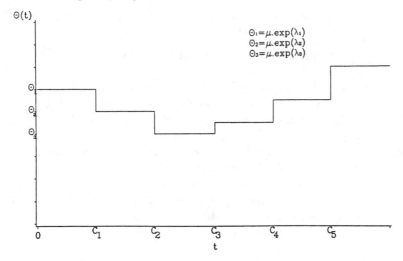

Figure 8.1.   A piecewise-constant hazard function.

equations and scores we shall assume μ to be $\exp\{\mathbf{x}'\gamma\}$, but it need not
have this form. Let

$$d_m(t) = \begin{cases} 1 & \text{if } c_{m-1} \leq t < c_m, \\ 0 & \text{otherwise,} \end{cases} \qquad m = 1, 2, \ldots, M. \qquad (2.44)$$

$$D_m(t) = \prod_{j=1}^{m}[1 - d_j(t)], \qquad m = 1, 2, \ldots, M - 1; \quad D_0(t) = 1 \qquad (2.45)$$

The $\{d_m\}$ are indicators of the section into which t falls, so that $d_m = 1$
if and only if t lies in the m'th interval. D_m is an indicator of whether or
not t fell at or after c_m, being one if it did so and zero otherwise. This
notation enables us to write the hazard for person i as

$$\theta_i(t) = \mu_i \exp\left\{ \sum_{m=1}^{M} \lambda_m d_{im}(t) \right\}. \qquad (2.46)$$

Notice that if $\mu_i = \exp\{\mathbf{x}_i'\gamma\}$ – there must be no constant term in $\mathbf{x}_i'\gamma$
because the $\{\lambda_m\}$ render it superfluous – then

$$\log \theta(t) = \mathbf{x}'\gamma + \sum_{m=1}^{M} \lambda_m d_m(t),$$

so that (2.43) is a log-linear hazard model and maximum likelihood
estimators will be unique by the argument of the last example.

The hazard integrated to the exit or censoring time t is

$$z = \int_0^t \theta(u)\,du = \mu \sum_{m=1}^{M} e^{\lambda_m}[(t - c_{m-1})d_m + (c_m - c_{m-1})D_m], \quad (2.47)$$

where $d_m = d_m(t)$, $D_m = D_m(t)$, and we have put $D_M \equiv 0$.

We shall now give the likelihood function for the model defined by (2.43) or (2.46) where we observe the exact value of the continuous random variable T for each of N people. We emphasise the nature of the data because in our next example we shall consider the same model, but where we know only the section into which each realisation of T fell, that is, where we have grouped data.

The survivor function for the model is $\exp\{-z(t)\}$ where $z(t)$ is given by (2.47) and the hazard is given by (2.43). The log likelihood contribution of person i who is observed to leave or be censored at t_i is

$$L_i = \delta_i \log \mu_i + \delta_i \sum_{m=1}^{M} d_{im}\lambda_m - \mu_i \sum_{m=1}^{M} e^{\lambda_m}[(t_i - c_{m-1})d_{im}$$
$$+ (c_m - c_{m-1})D_{im}]. \quad (2.48)$$

Here δ is the binary censoring indicator which equals one if the observation is uncensored, and $d_{im} = d_m(t_i)$, $D_{im} = D_m(t_i)$.

The term in square brackets in (2.48) is

$$T_{im} = (t_i - c_{m-1})d_{im} + (c_m - c_{m-1})D_{im}. \quad (2.49)$$

Now T_{im} equals $c_m - c_{m-1}$ if person i leaves or is censored at or after c_m; it equals $t_i - c_{m-1}$ if he leaves or is censored between c_{m-1} and c_m; and it equals zero otherwise. It follows that T_{im} is the total time known to be spent by person i in the m'th interval, and its sum over i, which we shall call T_m, is the total time spent by all people in that interval. Furthermore $\delta_i d_{im}$ is one if and only if person i is observed to leave in the m'th interval, so its sum over i, which we shall call E_m, is the total number of people observed to leave in the m'th interval.

The total log likelihood is got by summing terms like (2.48) over N observations and is

$$L = \sum_{i=1}^{N} \delta_i \log \mu_i + \sum_{m=1}^{M} \lambda_m \sum_{i=1}^{N} d_{im}\delta_i - \sum_{m=1}^{M} e^{\lambda_m} \sum_{i=1}^{N} \mu_i T_{im}. \quad (2.50)$$

Differentiation with respect to the $\{\lambda_m\}$ gives the scores

$$\frac{\partial L}{\partial \lambda_m} = \sum_{i=1}^{N} \delta_i d_{im} - e^{\lambda_m} \sum_{i=1}^{N} \mu_i T_{im}, \qquad m = 1, 2, \ldots, M. \quad (2.51)$$

These have the solutions

$$e^{\hat{\lambda}_m} = \frac{E_m}{\sum_{i=1}^{N} \mu_i T_{im}}, \qquad m = 1, 2, \ldots, M. \qquad (2.52)$$

If there are no regressors in the model so that $\mu_i \equiv 1$, $i = 1, 2 \ldots N$ the equations for the $\{\lambda_m\}$ become

$$e^{\hat{\lambda}_m} = \frac{E_m}{T_m} \qquad m = 1, 2, \ldots M, \qquad (2.53)$$

which is *the rate of leaving per unit time period, for example, per day, in the m'th time interval,* the natural estimator of the hazard function in that interval. If there are regressors then T_m is replaced by $\sum \mu_i T_{im}$ in (2.53). A term like $\mu_i T_{im}$ is a person-specific transformation of the time scale so that, for example, people who have large values of μ and who therefore tend to leave rapidly have clock time increased relative to those with small values of μ. The $\{\mu_i T_{im}\}$ are in this sense generalised times spent in the m'th interval.

If we substitute (2.52) into L we get the log likelihood function concentrated with respect to the $\{\lambda_m\}$. This may be written

$$L^*(\gamma) = \sum_{i=1}^{N} \delta_i \log \mu_i - \sum_{m=1}^{M} E_m \log \sum_{i=1}^{N} \mu_i T_{im} + \sum_{m=1}^{M} E_m (\log E_m - 1).$$

Or equivalently, remembering that $\hat{\lambda}_m$ is a function of γ,

$$L^*(\gamma) = \sum_{i=1}^{N} \delta_i \log \mu_i + \sum_{m=1}^{M} E_m (\hat{\lambda}_m - 1). \qquad (2.54)$$

Assuming that $\log \mu_i = \mathbf{x}_i' \gamma$, differentiation of $L^*(\gamma)$ gives the likelihood equations for γ as

$$\frac{\partial L^*}{\partial \gamma_j} = \sum_{i=1}^{N} \delta_i x_{ij} - \sum_{m=1}^{M} e^{\hat{\lambda}_m} \sum_{i=1}^{N} \mu_i x_{ij} T_{im} = 0, \qquad j = 1, 2, \ldots K. \quad (2.55)$$

The Hessian of the concentrated log likelihood has j, k'th element given by

$$\frac{\partial^2 L^*}{\partial \gamma_j \partial \gamma_k} = -\sum_{m=1}^{M} e^{\hat{\lambda}_m} \left[\sum_{i=1}^{N} \mu_i x_{ij} x_{ik} T_{im} \right.$$

$$\left. - \sum_{i=1}^{n} \mu_i x_{ij} T_{im} \sum_{i=1}^{N} \mu_i x_{ik} T_{im} / \sum_{i=1}^{N} \mu_i T_{im} \right] \quad (2.56)$$

In matrix notation this is

$$\mathbf{H}^*(\gamma) = -(\mathbf{X}'\mathbf{\Omega}\mathbf{X} - \mathbf{X}'\mathbf{S}\mathbf{E}^{-1}\mathbf{S}'\mathbf{X}), \qquad (2.57)$$

where $\mathbf{\Omega} = \text{diag}\{z_i\}$; $\mathbf{S} = \{\mu_i T_{im}\}$; $\mathbf{E} = \text{diag}\{E_m\}$; and $\mathbf{X}$ is the $N \times K$ regressor matrix.

Newton's method for solving (2.55) gives the iteration

$$\gamma_{p+1} = \gamma_p - \mathbf{H}^*(\gamma_p)^{-1}\frac{\partial L^*}{\partial \gamma_p}, \qquad (2.58)$$

which normally converges rapidly from an initial estimate of zero.

The Hessian of the full log likelihood, (2.50), is

$$\mathbf{H}(\lambda, \gamma) = -\begin{pmatrix} \mathbf{E} & \mathbf{S}'\mathbf{X} \\ \mathbf{X}'\mathbf{S} & \mathbf{X}'\mathbf{\Omega}\mathbf{X} \end{pmatrix} \qquad (2.59)$$

whose inverse is

$$\mathbf{H}^{-1} = -\begin{pmatrix} \mathbf{E}^{-1} + \mathbf{J}\mathbf{G}^{-1}\mathbf{J}' & -\mathbf{J}\mathbf{G}^{-1} \\ \mathbf{G}^{-1}\mathbf{J}' & \mathbf{G}^{-1} \end{pmatrix} \qquad (2.60)$$

for

$$\mathbf{G} = \mathbf{X}'\mathbf{\Omega}\mathbf{X} - \mathbf{X}'\mathbf{S}\mathbf{E}^{-1}\mathbf{S}'\mathbf{X}; \quad \mathbf{J} = \mathbf{E}^{-1}\mathbf{S}'\mathbf{X},$$

and where $\mathbf{\Omega} = \text{diag}\{z(t_i)\}$, as in (2.16). Since $\mathbf{E}$ is diagonal the only matrix inversion required is that of $\mathbf{G}$, which is of order $K \times K$. In the absence of regressors the Hessian is diagonal and the estimators of the $\{\lambda_m\}$ are asymptotically uncorrelated with variances estimated by var $\hat{\lambda}_m = E_m^{-1}$, the reciprocal of the total number of people observed to leave in interval m. When regressors are present the $\{\hat{\lambda}_m\}$ are generally correlated.

We now turn to consider estimation of the same model with grouped data.

Example 6 Piecewise-Constant Hazards – Grouped Data
Suppose that our data are grouped into intervals whose end points are the $\{c_m\}$ of the previous example, so that for each person we know only the interval into which his departure or censoring time falls. For someone who leaves in the m'th interval we know only that $c_{m-1} \leq T < c_m$; and for someone censored in that interval we know only that $T \geq c_{m-1}$. Thus the likelihood contribution from a single individual is

$$\mathcal{L} = \prod_{m=1}^{M} \left[\{\overline{G}(c_{m-1}) - \overline{G}(c_m)\}^{\delta} \, \overline{G}(c_{m-1})^{1-\delta} \right]^{d_m}$$

$$= \prod_{m=1}^{M} \left[\left\{ 1 - \frac{\overline{G}(c_m)}{\overline{G}(c_{m-1})} \right\}^{\delta} \overline{G}(c_{m-1}) \right]^{d_m}. \qquad (2.61)$$

Here d_m, defined in the last example, is the indicator of whether t fell in the m'th interval. The expressions appearing in (2.61) are, from (2.47), given by

$$\frac{\overline{G}(c_m)}{\overline{G}(c_{m-1})} = \begin{cases} \exp\{-\mu(c_m - c_{m-1})e^{\lambda_m}\} & m = 1, 2, \dots M-1, \\ 0 & m = M, \end{cases} \qquad (2.62)$$

and $$\overline{G}(c_{m-1}) = \exp\left\{ -\mu \sum_{l=1}^{m-1} (c_l - c_{l-1})e^{\lambda_l} \right\}, \qquad m = 2, 3, \dots (2.63)$$

Thus

$$\mathcal{L} = \prod_{m=1}^{M-1} [1 - \exp\{-\mu(c_m - c_{m-1})e^{\lambda_m}\}]^{\delta d_m}$$

$$\times \prod_{m=2}^{M} \exp\left\{ -d_m \mu \sum_{l=1}^{m-1} (c_l - c_{l-1})e^{\lambda_l} \right\} \qquad (2.64)$$

Note that λ_M does not appear in the likelihood. It is not identified from grouped data because such data contain no information about the rate at which people leave within the last interval. In effect, every observation that falls in the last interval is right censored at c_{M-1}, and estimation is not possible when all observations are censored.

It is notationally convenient to work not in terms of the parameters $\{\lambda_m\}$ as in the last example but in terms of new parameters $\{\beta_m\}$ defined by

$$(c_m - c_{m-1})e^{\lambda_m} = e^{\beta_m}, \qquad m = 1, 2, \dots, M-1. \qquad (2.65)$$

This just multiplies the old interval-specific parameters by the length of each of the intervals. It will also be helpful if we define

$$h_{im} = \exp\{-\mu_i e^{\beta_m}\}, \qquad m = 1, 2, \dots M-1. \qquad (2.66)$$

The h's are the ratios of successive survivor functions.

In this notation the log likelihood contribution from person i is

$$L_i = \delta_i \sum_{m=1}^{M-1} d_{im} \log[1 - h_{im}] - \sum_{m=2}^{M} d_{im} \mu_i \sum_{l=1}^{M-1} e^{\beta_l},$$

and the whole log likelihood is the sum of these terms over all people,

$$L = \sum_{i=1}^{N} \left\{ \delta_i \sum_{m=1}^{M-1} d_{im} \log[1 - h_{im}] - \sum_{m=2}^{M} d_{im} \mu_i \sum_{l=1}^{M-1} e^{\beta_l} \right\}. \quad (2.67)$$

The scores for the $\{\beta_m\}$ are given by

$$\frac{\partial L}{\partial \beta_m} = e^{\beta_m} \sum_{i=1}^{N} \mu_i \left[\frac{\delta_i d_{im} h_{im}}{1 - h_{im}} - D_{im} \right], \qquad m = 1, 2, \dots, M-1. \quad (2.68)$$

Here D_{im}, defined in the last example, is the indicator of whether t fell at or after c_m. The matrix of second derivatives with respect to the $\{\beta_m\}$ is diagonal as in the last example and the diagonal elements, evaluated at the maximum likelihood point, are

$$\frac{\partial^2 L}{\partial \beta_m{}^2} = -e^{2\beta_m} \sum_{i=1}^{N} \frac{\mu_i^2 \delta_i d_{im} h_{im}}{(1 - h_{im})^2}, \qquad m = 1, 2, \dots, M-1. \quad (2.69)$$

An important special case is where there are no regressors so that $\mu_i \equiv 1$, $i = 1, 2, \dots, N$, and the h_{im} are independent of i. In this case, when we equate (2.68) to zero we may solve explicitly to get

$$\hat{h}_m = \frac{\sum D_{im}}{\sum D_{im} + \sum \delta_i d_{im}}$$

$$= \frac{N_m}{N_m + E_m}, \qquad m = 1, 2, \dots, M-1. \quad (2.70)$$

E_m was defined in the last example to be the number of people observed to leave in the m'th interval, whereas N_m is the number of people who have neither left nor been censored before c_m. Their sum, $N_m + E_m$, is therefore the number of people who *could* have been observed to leave in the m'th interval, of which a total of E_m actually did so, and N_m did not.

If $(c_m - c_{m-1})e^{\lambda_m}$ is small, as it might be with a fine grouping of the data, then

$$\exp\{-(c_m - c_{m-1})e^{\lambda_m}\} \sim 1 - (c_m - c_{m-1})e^{\lambda_m},$$

implying that, from (2.70),

$$e^{\hat{\lambda}_m} = \frac{1}{(c_m - c_{m-1})} \frac{E_m}{N_m + E_m},$$

so that the estimated hazard function for the m'th interval is the fraction of those who could have been observed to leave who actually did so, per unit time period. This is a natural estimator of the hazard function.

The expressions (2.70) give maximum likelihood estimates of the ratios of successive values of the survivor function and imply the following maximum likelihood estimator of the survivor function itself,

$$\hat{\overline{G}}(c_m) = \prod_{l=1}^{m} \frac{N_l}{N_l + E_l}, \qquad m = 1, 2, \ldots, M - 1. \qquad (2.71)$$

This is the famous Kaplan–Meier, or product limit, survivor function estimator. It is obtained here in the context of a model that assumes the hazard function to be piecewise-constant but it is in fact the maximum likelihood estimator of the survivor function for homogeneous data in a much more general model. We shall point this out in the next example.

Continuing to assume the absence of regressors we now consider the asymptotic variances of the estimators of the betas, the h's, and the survivor function itself. The second derivatives, (2.69), reduce to

$$\frac{\partial^2 L}{\partial \beta_m{}^2} = -e^{2\beta_m} \frac{N_m(N_m + E_m)}{E_m},$$

which implies an estimate of the variance of $\hat{\beta}_m$ of

$$\mathrm{var}(\hat{\beta}_m) = e^{-2\beta_m} \frac{E_m}{N_m(N_m + E_m)}.$$

This we may then use, via (2.66), to deduce in turn estimators for the variances of the maximum likelihood estimators of h_m, $\log h_m$, and, since the survivor function is the product of the h's, $\log \overline{G}(c_m)$, and finally, of $\overline{G}(c_m)$ itself. The results are

$$\mathrm{var}(\hat{h}_m) = \frac{N_m E_m}{(N_m + E_m)^3},$$

$$\mathrm{var}(\log \hat{h}_m) = \frac{E_m}{N_m(N_m + E_m)},$$

$$\mathrm{var}(\log \hat{\overline{G}}(c_m)) = \sum_{l=1}^{m} \frac{E_l}{N_l(N_l + E_l)},$$

$$\mathrm{var}(\hat{\overline{G}}(c_m)) = \hat{\overline{G}}(c_m)^2 \sum_{l=1}^{m} \frac{E_l}{N_l(N_l + E_l)}. \qquad (2.72)$$

The step from the second to the third line above follows from the asymptotic uncorrelatedness of the $\{\hat{\beta}_m\}$, which implies the uncorrelatedness of the $\{\hat{h}_m\}$. The form of these results is easy to justify if we write

$$p = \frac{N_m}{N_m + E_m}, \qquad q = 1 - p.$$

Then the estimator of the variance of $\hat{h}_m$ which, from (2.70), is the proportion of those who could have been observed to survive through the m'th interval who did in fact do so, is just $pq/(N_m + E_m)$, which we recognise as the variance of a binomial proportion with $N_m + E_m$ trials and N_m successes.

Returning to the case where regressors are included, if $\mu_i = \exp\{\mathbf{x}_i'\gamma\}$, then the scores for the regression coefficients are

$$\frac{\partial L}{\partial \gamma_j} = \sum_{i=1}^{N} \sum_{m=1}^{M} x_{ij}\mu_i e^{\beta_m} \left\{ \frac{\delta_i d_{im} h_{im}}{1 - h_{im}} - D_{im} \right\}. \qquad (2.73)$$

The second derivatives can then be written down, but since they are involved and not particularly informative we shall omit them. The negative Hessian can be inverted in partitioned form exploiting the diagonality of the block referring to the $\{\beta_m\}$ as in the last example, so that a matrix only of order K need be inverted. The presence of regressors induces correlation among the $\{\hat{\beta}_m\}$ in general. ■

Example 7 Proportional Hazards – Grouped Data

Suppose now that we do not believe that the time dependence of the hazard function is a discontinuous, step function as in the piecewise-constant model of the last two sections – (2.43). Let us therefore write

$$\theta_i(t) = \mu_i \theta_0(t), \qquad 0 \le t < \infty. \qquad (2.74)$$

This model preserves the proportional hazards form since θ_0 is a positive function of t, common to all people, but otherwise arbitrary, whereas μ depends upon person-specific regressor variables. Let us consider what we can learn about μ and about θ_0 from data grouped as in example 1.6. The likelihood contribution from a single individual is, as before, (2.61), where now (2.62) and (2.63) are replaced by

$$\frac{\overline{G}(c_m)}{\overline{G}(c_{m-1})} = \exp\left\{ -\mu \int_{c_m}^{c_{m-1}} \theta_0(u)\, du \right\}, \quad m = 1, 2, \ldots, M-1, \qquad (2.62a)$$

$$\overline{G}(c_{m-1}) = \exp\left\{ -\mu \sum_{l=1}^{m-1} \int_{c_{l-1}}^{c_l} \theta_0(u)\, du \right\}, \quad m = 2, 3, \ldots, M. \qquad (2.63a)$$

The parameter transformation corresponding to (2.65) is

$$\int_{c_{m-1}}^{c_m} \theta_0(u)\, du = e^{\beta_m}, \qquad m = 1, 2, \ldots, M-1. \qquad (2.65a)$$

Inference about the $\{\beta_m\}$ then proceeds as in the last example. But since it is only the $\{\beta_m\}$ that can be identified, so far as the time-variation in the hazard is concerned, there is nothing to be gained by adopting the more elaborate model, (2.74), over the piecewise-constant one. Essentially, since with grouped data we can know nothing about the way the hazard varies within an interval, the best we can do is to estimate its average level and we might as well work with the simplest model, in which that level is constant. Note that even with the much more general model (2.74), the maximum likelihood estimator of the survivor function at the end points of the intervals remains the estimator, (2.71).   ■

Example 8 Time-Varying Regressors – Grouped Data
A more useful extension of the piecewise-constant model of (2.43) is to allow the regression component of the model, μ, to vary from interval to interval as well as between persons. One way of doing this is to admit the possibility of time-varying regressors which are constant within each interval but generally different between intervals. Thus the regressor vector for person i would be

$$\mathbf{x}_{mi}, \qquad m = 1, 2, \ldots, M, \quad i = 1, 2, \ldots, N. \qquad (2.75)$$

The term $\mathbf{x}_{mi}$ is the value of the regressor vector for person i in the m'th interval and it is assumed to be known to the investigator. The component μ_i of the model now becomes

$$\mu(\mathbf{x}_{mi}) = \mu_{mi}, \qquad m = 1, 2, \ldots, M, \quad i = 1, 2, \ldots N, \qquad (2.76)$$

for which a simple choice of functional form would be

$$\mu(\mathbf{x}_{mi}) = \exp\{\mathbf{x}'_{mi}\gamma\}. \qquad (2.77)$$

If we adopt the general form of (2.74) for the time dependence in the hazard we have the model

$$\theta_i(t) = \mu_{mi}\theta_0(t), \qquad c_{m-1} \le t < c_m, \quad m = 1, 2, \ldots, M. \qquad (2.78)$$

Inference about this model requires only minor modifications to our previous results, amounting to placing μ to the right of summations over m rather than to the left. Specifically, in (2.62a) and (2.63a) μ receives an m subscript, and the definition (2.66) is amended to

$$h_{mi} = \exp\{-\mu_{mi}e^{\beta_m}\} \qquad m = 1, 2, \ldots, M - 1. \qquad (2.66a)$$

In the scores and Hessian for the $\{\beta_m\}$, (2.68) and (2.69), μ receives an m subscript while the scores for the regression coefficients, on the model (2.77), become

$$\frac{\partial L}{\partial \gamma_j} = \sum_{i=1}^{N} \sum_{m=1}^{M-1} x_{mij}\mu_{mi}e^{\beta_m} \left[\delta_i d_{mi}\frac{h_{mi}}{1 - h_{mi}} - D_{im}\right], \qquad (2.73a)$$

where x_{mij} is the value of the j'th regressor for person i in the m'th interval.

There is another way of allowing the regression component of the model to vary between intervals and this is to allow the regression coefficients to so vary by writing, say,

$$\mu_{mi} = \exp\{\mathbf{x}'_{mi}\gamma_m\}, \qquad m = 1, 2, \ldots M. \tag{2.79}$$

This gives a model with a total of $KM + M - 1$ parameters which is feasible with the size of sample often available to econometricians. To implement this model is a rather straightforward extension of the algebra of the preceding sections, but this has not been done so far as the author is aware. In practice one might well wish to impose a certain amount of smoothness in the response of the hazard to variation in the regressors, which would mean constraining the gammas not to vary sharply between successive intervals. This could be done, though at the expense of additional complexity.   ∎

3   Other Single-Cycle Sampling Schemes

We remarked at the start of this chapter that the likelihood function depends both upon the model for the transition intensities and upon the way in which the data are collected. In the preceding section we considered inference from likelihoods based on the distributions of time and destination given the regressors, $g(t, \mathbf{d} \mid \mathbf{x})$. In effect the sampling scheme amounted to selecting a regressor vector $\mathbf{x}$ and then noting the corresponding duration of stay and destination state. This scheme could be carried out either by observing entrants to a state and their $\mathbf{x}$'s and waiting until t and $\mathbf{d}$ are revealed or by observing leavers and asking for $\mathbf{x}, t$, and $\mathbf{d}$. Of course the sampling need not be carried out contemporaneously with the state visit – a sample of people who were unemployed during the Great Depression could be analysed by studying $g(t, \mathbf{d} \mid \mathbf{x})$. The information about the parameters is contained in the comparison of $(t, \mathbf{d})$ for different $\mathbf{x}$'s, exactly as in the standard regression model where we compare the values of the dependent variable associated with different $\mathbf{x}$'s. The essential feature of this way of gathering information is that the probability that a person is selected for the sample does not depend upon either t or his destination. It is this independence which justifies the use of $g(t, \mathbf{d} \mid \mathbf{x})$ as the distribution providing the probabilities of what we observe.

In this section we shall examine other ways of collecting data which are potentially informative about the transition intensities and show how they lead to likelihoods different from the product of terms like

$g(t, \mathbf{d} \mid \mathbf{x})$. Such other ways of sampling are rather common with econometric data that are often collected for purposes unconnected with the needs of the applied economist. When deliberately designed by an investigator, alternative sampling schemes may be efficient ways of collecting information but, in practice, non-standard sampling schemes usually seem to arise as accidental consequences of the data collection process.

3.1   Observation Over a Fixed Interval

Suppose that we sample the residents of a state at a given time, t_0, note their elapsed durations, t, and then observe them for a fixed time interval of length, say, h. Suppose further that there exists a single destination state. Then we could observe whether or not each person left the state while we were watching him and we might also observe the time at which he left, if he did so. The time till he leaves is a forward recurrence time, and under an assumption of stationarity it will have density function $\overline{G}(t)/\mu$, as we saw in chapter 4. But conditionally on the elapsed duration t, the time to exit has a distribution which is just the entrant density function subject to the condition $T \geq t$. Thus for someone who has been resident for t days when first observed, the probability that he leaves in the interval $(t, t + h)$ given t is

$$\pi = P(t \leq T < t + h \mid T \geq t, h)$$

$$= \frac{\overline{G}(t) - \overline{G}(t + h)}{\overline{G}(t)}, \tag{3.1}$$

where $\overline{G}$ is the survivor function given $\mathbf{x}$. With N people for whom we observe only whether or not they left, the likelihood function would be

$$\mathcal{L} = \prod_{i=1}^{N} \pi_i^{d_i} (1 - \pi_i)^{1-d_i}, \tag{3.2}$$

where d is a binary indicator equal to 1 if a person left and 0 if he did not.

If we observe the time of departure of those that leave in the interval then the probability that someone leaves at $t + s$ given that he has been resident for t days when first observed is

$$P(\text{exit in } (t + s, t + s + ds) \mid \text{survival to } t) = \frac{g(t + s)\, ds}{\overline{G}(t)}, \tag{3.3}$$

for small ds. The likelihood for N people is then

$$\mathcal{L} = \prod_{i=1}^{N} \left[\frac{g(t_i + s_i)}{\overline{G}(t_i)} \right]^{d_i} \left[\frac{\overline{G}(t_i + h)}{\overline{G}(t_i)} \right]^{1-d_i}. \tag{3.4}$$

Notice that (3.4) contains the likelihood for a sample of entrants as the special case in which all the $\{d_i\}$ are one and all the $\{t_i\}$ are zero.

If there are multiple destinations, the transition intensities to which are θ_m, $m = 1, 2, \ldots, M$, then the probability that a person is observed to leave for destination m in the interval $(t + s, t + s + ds)$, given that he has been resident for t days, is, using (5.3) of chapter 3,

$$\frac{\theta_m(t + s)\overline{G}(t + s)\,ds}{\overline{G}(t)}, \tag{3.5}$$

where

$$\overline{G}(t) = \exp\left\{-\sum_{l=1}^{M} \int_0^t \theta_l(u)\,du\right\}. \tag{3.6}$$

The probability that he does not leave in the interval of observation, under the same condition, is

$$\frac{\overline{G}(t + h)}{\overline{G}(t)}.$$

The likelihood formed from observations on N people is then

$$\mathcal{L} = \prod_{i=1}^{N} \left[\frac{\overline{G}(t_i + h)}{\overline{G}(t_i)}\right]^{1-d_i} \prod_{m=1}^{M} \left[\frac{\theta_m(t_i + s_i)\overline{G}(t_i + s_i)}{\overline{G}(t_i)}\right]^{d_{im}}. \tag{3.7}$$

Here, $d_{im} = 1$ if person i leaves for m and zero otherwise, and $d_i = 1 - \sum_m d_{im}$. In the logarithm of this likelihood the transition intensities to different destinations and their integrals appear additively, so if they depend upon disjoint sets of parameters the likelihood can be maximised separately with respect to each subset of parameters. In particular, unspecified transition intensities, such as that associated with a censoring time, appear as additive constants and can be neglected.

It may be argued that there is a loss of information involved in constructing the likelihoods (3.2), (3.4), and (3.7) conditionally on the time, t, that each person has occupied the state. There appears to be information about the transition intensities in these elapsed durations themselves. The fact that individual i had been unemployed for two years when he appeared in the sample surely tells one something about the parameters of the hazard for leaving unemployment? We shall deal with this argument in section 3.3.

3.2   Observations Only of Destination

If we do not observe the transition time but only know the destination to which exit took place, together with $\mathbf{x}$, then we have in effect a qualitative response model. The probabilities of the destinations are, from (5.5.4),

$$P(\text{exit to destination } m) = \int_0^\infty \overline{G}(u)\theta_m(u)\,du = \pi_m, \qquad (3.8)$$

and the likelihood for N observations is

$$\mathcal{L} = \prod_{i=1}^N \prod_{m=1}^M [\pi_{im}]^{d_{im}}. \qquad (3.9)$$

The calculation of (3.9) requires the complete time paths of all time-varying regressors. Some parameters of the transition intensities may not be identifiable from (3.9). If the transition intensities are proportional – chapter 5, section 6 – no time-dependent parameters appear in this likelihood. If the transition intensities are of the proportional Weibull form then (3.9) is the likelihood for a multivariate Logit model. We shall omit further details of this case, as it is fully covered in the literature, for example by Amemiya (1985).

3.3   Stock Sampling

Suppose that we sample from the population of members of a state at a fixed calendar date – which we have defined as *stock sampling* in chapter 5 – and that what we observe is the length of time they have been resident together with their regressor vector. Our data are the elapsed duration or, in the language of point processes, the backward recurrence time, which we shall cal T. What distribution is appropriate for T and how is it connected to the transition intensities?

In chapter 5 we deduced this distribution under an hypothesis of stationarity. Let us look at the problem again without assuming that our data arise from observation of a stationary renewal process. One helpful way of thinking about this question is to think not in terms of probabilities but in terms of numbers and proportions of people. For the sake of a concrete example let us think of the state whose stock we sample, at a calendar time we shall label time 0, as the state of being registered as unemployed. Let $n(-y)$ be the number of people who have entered unemployment during a unit time period starting y days ago and let $n(-y)\,dy$ be the number of people who enter during a short interval of length dy. Then

$$\int_a^b n(-u)\,du$$

is the total number who enter in the time interval from $-b$ to $-a$. Let $\overline{G}_{-a}(x)$ be the fraction of people who enter unemployment at time $-a$ and stay unemployed for at least x days. It is the empirical counterpart of the survivor function at x applicable to the cohort who entered at time $-a$. Then the total number of registered unemployed at our sampling date is given by

$$\text{Size of the stock at time } 0 = \int_0^\infty n(-y)\overline{G}_{-y}(y)\,dy. \qquad (3.10)$$

This just adds up the entrants of all dates who are still unemployed at time 0. Of this total, the number who have been out of work for at least t days is

$$\text{Number of the stock at time 0 who have}$$
$$\text{been unemployed at least } t \text{ days } = \int_t^\infty n(-y)\overline{G}_{-y}(y)\,dy. \ (3.11)$$

This is the total number of people who entered at least t days ago and are still unemployed. The proportion of people in the population from which we sample who have been unemployed at least t days is the ratio of (3.10) to (3.11), and this is

$$\text{Proportion of people unemployed at time 0 who have been}$$
$$\text{out of work at least } t \text{ days} = \frac{\int_t^\infty n(-y)\overline{G}_{-y}(y)\,dy}{\int_0^\infty n(-y)\overline{G}_{-y}(y)\,dy} = \overline{F}(t). \qquad (3.12)$$

The function $\overline{F}(t)$ is the survivor function of the elapsed durations of people sampled from the stock of unemployed at time 0. If there are regressors present in the model then we regard the stock and inflow as composed of subgroups homogeneous with respect to the regressor vector, and the whole above argument applies if we add the qualification 'for people with regressor vector $\mathbf{x}$' after all statements about numbers and proportions. The expression (3.12) then becomes the survivor function for people with regressor vector $\mathbf{x}$.

Let us look at some special cases. If the survivor function is invariant over entry cohorts then

$$\overline{F}(t) = \frac{\int_t^\infty n(-y)\overline{G}(y)\,dy}{\int_0^\infty n(-y)\overline{G}(y)\,dy}. \qquad (3.13)$$

Notice that calculating this expression still requires knowledge of, or a model for, the time variation in the entry rate. Moreover, suppose the survivor functions $\overline{G}$ depend upon regressor variables that are functions of calendar time, for example, a measure of aggregate economic activity. Then the survivor functions for people entering at different calendar times will be different and they will not be invariant over entry cohorts. The move from (3.12) to (3.13) will be incorrect.

If both the survivor function is constant over entry cohorts and the entry rate itself is constant then

$$
\begin{aligned}
\overline{F}(t) &= \frac{\int_t^\infty n\,\overline{G}(y)\,dy}{\int_0^\infty n\,\overline{G}(y)\,dy}, \\[2mm]
&= \frac{\int_t^\infty \overline{G}(y)\,dy}{\int_0^\infty \overline{G}(y)\,dy}, \\[2mm]
&= \frac{\int_t^\infty \overline{G}(y)\,dy}{\mu}.
\end{aligned}
\tag{3.14}
$$

Here μ is the mean duration of unemployment of entrants and the last line follows from the fact that the mean is the integral of the survivor function. The expression (3.14) may be recognised as the survivor function of the backwards recurrence time distribution in a stationary process that we discussed in chapter 5. It arises here because the assumptions of a constant rate of entry and a constant survivor function imply a fully stationary, constant population size, model.

If the stationarity assumptions seem appropriate then it would be correct to base a likelihood function on (3.14) using as the density function of t

$$
f(t) = \frac{\overline{G}(t)}{\mu},
\tag{3.15}
$$

with likelihood function

$$
\mathcal{L} = \prod_{i=1}^N f_i(t_i).
\tag{3.16}
$$

If these assumptions are implausible then it will be necessary to base the likelihood function on (3.12) or (3.13). These require not only a model for the survivor function appropriate to each entry cohort but also a model for or historical data on the entry rate as a function both of calendar time and of the regressors. That this can be achieved with a limited amount of data as demonstrated in the following example.

Example 9 Nickell's Model for the Entry Rate

Let us emphasise the dependence of the entry numbers and the survivor functions on the regressors by writing (3.13) as

$$\overline{F}(t; \mathbf{x}) = \frac{\int_t^\infty n(-y; \mathbf{x}) \overline{G}(y; \mathbf{x}) \, dy}{\int_0^\infty n(-y; \mathbf{x}) \overline{G}(y; \mathbf{x}) \, dy}. \tag{3.17}$$

We shall suppose the regressors to be either time-invariant or if time-varying then varying only with elapsed duration and not as a function of calendar time. In this latter case we think of $\mathbf{x}$ as the set of numbers which determine the way in which the regressors change as a function of elapsed duration. As an example, the vector $\mathbf{x}$ might include the levels of unemployment benefit payable at different times in the course of a spell of unemployment. We now suppose that data are available on the aggregate numbers entering unemployment at each calendar date in the past and define

$N(-y) = $ the number of people entering unemployment y days ago.

The numbers $N(-y)$ are known for as far back in the past as is empirically relevant. The second assumption provides a model for $n(-y; \mathbf{x})$. We suppose that

$$\frac{n(-y; \mathbf{x})}{N(-y)} = c(\mathbf{x}). \tag{3.18}$$

For example, if $\mathbf{x}$ is age at entry then this model says that the number of young people becoming unemployed is a constant fraction of the total number of people becoming unemployed. If 10 percent of the people becoming unemployed a year ago were young people then the same was true two and three years ago and indeed at all times in the past. The consequence of this assumption is that the survivor function (3.17) now becomes

$$\overline{F}(t; \mathbf{x}) = \frac{\int_t^\infty c(\mathbf{x}) N(-y) \overline{G}(y; \mathbf{x}) \, dy}{\int_0^\infty c(\mathbf{x}) N(-y) \overline{G}(y; \mathbf{x}) \, dy}$$

$$= \frac{\int_t^\infty N(-y) \overline{G}(y; \mathbf{x}) \, dy}{\int_0^\infty N(-y) \overline{G}(y; \mathbf{x}) \, dy}, \tag{3.19}$$

with density function

$$f(t; \mathbf{x}) = \frac{N(-t) \overline{G}(t; \mathbf{x})}{\int_0^\infty N(-y) \overline{G}(y; \mathbf{x}) \, dy}. \tag{3.20}$$

The likelihood for N people becomes

$$\mathcal{L} = \prod_{i=1}^{N} f_i(t_i)^{\delta_i} \overline{F}_i(t_i)^{1-\delta_i}, \qquad (3.21)$$

where δ is the censoring indicator. A person will be censored if we only know that he has been unemployed for at least t days. To compute (3.21) is quite feasible but it will normally require the replacement of integrals by approximating sums. There would be no difficulty in allowing $\overline{G}$ to depend upon the entry date with this model. This ingenious device shows that it is possible to use elapsed duration data without making a strong stationarity assumption. But it does require additional data, and the reasonableness of (3.18) will depend upon the context of application. It was first used in Nickell (1979). ∎

The problem of the appropriate distribution for elapsed duration data has usually been discussed in the context of a sampling scheme in which we sample from the stock and observe both the elapsed duration and a portion of the future transition history. In this context it is an aspect of what is known as *the initial conditions problem*. In general, a fully satisfactory solution to the initial conditions problem appears to require a full model for the rate at which people enter the state in question. That is, we require to imbed the stock sampled data in a stochastic process describing the full state biography of each individual. Nickell's model is the only one which avoids this requirement, so far as the present author is aware.

If one stock samples and obtains data on the lengths of spells that commence *after* the sampling date then these spells have the ordinary, flow, density $g(t, \mathbf{d} \mid \mathbf{x})$, and they may be used to construct a flow data likelihood in the way described in section 2 of this chapter. A common treatment of stock sampled data with future spells observed is thus to ignore the elapsed duration data and to base inferences solely on those spells that begin after the sampling date. This is a sensible, and correct, way to proceed in models that do not involve unmeasured person-specific heterogeneity. Unfortunately, in models that do involve such heterogeneity there is a further complication to consider due to the fact that the distribution of *unobservable* quantities also depends upon the sampling scheme, as we pointed out in the overview of this chapter. We shall return to this point in sections 4.2 and 5.2.

The incorrect assumption of stationarity can lead to absurd results. As an example of this consider again the unemployment example. Most young people leave school in July and some register as unemployed. A sample of unemployed people taken in September will show that most young people have been unemployed for two months. This fact has little to do with the hazard function for leaving unemployment and largely reflects the variation in the entry flow. A model which assumes that the inflow is constant will lead to wrong conclusions about the hazard function. Incidentally, this seasonality in the inflow would tend to invalidate the assumption (3.18) of the Nickell model. It seems likely that young people comprise a higher fraction of the inflow in July than they do in other months.

3.4   Choice Based Sampling

When people are selected for a sample independently of their duration and destination the relevant density function is, as we have already remarked, $g(t, \mathbf{d} \mid \mathbf{x})$. Randomly sampling the stock is not independent of t because longer durations are relatively more likely and the appropriate density is that appropriate to length biased sampling, (3.14), or its non-stationary generalisations. An even more extreme case is where people are selected for inclusion in a sample on the basis of their duration or of their destination, or both. This is called *endogenous sampling* in Amemiya's terminology.

Consider the population of people who have completed a stay in a given state during a certain interval of time. Of that population a proportion $Q(m)$ exited to destination m, $m = 1, 2, \ldots, M$. If $\pi_m(\mathbf{x})$ given by (3.8) is the probability of exit to destination m given regressor vector $\mathbf{x}$ and if $h(\mathbf{x})$ is the distribution of the regressors over the population then by the law of conditional probability,

$$Q(m) = \int \pi_m(\mathbf{x}) \, h(\mathbf{x}) \, dx. \tag{3.22}$$

Suppose that we have a sampling scheme in which we first select a destination and then randomly select a person who exited to the destination and observe his regressor vector. If destination m is selected with probability p_m the relevant probability distribution is

$$h(\mathbf{x} \mid m)p_m = \frac{\pi_m(\mathbf{x})h(\mathbf{x})p_m}{Q(m)}, \tag{3.23}$$

where the equality follows from the law of conditional probability. This is the basis of the choice based sampling likelihood that has been extensively studied in the econometric literature to which we refer the reader. The reason that we mention it here is that, so far as we are aware, the relevance of choice based sampling to the analysis of transition data has not been pointed out.[5]

It is also possible to choose people on the basis of both their destination *and* their completed duration, and in this case the relevant likelihood is based on $h(\mathbf{x} \mid t, \mathbf{d})$. Or one might have a sampling scheme in which one selects a destination, takes a random sample from those who enter it, and observes both $\mathbf{x}$ and t. This leads to the likelihood function $h(\mathbf{x}, t \mid \mathbf{d})$. No analysis of either method has been published, but they would be worth studying.

3.5 Case-Control Sampling

A method of obtaining data that is closely related to choice based sampling, and that has been analysed, is the case-control method, which is as follows. We consider initially a single destination. Let us select a person, A, with a completed duration of t and match him with a second person, B, who has not left after t days. We have a complete duration of t and an incomplete duration of the same length. It seems reasonable that a comparison of the regressor vectors of these two people would be informative about the way in which the regressors affect the hazard function. Let us see how this can be done.

In this approach t has been fixed and the regressor vectors are the random variables. Think of a distribution of regressor vectors from which two realisations are taken and let the random pair of vectors to be drawn be denoted by $\mathbf{X} = \{\mathbf{X}_1, \mathbf{X}_2\}$ and let the particular realisations be $\mathbf{x}_1$ and $\mathbf{x}_2$, which together constitute the set S. Thus we observe $\mathbf{X} \in S$ and we shall argue conditionally on this fact. That is, we argue conditionally on the two regressor vectors but *not* upon their allocation to A and B. Let $\mathbf{X}_a$ and $\mathbf{X}_b$ be the vectors allocated to A and B, respectively. If we observe that, in fact, $\mathbf{X}_a = \mathbf{x}_1$ and $\mathbf{X}_b = \mathbf{x}_2$, the probability of this event is

$$\mathcal{L} = P(\mathbf{X}_a = \mathbf{x}_1, \mathbf{X}_b = \mathbf{x}_2 \mid T_a = t, T_b > t, \mathbf{X} \in S)$$

and by the law of conditional probability this may be written as

$$\mathcal{L} = \frac{P(\mathbf{X}_a = \mathbf{x}_1, \mathbf{X}_b = \mathbf{x}_2 \mid T_a = t, T_b > t)}{P(\mathbf{X} \in S \mid T_a = t, T_b > t)}. \tag{3.24}$$

The numerator probability is equal to $P(\mathbf{X}_a = \mathbf{x}_1 \mid T_a = t) \times P(\mathbf{X}_b = \mathbf{x}_2 \mid T_b > t)$ since the $\mathbf{X}$'s are selected independently given the t data.

[5] Except in Ridder's (1987) dissertation.

The denominator probability is

$$P(\mathbf{X}_a = \mathbf{x}_1, \mathbf{X}_b = \mathbf{x}_2 \mid T_a = t, T_b > t)$$
$$+ P(\mathbf{X}_a = \mathbf{x}_2, \mathbf{X}_b = \mathbf{x}_1 \mid T_a = t, T_b > t)$$
$$= P(\mathbf{X}_a = \mathbf{x}_1 \mid T_a = t) \times P(\mathbf{X}_b = \mathbf{x}_2 \mid T_b > t)$$
$$+ P(\mathbf{X}_a = \mathbf{x}_2 \mid T_a = t) \times P(\mathbf{X}_b = \mathbf{x}_1 \mid T_b > t). \qquad (3.25)$$

This is because there are only two ways of allocating the two vectors among the two people and because the vectors are independently selected. Thus $\mathcal{L}$ is equal to

$$P(\mathbf{X}_a = \mathbf{x}_1 \mid T_a = t) \times P(\mathbf{X}_b = \mathbf{x}_2 \mid T_b > t)$$
$$\div \{ P(\mathbf{X}_a = \mathbf{x}_1 \mid T_a = t) \times P(\mathbf{X}_b = \mathbf{x}_2 \mid T_b > t)$$
$$+ P(\mathbf{X}_a = \mathbf{x}_2 \mid T_a = t) \times P(\mathbf{X}_b = \mathbf{x}_1 \mid T_b > t) \}. \qquad (3.26)$$

This expression only involves the distribution of $\mathbf{x}$ given t, $g(\mathbf{x} \mid t)$. But by the law of conditional probability,

$$g(\mathbf{x} \mid t) = \frac{g(t \mid \mathbf{x}) \, h(\mathbf{x})}{g(t)} \qquad \text{and} \qquad g(\mathbf{x} \mid T > t) = \frac{P(T > t \mid \mathbf{x}) \, h(\mathbf{x})}{P(T > t)}. \qquad (3.27)$$

Inserting these expressions into $\mathcal{L}$ we find that $h(\mathbf{x})$, $g(t)$, and $P(T > t)$ all cancel, leaving

$$\mathcal{L} = \frac{g(t \mid \mathbf{x}_1) \times P(T > t \mid \mathbf{x}_2)}{g(t \mid \mathbf{x}_1) P(T > t \mid \mathbf{x}_2) + g(t \mid \mathbf{x}_2) P(T > t \mid \mathbf{x}_1)}.$$

But $g(t \mid \mathbf{x}_i) = \theta(t, \mathbf{x}_i) \times P(T > t \mid \mathbf{x}_i)$, $i = 1, 2$, so that

$$\mathcal{L} = \frac{\theta(t, \mathbf{x}_1)}{\theta(t, \mathbf{x}_1) + \theta(t, \mathbf{x}_2)}. \qquad (3.28)$$

This is the required likelihood and it will be seen that it amounts to a comparison of the two hazard functions at the same time t.

Example 10 Case-Control Sampling with Weibull Hazards
The Weibull model provides a simple case. If $\theta(t, \mathbf{x}) = \alpha \exp\{\mathbf{x}_i'\beta\} t^{\alpha-1}$ then

$$\mathcal{L} = \frac{e^{\mathbf{x}_1'\beta}}{e^{\mathbf{x}_1'\beta} + e^{\mathbf{x}_2'\beta}}, \qquad (3.29)$$

which is a Logit model. Note how the time-dependent parameter – and the constant term – vanish from $\mathcal{L}$, which is understandable since we are arguing conditionally on the t data. $\mathcal{L}$ just depends upon the difference of the regressor vectors. ∎

This method generalises to the case in which there is one person observed exiting at t, to destination m, and n people observed not to have left by time t. Moreover, we can allow for time-dependent regressors $\mathbf{x}(t)$. For any t we define the set S to be

$$S = \{\mathbf{x}_1(t), \mathbf{x}_2(t), \ldots, \mathbf{x}_{n+1}(t)\}, \tag{3.30}$$

and argue conditionally on $\mathbf{X} \in S$, but not upon the way in which the elements of S are allocated to the $n + 1$ people. An easy generalisation of the preceding argument then gives

$$\mathcal{L}_m = \frac{\theta_m(\mathbf{x}_1(t))}{\sum_{i=1}^{n+1} \theta_m(\mathbf{x}_i(t))}, \tag{3.31}$$

where $\mathbf{x}_1$ is the regressor vector of the person observed to leave at t.

More generally still, if we observe an exit to m at s distinct times, t_1, t_2, ... t_s, each time observing also n_l people who have not left by that time, the likelihood function for the parameters of the transition intensity to state m, θ_m, is

$$\mathcal{L}_m = \prod_{l=1}^{s} \frac{\theta_m(\mathbf{x}_1(t_l))}{\sum_{i=1}^{n_l+1} \theta_m(\mathbf{x}_i(t_l))}. \tag{3.32}$$

Finally, the likelihood for all M destinations is formed from the product of terms like $\mathcal{L}_m$.

It is also possible to allow for more than one leaver at each exit time. The asymptotic covariance matrix would be estimated in the usual way by the inverse of the negative Hessian of $\log \mathcal{L}$ evaluated at the maximum likelihood point. The relevant asymptotic distribution theory is the one appropriate as the number of people observed to exit becomes large.

This approach would seem to be useful in econometrics though it has not apparently yet been applied. It does have the drawback that components of the transition intensity that are the same for all people at the same time – such as $\alpha t^{\alpha-1}$ in the Weibull model – are not identifiable. It would also be rather difficult to allow for unmeasured heterogeneity in the transition intensities. The heterogeneity components, $\{v_i\}$, would have to be integrated out with respect to $g(v \mid t)$ or $g(v \mid T > t)$ depending on whether the person concerned was a leaver or not. On the other hand, if the data were drawn from two spells for the same person the person-specific heterogeneity would cancel from the likelihood but so also would all regressors that were the same for both spells. We shall have more to say in chapter 9 about the the use of multiple spell data in eliminating person-specific heterogeneity.

4   Unmeasured Heterogeneity in Single-Cycle
       Data

We now turn to consider problems that arise with unmeasured person-specific heterogeneity in the hazard function of a fully parametrically specified model. Suppose that the hazard function, given a scalar v, is

$$v\theta(t, \mathbf{x}; \gamma). \tag{4.1}$$

The function θ is specified up to the unknown parameter vector γ, of dimension k_γ, as a function of time and regressor variables $\mathbf{x}$.[6] The survivor function for the duration of stay, T, of an entrant to the state, conditional on v, is

$$\overline{G}(t \mid v; \mathbf{x}) = \exp\left\{-v \int_0^t \theta(u; \mathbf{x})\, du\right\}$$
$$= \exp\{-v\, z(t)\}, \qquad 0 \leq t < \infty. \tag{4.2}$$

The unmeasured heterogeneity term will be regarded as a realisation of a random variable V with distribution function $H(v; \mathbf{x})$.

When we allow for unmeasured heterogeneity in the hazard function we must normally eliminate such terms from the likelihood function in order to obtain consistent estimates of the parameters of the conditional hazard, for otherwise the number of unknown parameters will increase at the same rate as the number of people in the sample. There are several ways to do this. The use of partial or conditional likelihoods can eliminate such effects, as we shall explain in chapter 9. But they may also be eliminated by integration, in which we form the joint distribution of the data and the individual effect and then integrate out the latter. This then gives us a likelihood based on a mixture model of the type dealt with in chapter 4. Such mixture likelihood functions raise two sets of problems. The first set are computational, and we present these in the next section, 4.1. The second, more severe, set of problems are connected the choice of mixing distribution. We describe these in section 4.2.

4.1   Computational Issues in Fitting Parametric Mixtures

We assume that an investigator proposes to fit a model to flow data with a single destination with right censoring. The model involves a paramet-

---

[6] There is no reason why the regressors should not be time varying, if the hazard is defined conditionally on the complete path, $\mathbf{X}$, in the notation of section 2 of chapter 2. If, however, the hazard is defined conditionally only on the path to date the argument of this section does not apply.

rically specified conditional hazard, such as (4.1), and a parametrically specified mixing distribution $H(v; \mathbf{x})$. The unconditional survivor function, which is the one relevant to inference when V is unmeasured and variable, is

$$\overline{G}(t; \mathbf{x}) = \int_0^\infty \exp\{-v\, z(t)\}\, dH(v; \mathbf{x}). \qquad (4.3)$$

In this section we shall suppose that the distribution H is specified up to some unknown parameter vector η of dimension k_η. The total set of parameters we shall call ϕ of dimension $k = k_\gamma + k_\eta$. The mixture density function is

$$g(t; \mathbf{x}, \phi) = \int_0^\infty v\theta(t; \mathbf{x}, \gamma) \exp\{-vz(t; \gamma)\}\, dH(v; \mathbf{x}, \eta). \qquad (4.4)$$

For N possibly right censored observations the flow data log likelihood will be

$$L(\boldsymbol{\Phi}) = \sum_{i=1}^N [\delta_i \log g_i(t_i; \boldsymbol{\Phi}) + (1 - \delta_i) \log \overline{G}_i(t_i; \boldsymbol{\Phi})]. \qquad (4.5)$$

In one sense (4.3) is just another parametrically specified model of the type that occupied us in section 2 of this chapter. But the fact that it is a mixture model raises a number of special issues, two of which we shall deal with in this section. The first of these arises from the possibility that the mixture likelihood does not have a maximum interior to the parameter space. The second is the question of how best to maximise the mixture likelihood function. In order to focus on these issues we shall assume that the mixing distribution is specified up to a finite parameter vector and that it does not depend upon the regressor vector $\mathbf{x}$. This latter hypothesis may be difficult to defend, as we shall argue in section 4.2.

4.1.1   Non-Existence of an Interior Maximum

The first point about the fitting of a mixture distribution is that the data may be inconsistent with a mixture model, and this can lead to maximum likelihood estimates that lie on the boundary of the natural parameter space *at which the derivative of the log likelihood function is not zero*. In this case algorithms which seek a maximum by solving the likelihood equations will fail. An example will make the point.

Example 11 A Gamma Mixture
Suppose that the conditional distribution $g(t \mid v)$ is $\mathcal{E}(v)$ and thus has no unknown parameters and let $h(v)$ be the unit mean Gamma density

$\mathcal{G}(1, \eta)$, where η is the reciprocal of σ^2 which is the variance of V. Thus the only element of ϕ is σ^2. Then the mixture density function, (4.4), is

$$g(t; \sigma^2) = (1 + \sigma^2 t)^{1 + \sigma^{-2}}, \qquad (4.6)$$

and the log likelihood function is

$$L(\sigma^2) = -(1 + \sigma^{-2}) \sum_{i=1}^{N} \log(1 + \sigma^2 t_i). \qquad (4.7)$$

The natural parameter space for σ^2 is

$$\Omega = \{\sigma^2 \mid 0 \leq \sigma^2\}.$$

As $\sigma^2 \to \infty, L \to -\infty$, and as $\sigma^2 \to 0$ an application of l'Hôpital's rule shows that

$$\lim_{\sigma^2 \to 0} L = -\sum_{i=1}^{N} t_i.$$

The first derivative of the log likelihood is given by

$$\frac{\partial L}{\partial \sigma^2} = \sigma^{-4} \sum_{i=1}^{N} [\log(1 + \sigma^2 t_i) - \sigma^2 (1 + \sigma^2) t_i / (1 + \sigma^2 t_i)].$$

This derivative approaches zero as $\sigma^2 \to \infty$ and another application of l'Hôpital's rule shows that

$$\lim_{\sigma^2 \to 0} \frac{\partial L}{\partial \sigma^2} = \frac{1}{2} \left[\sum_{i=1}^{N} t_i^2 - 2 \sum_{i=1}^{N} t_i \right]$$
$$= S, \quad \text{say.} \qquad (4.8)$$

This statistic may be positive, negative, or zero. If it is positive the log likelihood is increasing at the origin and has a single maximum at a positive value of σ^2. If it is zero the log likelihood is decreasing for every positive value of σ^2 and the maximum likelihood estimate of σ^2 is zero. If it is negative the log likelihood is decreasing at the origin and may be shown to be always decreasing in Ω. In this case an algorithm that searches for a solution of the likelihood equation will produce a sequence of values for σ^2 that diverge to infinity. ∎

Since $\partial L / \partial \sigma^2$ is the score for σ^2 evaluated at the point $\sigma^2 = 0$ it forms the basis of a score test of the hypothesis that the mixture is degenerate with all its probability concentrated at the unit mean. We shall give the general version of this statistic in chapter 11. The implication of this example is that it is sensible to conduct a test for the plausibility of a mixture model before attempting to fit one. A score statistic which – in standard Normal form – is negative indicates potential computing problems in trying to fit a mixture model.

4.1.2   The EM Algorithm

We turn next to the appropriate choice of algorithm for fitting a mixture model. Consider the following argument. If the v_i were known, then inference about ϕ would be based on the log likelihood function constructed from the joint distribution of T and V, which is

$$L_0(\phi; \mathbf{t}, \mathbf{v}) = \sum_{i=1}^{N} [\log g(t_i \mid v_i; \gamma) + \log h(v_i \mid \eta)],$$

$$= \sum_{i=1}^{N} [\log v_i + \log \theta(t_i; \gamma) - v_i z(t_i; \gamma) + \log h(v_i; \eta)]. \qquad (4.9)$$

It may well be that the maximisation of L_0 is numerically straightforward. But, of course, the v_i are not known, and so L_0 cannot be calculated – *but it can be estimated.*

Let us take an initial guess at the parameter vector ϕ and call it ϕ^p. We then calculate the conditional distribution of V given t, with the parameters of that distribution set equal to ϕ^p, for each person. We then use these distributions to calculate the expected value of $L_0(\phi)$ with respect to the $\{V_i\}$ given the $\{t_i\}$. The result will be an expression depending upon two sets of parameters, the parameters ϕ^p used to calculate the conditional distributions of V given t, and the parameter vector ϕ which is the point at which L_0 is calculated. We call this conditional expectation

$$Q(\phi, \phi^p) = \mathrm{E}\,[L_0(\phi); \mathbf{V} \mid \mathbf{t}, \phi^p]. \qquad (4.10)$$

Q gives us an estimate of the full-data log likelihood, which we would like to maximise if only the v_i were known.

The next step is to maximise, not the unknown L_0, but our estimate of it, (4.10), *with respect to* ϕ. Then we let the maximising vector ϕ replace the initial guess ϕ^p, recalculate the conditional distributions using the new value of ϕ^p, recalculate Q, and maximise it again. This yields a new maximising vector and the cycle is repeated. Such a sequence of calculations is called the EM algorithm. The E refers to the calculation of Q, the Expectation of L_0, and the M refers to the Maximisation of Q, the E and M steps being undertaken alternately. The EM algorithm was originally invented to cope with inference in models with missing data, and since the heterogeneity problem is essentially a problem of missing data, it is the logical optimisation technique for econometricians to use in this context. We shall give some examples to illustrate the method.

Example 12 Gamma Mixtures in General

Consider a model in which the conditional hazard is arbitrary but the mixing distribution is unit mean Gamma. To calculate $Q(\phi, \phi^p)$ we must take expectations of (4.9) with respect to V_i and $\log V_i$ using the conditional distribution of V_i given t_i, the parameters of this conditional distribution being set equal to ϕ^p. Now since

$$h(v) \propto v^{\eta-1} e^{-\eta v} \qquad \text{and} \qquad g(t \mid v) \propto v\theta \exp\{-vz\},$$

the conditional distribution of V given t is

$$g(v \mid t) \propto v^\eta \exp\{-v[z(t; \gamma) + \eta]\}, \tag{4.11}$$

which is a Gamma distribution and, from appendix 1, we find that

$$E\,(V \mid t) = \frac{1 + \eta^p}{z(t; \gamma^p) + \eta^p},$$

$$E\,(\log V \mid t) = \psi(1 + \eta^p) - \log(z(t; \gamma^p) + \eta^p). \tag{4.12}$$

Here the p superscript indicates parameters calculated at the initial guess. Using these results to take expectations of (4.9) given t we get

$$Q(\phi, \phi^p) = \sum_{i=1}^{N} [\eta\{\psi(1 + \eta^p) - \log(z(t_i; \gamma^p))\}$$

$$- (z(t_i; \gamma) + \eta)\frac{1 + \eta^p}{z(t_i; \gamma^p) + \eta^p}$$

$$+ \log \theta(t; \gamma) - \log \Gamma(\eta) + \eta \log \eta]. \tag{4.13}$$

Notice the essential distinction between γ, η and γ^p, η^p. Construction of (4.13) is the E step of the algorithm. In the M step we maximise $Q(\phi, \phi^p)$ with respect to ϕ, that is, with respect to η and γ. The first-order condition for η is

$$\frac{\partial Q}{\partial \eta} = \sum_{i=1}^{N} \left[\psi(1 + \eta^p) - \log(z(t_i; \gamma^p)) - \frac{1 + \eta^p}{z(t_i; \gamma^p) + \eta^p} \right.$$

$$\left. + 1 - \psi(\eta) + \log \eta \phantom{\frac{1}{1}} \right] = 0. \tag{4.14}$$

This equation is of the form

$$c - \psi(\eta) + \log \eta = 0$$

and it has a unique positive solution if and only if $c < 0$. The equations to determine γ are

$$\frac{\partial Q}{\partial \gamma_j} = \sum_{i=1}^{N} \left[-v_i^p \frac{\partial z(t_i; \gamma)}{\partial \gamma_j} + \frac{\partial \log \theta(t_i; \gamma)}{\partial \gamma_j} \right] = 0, \qquad j = 1, 2, \ldots, K_\gamma,$$
(4.15)

where v_i^p is given by the first equation of (4.12) at $t = t_i$. These equations are those that would arise if the $\{\log v_i^p\}$ were known regressors appearing linearly in the log hazard with known unit coefficient. So if the conditional model is easy to maximise when the v_i are known the equations (4.15) will be equally easy to solve. ∎

For a numerical example consider

Example 13 Gamma Mixtures of Homogeneous Exponentials
Let $\theta(t_i; \gamma) = e^\gamma$ and $z(t_i; \gamma) = t_i e^\gamma$, so that the equation (4.15) becomes

$$\frac{\partial Q}{\partial \gamma} = \sum_{i=1}^{N} \left[-\frac{1+\eta^p}{t_i e^{\gamma^p} + \eta^p} t_i e^\gamma + 1 \right] = 0$$
(4.16)

with solution

$$e^{\gamma^{p+1}} = \frac{N}{\sum w_i t_i}; \qquad w_i = \frac{1+\eta^p}{t_i e^{\gamma^p} + \eta^p}.$$
(4.17)

Thus both expectation and maximisation steps are easy in this case. To illustrate the calculations we generated $N = 100$ observations from a Gamma mixture of Exponential distributions with $\sigma^2 = \eta = 1.0$ and $\gamma = 1$. The initial guesses were $\gamma^p = 0$ and $\eta^p = 2.0$. We then solved (4.17), for $\gamma^{p+1} = 0.455$ and (4.14) for $\eta^{p+1} = 1/0.498$. These were then used as new initial guesses in resolving (4.14) and (4.17) giving in turn new values of $\gamma = 0.677$ and $\eta = 1/0.534$. The complete iteration, in terms of σ^2 is shown it table 8.1.

The final column of the table gives the value of the log-likelihood function at each iteration. This log likelihood is the expression (4.5) specialised to the case of a Gamma mixture of a homogeneous Exponential distribution and without censoring. It is

$$L(\gamma, \eta) = \sum_{i=1}^{N} [\gamma - (1 + \sigma^{-2}) \log(1 + \sigma^2 t_i e^\gamma)].$$
(4.18)

Note that it is the object of the exercise to maximise L, *not* Q. Table 8.1 shows some typical characteristics of the EM algorithm; a rather large number of iterations are required compared to, say, an iteration

Table 8.1.   Example of the EM Algorithm

Iteration	γ	σ^2	$L(\gamma, \sigma^2)$
Initial Values	0.000	0.500	−94.786
1	0.455	0.498	−82.017
2	0.677	0.534	−78.368
5	0.947	0.694	−75.229
10	1.081	0.827	−74.550
15	1.114	0.859	−74.514
20	1.121	0.867	−74.512
26	1.123	0.869	−74.512
27	1.124	0.869	−74.512

using Newton's method, but at each iteration the likelihood never decreases.[7]   ∎

The EM algorithm would appear to be the most suitable general method for parametric mixtures; it also arises as a component of the most natural algorithm for fitting models in which the mixing distribution is estimated non-parametrically, as we shall see in chapter 9.

An iterative calculation needs an initial estimate of ϕ, and one way of getting these for a mixture model is by the method of moments. Denote the conditional integrated hazard by

$$vz = v \int_0^t \theta(u)\, du. \qquad (4.19)$$

Then since vZ is unit Exponential given v, when the covariates are exogenous, we have

$$\mathrm{E}\,(vZ \mid v) = 1 \Rightarrow \mathrm{E}\,(Z \mid v) = \frac{1}{v} \Rightarrow \mathrm{E}\,(Z) = \mathrm{E}\left(\frac{1}{V}\right); \qquad (4.20)$$

and

$$\mathrm{E}\,(Z^2 v^2 \mid v) = 2 \Rightarrow \mathrm{E}\,(Z^2 \mid v) = \left(\frac{2}{v^2}\right) \Rightarrow \mathrm{E}\,(Z^2) = \mathrm{E}\,\frac{2}{V^2}. \qquad (4.21)$$

Given a parametric model for the mixing distribution the expressions on the right can be evaluated in terms of η, while the sample moments of z can be expressed in terms of the data and of γ. Thus the system (4.20)

---

[7] Methods for speeding the convergence of the EM algorithm are becoming available; see Laird, Lange, and Stram (1987).

and (4.21), and higher moments if necessary, can be used to determine
initial estimates of the parameters. To illustrate the method, consider

Example 14 Initial Values for Example 13
For the unit mean Gamma mixing distribution we find from appendix
1 that

$$E\left(\frac{1}{V}\right) = \frac{1}{1-\sigma^2}, \qquad \sigma^2 < 1;$$

$$E\left(\frac{1}{V^2}\right) = \frac{1}{(1-\sigma^2)(1-2\sigma^2)}, \qquad \sigma^2 < \frac{1}{2}. \qquad (4.22)$$

In the model of example 4.3, $z = tc^\gamma = t\theta$ so the relations (4.22) imply

$$\bar{t} = \frac{1}{\theta(1-\sigma^2)},$$

$$\overline{t^2} = \frac{2}{\theta^2(1-\sigma^2)(1-2\sigma^2)}.$$

These equations may be solved to give the initial estimates of σ^2 and θ,

$$\tilde{\sigma}^2 = \frac{1-2R}{2-2R}, \qquad R = (\bar{t})^2/\overline{t^2};$$

$$\tilde{\theta} = \frac{1}{\bar{t}(1-\tilde{\sigma}^2)}. \qquad (4.23)$$

Note that this method gives a positive estimate of σ^2 only if $R < 1/2$,
which requires that the variance of T exceed the squared mean. Since T
is assumed to be Exponentially distributed given v and the presence of
v will raise the variance relative to the mean there would be no point in
trying to fit a mixture model if in fact the sample variance were found
to be *less than* the squared mean, for this evidence is inconsistent with
the presence of neglected heterogeneity – compare (4.8). One could also
use the moments of $\log ZV$ rather than those of ZV itself to provide
starting values, provided it is sensible to try to fit a mixture at all.
These moments always exist regardless of the value of σ^2.   ■

There is no need to confine oneself to the Gamma mixing distribution,
though as we have seen the algebra is particularly simple in that case.
A rather tractable alternative mixing distribution is a discrete mixture
over M points. Such finite mixtures have been intensively studied and
a good deal is known about their properties. We shall give an account
of such mixtures in the next chapter.

4.1.3   Mixture Models with Grouped Data

The equations (4.4) and (4.5) presume that we observe the individual duration or censoring times and must be modified if all we have are grouped data. In this case, conditional on the value of v, the probability that an observation falls into the m'th interval is

$$P(c_{m-1} \leq T < c_m \mid v) = \overline{G}(c_{m-1} \mid v) - \overline{G}(c_m \mid v),$$

and the unconditional probability is

$$P(c_{m-1} \leq T < c_m) = \int_0^\infty [\overline{G}(c_{m-1} \mid v) - \overline{G}(c_m \mid v)] \, dH(v) = \pi_m. \tag{4.24}$$

If we adopt the proportional hazards model with interval-specific regressors, (2.78), the hazard for person i, integrated to c_m, is,

$$\int_0^{c_m} \theta_i(s) \, ds = v \sum_{l=1}^m \mu_{li} e^{\beta l} = v S_m^i, \qquad m = 1, 2, \ldots, M-1,$$

so (4.24) becomes

$$P(c_{m-1} \leq T < c_m) = \int_0^\infty [e^{-v S_{m-1}^i} - e^{-v S_m^i}] \, dH(v)$$
$$= M(-s_{m-1}^i) - M(-s_m^i) = \pi_m^i, \tag{4.25}$$

where $M(s)$ is the moment generating function of $H(v)$ at s.

The likelihood contribution of person i who leaves in the m'th interval is just π_m^i. Calculation of these unconditional probabilities is straightforward when H has a moment generating function which can be expressed in closed form.

Example 15 Gamma Heterogeneity with Grouped Data
Since the unit mean Gamma distribution has moment generating function given by $M(s) = (1 - s\sigma^2)^{-1/\sigma^2}$ we find that

$$\pi_m = (1 + S_{m-1}\sigma^2)^{-1/\sigma^2} - (1 + S_m\sigma^2)^{-1/\sigma^2}, \qquad m = 1, 2, \ldots, M-1. \tag{4.26} \blacksquare$$

The Stable family of mixing distributions discussed in chapter 4, section 6.2 which has a closed form moment generating function, also appears to yield tractable expressions with grouped data though it has not been applied in this way as yet.

It should also be noted that the same considerations that we discussed in section 4.1.1 of this chapter apply here and it would be important to evaluate the score for σ^2 at $\sigma^2 = 0$ and with the remaining parameters at their maximum likelihood estimates on the same hypothesis. A negative score argues against the mixing hypothesis and points to computational problems in trying to estimate a mixture. A straightforward application of l'Hôpital's rule applied to the logarithmic derivatives of the π_m enables this score statistic to be calculated.

To apply the EM algorithm to fit a mixture we need the full data likelihood, which is

$$P\left(c_{m-1} \leq T < c_m, v\right) = [e^{-vS_{m-1}} - e^{-vS_m}]h(v). \qquad (4.27)$$

To form Q we take the expectation of the logarithm of this expression with respect to the distribution $p(v \mid c_{m-1} \leq t < c_m)$. Due to the form of the expression in square brackets this expectation will not, in general, be easy to calculate. This suggests that the EM algorithm may not be as appealing a procedure with grouped data as it is with raw data.

4.2   Mixing Distributions and the Sampling Scheme

The mixing distribution must be appropriate to the sampling scheme. If we are randomly stock sampling it must describe the variation of V over the stock and if we are sampling from the flow it must describe the variation of V over members of the flow. These distributions will differ. Different sampling schemes imply different data distributions. In this section we shall explore these differences and in particular we shall study what these differences imply for the appropriate choice of mixing distribution in a model with neglected heterogeneity. We shall postulate that our data derive from a rather simple stationary stochastic process, but our conclusions will hold much more generally.

We shall assume an alternating renewal process and denote the durations of stay in the two-states by T_1 and T_2 with means

$$E\left(T_m\right) = \mu_m(\mathbf{x}), \qquad m = 1, 2, \qquad (4.28)$$

given a time-constant regressor vector $\mathbf{x}$, which we shall later on suppose to have two components, one measured and the other not. We shall suppose the process is in equilibrium so that, from the results of chapter 5, the probability that at an arbitrary time point a person, randomly sampled from those with regressor vector $\mathbf{x}$, is in state m is

$$P \left(\text{state } m \text{ occupied at a fixed time point} \mid \mathbf{x}\right) = \frac{\mu_m(\mathbf{x})}{\mu_1(\mathbf{x}) + \mu_2(\mathbf{x})}.$$
$$(4.29)$$

We shall write $\mu(\mathbf{x}) = \mu_1(\mathbf{x}) + \mu_2(\mathbf{x})$. The sequence of times between entrances to state 1 or between entrances to state 2 form ordinary renewal processes each with renewal density $\mu(\mathbf{x})^{-1}$. It follows that the probability of observing a renewal, that is, a movement between states in a short interval of time of length dt, among those with regressor vector $\mathbf{x}$, is

$$P\,(\text{a change of state in the interval } dt \mid \mathbf{x}) = \frac{2dt}{\mu(\mathbf{x})}. \qquad (4.30)$$

We now think of a large population of people over whom the vector $\mathbf{x}$ is distributed with density function $f(\mathbf{x})$. Each person moves through time between states 1 and 2 according to the renewal process appropriate to his vector $\mathbf{x}$. At any particular time there will be a distribution of $\mathbf{x}$ over the people who are in state 1 at that time and similarly there will be a distribution of $\mathbf{x}$ over the people who are in state 2 at that time. There will also be a distribution of $\mathbf{x}$ over the people who move between states during an interval of time of length dt. We shall call $f(\mathbf{x})$ the *population distribution*; we shall call the distributions of $\mathbf{x}$ over the members of each state at a point of time the *stock distributions*; and we shall call the distribution of $\mathbf{x}$ over the movers during dt the *flow distribution*. We shall now deduce the stock and flow distributions.

We first consider the distributions of $\mathbf{x}$ over the members of each stock at an arbitrary point of time. These are

$$f(\mathbf{x} \mid \text{stock } m) = \frac{P\,(\text{stock } m \mid \mathbf{x}) f(\mathbf{x})}{\int P\,(\text{stock } m \mid \mathbf{u}) f(\mathbf{u})\,d\mathbf{u}}$$

$$\propto \frac{\mu_m(\mathbf{x})}{\mu(\mathbf{x})}\,f(\mathbf{x}), \qquad m = 1, 2. \qquad (4.31)$$

The missing factors of proportionality are the reciprocals of the proportions of the whole population in each stock. The first line of (4.31) follows from the law of conditional probability and the second line follows from (4.29). It will be seen that the distributions of $\mathbf{x}$ in the two stocks are generally different both from each other and from the population distribution.

Next we deduce the distribution of $\mathbf{x}$ among those changing states during a time period of length dt. This is

$$f(\mathbf{x} \mid \text{flow}) = \frac{P\,(\text{flow} \mid \mathbf{x})\,f(\mathbf{x})}{\int P\,(\text{flow} \mid \mathbf{u})\,f(\mathbf{u})\,d\mathbf{u}}$$

$$= \frac{dt\mu(\mathbf{x})^{-1}\,f(\mathbf{x})}{\int dt\mu(\mathbf{u})^{-1}\,f(\mathbf{u})\,d\mathbf{u}}$$

$$\propto \frac{f(\mathbf{x})}{\mu(\mathbf{x})}. \qquad (4.32)$$

The second line follows from (4.30). We see that the flow, stock, and whole population distributions are all different, in general.

Example 16 Multivariate Normality in the Flow
Suppose, for example, that the vector $\mathbf{x}$ has a multivariate Normal distribution *in the flow*, with mean zero and covariance matrix Σ.

$$\frac{f(\mathbf{x})}{\mu(\mathbf{x})} \propto \exp\{-\mathbf{x}'\Sigma^{-1}\mathbf{x}/2\},$$

and that

$$\mu_m(\mathbf{x}) = e^{\mathbf{x}'\gamma_m}, \qquad m = 1, 2.$$

Then the density of $\mathbf{x}$ in stock m is

$$f(\mathbf{x} \mid \text{stock } m) \propto \exp\{\mathbf{x}'\gamma_m - \mathbf{x}'\Sigma^{-1}\mathbf{x}/2\}$$
$$\propto \exp\{-(\mathbf{x} - \Sigma\gamma_m)'\Sigma^{-1}(\mathbf{x} - \Sigma\gamma_m)/2\}, \quad (4.33)$$

which is a Normal distribution of mean $\Sigma\gamma_m$ and covariance matrix Σ. As compared with the flow, the stock distributions have their means shifted away from zero but their correlations and variances remain the same. The whole population distribution is

$$f(\mathbf{x}) \propto [e^{\mathbf{x}'\gamma_1} + e^{\mathbf{x}'\gamma_2}]e^{-\mathbf{x}'\Sigma^{-1}\mathbf{x}/2}, \qquad (4.34)$$

which is a (non-Normal) mixture of two Normal distributions and is generally bimodal. ∎

It follows from (4.31) and (4.32) that

$$\frac{f(\mathbf{x} \mid \text{stock } m)}{f(\mathbf{x} \mid \text{flow })} \propto \mu_m(\mathbf{x}), \qquad m = 1, 2, \qquad (4.35)$$

where the constant of proportionality does not involve $\mathbf{x}$. The intuition behind (4.35) is straightforward. If there is some $\mathbf{x}$, that is some class of person, who, if they enter state m, stay there only briefly, then that value of $\mathbf{x}$ will be underrepresented in stock m relative to its frequency in the flow.

Let us now examine the implication of these results for the question of unmeasured heterogeneity in econometric models. Suppose that $\mathbf{x}$ has two components, an observed vector $\mathbf{x}_o$ and a vector $\mathbf{x}_u$ unobserved by the econometrician. Thus $\mathbf{x} = (\mathbf{x}_o \, \mathbf{x}_u)$, and we can write (4.35) as

$$\frac{f(\mathbf{x}_o, \mathbf{x}_u \mid \text{stock } m)}{f(\mathbf{x}_o, \mathbf{x}_u \mid \text{flow})} \propto \mu_m(\mathbf{x}_o, \mathbf{x}_u). \qquad (4.36)$$

Now if any two of the three terms in (4.36) factor into the product of a function of $\mathbf{x}_o$ alone and a function of $\mathbf{x}_u$ alone then the third one must also factor in this way. This remark has the following implications.

1. If μ_m factors and $\mathbf{x}_o$ and $\mathbf{x}_u$ are independent in the flow, then they are independent in stock m.

2. If μ_m factors and $\mathbf{x}_o$ and $\mathbf{x}_u$ are independent in stock m, then they are independent in the flow.

3. If $\mathbf{x}_o$ and $\mathbf{x}_u$ are independent in both stock m and in the flow then μ_m factors.

The last implication is particularly important for it tells us that if μ_m does *not* factor into the product of functions of $\mathbf{x}_o$ alone and $\mathbf{x}_u$ alone then they cannot be distributed independently in both stock m and in the flow. This in turn implies that if two econometricians estimate the same model which has a mean which does not factor and assume independence of the observed regressors $\mathbf{x}_o$ and the unobserved ones $\mathbf{x}_u$, but one samples the flow and the other the stock, they cannot both have a correct model. At least one must be mistaken. We give some examples to illustrate the point.

Example 17 Some Examples of Factoring
1. Let the unmeasured regressors $\mathbf{x}_u$ enter the model through the scalar $v = v(\mathbf{x}_u)$, which multiplies the hazard for stays in state m, and let the hazard itself be Weibull so that

$$\theta(t) = v(\mathbf{x}_u)\psi_1(\mathbf{x}_o)\alpha t^{\alpha-1}.$$

Then from (2.7) of chapter 2

$$\mu_m(\mathbf{x}_o, \mathbf{x}_u) = \{v(\mathbf{x}_u)\psi_1(\mathbf{x}_o)\}^{-1/\alpha},$$

which does factor into the product of functions of $\mathbf{x}_o$ alone and of $\mathbf{x}_u$ alone. Thus independence of $\mathbf{x}_o$ and $\mathbf{x}_u$ in the flow implies and is implied by their independence in stock m.

2. Suppose that the model for stays in state m is Inverse Gaussian with drift parameter $\mu = v(\mathbf{x}_u)\psi_1(\mathbf{x}_o)$. Then since the mean of an Inverse Gaussian variate is the reciprocal of the (positive) rate of drift we see that this model also implies the factoring property.

3. Suppose that the model for stays in state m – given $\mathbf{x}$ – is Log-normal with parameters $\mu = v(\mathbf{x}_u) + \psi_1(\mathbf{x}_o)$ and σ^2. Then from (4.5) of chapter 2

$$\mu_m(\mathbf{x}_o, \mathbf{x}_u) = \exp\{v(\mathbf{x}_u) + \psi_1(\mathbf{x}_o) + \sigma^2/2\},$$

so again the factoring property holds if σ^2 does not depend upon $\mathbf{x}$. ∎

The next example gives a large class of models for which the factoring property fails to hold.

Example 18 Factoring Fails in General Proportional Hazard Models
Consider the general proportional hazard model

$$\theta(t) = v(\mathbf{x}_u)\psi_1(\mathbf{x}_o)\psi_2(t)$$

so that

$$\mu_m = \mathrm{E}\,(T) = \int_0^\infty \exp\left\{-v\psi_1 \int_0^t \psi_2(s)\,ds\right\}\,dt. \qquad (4.37)$$

Now we have seen in example 17 that if $\psi_2 \propto t^{\alpha-1}$ then μ_m factors. It may be shown that the converse is true. This implies that the only proportional hazard model with multiplicative neglected heterogeneity for which the factoring condition holds is the Weibull. With this exception PH models do not have means that factor into the product of functions of $\mathbf{x}_o$ alone and $\mathbf{x}_u$ alone. Hence for such models $\mathbf{x}_u$ and $\mathbf{x}_o$ cannot be independent in both flow and stock.   ∎

Example 18 is a damaging one for econometricians who wish to allow for neglected heterogeneity in their models since it indicates that most models that econometricians would wish to entertain are likely to have correlation between neglected and included regressors over some population from which they could reasonably sample. It suggests that econometricians should look to methods of inference – and the data which they require – that do not require the hypothesis of independence of neglected and included regressors. One such class of methods involves treating the effect of neglected regressors as fixed effects and eliminating that effect by, for example, conditioning arguments. We shall discuss such methods in chapter 9.

There are reasons quite apart from the effect of alternative sampling schemes why one might expect to have the mixing distribution dependent upon the regressor vector. A simple example is that in which the regressor vector includes some aspect of the previous state history, for example, the length of the previous spell. There is a strong presumption that that regressor is informative about the value of V since if V affects the length of the current spell it presumably affects the length of the previous one. This situation is somewhat analogous to the correlation between an autocorrelated error term – V is autocorrelated because it is time-invariant – and a lagged value of the dependent variable in times series analysis. In this case one would want to have $H(v; \mathbf{x})$ depend upon

x. We shall comment further on this point in the next section, which deals with multiple-cycle data.[8]

As we observed at the beginning of this section, the discussion we have given does not apply in models with time-varying covariates and where the hazard at time t is defined conditionally on the covariate path to t. In this case it will be necessary to base the argument on the joint distribution of the exit time *and* the covariate path conditional on the heterogeneity term. It is this joint distribution which will be integrated with respect to the mixing distribution $H(v)$ to get the unconditional data distribution. It seems likely that the argument of this section can be suitably modified if the covariate process satisfies the exogeneity condition of chapter 2. But if it does not some difficult new problems arise. So far as the author is aware there is no published literature on the problems of mixture models with time-varying covariates and the problem awaits study.[9]

5   Multiple Cycle/Flow Data

We shall now give some results on fully parametric inference when the data consist of observations on N people each of whom passes though a sequence of discrete-states. This is sometimes called *event history* data. Each person is first observed on entry to some initial state and his subsequent transitions are determined by a matrix of transition intensities of the form given in equation (6.1) of chapter 5. The fact that people are selected from among the entrants to a given state is the flow character of the data; and the fact that people will experience multiple transitions is the multiple-cycle aspect of the data. We shall deal in this section with models which do not involve unmeasured heterogeneity.

Given that state l is entered at calendar time t and is still occupied at $t + s$, the transition out of l is determined by the set of $M - 1$ transition intensities $\theta_{lm}(t, s)$ which are such that $\theta_{lm}(t, s)\, ds$ gives the probability of a departure to state m in the short interval from $t+s$ to $t+s+ds$. This probability is conditional on occupation of l for s and upon the previous transition history. It is also conditional upon the level and time paths of regressor vectors to $t + s$. In particular, θ may depend upon the number

---

[8] Chamberlain (1985) has argued that there are often good economic reasons why there should be dependence between neglected heterogeneity terms and measured regressor variables.

[9] The work of Heckman and Singer (1985) seems to refer to models in which the hazard is conditional on the entire covariate path.

of previous entries to l, which is known as occurrence dependence, and it may depend upon the lengths of previous visits to state l, or indeed to other states, which is known as lagged duration dependence. Duration dependence without the qualification refers to the dependence of θ on s, the length of time state l has been occupied.

An example of occurrence dependence would be where the probability of leaving unemployment for employment depends upon the number of previous spells of unemployment that a person has undergone. An example of lagged duration dependence would be where that same probability depends upon the duration of previous spells of unemployment, if there were any.

The notation must recognise two-states, the origin and destination, two times, the calendar time and the elapsed duration, and it must also label both the person and the cycle. Notational complexity is thus inevitable. The notation we use attempts to improve on some previous efforts in econometrics, though it may not succeed. In section 5 of chapter 5 we defined binary indicators $\{d_m\}$ which equalled 1 if destination m was entered and 0 otherwise. Let us extend this by defining

$$d_{cm} = \begin{cases} 1, & \text{if } m \text{ is entered at the end of the } c\text{'th cycle,} \\ 0, & \text{otherwise.} \end{cases} \tag{5.1}$$

We shall write the transition intensities as

$$\theta^c_{lm}(t_c, s); \qquad l, m = 1, 2, \ldots, M, \quad l \neq m, \tag{5.2}$$

for the transition intensity from l to m in the c'th cycle where l was entered at calendar time t_c and has been occupied for s days. And, following previous notation, we shall write

$$z^c_{lm}(t_c, s) = \int_0^s \theta^c_{lm}(t_c, u)\, du; \qquad l, m = 1, 2, \ldots M, \quad l \neq m, \tag{5.3}$$

for the integrated transition intensities. Notice that we suppress the dependence of the transition intensities on parameters and regressors in this notation. The person identifier will be the superscript i.

If we observe person i through C_i cycles, his contribution to the log likelihood will be

$$L_i = \sum_{c=1}^{C_i} \sum_{l=1}^{M} \sum_{m=1}^{M} d^i_{c-1,l}[d^i_{cm} \log \theta^{ci}_{lm}(t^i_c, s^i_c) - z^{ci}_{lm}(t^i_c, s^i_c)]. \tag{5.4}$$

This is a direct generalisation of equation (5.13) of chapter 4, and of equation (2.1) of this chapter. The $\{s_c\}$ are the completed durations of each cycle and the $\{t_c\}$ the calendar times at which the cycles were commenced – if the cycles are contiguous in time then $t_{c+1} = t_c + s_c$. If observation ceases at a censoring time then the final cycle is concluded by entry to a dummy censoring destination whose transition intensity may be unspecified. Some transition intensities may be identically zero. The summations over l, m are taken to exclude the case $l = m$. If there are in fact repeat spells of the same type, these can be allowed for by use of the device described in chapter 5, section 6, example 15. The indicators $\{d_{0,l}\}$ identify the initial state. The likelihood is conditional on the initial state and on the state history prior to the start of observation. The total log likelihood is the sum of the $\{L_i\}$ over persons,

$$L = \sum_{i=1}^{N} L_i. \tag{5.5}$$

The asymptotic distribution theory is that appropriate as the number of people, N, becomes large, with the lengths of each history remaining fixed. It must be assumed that as N becomes large the numbers of each type of transition that are observed also increase.

The log likelihood (5.5) breaks up into separate contributions from each type of transition. If the transition intensities depend upon disjoint sets of parameters, $\{\gamma_{lm}\}$, possibly cycle-specific, the sub-log likelihoods can be maximised separately and the Hessian will be block diagonal.

If the model only has one type of state which is repeatedly re-entered, as with observations on a sequence of job tenures, the full complexity of (5.4) is really superfluous and a simpler log likelihood can be written down. Let $\theta^c(t, s)$ be the hazard function for the c'th cycle at calendar time t and elapsed duration s. Then for a person whom we observe for C_i cycles the last of which may be right censored, the log likelihood contribution will be

$$L_i = \sum_{c=1}^{C_{i-1}} [\log \theta^{ci}(t_c^i, s_c^i) - z^{ci}(t_c^i, s_c^i)] + d^i \log \theta^{C_i}(t_{C_i}, s_{C_i}) - z^{C_i}(t_{C_i}, s_{C_i}), \tag{5.6}$$

where z^c is the integrated hazard for the c'th cycle and d is a censoring indicator.

The number of econometric applications of this type of likelihood has so far been very few. Our aim in this section will be to enable the reader to follow and to contribute to that applied literature and to use the available software. We shall not attempt an exhaustive discussion but rather we shall make what we see as the important points in the context of a discussion of particular cases. In the next section we shall offer some comments on alternative ways of sampling multiple-state processes and their implications for the estimation of models with neglected heterogeneity.

Example 19 A Poisson Process

For a single state model whose hazard is θ independent of t, s, c, and the transition history, we have a Poisson process, that is, repeated, independent, $\mathcal{E}(\theta)$ variates. If $\log \theta^i = \mathbf{x}_i'\gamma$ we have the model studied in example 2.1 of this chapter with $\sum C_i$ observations of which up to N are right censored. ∎

Example 20 Occurrence Dependence

Let us modify the last example by allowing θ to vary from cycle to cycle. This gives us a model for occurrence dependence in a one-state model. It might be a simple model for the intervals between births to a particular woman. The waiting time to the next birth depends on the number of previous pregnancies. The simplest version of this model might be

$$\log \theta^c = \alpha_c + \mathbf{x}'\gamma \qquad (5.7)$$

in which the log hazards differ only in the constant term. The analysis of this model is a simple extension of that of example 1 and we omit it.

Equation (5.7) is a reduced form model for occurrence dependence – there is no economic reason why it should be modelled this way and the parameters have not been given any economic-theoretical interpretation. Flinn and Heckman (1982) have suggested a simple structural model for occurrence dependence in the context of optimal job search – chapter 6, section 2 – in which the wage offer distribution faced by an individual depends upon his job history. This gives rise to a specification in which the hazard for leaving a spell of unemployment depends upon the number of previous spells that have occurred. ∎

Example 21 Time-Dependent Poisson Process

In this model the hazard is

$$\theta(t, s) = \theta(t + s), \qquad (5.8)$$

which varies only with the current calendar time. An example would be where the hazard depends upon a calendar-time-varying regressor $\mathbf{x}(t)$. The log likelihood for a particular person for whom we observe C complete spells is

$$L = \sum_{c=1}^{C} [\log \theta \{\mathbf{x}(t_{c-1} + s_c)\} - z(t_{c-1} + s_c)], \qquad (5.9)$$

where

$$z(t_{c-1} + s_c) = \int_0^{s_c} \theta\{\mathbf{x}(t_{c-1} + u)\}\, du = \int_{t_{c-1}}^{t_{c-1}+s_c} \theta\{\mathbf{x}(u)\}\, du. \qquad (5.10)$$

If the spells are contiguous in time so that $t_{c-1} + s_c = t_c$, L simplifies to

$$L = \sum_{c=1}^{C} [\log \theta\{\mathbf{x}(t_c)\} - z(t_c)].$$ (5.11)

A simple parametric form might be

$$\log \theta(t) = \alpha + \mathbf{x}_1 \gamma_1 + \gamma_2 x_2(t),$$ (5.12)

in which $\mathbf{x}_1$ contains time-constant regressors and t is calendar time.

It would be possible to combine (5.12) and (5.7) to obtain a model with both occurrence dependence and a time-varying regressor. In the birth interval example x_2 might be some function of the woman's age, giving a model in which birth probabilities depend upon both age and parity. ∎

Example 22 Lagged Duration Dependence
The hazard for cycle c might be allowed to depend upon the length of the previous spell, for example, as

$$\log \theta^c = \alpha_c + \mathbf{x}' \gamma + \beta s_{c-1}.$$ (5.13)

This gives a model analogous to a first-order autoregression. One would need to know the duration of the spell prior to the start of observation, if there was one. If there was not, put $s_0 = 0$, but it would be important to allow for the cycle-specific intercept in this case. In this model the lagged duration, s_{c-1}, effectively acts as an extra, cycle-specific regressor variable.

The log likelihood for the model (5.13) with C complete spells observed for each of N people is

$$L = \sum_{i=1}^{N} \sum_{c=1}^{C} [\alpha_c + \mathbf{x}_i' \gamma + \beta s_{c-1,i} - s_{ci} \exp\{\alpha_c + \mathbf{x}_i' \gamma + \beta s_{c-1,i}\}],$$

and the scores are

$$\frac{\partial L}{\partial \alpha_c} = \sum_{i=1}^{N} [1 - s_{ci} \theta^{ci}], \qquad c = 1, 2, \ldots, C,$$ (5.14)

$$\frac{\partial L}{\partial \gamma_j} = \sum_{i=1}^{N} \sum_{c=1}^{C} x_{ij} [1 - s_{ci} \theta^{ci}], \qquad j = 1, 2, \ldots, K,$$ (5.15)

$$\frac{\partial L}{\partial \beta} = \sum_{i=1}^{N} \sum_{c=1}^{C} s_{c-1,i} [1 - s_{ci} \theta^{ci}].$$ (5.16)

One interesting consequence of these equations is the form taken by the score statistic for the null hypothesis of no lagged duration dependence, $\beta = 0$. Using the likelihood equations for α_c and γ we find that, at $\beta = 0$,

$$\frac{\partial L}{\partial \beta} \propto \sum_{c=1}^{C} \text{cov}(s_c \, s_{c-1}). \tag{5.17}$$

The score test for no lagged duration dependence is based on the sum of the (cross-sectional) first-order autocovariances of the durations.   ∎

We shall now examine some multiple-state models.

Example 23 The Continuous-Time Markov Chain

In this model, which we discussed in chapter 5, section 6, the transition intensities are independent of t, s, c, and the transition history. Thus they can be written as the constants $\{\theta^i_{lm}\}$ and the integrated transition intensities are

$$z^{ci}_{lm} = s^i_c \theta^i_{lm}. \tag{5.18}$$

The log likelihood contribution of person i, (5.4), reduces to

$$L_i = \sum_{c=1}^{C_i} \sum_{l=1}^{M} \sum_{m=1}^{M} d^i_{c-1,l}[d^i_{cm} \log \theta^i_{lm} - s^i_c \theta^i_{lm}],$$

$$= \sum_{l=1}^{M} \sum_{m=1}^{M} [N^i_{lm} \log \theta^i_{lm} - T^i_l \theta^i_{lm}],$$

where

$$N^i_{lm} = \sum_{c-1}^{C_i} d^i_{c-1,l} d^i_{cm}; \qquad T^i_l = \sum_{c=1}^{C_i} s^i_c. \tag{5.19}$$

The interpretation of these quantities is that N^i_{lm} is the total number of $l \rightarrow m$ transitions made by person i, and T^i_l is the total time spent by person i in state l. The total log likelihood is

$$L = \sum_{l=1}^{M} \sum_{m=1}^{M} \sum_{i=1}^{N} [N^i_{lm} \log \theta^i_{lm} - T^i_l \theta^i_{lm}]. \tag{5.20}$$

If θ does not depend upon i the log likelihood reduces further to

$$L = \sum_{l=1}^{M} \sum_{m=1}^{M} [N_{lm} \log \theta_{lm} - T_l \theta_{lm}], \tag{5.21}$$

where N_{lm} and T_l are the sums of (5.19) over people. The likelihood equations for the $\{\theta_{lm}\}$ become

$$\frac{\partial L}{\partial \theta_{lm}} = \frac{N_{lm}}{\theta_{lm}} - T_l = 0, \tag{5.22}$$

with diagonal Hessian

$$\frac{\partial^2 L}{\partial \theta_{lm}^2} = -\frac{N_{lm}}{\theta_{lm}^2}. \tag{5.23}$$

If one state is a censoring destination, to which the transition intensities are unspecified, these equations remain valid for transitions among the remaining states.

From (5.22) we see that the maximum likelihood estimator of the $l \to m$ transition intensity is given by

$$\hat{\theta}_{lm} = \frac{N_{lm}}{T_l}, \tag{5.24}$$

which is the rate of leaving l for m per unit time period, sometimes known as the empirical transition intensity. Equation (5.24) can also be written as

$$\hat{\theta}_{lm} = \frac{N_{lm}}{N_l} \frac{N_l}{T_l} = \frac{\hat{\pi}_{lm}}{\bar{t}_l}. \tag{5.25}$$

Here N_l is the total number of visits to state l. The numerator in (5.25) is the maximum likelihood estimator of the probability that when departure from l occurs, it is to m. This probability is an element of the transition probability matrix for the discrete-time Markov chain imbedded in the CTMC, and $\hat{\pi}$ is the estimator that would be formed if we knew only the sequences of states visited and were ignorant of the durations of stay. The denominator in (5.25) is the mean time spent in l and is the estimator of the expected time spent in visits to l that we would construct if we knew the times spent in each state but were ignorant of the order in which those states were visited. Equation (5.25) is the empirical counterpart of the theoretical identity

$$\theta_{lm} = \frac{\theta_{lm}}{\theta_l} \theta_l$$

since the first term in the product is just π_{lm} and the second is the hazard for leaving l which is the reciprocal of the mean duration of stays in l.

Equation (5.23) shows that the estimator is unique with asymptotic variance, which can be estimated by

$$\text{var}(\hat{\theta}_{lm}) = \frac{\hat{\theta}_{lm}}{T_l}. \tag{5.26}$$

This shows that the effective sample size so far as estimation of θ_{lm} is concerned is T_l, the total time spent in state l by all people.   ∎

The algebra of the flow data likelihood function for other multiple-cycle and -state models raises no new issues of principle since they are obtained by multiplying together single-cycle likelihoods in the manner described at the start of this section and in chapter 5. Important new issues do arise, however, when we sample such processes in other ways, and in the next section we shall examine one of these.

6   Other Multiple-Cycle Sampling Schemes

There are many other ways of collecting multiple-cycle data that are informative about a set of parametrically specified transition intensities besides sampling the flow between states. We shall give an account in this section of one such method of which a study has appeared in the otherwise rather sparse econometric literature. In the notes to this chapter we refer to some published work on these problems that has appeared in related branches of statistics.

6.1   Discrete-Time Sampling

Suppose that we observe a continuous-time, multiple-state, process at $n+1$ equally spaced discrete-time points and that at each point we obtain less than complete information about the transitions that have been experienced since the previous observation time. As compared with full observation of the process we lose information and a number of questions arise. What are likelihoods for such discrete-time sampling? How much information is lost by the incomplete observation of the process? We shall study these questions by examining a tractable example which points the way to more complex generalisations. The exposition follows De Stavola (1986).

We assume that the process being studied is known to be an alternating Poisson process with unknown transition intensities θ_{12}, θ_{21}. The process is observed at times we shall label 0, δ, 2δ, ..., $n\delta$ and the information collected at each time point is the identity of the state then occupied. Let $Y_t = 1$ or 2 indicate the state occupied at discrete sampling time t. Then the likelihood may be constructed by calculating the probability distributions of Y_t given Y_{t-1}, where $t-1$ is the observation point preceding t. It is unnecessary to condition on earlier values of Y because of the Markov property of the process. To show how these calculations are done consider the distributions of Y_δ given Y_0 which, from (4.6.15), are

$$P\,(Y_\delta = 1 \mid Y_0 = 1) = \{\theta_{21} + \theta_{12}e^{-\theta\delta}\}/\theta = \pi_{11},$$
$$P\,(Y_\delta = 1 \mid Y_0 = 2) = \{\theta_{21} - \theta_{21}e^{-\theta\delta}\}/\theta = \pi_{21},$$
$$P\,(Y_\delta = 2 \mid Y_0 = 1) = \{\theta_{12} - \theta_{12}e^{-\theta\delta}\}/\theta = \pi_{12},$$
$$P\,(Y_\delta = 2 \mid Y_0 = 2) = \{\theta_{12} + \theta_{21}e^{-\theta\delta}\}/\theta = \pi_{22}, \qquad (6.1)$$

for $\theta = \theta_{12} + \theta_{21}$. These expressions give the distributions of Y_δ conditional on Y_0, and, in general, of Y_t given Y_{t-1}. The likelihood contribution of one person observed at $n+1$ points and conditional on the state occupied at time 0 is then

$$\mathcal{L}(\theta_{12}, \theta_{21}) = \prod_{t=1}^{n} p(Y_t \mid Y_{t-1}). \qquad (6.2)$$

If the process is assumed to be in equilibrium when first observed the probability that state 1 is occupied at time 0 is, from chapter 5, given by θ_{21}/θ and the likelihood unconditional on the initial state is arrived at by multiplying (6.2) by the initial state probability.

Let us now use this likelihood to study the loss of efficiency in estimation due to incomplete observation. To do this we need to evaluate the information matrix corresponding to (6.2) and the information matrix corresponding to the same process fully observed from time 0 to time $n\delta$. This latter, or rather its logarithm, is a special case of (5.4) of this chapter. The calculation of these expectations is quite feasible because of the simple character of the alternating Poisson process. The details are explained in de Stavola (1986). Having obtained the two information matrices, they may be inverted to obtain the asymptotic covariance matrices of the maximum likelihood estimators of θ_{12} and θ_{21} and from these, comparisons of efficiency may be made. The asymptotic relative efficiency (ARE) of an estimator is defined to be the ratio of its asymptotic variance for the fully observed process to its variance for the discretely observed process. ARE will generally be a positive fraction. The asymptotic distribution theory is that arising as the number of people becomes large with n and δ fixed.

The results of these calculations depend upon n, the number of sampling points, δ, the interval between them, and the functions of θ_{12} and θ_{21} which are to be estimated. This last point is important for it may be the case that one is interested in estimating not the theta's themselves but rather, say, $\lambda = \theta_{21}/\theta$, the long-run proportion of time spent in state 2. The ratio λ might correspond to the unemployment rate if the states are employed and not employed. The main conclusions of the calculations of ARE are as follows.

For estimation of λ ARE depends upon the products $\theta_{12}\delta$ and $\theta_{21}\delta$, and the greater these products the greater is the efficiency of discrete sampling. The reason for this is that these products are the ratios of the sampling interval to the mean durations of stay in each state. Large values of these ratios imply that few state occupations fail to be observed by the discrete-time sampling scheme. Very little efficiency is lost by the discrete-time sampling scheme if the products $\theta\delta$ are both near unity so that the sampling interval is about the same as the mean durations.

For estimation of the $\{\theta_{lm}\}$ themselves the conclusions are rather different. As for λ the efficiency of discrete-time sampling increases with the products $\theta\delta$ but the efficiency loss is much greater for the same values of $\theta\delta$. One needs an observation interval much smaller than the mean durations before the loss of efficiency due to discrete-time sampling becomes negligible. The loss of the possibility of observing such state occupations as occur wholly within the sampling interval is much more damaging for estimation of the theta's than for estimation of λ.

The moral of this study is that sometimes little information is lost by observing a continuous-time process at discrete-time points – and presumably there would be a saving in sampling cost – but the loss depends upon precisely which parameters are the object of estimation.

7 Unmeasured Heterogeneity in Multiple-Cycle Data

We shall now consider some consequences of models in which an unmeasured person-specific heterogeneity term appears in the specification of the transition intensities. The important points can be made by considering a process which starts at time $t = 0$ and is observed, for each person, for exactly two cycles. There are M states and we condition on the initial state which we shall label state l. The heterogeneity term will be labelled v, as usual, and it is regarded as a realisation of a random variable V. The distribution function of V among entrants to state l at time $t = 0$ is $H_l(v)$ independently of the values of any regressor variables at that time. There are two types of regressor. The first are regressors which are independent of the elapsed duration within a spell, but may vary from spell to spell. They are denoted x^c in spell c. The second are defined external regressors or covariates which vary as a function of time measured from the start of the process. Conditional on their values at the start of each spell they are exogenous covariates in the sense of chapter 2, section 3. Their paths to t are denoted $\mathbf{X}(t)$. The duration of spell j, measured from entry to the state then occupied, is T_j. The hazard function for exit from the initial state is

$$\theta^1_{lm}(s; \mathbf{X}(s), \mathbf{x}^1, v), \qquad m = 1, 2, \ldots, M \quad l \neq m.$$

If we observe a person leave for state m at t_1 the probability of this, given $V = v$, is

$$\theta^1_{lm}(t_1; \mathbf{X}(t_1), \mathbf{x}^1, v) \exp\left\{-\int_0^{t_1} \theta^1_l(s; \mathbf{X}(s), \mathbf{x}^1, v)\, ds\right\}, \qquad (7.1)$$

where, as in chapter 5, $\theta_l = \sum_{l \neq m} \theta_{lm}$. For the second spell the transition intensities, conditional on the origin state being m and the origin time being t_1 and upon v are

$$\theta^2_{mn}(s; \mathbf{X}(t_1 + s), \mathbf{x}^2, v), \qquad n = 1, 2, \ldots, M, \quad n \neq m.$$

The probability of the second cycle of information, conditional on the origin state, the start time, and v is then

$$\theta^2_{mn}(t_2; \mathbf{X}(t_1 + t_2), \mathbf{x}^2, v) \exp\left\{-\int_0^{t_2} \theta^2_m(s; \mathbf{X}(t_1 + s), \mathbf{x}^2, v)\, ds\right\}. \quad (7.2)$$

The likelihood formed from the two cycles of information, given v, is then the product of (7.1) and (7.2) and unconditional on v it is this product integrated with respect to $H_l(v)$. This is a correct likelihood, and provided the assumptions of the model are right, maximum likelihood estimators would be consistent for the parameters of the transition intensities and of H.

On the other hand, it may be that an investigator proposes to base his inference solely on the second cycle data and constructs his likelihood from

$$\int \theta^2_{mn}(t_2; \mathbf{X}(t_1 + t_2), \mathbf{x}^2, v)$$

$$\times \exp\left\{-\int_0^{t_2} \theta^2_m(s; \mathbf{X}(t_1 + s), \mathbf{x}^2, v)\, ds\right\} dH_m(v). \quad (7.3)$$

This would be the wrong density because the choice of mixing distribution neglects the conditioning on t_1, and V and T_1 must generally be correlated. Essentially, there is a correlation here between the 'autocorrelated error term', V, and a regressor variable because that variable depends upon the previous state history in the form of t_1. The same difficulty would arise even in the absence of time-varying covariates if the duration-invariant regressor for any spell depended upon some aspect of the state history, as with occurrence or lagged duration dependence.

This is very similar to the standard time-series problem of estimating a regression model with regressors which include lagged values of the dependent variable and where the errors are autocorrelated. A common way of obtaining consistent estimates for that problem is by the method of instrumental variables. It may be possible to use the same approach in the present context, but the possibility has not, apparently, been studied.

Flinn and Heckman (1982) have proposed parametric forms for the way in which a scalar v enters the transition intensities. They allow the same v in each transition intensity but let it have coefficient α_{lm} when v appears in the l to m transition intensity. This specification goes some way towards allowing the heterogeneity to vary among transitions yet ensures that the integration in (7.3) remains one-dimensional in the interests of tractability.

Practical econometric experience with multiple-cycle models including unobserved heterogeneity is so far extremely limited. Moreover, the theory needs a good deal of further study, particularly with regard to the role of endogenous time-varying covariates and to the possibilities of instrumental variable type estimators.

8   Least Squares Estimators

In this section we shall examine some Least Squares (LS) estimators. We saw in chapter 3 that a number of parametric models imply that the logarithm of duration has a homoscedastic linear regression on a set of time-invariant regressor variables,

$$\log T = \mathbf{x}'\gamma + U, \tag{8.1}$$

where U has mean zero and constant variance σ^2. Now this relation applies only in the absence of time-varying regressors and estimation of this model is straightforward only in the absence of censoring. Moreover, models based in economic theory usually are more naturally specified in terms of the hazard rather than the regression function. For these reasons econometricians working with duration and transition data have found Least Squares regression procedures to be of only marginal interest. But since this approach has historically been central to econometrics we shall devote some space to an account of LS procedures. We deal first with the case in which we have uncensored flow data on a single duration for each of N individuals together with the time-constant regressor vector.

Least Squares regression applied to (8.1) will give unbiased estimators of γ which are of minimum variance in the class of estimators which are linear functions of $\log T$, but which are, in general, inefficient compared to maximum likelihood estimators. Remaining parameters of the model can be determined from the second and higher moments of the residuals. These method of moments estimators are consistent under the weak conditions that ensure that sample moments consistently estimate population ones. Let us consider some examples.

Example 24 The Exponential Model
We saw in chapter 2, section 2, that the hazard model $\log \theta = -\gamma_0' - \mathbf{x}'\gamma_1$ implies the linear model

$$\log T = \gamma_0 + \mathbf{x}'\gamma_1 + U, \qquad \mathrm{E}(U) = 0, \quad \mathrm{var}(U) = \psi'(1), \qquad (8.2)$$

where $\gamma_0 = \gamma_0' + \psi(1)$. The Least Squares estimator of $\gamma = (\gamma_0 \, \gamma_1)$ denoted by $\tilde\gamma$ has mean γ and covariance matrix

$$\mathrm{var}(\tilde\gamma) = \psi'(1)(\mathbf{X}'\mathbf{X})^{-1}, \qquad (8.3)$$

from standard Least Squares theory. Here $\mathbf{X}$ is the usual regressor matrix. From (2.23) the inverse of the information matrix for maximum likelihood estimation is

$$\mathcal{I}^{-1} = (\mathbf{X}'\mathbf{X})^{-1}. \qquad (8.4)$$

Comparing (8.3) and (8.4) we see that asymptotically every element of $\tilde\gamma$ has efficiency $1/\psi'(1) = 0.61$. Use of Least Squares on such data, given that the correct model is Exponential, is equivalent to throwing away 39 percent of one's data, which is not recommended. ∎

Example 25 The Weibull Model
The Weibull hazard model $\log \theta = \gamma_0 + \mathbf{x}'\gamma_1 + \log \alpha + (\alpha - 1)\log t$ implies the linear model

$$\log T = \beta_0 + \mathbf{x}'\beta_1 + U; \qquad \mathrm{E}(U) = 0, \quad \mathrm{var}(U) = \frac{\psi'(1)}{\alpha^2}, \qquad (8.5)$$

where

$$\beta_0 = \frac{-\gamma_0 + \psi(1)}{\alpha}, \quad \beta_1 = -\frac{\gamma_1}{\alpha}. \qquad (8.6)$$

Again from standard theory the Least Squares estimator of β has covariance matrix

$$\mathrm{var}(\tilde\beta) = \frac{\psi'(1)}{\alpha^2}(\mathbf{X}'\mathbf{X})^{-1}. \qquad (8.7)$$

The parametrisation used in the treatment of the Weibull model in example 1.4 of this chapter is in terms of γ rather than β, but a little algebra applied to (2.37) yields the inverse information matrix for β_1 as

$$\mathcal{I}^{-1} = \frac{1}{\alpha^2}(\mathbf{X}'\mathbf{X})^{-1},$$

so that the inefficiency of the LS estimators of the slope coefficients is the same as in the Exponential model.

More interesting is the LS estimator of α, which would be

$$\tilde{\alpha} = \frac{\sqrt{\psi'(1)}}{s}, \tag{8.8}$$

where s^2 is the LS residual variance in the regression (8.5). Recalling that αU is the logarithm of an $\mathcal{E}(1)$ variate and using the formulae of appendix 1 and standard results for the variance of a function of quantities with variances of $O(N^{-1})$ we find that

$$\text{var}(\tilde{\alpha}) = N^{-1}\alpha^2(1.1000)$$

asymptotically. Comparing this with the asymptotic variance of the maximum likelihood estimator from the last element of (2.38) we see that $\tilde{\alpha}$ has asymptotic efficiency equal to $1/(1.1 \times \psi'(1)) = 0.55$. The LS estimator of α is even less efficient than that of β_1. Its use amounts to discarding 45 percent of one's data, given that the Weibull model is correct.

These efficiency losses are severe but to set against them it might be argued that Least Squares estimators could be expected to retain consistency for a wider set of data generating processes than fully parametric maximum likelihood estimators. It is not obvious that this is true, and we shall consider the point further in chapter 9, which deals with issues of misspecification.

With right censoring so that we observe only the minimum of two quantities, one of which satisfies a linear model and the other being a censoring time, the situation is more complicated. The observed dependent variable does not satisfy a linear regression model and so Least Squares is inappropriate. One can construct a dependent variable which does satisfy such a model but to do so requires an estimate of the error distribution. If this distribution is known up to a finite set of parameters then there is no point in doing Least Squares since the method of maximum likelihood is available and efficient. If it is not so known then it must be estimated non-parametrically. There is a small but growing recent literature on the semi-parametric estimation of censored regression models which we shall not attempt to exposit in this book. We refer the reader, in particular, to the paper by Horowitz (1987).

9   Inference about Structural Models

In chapter 6 we described some structural models and gave the likelihood functions to which they lead. In this section we shall describe the principal issues that arise in using data from N people to make inferences about the parameters of those models. To a large extent standard likelihood theory may be applied and where this is so we have no special remarks to make, but there are three special issues that arise with these models that merit some discussion.

1. Minima and maxima typically occur in structural econometric models, which is natural enough since much of microeconomics is concerned with minimisation and maximisation problems. But the asymptotic distribution theory of sample extremes is not the same theory as that of sample means and other central moments, which features in standard likelihood problems. Hence non-standard distribution theory of estimators is common in inference about structural models.

2. Allowance for sources of heterogeneity between people that have not been measured by the econometrician is usually necessary to ensure consistent estimation of structural parameters. Such allowance is made more complicated by the role of sample extremes in the likelihood function.

3. Severe computational problems arise in estimating non-stationary structural models and in examining their goodness of fit.

We shall, as usual, exposit these problems and their solution through a series of examples.

Example 26 Stationary Job Search with Accepted Wages
In chapter 6, equation (2.10), we gave the joint density function of the completed search duration and the wage accepted in a stationary optimal job search model as

$$g(w,t) = \lambda f(w) \exp\{-\lambda \overline{F}(\xi)t\}, \qquad w \geq \xi \geq 0. \qquad (9.1)$$

To avoid inessential complications let us neglect censoring and assume that we observe both T and W for each of N people. Initially we shall also suppose that λ and ξ are unknown constants, the same for everyone. Thus we shall not use the optimality condition, (2.6) of chapter 5, in the estimation method. We denote the unknowns of a specified parametric model for the wage offer distribution, $f(w)$, by γ. Thus the log likelihood function will be

$$L(\lambda, \xi, \gamma) = \sum_{i=1}^{N} [\log \lambda + \log f(w_i; \gamma) - \lambda \overline{F}(\xi; \gamma)t_i];$$

$$w_i \geq \xi \geq 0, \quad i = 1, 2, \ldots, N. \tag{9.2}$$

Consider maximising L with respect to λ, ξ, γ. Since a survivor function, such as $\overline{F}$, is a decreasing function the likelihood function is increasing in ξ. In view of the sample space constraint in (9.2) the value of ξ which maximises the likelihood will be

$$\hat{\xi} = \min\{w_i\} = w_{(1)}. \tag{9.3}$$

The ML estimator of ξ is the sample minimum wage.

We can now substitute this estimate into L – concentrating it with respect to this parameter – to get

$$L(\lambda, \gamma) = N \log \lambda + \sum_{i=1}^{N} \log f(w_i; \gamma) - \lambda \overline{F}(w_{(1)}; \gamma) \sum_{i=1}^{N} t_i. \tag{9.4}$$

This concentrated log likelihood function can now be maximised in the usual way and the likelihood equations may be written

$$\frac{\partial L}{\partial \lambda} = \frac{N}{\lambda} - \overline{F}(w_{(1)}; \gamma) \sum_{i=1}^{N} t_i = 0, \tag{9.5}$$

$$\frac{\partial L}{\partial \gamma_j} = \sum_{i=1}^{N} \frac{\partial \log f(w_i; \gamma)}{\partial \gamma_j} - N \frac{\partial \log \overline{F}(w_{(1)}; \gamma)}{\partial \gamma_j} = 0, \quad j = 1, 2, \ldots, K. \tag{9.6}$$

The solutions of these equations have easy interpretations. The ML estimator of λ, from (9.5), satisfies

$$\hat{\lambda} = \frac{1}{\bar{t} \, \overline{F}(w_{(1)}; \hat{\gamma})}. \tag{9.7}$$

We saw in chapter 6, section 2, that acceptable job offers in this model arrive in a Poisson stream at rate $\lambda \overline{F}(\xi)$ so the mean waiting time to the first acceptable offer is

$$\mathrm{E}\,(T) = \frac{1}{\lambda \overline{F}(\xi; \gamma)}.$$

Equation (9.7) is just the sample analogue of this relation. The equations for γ, (9.6), are those which would have arisen if the likelihood for γ had been

$$\mathcal{L}(\gamma) = \prod_{i=1}^{N} \frac{f(w_i; \gamma)}{\overline{F}(w_{(1)}; \gamma)}.$$

This is the likelihood for random samples from the wage offer distribution truncated on the left at the known point $w_{(1)}$ so the estimates of Gamma are got by maximising a pseudo likelihood in which the unknown reservation wage is replaced by its maximum likelihood estimate. Again, this is a common sense procedure.

Now let us consider the asymptotic distribution theory for $\hat{\xi} = w_{(1)}$ in this model. The variate $w_{(1)}$ is the minimum in a random sample of N observations from the wage offer distribution $f(w)$ truncated on the left at ξ. It is clear that $w_{(1)}$ will converge stochastically to ξ, so let us consider the asymptotic distribution of

$$z_N = \sqrt{N}(w_{(1)} - \xi).$$

For reasonable wage offer distributions this random variable has a limiting distribution which is degenerate at the point zero. A necessary and sufficient condition for this is provided by the following theorem.

Theorem 1   *The limiting distribution of z_N is degenerate at zero if and only if*

$$\lim_{N \to \infty} \left[\frac{\overline{F}(\xi + z/\sqrt{N})}{\overline{F}(\xi)} \right]^N = 0, \qquad z > 0. \qquad (9.8)$$

Proof: The probability that the smallest of N observations from F exceeds z is the same as the probability that they all do – if the smallest exceeds z they all do, and if they all do then the smallest does. Hence the survivor function of $w_{(1)}$ at z is

$$\overline{G}(z) = \left[\frac{\overline{F}(z)}{\overline{F}(\xi)} \right]^N, \qquad z \geq \xi,$$

and the survivor function of z_N at z is

$$\mathrm{P}\left(z_N > z\right) = \mathrm{P}\left(w_{(1)} - \xi > z/\sqrt{N}\right) = \left[\frac{\overline{F}(\xi + z/\sqrt{N})}{\overline{F}(\xi)} \right]^N, \qquad z \geq 0,$$

from which the theorem follows.   ■

A necessary condition for (9.8), if the wage offer distribution is twice continuously differentiable with bounded second derivative, is

$$f(\xi) = 0.$$

The proof is by Taylor series expansion of $N \log[\overline{F}(\xi + z/\sqrt{N})]$ about $z = 0$ up to the quadratic term. This condition seems unreasonable in applications, implying that z_N will in fact have a degenerate limiting distribution. A simple, though economically unreasonable, example would be to take $\overline{F}(w)$ as itself Exponential with mean μ, $\overline{F}(w) = \exp\{-w/\mu\}$. In this case the exact distribution of $w_{(1)} - \xi$ is

$$
\begin{aligned}
P\left(w_{(1)} - \xi > z\right) &= P\left(\text{all } \{w_i\} > z + \xi\right), \\
&= [\overline{F}(z + \xi)/\overline{F}(\xi)]^N, \\
&= \exp\{-Nz/\mu\}.
\end{aligned}
$$

This result shows that $N(w_{(1)} - \xi)/\mu \sim \mathcal{E}(1)$ and that var $(w_{(1)}) \propto N^{-1}$ rather than $N^{-1/2}$ as in regular cases. Generally, $w_{(1)} - \xi$ will go to zero more rapidly than $N^{-1/2}$.

On the other hand, the asymptotic distribution theory for the estimators of λ and γ is entirely regular. The reason for this is that the rapid convergence of $w_{(1)}$ to ξ means that the ML estimators of λ and γ behave in large samples as though they were the solutions of (9.5) and (9.6) with $w_{(1)}$ replaced by ξ; that is, the difference between these two quantities can be neglected. With this substitution, standard arguments applied to these equations show that $\sqrt{N}(\hat{\lambda} - \lambda)$ and $\sqrt{N}(\hat{\gamma} - \gamma)$ are asymptotically Normally distributed with mean zero and covariance matrix which can be estimated by the inverse of the negative Hessian of the concentrated log likelihood after substituting ξ for $\hat{\xi}$.   ∎

The purpose of this example has been to show how the presence of sample minima in inference about structural models leads to non-regular asymptotic distribution theory and how extreme value theory must then be used to calculate the asymptotic distribution of ML estimators. It is perfectly feasible to extend the example by allowing for λ and some elements of γ to be parametric functions of regressor variables, or by eliminating ξ from the estimation problem using (2.6) of chapter 5, but little additional insight is gained by doing so and we shall turn to other issues.

In the next example we shall examine the problem of neglected heterogeneity in structural models by extending the model of exampl 26.

Example 27 Neglected Heterogeneity in a Structural Model
Let us suppose that in the stationary job search model of example 26 the reservation wage, ξ, for person i takes the form

$$\xi_i = \xi v_i, \qquad i = 1, 2, \ldots, N. \tag{9.9}$$

The quantities $\{v_i\}$ are unknown realisations of a non-negative random variable with distribution function $H(v)$ whose mean is normalised to one. The joint density function of W, T conditional on v is then

$$g(w, t \mid v) = \lambda f(w) \exp\{-\lambda \overline{F}(\xi v)t\}, \qquad w \geq \xi v \geq 0, \tag{9.10}$$

but the distribution relevant for inference is that unconditional on v which is obtained by integrating v out the joint distribution of T, W, and V. This distribution is

$$g(w,t) = \lambda f(w) \int_0^{w/\xi} \exp\{-\lambda \overline{F}(\xi v)t\}\, dH(v). \qquad (9.11)$$

The crucial feature of this expression is the range of integration, which follows from the constraint appearing in the conditional distribution, (9.10). The constraint $w \geq \xi$, which in example 26 implied that the ML estimator of ξ would be the smallest wage, which in turn led to the non-standard distribution theory for $\hat{\xi}$, has disappeared when we introduce unmeasured heterogeneity. But a new problem arises since, in general, the integration in (9.11) will have to be carried out numerically and separately for every person, or rather every distinct wage, since for person i the range of integration will be from zero to w_i/ξ. That is, the range of integration will differ from person to person, and up to N numerical integrations will be needed each time the value of the likelihood function is to be calculated. This is feasible in principle but in the only practical example of which I am aware – unpublished work by the present author and A. D. Chesher – it proved difficult to determine whether or not the iterative calculation of the ML estimates had converged and, if it had, whether the solution was a local or a global maximum. These calculations were for a model, more general than (9.10), with regressor variables and in which the reservation wage was allowed to vary over time.

It must also be observed that there is a certain arbitrariness in the choice of where to place the heterogeneity term in the model – it is not obvious that it should enter multiplicatively into the reservation wage. Flinn and Heckman (1982) remark that 'the greater simplicity in the asymptotic distribution theory (gained by the introduction of unmeasured heterogeneity terms) is offset by the arbitrariness inherent in controlling for unmeasured heterogeneity'. This seems a fair assessment. ∎

The complexities in the estimation of structural models revealed by the last example suggest the search for alternative ways of confronting structural models with data. One such is described in the next example.

Example 28 Simultaneous Equations in Non-stationary Job Search
We shall assume the non-stationary job search model in which the reservation wage varies deterministically as a function of time, the likelihood function being given by (4.10) of chapter 6. Suppose that all people follow a policy of choosing a decreasing sequence of reservation wages such

that the longer they have been unemployed the less they ask. Then if
we observe someone out of work for a long time we might reasonably
guess that he had set a high reservation wage. On the other hand, since
ξ is a decreasing function of time, the longer he has been searching the
lower his reservation wage must be. Evidently there are two causal relations between ξ and t. In one, ξ is a decreasing function of time, and
in the other, the duration (time) is a stochastically increasing function
of ξ. The t we observe is *both* the calendar time and a realisation of the
random duration in a way rather analogous to a market model in which
the quantity we observe is both the quantity demanded and the quantity
supplied. And since the realised wage, w, is an increasing function of ξ
this heuristic argument suggests that there will be two causal relations
between w and t. This argument indicates that when we write down a
model for w (or ξ) and t we are in effect writing down a simultaneous
equations model. There should therefore be a structural and a reduced
form and a set of conditions telling us when we can and cannot identify
structural parameters. One way of proceding is therefore to search for
these forms and see if we can apply simultaneous equations estimation
procedures. One way of viewing this approach is as a bivariate version of
searching for an approximate linear regression model contained within
a rather complex non-linear problem.

Suppose we adopt the following functional forms;

$$\overline{F}(w) = (w_0/w)^\alpha, \qquad w \geq w_0, \quad \alpha > 0; \qquad (9.12)$$

$$\xi(t) = \begin{cases} \xi_0 t^{-\rho}, & t \leq t_0, \\ \xi_0 t_0^{-\rho}, & t > t_0. \end{cases} \qquad (9.13)$$

These amount to a Pareto wage offer distribution with lower bound w_0
and with

$$t_0 = \begin{cases} (w_0/\xi_0)^{-1/\rho}, & \rho > 0, \\ \infty, & \rho = 0, \end{cases} \qquad (9.14)$$

a reservation wage which is either constant ($\rho = 0$) or falls until it equals
w_0 and then remains constant. To introduce time-constant regressors
into the model we write

$$\lambda w_0^\alpha = \exp\{\mathbf{x}'\gamma + u_1\}, \qquad (9.15)$$

$$\xi_0 = \exp\{\mathbf{x}'\beta + u_2\}. \qquad (9.16)$$

The scalars u_1 and u_2 are unobserved heterogeneity terms – errors in
the two regression components of the model. In this parametrisation one
cannot separately identify the rate of arrival of offers, λ, and the origin
of the offer distribution, w_0, so we must model them together, which is

what (9.15) does. Equation (9.16) shows how the level of the reservation wage function – until that wage falls to w_0 – varies between people with different measured, $\mathbf{x}$, and unmeasured, u_2, characteristics. The functional forms (9.12) to (9.16) are chosen with an eye to extracting an approximate pair of linear relations between t and w from the joint distribution (4.10) of chapter 6. In particular, the time path of the reservation wage, (9.13), is ad hoc and does not emerge from non-stationary optimising behaviour, so in this example we are to some extent departing from strictly structural modelling.

The Pareto offer distribution combines with the functional form for $\xi(t)$ to yield the hazard function

$$\theta(t) = \lambda \overline{F}(\xi(t)) = \left\{ \begin{array}{ll} \lambda(t/t_0)^{\alpha\rho}, & t \leq t_0; \\ \lambda, & t > t_0. \end{array} \right. \tag{9.17}$$

This is of Weibull form until t_0 and constant thereafter. To derive the simultaneous model we work out the joint moment generating function of t and w, given u_1, u_2, and calculate the means of $\log t$ and $\log w$ given the u's. After some algebra – details are in Lancaster (1985) – these are found to be approximately

$$\mathrm{E}\,(\log w) = c_1' + a\mathbf{x}'(\beta + \rho\gamma) + a(u_2 + \rho u_1), \tag{9.18}$$
$$\mathrm{E}\,(\log t) = c_2' + a\mathbf{x}'(\alpha\beta - \gamma) + a(\alpha u_2 - u_1), \tag{9.19}$$

for $a = (1 + \alpha\rho)^{-1}$ and where the c's are two constants. The approximation will be accurate if almost all people return to work before the reservation wage has fallen to the smallest possible offer w_0. Thus we have approximately a linear model for the logarithms of the data implied by our choice of functional forms. We now take the final step of adding two error terms v_1 and v_2 to the relations (9.18) and (9.19) and taking two linear combinations of the resulting equations. Specifically, we add ρ times the second equation to the first and subtract α times the first equation from the second to get

$$\log w = c_1 - \rho \log t + \mathbf{x}'\beta + (u_2 + v_2 + \rho v_1), \tag{9.20}$$
$$\log t = c_2 + \alpha \log w - \mathbf{x}'\gamma - (u_1 - v_1 + \alpha v_2). \tag{9.21}$$

This is a linear simultaneous equations model whose coefficients, ρ, α, β, γ, are the coefficients that appear in our specification of the structure, (9.12) to (9.16). For this reason it seems reasonable to call this, rather than some other linear combination of the means, *the* structural form of the model. The equations (9.18) and (9.19) are the reduced form of the model. The structural form exhibits clearly the two causal relations that we argued earlier should obtain between t and w. The first equation corresponds to the heuristic argument that people who have been searching a long time should have cut their asking price a lot (if $\rho > 0$) and therefore get a low wage in the new job. The second equation corresponds to the idea that people who go back to work at a high wage must have had a high asking price and therefore have taken a long time to get an acceptable offer.

Apart from their revealing the simultaneous equations structure underlying a family of rather complicated non-linear models there are two advantages to putting the model in the form (9.20) and (9.21). The first is that the neglected heterogeneity terms u_1, u_2 appear additively in the structural form errors and so nothing needs to be assumed about their distribution apart from the first two moments in order to get consistent estimates of identifiable structural parameters. There is no question of integrating them out in order to get the correct data distribution. Note also that we can allow for two such terms and not only one as in example 27.

The second advantage is that standard theorems on identifiability in linear simultaneous equations models can be applied to see which structural parameters can be identified from the first moments of the data alone. One of the difficulties of complex non-linear models such as (4.10) of chapter 6 is that it is difficult to see which parameters are identifiable and, for those that are, which aspects of the specification lead to that identifiability. Light is thrown on these questions if we can reduce the model approximately to one whose identifiability properties are well understood. In particular, from standard results on identifiability in linear models, we see that exclusion restrictions on β and γ will give identifiability of structural parameters. For example, if at least one element of γ is zero a priori while the corresponding element of β is not, then α and the remaining elements of γ can be identified regardless of the distribution of the error terms u_1, u_2 as long as these have means that do not depend upon $\mathbf{x}$.

Given identifiability, standard simultaneous equations estimators will provide consistent structural parameter estimates under weak additional assumptions. So this approach avoids the complications discussed in our first two examples at the expense of rather strong functional form assumptions. It may, however, be possible to pursue this approach by developing approximating non-linear simultaneous equations models from more reasonable hypotheses about structural functional forms, and this seems a promising line of research. Further details and an empirical application of the method of this example are given in Lancaster (1985a), which refers to earlier work with A. D. Chesher.   ∎

Our final example in this section represents another response to the difficulties in maximum likelihood estimation of structural models with

neglected heterogeneity, and indeed it originated in the frustrations arising from the calculations referred to at the end of example 27.

Example 29 Non-statistical Inference about Optimal Search
Optimal search models are rich in their refutable implications, which
extend well beyond a joint density function for unemployment durations
and wages. There are many quantities which can, in principle, be measured and which can tell us if the model is true and, if so, about the
numerical value of interesting and useful parameters. One such pair of
numbers are the reservation wage itself, ξ, and the wage which a person
expects to earn once he has found employment, x, say. Let us see how
we might use such data if we adopt as our model the stationary optimal
job search theory of chapter 6.

   The wage which a person expects to earn in a new job, x, must be
equal to the expectation in the wage offer distribution given that the
wage exceeds the reservation wage. This is

$$x = \mathrm{E}\,(W \mid W > \xi) = \xi + \frac{\int_\xi^\infty \overline{F}(w)\,dw}{\overline{F}(\xi)}, \qquad (9.22)$$

since the mean is the integral of the survivor function. The equation
which defines the optimal reservation wage is, from section 2 of chapter 6,

$$\xi = -c + \frac{\lambda}{\rho}\int_\xi^\infty (w - \xi)dF(w). \qquad (9.23)$$

Using (9.22) this may also be written

$$\xi = -c + \frac{\lambda}{\rho}\overline{F}(\xi)(x - \xi). \qquad (9.24)$$

Now suppose the cost per unit time period of job search, c, can be
approximated by the negative of the level of unemployment benefit re-
ceivable, b, and consider the effect on the optimal reservation wage of
an increase in b. Differentiating the optimality condition, (9.23), with
respect to b we get

$$\frac{\partial\xi}{\partial b} = \left(1 + \frac{\lambda\overline{F}(\xi)}{\rho}\right)^{-1}$$

$$= \left(1 + \frac{\xi - b}{x - \xi}\right)^{-1}$$

$$= \frac{x - \xi}{x - b}. \qquad (9.25)$$

Here the second line follows by use of (9.24). It follows that, if, for any person, we could observe x, ξ, and b we could deduce the way he would respond to a change in the level of his unemployment income. But such a derivative is precisely one of the key parameters of the model. It can be deduced exactly by simple arithmetic using a combination of data and theory. No statistical inference, possibly involving complex numerical maximisation and arbitrary hypotheses about the role of unmeasured heterogeneity, is necessary. Pencil and paper and theory suffice.

To determine the response of the unemployment duration to a variation in b is less easy. The derivative of the hazard – the reciprocal of the mean duration – is

$$\frac{\partial \theta}{\partial b} = \lambda \frac{\partial \overline{F}(\xi)}{\partial b}$$

$$= -\lambda f(\xi) \frac{\partial \xi}{\partial b}$$

$$= -\lambda f(\xi) \frac{x - \xi}{x - b}. \tag{9.26}$$

This cannot be computed from a knowledge of x, ξ, and b alone. Some information about the density of the offer distribution in the neighbourhood of the reservation wage is needed. There is no reason why, in principle, such information could not be obtained in a suitably designed survey, but I am not aware that this has ever been done.   ∎

In the next chapter we shall examine methods of inference which require less than a fully parametric specification of the data distribution.

NOTE

The Exponential and Weibull models are the basic parametric models and have been exposited in many places. We might mention Cox and Oakes (1984), Kalbfleisch and Prentice (1980), and Miller (1981) in the statistics literature and Lancaster (1983, 1985a) in the econometrics journals. The properties of log-linear hazards models are described in Lancaster and Imbens (1986). The grouped data proportional hazards models of examples 7 and 8 are due to Prentice and Gloeckler (1978). They have been applied and extended to allow for both parametric and non-parametric unmeasured heterogeneity by Meyer (1986), who argues for the importance in econometrics of robust ways of handling grouped data. The basic reference on the EM algorithm is Dempster, Laird, and Rubin (1977), and Wu (1983) discusses its convergence properties. The Gamma mixing distribution was used in Lancaster (1979) where the conditional likelihood was of the type discussed in section 3.1. Titterington, Smith and Makov (1986) is a useful recent reference on inference in mixture models.

Nickell's model of example 3.1 was given in Nickell (1979). The case-control approach of section 3.5 is fully described in Prentice and Breslow (1978). The main econometric references on multiple-cycle/multiple-state data are papers coauthored with Heckman, particularly Flinn and Heckman (1982), Heckman and Borjas (1980), and Heckman and Singer (1985). Ridder with coauthors (1982, 1984, 1986) has written extensively about estimation of continuous-time Markov chains and has given applications. In particular, Ridder (1987) has developed methods of inference suitable for stock sampled continuous-time Markov chains, building on earlier work by Hoem (1969). Kalbfleisch and Lawless (1985) give a lucid account of estimation of the parameters of a continuous-time Markov chain when the data consist of the states occupied by each person at a set of discrete-time points. The sociological literature contains work on such data, a reference being Tuma, Hanna, and Groeneveld (1979). The stock and flow sampling material of section 4.2 was given in Chesher and Lancaster (1983). Section 6.1 is based on the work of de Tavola (1985, 1986). The material on unmeasured heterogeneity in multiple-cycle models given in section 7 draws on Heckman and Singer (1985). The discussion of Least Squares methods in section 8 draws on Lancaster (1983, 1985a). Section 9 draws on Flinn and Heckman (1982) and on unpublished work by the present author with Chesher. David (1970) and Galambos (1978) are the standard references on the distribution of order statistics, including sample extreme values. Example 9.3 is based on Lancaster (1985). The methods of Example 29 were devised in Lancaster and Chesher, (1983) which gives further results and an empirical application. They have since been applied by a number of authors including Lynch (1983), Main (1986), and Jones (1988).

CHAPTER 9

Limited Information Inference

1   Introduction and Overview

To construct the likelihood functions described in chapter 8 requires that an investigator assume a form for the joint probability density function of the data up to a finite set of unknown parameters. That assumption constitutes information supplied by the investigator, and since it gives the complete joint data distribution it is appropriate to call it *full information*. It is possible to carry out an econometric analysis using assumptions that amount to less than such a full specification. It seems useful to call such analyses *limited information* by analogy with the econometric simultaneous equations model in which limited information analysi requires less than a full specification of all equations in the system. These methods are also called *semi-parametric*.

The situation in which economic theory suggests only part of the model for data is rather common in econometrics. It corresponds to the idea that there may be components of a model specification that are, from the economic point of view, at best uncertain and at worst entirely arbitrary. We have already considered at some length the case in which theory might indicate a specification of the hazard function of the form $\theta = v\mu(\mathbf{x}'\beta)$ given the regressor vector $\mathbf{x}$ and the unobserved scalar v. A complete model then requires us to specify the density function of V given $\mathbf{x}$, and economic theory offers little guidance on this. In this case, theory does not lead us to a complete model and the question then arises as to whether we can devise a likelihood function that will enable us to make inferences about β while allowing us to avoid specifying the distribution of V.

A second example of theory providing only part of the model arises in discrete choice analysis. Here theory will suggest reasons, relative prices, for example, why one alternative rather than another is likely to be chosen, but a complete model requires an assumption about the

233

distribution of tastes over the population of interest. Economics does not provide such information.

A third example is the case of a simultaneous equations system referred to earlier. A theory may indicate the form taken by a single equation in a simultaneous system but it may be silent on the form of the remaining equations. In this case it is appropriate to analyse the data using a limited information likelihood.

A fourth, and most important, example arises in models for duration data in which the hazard depends upon time-varying covariates, which we discussed in chapter 2 and again in section 2.11 of chapter 8. Here the 'data' consist of both the exit time and the covariate path. An economist may have a model for the probabilities of exit given the covariate path but not for that path itself. Again a limited information likelihood is called for.

All these examples call for an analysis that permits the investigator to specify parametrically something less than the full joint distribution of the data. There exists a somewhat heterogeneous collection of procedures which enable an investigator to do this and which are relevant to the analysis of transition data and we shall give an account of them in this chapter. But by far the most important of these in econometrics is the method of *partial likelihood.*

Section 2 gives a rather detailed account of inference based on partial likelihoods. We not only give the basic approach but also describe some recent extensions of the method to deal with models containing unmeasured heterogeneity. In section 2.11 we show how econometric inferences in models with time-varying regressors are, in general, partial likelihood inferences.

In section 3 we describe a miscellaneous collection of other limited information likelihoods that are applicable with special, rather than general, models. Section 4 deals with non-parametric estimation of survivor functions in the presence of right censoring, results which are important in testing the specification of econometric duration models. It then goes on to present techniques for non-parametric estimation of mixing distributions in models containing unmeasured heterogeneity. We begin with an account of *partial likelihoods.*

2   Partial Likelihood

2.1   Rank and Order Data

Suppose we have the completed unemployment durations of N people, randomly sampled from the flow, and let the duration of the person who appears first on our list of data be called t_1, let that of the person next on the list be t_2, and so on, down to the duration of the person last on the list t_N. The methods of the last chapter have been based on writing down a model for the probability distribution of the duration of unemployment, T, of any particular person and then regarding t_i as a realisation of the random variable T_i for someone with the characteristics of person i, for each $i = 1, 2 \ldots, N$. The joint probability of the data in our list is then given by the joint density function of the N random variables $T_1, \ldots, T_N$. Evaluated at the particular point $t_1, \ldots, t_N$ this is the likelihood function. Thus our method is based on a theory about why person 1 was unemployed for t_1 weeks, person 2 for t_2 weeks, and so on. But we can regard the data as actually consisting of two separate pieces of information. The first piece is the ranks of the N people when their durations are arranged in order of magnitude – who had the shortest duration, who the next shortest, and so on. The second piece of information is the list of actual durations, in order of magnitude, *without the labels* which indicate to whom they belong. Suppose our data list is as follows.

Person	Duration of Unemployment	
1	17 weeks	
2	13 weeks	(2.1)
3	14 weeks	

The information in this table consists of the *rank* information;

$$\begin{array}{cc} \text{person 2 had the shortest duration,} & \\ \text{person 3 had the second shortest duration,} & (2.2) \\ \text{person 1 had the longest duration;} & \end{array}$$

and the *order statistic* information;

$$\begin{array}{cc} \text{the shortest duration was 13 weeks,} & \\ \text{the second shortest duration was 14 weeks,} & (2.3) \\ \text{the longest duration was 17 weeks.} & \end{array}$$

If we knew the data in table (2.1) we could deduce that in tables (2.2) and (2.3), and if we knew tables (2.2) and (2.3) we could deduce table (2.1). Thus the data in the first table have the same probability as those in the second and third taken together. When we write down a joint probability density function for our data we are implicitly writing down a theory for the data of tables (2.2) and (2.3) taken together. But our economics may not provide a theory of why someone with the characteristics of person 2 should be unemployed for 13 weeks. It may, however, provide a theory about why someone with the characteristics of person 2 should have a shorter duration than someone like person 1 or person 3. Thus we may have an economically well-founded theory for the rank data (2.2) but not for the whole data (2.1). In this case it would be reasonable to apply our theory to the rank data alone, in effect throwing away the order statistic information. Of course, to jettison data is usually unwise, but if one does not have an economic theory about part of the data it is not very clear in what sense that data constitutes information at all.

What we shall do in the next subsection is give a general expression for the likelihood function when the data vector $\mathbf{t} = (t_1, \ldots, t_N)$ is equivalent to two other vectors, say, $\mathbf{x}$ and $\mathbf{s}$, in the sense that $\mathbf{t}$ can be deduced from $\mathbf{x}$ and $\mathbf{s}$, and $\mathbf{x}$ and $\mathbf{s}$ can be deduced from $\mathbf{t}$. We shall then study different ways in which one may choose to utilise only part of the information in that likelihood function and give examples. As a by-product of our argument we shall give the distribution of the rank and order statistic vectors for a set of independent but not necessarily identically distributed Exponential variates. This distribution will be important in our later work.

2.2   Partial Likelihood

Suppose that the data $\mathbf{t}$ are equivalent to M pairs of random variables $x_1 s_1, x_2 s_2, \ldots, x_M s_M$. To make the argument concrete one could think of $M = N$ and $\mathbf{s}$ and $\mathbf{x}$ as giving the rank and order statistics, as in the example of the previous section, but our argument will be more general than this. Thus the joint probability density function, or full likelihood function, of what we can observe can be written in terms of $\mathbf{x}$ and $\mathbf{s}$ as

$$\mathcal{L} = f(x_1, s_1, x_2, s_2, \ldots, x_M, s_M). \tag{2.4}$$

Note that even if the t's are independent the pairs (x_i, s_i) and (x_j, s_j) will in general be dependent. This is obvious from the rank and order statistic example in which the rank of person i must necessarily depend on that of person j – think of the case $N = 2$. Now let $\mathbf{x}^{(j)} = (x_1, \ldots, x_j)$ and $\mathbf{s}^{(j)} = (s_1, \ldots, s_j)$ for $j = 1, 2 \ldots, M$. Then by the product law of probability we can write the full likelihood (2.4) in the form

$$
\begin{aligned}
\mathcal{L} &= f(x_1, s_1) f(x_2, s_2 \mid x_1, s_1) f(x_3, s_3 \mid x_2, s_2, x_1, s_1) \\
&\quad \times f(x_M, s_M \mid x_1, s_1, x_2, s_2, \ldots, x_{M-1}, s_{M-1}) \\
&= \prod_{j=1}^{M} f(x_j, s_j \mid \mathbf{x}^{(j-1)}, \mathbf{s}^{(j-1)})
\end{aligned}
\tag{2.5}
$$

if we take $\mathbf{x}^0$ and $\mathbf{s}^0$ as null. We can further decompose (2.5) by noting that, again by the product law,

$$f(x_j, s_j \mid \mathbf{x}^{(j-1)}, \mathbf{s}^{(j-1)}) = f(x_j \mid \mathbf{x}^{(j-1)}, \mathbf{s}^{(j-1)}) f(s_j \mid \mathbf{x}^{(j)}, \mathbf{s}^{(j-1)})$$

since $\mathbf{x}^{(j)}$ is $\mathbf{x}^{(j-1)}$ together with x_j. Thus we can decompose the full likelihood (2.4) into

$$\mathcal{L} = \prod_{j=1}^{M} f(x_j \mid \mathbf{x}^{(j-1)}, \mathbf{s}^{(j-1)}) \times \prod_{j=1}^{M} f(s_j \mid \mathbf{x}^{(j)}, \mathbf{s}^{(j-1)}) \qquad (2.6)$$

The second factor in (2.6) is called the *partial likelihood* based on s. It is possible to base an analysis of data on a partial likelihood alone since it may be shown (Johansen (1978), Gill (1982)) that it has all the essential properties of a likelihood function so far as statistical inference is concerned. In particular, maximum partial likelihood estimates of unknown parameters have all the standard asymptotic properties, and a consistent estimate of their covariance matrix is provided by the inverse of the negative Hessian of the partial likelihood with unknown parameters replaced by maximum partial likelihood estimates. Before going on to look at particular cases let us look at the partial likelihood for s a little more closely.

The first point is that the partial likelihood for s is not generally the same as the likelihood based on the marginal distribution of s alone. This marginal distribution is

$$\begin{aligned}
\mathcal{L}_M(\mathbf{s}) &= f(s_1, s_2, \ldots, s_M) \\
&= f(s_1) f(s_2 \mid s_1). f(s_3 \mid s_2, s_1) \cdots f(s_M \mid s_1, s_2, \ldots, s_{M-1}) \\
&= \prod_{j=1}^{M} f(s_j \mid \mathbf{s}^{(j-1)}),
\end{aligned} \qquad (2.7)$$

again by the product law. Clearly (2.7) is not, in general, the same as the partial likelihood based on s,

$$\mathcal{L}_P(\mathbf{s}) = \prod_{j=1}^{M} f(s_j \mid \mathbf{x}^{(j)}, \mathbf{s}^{(j-1)}). \qquad (2.8)$$

The two would be the same if $\mathbf{x}$ and $\mathbf{s}$ were stochastically independent, for then

$$\begin{aligned}
\mathcal{L} &= f(\mathbf{x}) f(\mathbf{s}) \\
&= \prod_{j=1}^{M} f(x_j \mid \mathbf{x}^{(j-1)}) \times \prod_{j=1}^{M} f(s_j \mid \mathbf{s}^{(j-1)}) \\
&= \mathcal{L}_M(\mathbf{x}) \mathcal{L}_M(\mathbf{s}).
\end{aligned} \qquad (2.9)$$

An analysis based on the marginal distribution of $\mathbf{x}$ (or $\mathbf{s}$) alone is called a *marginal likelihood* analysis.

The second point is that the partial likelihood for s is generally different from the conditional distribution of s given x. This conditional distribution is

$$
\begin{aligned}
\mathcal{L}_C(\mathbf{s} \mid \mathbf{x}) &= f(s_1, s_2, \ldots, s_M \mid x_1, x_2, \ldots, x_M) \\
&= f(s_1 \mid \mathbf{x}) f(s_2 \mid s_1, \mathbf{x}) \cdots f(s_M \mid \mathbf{s}^{(M-1)}, \mathbf{x}) \\
&= \prod_{j=1}^{M} f(s_j \mid \mathbf{x}, \mathbf{s}^{(j-1)}).
\end{aligned}
\tag{2.10}
$$

Since each term in (2.10) depends on all the elements of x whereas each term in (2.8) depends only on the current and preceding x's the two expressions generally differ. An analysis based on $\mathcal{L}_C(\mathbf{s} \mid \mathbf{x})$ is called a *conditional likelihood* analysis. Partial, marginal, and conditional likelihoods might be collectively referred to as *limited information likelihoods* since they use only part of the information in the full likelihood.

These rather abstract ideas are best understood by looking closely at some examples, which we shall do in the next few sections. We shall begin with just about the simplest case in which our data consist of N independent observations which are $\mathcal{E}(\theta_i)$ variates, where the $\{\theta_i\}$ are generally all distinct. Thus we have N independent but non-identically distributed Exponential variates. We shall give a partial likelihood factoring for this case and, as a useful by-product of the example, we shall derive the distribution of the rank and order statistic vectors for such data. In the following sections we shall extend the example by allowing our observations to be possibly right censored and to have distributions much more general than the Exponential.

2.3   Likelihood Factoring for Exponential Data

With N independent $\mathcal{E}(\theta_i)$ variates the likelihood function is

$$
\mathcal{L} = \prod_{i=1}^{N} \theta_i \exp\{-\theta_i t_i\}.
\tag{2.11}
$$

As we pointed out in section 2.1 a set of data equivalent to $\mathbf{t} = (t_1, \ldots, t_N)$ is the rank vector, which shall be our s, and the order statistic vector, which shall be our x. Let us then write $\mathcal{L}$ in terms of s and x and examine the two factors in (2.6).

The vector s contains the labels of N people arranged in order of magnitude of their t's so its elements consist of some permutation of the integers 1, 2, ... N. In the example of section 2.1, where $N = 3$, $\mathbf{s} = (2, 3, 1)$. The x vector contains the t's in order of magnitude so that for the example of section 1, $\mathbf{x} = (13, 14, 17)$. Let us write the j'th element of the rank vector as i_j and that of the order statistic vector as $t_{(j)}$, $j = 1, 2 \ldots, N$. Thus

$$s = (i_1 \, i_2 \ldots i_N)$$
$$x = (t_{(1)} \, t_{(2)} \cdots t_{(N)}).$$

We shall now give the partial likelihood factoring for s, which, it will be recalled, is

$$\mathcal{L}_P(s) = \prod_{j=1}^{N} f(s_j \mid x^{(j)}, s^{(j-1)}). \qquad (2.12)$$

In order to do so we need to establish some convenient notation for the set of people who have not exited by $t_{(j)}$.

Definition 1 $\mathcal{R}_j$ *is the set of people who have not exited the instant before $t_{(j)}$; $\mathcal{R}_j = \{i_j, i_{j+1}, \ldots, i_N\}$, $j = 1, 2 \ldots, N$. Since $\mathcal{R}_j$ is the set of people* at risk *of exiting at $t_{(j)}$ it is usually called the* **risk set** *at $t_{(j)}$.*

We also need a concise notation for the sum of the thetas over $\mathcal{R}_j$.

Definition 2 Ψ_j *is the sum of the thetas for the people in $\mathcal{R}_j$. We can write this algebraically in several equivalent ways as*

$$\Psi_j = \sum_{i \in \mathcal{R}_j} \theta_i$$

$$= \sum_{l=j}^{N} \theta_{i_l}$$

$$= \sum_{t_{(j)} \le t_i} \theta_i; \qquad j = 1, 2 \ldots, N.$$

For the example of section 1, $\Psi_1 = \theta_1 + \theta_2 + \theta_3, \Psi_2 = \theta_1 + \theta_3, \Psi_3 = \theta_1$.

Theorem 1

$$\mathcal{L}_P(s) = \prod_{j=1}^{N} \theta_{i_j} / \Psi_j \qquad (2.13)$$

Proof: The first term in $\mathcal{L}_P(s)$ is $f(s_1 \mid x^{(1)}) = f(i_1 \mid t_{(1)})$, which is the (discrete) probability distribution of the label attached to the first person to exit given that first exit occurred at time $t_{(1)}$. The probability that person i_1 exits at $t_{(1)}$ given that someone does is

$$f(i_1 \mid t_{(1)}) = P(i_1 \text{exits at } t_{(1)} \mid \text{someone does})$$

$$= \frac{P(i_1 \text{exits at } t_{(1)} \cap \text{someone does})}{P(\text{someone exits at } t_{(1)})}$$

$$= \theta_{i_1} dt_{(1)} / \sum_{i=1}^{N} \theta_i \, dt_{(1)}$$

$$= \theta_{i_1} / \Psi_1,$$

which is the first term in the product (2.13). The second term in the partial likelihood is $f(s_2 \mid \mathbf{x}^{(2)}, \mathbf{s}^{(1)}) = f(i_2 \mid t_{(2)}, t_{(1)}, i_1)$, which is the discrete distribution of the label attached to the second person to leave given the times at which the first and second exits occurred and the identity of the first person to leave. At the time of the second exit the people who could be observed to leave then are those in $\mathcal{R}_2$, and by the same reasoning as before the probability that it is i_2 who leaves then is θ_{i_2} / Ψ_2. Similar reasoning applies to all subsequent terms and the theorem is proved. ∎

Notice that, in fact, $\mathcal{L}_P(\mathbf{s})$ does not depend upon the *times* of exit and that the only reason why it depends upon $\mathbf{s}^{(j-1)}$ is because the labels of previous leavers establish, by subtraction, the set of people who could possibly be observed to leave at $t_{(j)}$. We shall return to these points after giving two examples.

Example 1
If the models for t's in the example of section 1 specified that they were independently $\mathcal{E}(\theta_i)$ distributed then the partial likelihood for the data of that example would be

$$\mathcal{L}_P(\mathbf{s}) = \frac{\theta_2}{\theta_1 + \theta_2 + \theta_3} \cdot \frac{\theta_3}{\theta_1 + \theta_3} \cdot \frac{\theta_1}{\theta_1}. \qquad (2.14)$$

This may be compared to the full information likelihood for the same data

$$\mathcal{L}(\mathbf{t}) = \prod_{i=1}^{3} \theta_j \exp\{-\theta_i t_i\}$$

$$= \theta_1 \theta_2 \theta_3 \exp\{-17\theta_1 - 13\theta_2 - 14\theta_3\}.$$

Of course in this parametrisation we have as many parameters as observations but the example may be made more reasonable by writing, say, $\theta_j = \exp\{\alpha + \beta z_j\}$ for given regressor values z_1, z_2, z_3. This gives a two-parameter (α, β) full likelihood though only a one-parameter (β) partial likelihood. The parameter α is not identifiable from the partial likelihood.   ∎

Example 2
A special case is that in which the data are identically distributed so that all the N thetas are equal, say, to θ. Then $\Psi_1 = N\theta$, $\Psi_2 = (N-1)\theta$, $\ldots$, $\Psi_N = \theta$ and the partial likelihood is

$$\mathcal{L}_P(\mathbf{s}) = \theta^N / \theta^N . N . (N-1) \cdots 2.1$$
$$= 1/N! \tag{2.15}$$

∎

Let us return to the point made above that for the present case of uncensored sampling of Exponential variates the partial likelihood for **s** does not in fact depend upon **x**, the times at which exits occur. That is,

$$\mathcal{L}_P(\mathbf{s}) = \prod_{j=1}^{N} f(s_j \mid \mathbf{x}^{(j)}, \mathbf{s}^{(j-1)})$$

$$= \prod_{j=1}^{N} f(s_j \mid \mathbf{s}^{(j-1)}).$$

Thus we are in the special case in which the partial likelihood for **s** happens to be identical to the marginal likelihood for **s**, that is, the likelihood based on the marginal joint distribution of the ranks (2.7) and we have

Theorem 2   *In a sample of N independent $\mathcal{E}(\theta_i)$ variates the marginal joint distribution of the rank vector is*

$$f(\mathbf{s}) = f(i_1, \ldots, i_N) = \prod_{j=1}^{N} \theta_{i_j} / \Psi_j$$

over a sample space consisting of all permutations of the first N integers.

This result then explains (2.15), for if the thetas are all the same then all $N!$ permutations of the N labels, that is, all possible distinct orders in which people could leave, are equally likely and each must have probability $1/N!$

We have just found the distribution of the rank vector as a by-product of our investigation of the partial likelihood for **s** in random sampling of

Exponential variates. We could have got this distribution by the following more direct argument, which we shall give because it will be useful for later work. The probability of the rank vector $\mathbf{s} = (i_1, \ldots, i_N)$ is the probability that the t's are such that $t_{i_1} < t_{i_2} < \cdots < t_{i_N}$ and this in turn can be found by integrating the joint density funtion of $\mathbf{t}$ over the region defined by these inequalities. Thus we have

Theorem 3   *In samples of N independent $\mathcal{E}(\theta_i)$ variates the distribution of the rank vector is*

$$f(i_1, \ldots, i_N) = \int_0^\infty \int_{t_{i_1}}^\infty \cdots \int_{t_{i_{N-1}}}^\infty \prod_{j=1}^N \theta_{i_j} \exp\{-\theta_{i_j} t_{i_j}\} dt_{i_N} dt_{i_{N-1}} \cdots dt_{i_1}$$

$$= \prod_{j=1}^N \theta_{i_j} / \Psi_j \qquad\qquad (2.16)$$

Proof: The proof uses the formula $\int_t^\infty \theta \exp\{-\theta s\} ds = \exp\{-\theta t\}$ in repeated integration.   ∎

Example 3
To exemplify the evaluation of the integral of Theorem 3 consider the data of our numerical example.

$$f(2,3,1) = \int_0^\infty \int_{t_2}^\infty \int_{t_3}^\infty \theta_2 \theta_3 \theta_1 \exp\{-\theta_2 t_2 - \theta_3 t_3 - \theta_1 t_1\} dt_1 dt_3 dt_2$$

$$= \int_0^\infty \int_{t_2}^\infty \theta_2 \theta_3 \exp\{-\theta_2 t_2 - (\theta_3 + \theta_1) t_3\} dt_3 dt_2$$

$$= \frac{1}{\theta_3 + \theta_1} \cdot \int_0^\infty \theta_2 \theta_3 \exp\{-(\theta_2 + \theta_3 + \theta_1) t_2\} dt_2$$

$$= \frac{\theta_3}{\theta_3 + \theta_1} \cdot \frac{\theta_2}{\theta_2 + \theta_3 + \theta_1},$$

which is (2.14).   ∎

We now know that in uncensored sampling from Exponential distributions the partial likelihood for the rank data ($\mathbf{s}$) is also the marginal likelihood based on the density of the rank vector and is given in theorem 2. Let us now look at the other component of the likelihood function in (2.6), which is $\prod_{j=1}^N f(x_j \mid \mathbf{x}^{(j-1)}, \mathbf{s}^{(j-1)})$ in which x_j is the j'th ordered exit time. A simple way to deduce this term is to note that it is equal to the full likelihood divided by the partial likelihood for $\mathbf{s}$. The full likelihood is (2.11), which by relabelling can be written

$$\mathcal{L} = \prod_{j=1}^{N} \theta_{i_j} \exp\{-\theta_{i_j} t_{(j)}\}. \tag{2.17}$$

Dividing this by $\mathcal{L}_P(\mathbf{s})$ given in theorem 2 we find that

$$\prod_{j=1}^{N} f(x_j \mid \mathbf{x}^{(j-1)}, \mathbf{s}^{(j-1)}) = \frac{\prod_{j=1}^{N} \theta_{i_j} \exp\{-\theta_{i_j} t_{(j)}\}}{\prod_{j=1}^{N} \theta_{i_j} / \Psi_j}$$

$$= \left(\prod_{j=1}^{N} \Psi_j\right) \exp\left\{-\sum_{j=1}^{N} \theta_{i_j} t_{(j)}\right\}. \tag{2.18}$$

The term in braces is

$$-(\theta_{i_1} t_{(1)} + \cdots + \theta_{i_N} t_{(N)}) = -\{(\Psi_1 - \Psi_2)t_{(1)} + (\Psi_2 - \Psi_3)t_{(2)} + \cdots$$
$$+ (\Psi_{N-1} - \Psi_N)t_{(N-1)} + \Psi_N t_{(N)}\}$$
$$= \{\Psi_1 t_{(1)} + \Psi_2(t_{(2)} - t_{(1)}) + \cdots$$
$$+ \Psi_N(t_{(N)} - t_{(N-1)})\}.$$

Hence,

$$\prod_{j=1}^{N} f(x_j \mid \mathbf{x}^{(j-1)}, \mathbf{s}^{(j-1)}) = \left(\prod_{j=1}^{N} \Psi_j\right) \exp\left\{-\sum_{j=1}^{N} \Psi_j(t_{(j)} - t_{(j-1)})\right\}$$

$$\tag{2.19}$$

over the sample space $t_{(1)} \le t_{(2)} \le \cdots \le t_{(N)}$.

How do we interpret this expression? The full likelihood is the joint density function of $\mathbf{x}$ and $\mathbf{s}$ which can be written as the product of the conditional distribution of $\mathbf{x}$ given $\mathbf{s}$ and the marginal distribution of $\mathbf{s}$, $\mathcal{L} = f(\mathbf{x} \mid \mathbf{s})f(\mathbf{s})$, and it may also be written as the product (2.6). But for uncensored sampling from Exponential distributions the second factor in (2.6) is $f(\mathbf{s})$. Hence it must be that (2.19) gives the conditional distribution of the order statistic vector given the rank vector and we have

Theorem 4 *In uncensored random sampling from N Exponential distributions the joint distribution of the vector of order statistics given the rank vector is*

$$f(\mathbf{x} \mid \mathbf{s}) = \left(\prod_{j=1}^{N} \Psi_j\right) \exp\left\{-\sum_{j=1}^{N} \Psi_j(t_{(j)} - t_{(j-1)})\right\}, \qquad t_{(0)} = 0,$$

$$\tag{2.20}$$

over the sample space $t_{(1)} \leq t_{(2)} \leq \cdots \leq t_{(N)}$.

This distribution has an elegantly simple form. If we change the variates in (2.20) to

$$y_j = \Psi_j(t_{(j)} - t_{(j-1)}), \qquad j = 1, 2 \ldots, N, \qquad (2.21)$$

with Jacobian equal to $\prod_{j=1}^{N} \Psi_j$ we see that the new variates $Y_1, \ldots, Y_N$ are independently unit Exponential. Or, to put it another way, the intervals between successive exits are independently $\mathcal{E}(\Psi_j)$ given the order in which people leave. Since we know the moments of the unit Exponential distribution we can readily deduce those of the order statistics by solving the system (2.21) for the $t_{(.)}$'s to give

$$t_{(j)} = \sum_{i=1}^{j}(y_i/\Psi_i), \qquad j = 1, 2 \ldots, N, \qquad (2.22)$$

Then since $\mathrm{E}\,(Y) = \mathrm{var}(Y) = 1$ and $\mathrm{cov}(Y_i Y_j) = 0, \quad i \neq j,$

$$\mathrm{E}\,(T_{(j)}) = \sum_{i=1}^{j} \Psi_i^{-1},$$

$$\mathrm{var}(T_{(j)}) = \sum_{i=1}^{j} \Psi_i^{-2},$$

$$\mathrm{cov}(T_{(j)} T_{(k)}) = \sum_{i=1}^{k} \Psi_i^{-2}, \qquad k \leq j. \qquad (2.23)$$

Example 4
In the special case in which the sample is homogeneous, $\theta_1 = \theta_2 = \cdots = \theta_N = \theta$, say, so that $\Psi_j = (N - j + 1)\theta$, then (2.23) reduces to

$$\mathrm{E}\,(T_{(j)}) = \theta^{-1} \sum_{i=1}^{j}(N - j + 1)^{-1},$$

$$\mathrm{cov}(T_{(j)} T_{(k)}) = \theta^{-2} \sum_{i=1}^{k}(N - i + 1)^{-2}, \qquad k \leq j. \qquad (2.24)$$

With a homogeneous sample the conditioning on the order in which people leave – the rank vector – is obviously irrelevant so the moments (2.24) hold unconditionally. In the special case in which $\theta = 1$ the first moments in (2.24) are called the *Exponential scores* – the expected order statistics in random samples of size N from the unit Exponential distribution. ∎

A particularly interesting order statistic is the minimum, $T_{(1)}$, whose distribution, from (2.22), is that of a unit Exponential variate divided by Ψ_1 so that $T_{(1)} \sim \mathcal{E}(\sum_{i=1}^{N} \theta_i)$ given the rank vector. But since neither the density function nor the sample space depends upon the rank vector, $T_{(1)} \sim \mathcal{E}(\sum_{i=1}^{N} \theta_i)$ unconditionally. This is a rather remarkable result. For example, if one has two Exponential variates, T_1 and T_2, with parameters $\theta_1 = 0.1$ and $\theta_2 = 1.0$ and means of 10 and 1, the probability that the smaller of them exceeds, say, 8 does not depend on whether T_1 or T_2 was the smaller. It is worth noting that for a homogeneous sample the minimum has mean equal to $(N\theta)^{-1}$ and variance $(N\theta)^{-2}$.

2.4 Partial Likelihood for Proportional Hazard Distributions

Consideration of partial likelihood would be of limited use if $\mathcal{L}_P$ only took a simple form when the data were Exponentially distributed but, in fact, the method applies much more generally. In this section we shall give the extension from Exponential distributions to distributions whose hazard functions factor as in the proportional hazard (PH) models discussed earlier. Thus we replace the hypothesis that the hazard for T_i is time-invariant with the hypothesis that the hazard takes the form $\theta_i(t_i) = \mu_i \theta_0(t_i)$, where μ_i is some person-specific term, for example, $\mu_i = \exp\{\mathbf{x}_i'\beta\}$, and θ_0 is a function of t common to all N people. The function $\theta_0(t)$ is the *baseline hazard*. Of course, this family includes the Exponential distribution as the particular case $\theta_0 = $ constant.

Let us retain our definitions of $\mathbf{s}$ and $\mathbf{x}$ as the rank and order statistic vectors for the data $t_1, \ldots, t_N$, but we shall redefine the Ψ_j as the sums not of the θ's but of the μ's.

Definition 3 Ψ_j *is the sum of the $\{\mu_i\}$ for the people in $\mathcal{R}_j$.*

The first term in the partial likelihood for $\mathbf{s}$ is, from the proof of theorem 1,

$$f(i_1 \mid t_{(1)}) = \frac{P(i_1 \text{exits at } t_{(1)})}{P(\text{someone exits at } t_{(1)})}.$$

This is equal to

$$f(i_1 \mid t_{(1)}) = \frac{\theta_{i_1}(t_{(1)}) \, dt_{(1)}}{\sum_{i=1}^{N} \theta_i(t_{(1)}) \, dt_{(1)}},$$

which, on substituting the proportional hazard form for θ, is

$$= \frac{\mu_{i_1}\theta_0(t_{(1)})\,dt_{(1)}}{(\sum_{i=1}^{N}\mu_i)\theta_0(t_{(1)})\,dt_{(1)}}$$

$$= \mu_{i_1}/\Psi_1.$$

The second term in $\mathcal{L}_P$ is the probability that the second person to exit is i_2 given that someone exits at $t_{(2)}$ and that person i_1 had left earlier. This is

$$f(i_2 \mid t_{(2)}, i_1) = \frac{\theta_{i_2}(t_{(2)})\,dt_{(2)}}{\sum_{j\in\mathcal{R}_2}\theta_j(t_{(2)})\,dt_{(2)}}$$

$$= \frac{\mu_{i_2}}{\Psi_2}$$

after substituting the PH form for the θ's. The same type of argument applies to every term in $\mathcal{L}_P$ and we have

Theorem 5   *In uncensored random sampling from distributions with proportional hazards $\theta_i(t) = \mu_i\theta_0(t)$ the partial likelihood based on the rank vector* **s** *is*

$$\mathcal{L}_P(\mathbf{s}) = \prod_{j=1}^{N} \mu_{i_j}/\Psi_j, \qquad (2.25)$$

where $\Psi_j = \sum_{i\in\mathcal{R}_j}\mu_i, \quad j = 1,2\ldots,N.$

One important feature of this result is that, just as in the Exponential case, the partial likelihood does not involve the times at which exits occur. Or, in the $\mathbf{s}, \mathbf{x}$ notation,

$$\mathcal{L}_P(\mathbf{s}) = \prod_{j=1}^{N} f(s_j \mid \mathbf{x}^j, \mathbf{s}^{(j-1)})$$

$$= \prod_{j=1}^{N} f(s_j \mid \mathbf{s}^{(j-1)}).$$

Thus the partial likelihood based on **s** is still the same as the marginal likelihood based on **s**, so (2.25) must be the joint density function of the rank vector **s** and we can state

Theorem 6   *In uncensored random sampling from distributions with proportional hazards the joint density function of the vector of ranks of*

the $\{t_i\}$ is

$$f(\mathbf{s}) = f(i_1, \ldots, i_N) = \prod_{j=1}^{N} \mu_{i_j} / \Psi_j$$

over the sample space which consists of all permutations of the integers 1, 2, ... N.

A direct proof of this result is by integration of the joint density function of the t's over the region $t_{i_1} < t_{i_2} < \cdots < t_{i_N}$, giving

$$f(\mathbf{s}) = \int_0^\infty \int_{t_{i_1}}^\infty \cdots \int_{t_{i_{N-1}}}^\infty \left(\prod_{j=1}^{N} \mu_{i_j} \theta_0(t_{i_j}) \right)$$

$$\exp \left\{ -\sum_{j=1}^{N} \mu_{i_j} \int_0^{t_{i_j}} \theta_0(s)ds \right\} dt_{i_N} \cdots dt_{i_2} dt_{i_1}. \quad (2.26)$$

Since we shall have further occasion to write down integrals of the form (2.26) and these involve a rather confusing subscripting we shall adopt some simplifying notation and write (2.26) as

$$f(\mathbf{s}) = \int_R \left(\prod_{i=1}^{N} \mu_i \theta_0(t_i) \right) \exp \left\{ -\sum_{i=1}^{N} \mu_i \int_0^{t_i} \theta_0(s)ds \right\} dt$$

$$= \int_R f(\mathbf{t})\, dt. \quad (2.27)$$

Here the expression $\int_R dt$ means integrate over the region in $\mathbf{t}$ space defined by the (R)ank information, which in the present, uncensored case is $0 < t_{i_1} < t_{i_2} < \cdots < t_{i_N} < \infty$. The change of variables $z_i = \int_0^{t_i} \theta_0(s)ds$, $i = 1, 2 \ldots, N$, in (2.27), with Jacobian $\prod_{i=1}^{N} \theta_0(t_i)$, gives

$$f(\mathbf{s}) = \int_R \left(\prod_{i=1}^{N} \mu_i \right) \exp \left\{ -\sum_{i=1}^{N} \mu_i z_i \right\} d\mathbf{z}, \quad (2.28)$$

where again R is the region defined by the rank information which, since z_i is a monotonic increasing function of t_i, is the region $0 < z_{i_1} < z_{i_2} < \cdots < z_{i_N} < \infty$. (Note the new notation – we have previously used z to denote the whole integrated hazard, and here it is the integral only of the time-varying component.) But in view of this we see that (2.28) is identical to the integral considered earlier in theorem 3 with θ replaced by μ, which is the required direct proof of theorem 6. Essentially, the change of variables to the $\{z_i\}$ reduces the integral (2.26) to the Exponential case considered earlier. The proportional hazard form is crucial to this argument because the fact that the time-dependent component of the hazard, θ_0, is common to all people means that the region $0 < t_{i_1} < t_{i_2} < \cdots < t_{i_N} < \infty$ is transformed into the region $0 < z_{i_1} < z_{i_2} < \cdots < z_{i_N} < \infty$. When the hazards are not proportional this argument will not work and the distribution of the rank vector will not be the same for both **z** and **t**.

In our discussion of the Exponential case we noted – theorem 4 – that the other component of the full likelihood was interpretable as the density of the order statistic vector given the rank vector, $f(\mathbf{x} \mid \mathbf{s})$. In the present, more general case we can exploit the fact that the transformation $z_i = \int_0^{t_i} \theta_0(s)ds$ returns us to the Exponential case – specifically, $z_i \sim \mathcal{E}(\mu_i)$ $i = 1,2\ldots,N$ – to deduce

Theorem 7   *The joint density function of the order statistics of the* $\{z_i = \int_0^{t_i} \theta_0(s)ds\}$, $\quad i = 1,2\ldots,N$, *given the rank vector of the* $\{t_i\}$, *or, equivalently, that of the* $\{z_i\}$ *is*

$$f(z_{(1)}, z_{(2)}, \ldots z_{(N)}) = \left(\prod_{i=1}^{N} \Psi_i\right) \exp\left\{-\sum_{i=1}^{N} \Psi_i(z_{(i)} - z_{(i-1)})\right\}, \quad (2.29)$$

over the sample space $0 < z_{(1)} < z_{(2)} < \cdots z_{(N)} < \infty$, *and where* $z_{(0)} = 0$.

Proof: The proof proceeds by changing the variables in the full likelihood from $\{t_i\}$ to $\{z_i\}$ and arguing as for theorem 4.   ∎

A consequence of this result is that the means and variances of the ordered z's are

$$\mathrm{E}\left(Z_{(j)}\right) = \sum_{i=1}^{j} \Psi_i^{-1}, \qquad j = 1,2\ldots,N$$

$$\mathrm{cov}(Z_{(j)}Z_{(k)}) = \sum_{i=1}^{k} \Psi_i^{-2}, \qquad k \le j, \quad (2.30)$$

for $\Psi_j = \sum_{l \in \mathcal{R}_j} \mu_l$. These follow from the same argument as that which gave the moments of the ordered T's in the Exponential case, (2.23). It is worth noting that these moments could also have been obtained by the following slightly shorter route.

Consider the integral representation of $\mathcal{L}_P$,

$$\prod_{j=1}^{N} \mu_{i_j}/\Psi_j = \int_R \left(\prod_{i=1}^{N} \mu_i\right) \exp\left\{-\sum_{i=1}^{N} \mu_i z_i\right\} d\mathbf{z}. \qquad (2.28)$$

Taking logarithms and differentiating with respect to μ_{i_k} gives

$$\frac{1}{\mu_{i_k}} - \sum_{j=1}^{k} \frac{1}{\Psi_j} = \int_R \left\{\frac{1}{\mu_{i_k}} - z_{i_k}\right\} f(\mathbf{z}) d\mathbf{z} / \int_R f(\mathbf{z}) d\mathbf{z}$$

$$= \frac{1}{\mu_{i_k}} - \mathrm{E}\left(Z_{i_k} \mid R\right)$$

$$= \frac{1}{\mu_{i_k}} - \mathrm{E}\left(Z_{(k)} \mid R\right)$$

since $f(\mathbf{z})/\int_R f(\mathbf{z}) d\mathbf{z}$ is the joint p.d.f. of $\mathbf{Z}$ given $\mathbf{z} \in R$, that is, given the rank information about $\mathbf{Z}$. Subtracting $\mu_{i_k}^{-1}$ from both sides then gives the first moments of (2.30). Further differentiation gives the higher moments. Thus the moments of the $Z_{(j)}$ can be obtained by differentiation of the logarithm of the partial likelihood with respect to the μ_{i_j}. This is a point to which we shall return.

Let us look at an example of a partial likelihood for a proportional hazard model.

Example 5 Partial Likelihood for the Weibull Model
The model $\theta_i(t) = \exp\{\beta_0 + \mathbf{x}_i'\beta_1\}\alpha t^{\alpha-1}$ has been considered several times already. This hazard function is of the PH form with $\mu_i = \exp\{\mathbf{x}_i'\beta_1\}$ and $\theta_0(t) = \alpha \exp\{\beta_0\}t^{\alpha-1}$. Note in particular how the constant term in $\mathbf{x}'\beta$ is part of θ_0, not of μ_i. The typical term in $\mathcal{L}_P$ is $\mu_i/\Psi_i = \exp\{\mathbf{x}_i'\beta_1\}/\sum_{l\in\mathcal{R}_i} \exp\{\mathbf{x}_l'\beta_1\}$. Note also how β_0 and α do not appear in $\mathcal{L}_P$ – they are not identifiable from it. ∎

This lack of identifiability, from $\mathcal{L}_P$, of unknown parameters appearing in the common component of the hazard function is a general feature of $\mathcal{L}_P$ for PH models. Indeed, it is the great advantage of this approach that any common function θ_0 cancels from the ratios whose product forms the partial likelihood. This means that an investigator whose theory does not provide him with a complete model for the hazard function can refrain from specifying such a complete model as long as he is willing to assume that what he has not specified (a) enters the hazard multiplicatively and (b) is common to all people. Where these assumptions can be made, inference about parameters of μ can be made without any further hypotheses about the remainder of the hazard function. This is why partial likelihood is a *limited information* likelihood; it does not require the investigator to provide the information that would be contained in a parametric form for θ_0. It is also why inferences based on partial likelihoods are sometimes called *semi-parametric*; only μ needs to be specified parametrically and no parametric specification of θ_0 is required. The reader should note that this does not mean that no inferences about θ_0 can be made in the partial likelihood approach, they can, but they are non-parametric inferences, as we shall explain in later sections.

In the next section we shall describe how the partial likelihood function is defined in the presence of random right censoring, and in the following section we shall give the form taken by $\mathcal{L}_P$ when the observations do not necessarily follow proportional hazard distributions.

2.5   Partial Likelihood with Right Censoring

With right censoring our data will consist of a list of times, M of which are exit times and $N - M$ of which are censoring times, usually marked with a star. For a censored t we know only that the exit time was greater than the censoring time. We can break up the information in this list into **x** and **s** components by defining $t_{(1)}, t_{(2)}, \ldots, t_{(M)}$ to be the ordered *observed* exit times and letting

$s_j = $ the label of the person observed exiting at $t_{(j)}$,

$x_j = $ the time $t_{(j)}$ and the list of people censored in $[t_{(j-1)}, t_{(j)})$,

for $j = 1, 2 \ldots, M$.

Example 6
Thus if our data are

Person	Time
1	17
2	16*
3	12
4	23

then $N = 4$, $M = 3$, and

$$s_1 = 3, \qquad\qquad s_2 = 1, \qquad\qquad s_3 = 4;$$
$$x_1 = 12, \quad x_2 = 17 \text{ and person 2 was censored at 16,} \quad x_3 = 23. \quad \blacksquare$$

As before the partial likelihood for $\mathbf{s}$ is $\mathcal{L}_P = \prod_{j=1}^{M} f(s_j \mid \mathbf{x}^{(j)}, \mathbf{s}^{(j-1)})$ and the first term in this product is the discrete probability distribution of the label attached to the person observed to exit first, at $t_{(1)}$, given the time, $t_{(1)}$, and the list of censorings prior to $t_{(1)}$. This is, using the rule that $P(A \mid B \cap C) = P(A \cap B \mid C)/P(B \mid C)$,

$$f(i_1 \mid \text{first exit at } t_{(1)} \text{and the censorings before } t_{(1)})$$

$$= \frac{P(i_1 \text{ leaves at } t_{(1)} \mid \text{ the censorings before } t_{(1)})}{P(\text{first exit at } t_{(1)} \mid \text{the censorings before } t_{(1)})}.$$

The numerator event has probability $\theta_{i_1}(t_{(1)})dt_{(1)}$. The denominator event is that someone is observed to leave at $t_{(1)}$ given that none had been observed to leave earlier and given the people who had already been censored. The set of people who could be observed to leave at $t_{(1)}$ is all N people less those already censored, which defines the risk set $\mathcal{R}_1$ at $t_{(1)}$. The probability that someone of those in the risk set at $t_{(1)}$ does leave is $\sum_{j \in \mathcal{R}_1} \theta_j(t_{(1)}) dt_{(1)}$. Hence the first term is

$$\frac{\theta_{i_1}(t_{(1)}) dt_{(1)}}{\sum_{j \in \mathcal{R}_1} \theta_j(t_{(1)}) dt_{(1)}},$$

which, under the proportional hazard form for the $\{\theta_i\}$, becomes

$$\frac{\mu_{i_1}}{\sum_{j \in \mathcal{R}_1} \mu_j}.$$

The second term in $\mathcal{L}_P$ is $f(i_2 \mid \text{second exit at } t_{(2)}, \text{first exit at } t_{(1)}$, and the censorings before $t_{(2)})$. The conditioning information serves to define the risk set at $t_{(2)}$, which consists of all N people less those censored before $t_{(2)}$ and less person i_1. By the same reasoning as before we see that this second term is equal to

$$\frac{\theta_{i_2}(t_{(2)}) dt_{(2)}}{\sum_{j \in \mathcal{R}_2} \theta_j(t_{(2)}) dt_{(2)}},$$

which again on the PH hypothesis reduces to

$$\frac{\mu_{i_2}}{\sum_{j \in \mathcal{R}_2} \mu_j}.$$

The argument proceeds in the same way for each term in $\mathcal{L}_P$ and we see that we have

Theorem 8   *The partial likelihood for proportional hazard models with random right censoring is*

$$\mathcal{L}_P = \prod_{j=1}^{M} \mu_{i_j}/\Psi_j, \tag{2.31}$$

where there are M observed exit times and Ψ_j is the sum of the $\{\mu_i\}$ over the risk set at $t_{(j)}$.

Example 7

To exemplify the method let us consider the full and partial likelihood functions for a small data set. Suppose that our model for theta is $\theta = \exp\{\mathbf{x}'\beta\}\theta_0(t)$ and that we have five observations of which one is right censored.

Person	x	t
1	-2	1.75*
2	-1	1.59
3	0	1.83
4	1	1.15
5	2	0.14

Thus $N = 5$, $M = 4$ and the risk sets are $\mathcal{R}_1 = \{1, 2, 3, 4, 5\}$, $\mathcal{R}_2 = \{1, 2, 3, 4\}$, $\mathcal{R}_3 = \{1, 2, 3\}$, $\mathcal{R}_4 = \{3\}$, and the Ψ's are $\Psi_1 = \mu_1 + \mu_2 + \mu_3 + \mu_4 + \mu_5$, $\Psi_2 = \mu_1 + \mu_2 + \mu_3 + \mu_4$, $\Psi_3 = \mu_1 + \mu_2 + \mu_3$, $\Psi_4 = \mu_3$ for $\mu_j = \exp\{\mathbf{x}'_j\beta\}$. The log partial likelihood is

$$L_P = \beta\{x_2 + x_3 + x_4 + x_5\} - \sum_{j=1}^{4} \log \Psi_j$$

$$= 2\beta - \sum_{j=1}^{4} \log \Psi_j$$

This function is sketched in figure 9.1.

If we had been prepared to assume that $\theta_0(t)$ was constant, implying an Exponential model for the data, the log likelihood would have been

$$L_F = \sum_{i=1}^{5} \delta_i \log\{e^{\mathbf{x}'_i\beta}\theta_0\} - \sum_{i=1}^{5} t_i e^{\mathbf{x}'_i\beta}\theta_0$$

$$= \beta(x_2 + x_3 + x_4 + x_5) + 4\log\theta_0 - \theta_0\sum_{i=1}^{5} t_i e^{\mathbf{x}'_i\beta}$$

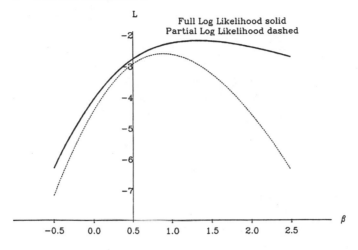

Figure 9.1.   Full (—) and partial (--) log likelihoods for $N = 5$.

$$= 2\beta + 4\log\theta_0 - \theta_0 \sum_{i=1}^{5} t_i e^{\mathbf{x}_i'\beta},$$

where the $\{\delta_i\}$ are the censoring indicators. Differentiating with respect to θ_0 and equating to zero gives

$$\hat{\theta}_0 = 4 / \sum_{i=1}^{5} t_i e^{\mathbf{x}_i'\beta}.$$

Substituting this into L_F gives the log likelihood function concentrated with respect to θ_0,

$$L_F(\beta) = 2\beta - 4\log \sum_{i=1}^{5} t_i e^{\mathbf{x}_i'\beta},$$

apart from an additive constant. This curve is also sketched in figure 9.1 after adjusting the constant to make it comparable in height to $L_P(\beta)$.

Comparing the two curves we see that L_P is flatter than L_F, markedly so for large positive beta. This greater uncertainty about β is the price paid for avoiding making an assumption about the form of θ_0 – the price of limited information. The greater precision attached to inference from L_F would be illusory if, in fact, the assumption $\theta(t) = $ constant was wrong.   ■

The partial likelihood with censoring depends upon the censoring information since the risk sets at each observed exit time depend upon the identities of the people previously censored. But the censoring information is, by definition, contained in $\mathbf{x}$, hence $\mathcal{L}_P$ *depends* upon $\mathbf{x}$ when there is censoring. It follows that $\mathcal{L}_P$ is not, in this case, equal to the marginal distribution of the rank vector; indeed, since the number of uncensored exits will vary from sample to sample the number of items to be ranked will itself vary and this marginal joint distribution does not have a clear meaning. Right censoring therefore destroys this simple interpretation of $\mathcal{L}_P$. Can it be given some other clear probabilistic interpretation? The answer is yes, we can find such an interpretation and we can write $\mathcal{L}_P$ as an integral analogously to (2.28).

Consider the ranks of all N exit times regardless of whether we observe them. With censoring we cannot observe this complete rank vector but we do know something about it. In example 6 we know that the complete rank vector can only be one of the three vectors

$$\begin{matrix} \{3 & 1 & 4 & 2\} \\ \{3 & 1 & 2 & 4\} \\ \{3 & 2 & 1 & 4\} \end{matrix} \qquad (2.32)$$

since we know definitely that person 3 was the first to leave and that person 1 left before person 4. The only uncertainty is about the censored exit time, that of person 2, about which we know only that it came after that of person 3. Notice that there are $4! = 24$ possible complete rank vectors and the censored sample information tells us that the actual one must be one of the three given in (2.32). Let us therefore work out the probability that the complete (N observation) rank vector should be one of those possible in the light of our data. This probability is got by adding up the probabilities attached to every vector $t_1, \ldots, t_N$ whose elements are rank ordered in a way consistent with our sample information. In our numerical example this means integrating the joint distribution of $T_1, \ldots, T_4$ over the region R given by

$$t_2 > t_3, \quad t_4 > t_1 > t_3 > 0 \qquad (2.33)$$

since every $\mathbf{t}$ vector in R has a rank vector consistent with our sample information and every $\mathbf{t}$ vector outside it is inconsistent with that information. Notice that in the region defined by (2.32) each T, censored or not, is integrated from the immediately preceding observed exit time, zero if there was none. A little thought indicates that this is generally true of the region in $\mathbf{t}$ space that is consistent with the sample information about the complete rank vector.

Example 8

Let us exemplify this calculation with the data of our numerical example where R is given by (2.33). The joint density of the N uncensored T's is

$$f(\mathbf{t}) = \prod_{i=1}^{4} \mu_i \theta_0(t_i) \exp\left\{ -\mu_i \int_0^{t_i} \theta_0(s) ds \right\}.$$

Changing the variables to $z_i = \int_0^{t_i} \theta_0(s) ds$, $i = 1, 2 \ldots, N$, we reduce the joint density function to that of four $\mathcal{E}(\mu_i)$ variates,

$$f(\mathbf{z}) = \prod_{i=1}^{4} \mu_i e^{-\mu_i z_i},$$

and the region of integration to $R = \{\mathbf{z}; z_2 > z_3, z_4 > z_1 > z_3 > 0\}$. The probability we require is

$$P = \int_R f(\mathbf{z}) d\mathbf{z}.$$

If we first integrate out the z corresponding to the censored observation the integral becomes

$$P = \int_{z_4 > z_1 > z_3 > 0} \mu_3 \mu_1 \mu_4 \exp\{-\mu_1 z_1 - (\mu_2 + \mu_3) z_3 - \mu_4 z_4\} d\mathbf{z}$$

$$= \frac{\mu_3}{\mu_1 + \mu_2 + \mu_3 + \mu_4} \cdot \frac{\mu_1}{\mu_1 + \mu_4},$$

which is (2.31) for these data. ∎

Thus the partial likelihood in this case is equal to the probability that the full data rank vector should be one of those consistent with our sample information. It is not difficult to show that this is generally true and we can state

Theorem 9 *In right censored random sampling from distributions with proportional hazards the partial likelihood is equal to the probability that the complete rank vector is one of those consistent with the (censored) sample information. It is given by the equivalent integrals*

$$\mathcal{L}_P = \int_R \left(\prod_{i=1}^{N} \mu_i \theta_0(t_i) \right) \exp\left\{ -\sum_{i=1}^{N} \mu_i \int_0^{t_i} \theta_0(s) ds \right\} d\mathbf{t} \qquad (2.34)$$

and

$$\mathcal{L}_P = \int_R \left(\prod_{i=1}^{N} \mu_i \right) \exp\left\{ -\sum_{i=1}^{N} \mu_i z_i \right\} d\mathbf{z}, \qquad (2.35)$$

where R is the region in which each t_i is integrated from the immediately preceding uncensored exit time or zero if there was none.

Example 9
Suppose, in example 6, that the $\{\mu_i\}$ are identical so the observations are homogeneous. Then the twenty-four possible rank orderings of the exit times are equally likely and each must have probability $1/24$. What we observe is that this rank vector must in fact be one of the three given in (2.32), and what we observe must therefore have probability $3/24$, which is the value of $\mathcal{L}_P$, (2.31), in this case. ∎

Finally, let us observe that we can obtain the moments of the $\{z_i\}$ given the information in the sample about the complete rank vector by differentiating under the integral sign just as in the uncensored case considered earlier. Taking the integral representation of $\mathcal{L}_P$ given in (2.35), taking logarithms, and differentiating both sides with respect to μ_i we get

$$\frac{\partial \log \mathcal{L}_P}{\partial \mu_i} = \frac{\int_R (\mu_i^{-1} - z_i)(\prod_{i=1}^N \mu_i)\exp\{-\sum_{i=1}^N \mu_i z_i\}d\mathbf{z}}{\int_R (\prod_{i=1}^N \mu_i)\exp\{-\sum_{i=1}^N \mu_i z_i\}d\mathbf{z}}$$

$$= \mu_i^{-1} - \mathrm{E}\,(z_i \mid \mathbf{z} \in R). \tag{2.36}$$

But $\mathcal{L}_P = \prod_{j=1}^M \mu_{i_j}/\Psi_j$, whose logarithmic derivative with respect to μ_i is

$$\frac{\partial \log \mathcal{L}_P}{\partial \mu_i} = \frac{\delta_i}{\mu_i} - \sum_{t_{(j)} \leq t_i} \Psi_j^{-1}, \tag{2.37}$$

where δ_i is the censoring indicator. The first term on the right of (2.37) arises because μ_i only appears in the numerator of $\mathcal{L}_P$ if $Z_i(t_i)$ was uncensored. The second term is the sum of the reciprocals of the psi's for all risk sets containing μ_i. Equating (2.36) and (2.37) we get

Theorem 10   *In right censored random sampling from distributions with proportional hazards of the form $\theta_i(t) = \mu_i\theta_0(t)$ the variates $z_i = \int_0^{t_i} \theta_0(s)ds$ have means*

$$\mathrm{E}\,(Z_i \mid \mathbf{z} \in R) = \frac{1 - \delta_i}{\mu_i} + \sum_{t_{(j)} \leq t_i} \Psi_j^{-1}, \tag{2.38}$$

given the information in the sample about the full rank vector.

If the sample is uncensored so that we know exactly the complete rank vector, and all $\{\delta_i\} = 1$, this result reduces to the first moments of (2.30). For any censored observation (2.38) is equal to the expectation of the immediately preceding uncensored observation plus $1/\mu_i$, the marginal expectation of Z_i.

2.6   The EM algorithm

Programs to maximise the partial likelihood are now widely available, so an account of computational methods is scarcely necessary. We shall, however, briefly indicate the form taken by the EM algorithm when hazards are proportional, partly because of its simplicity and partly because it provides the basis for calculations in the more complicated heterogeneous proportional hazards models that we shall descibe later in this chapter.

To apply the algorithm we write down the scores from the full data log likelihood for the vector of parameters γ entering into the $\{\mu_i\}$ and take expectations with respect to the data distribution given what we can observe, evaluated at the parameter point γ^p. The solution of the expected score equations then gives a new γ^p and the process is repeated until convergence. We take the full data to be the N values of $z_i = \int_0^{t_i} \theta_0(s)ds$ and the observed data to be the information in the sample about the complete rank vector. The hazard of course is $\mu_i(\gamma)\theta_0(t)$, and we shall assume the parametric form $\mu_i = \exp\{\mathbf{x}_i'\gamma\}$ though the method applies to other forms. The full data likelihood is the product of N $\mathcal{E}(\mu_i)$ distributions with scores

$$\frac{\partial L}{\partial \gamma_j} = \sum_{i=1}^{N} x_{ij}\{1 - \mu_i z_i\} \qquad j = 1, 2 \dots, K. \tag{2.39}$$

The expectation of these with respect to the distribution of the $\{z_i\}$ given the information in the sample about the full rank vector is (2.39) with each z_i replaced by $\bar{z}_i$ given by (2.38) with γ replaced by γ^p. We then solve the equations

$$\sum_{i=1}^{N} x_{ij}\{1 - \mu_i(\gamma)\bar{z}_i\} = 0 \qquad j = 1, 2 \dots, K \tag{2.40}$$

for γ, recompute the $\{\bar{z}_i\}$ and solve again, and so on. Solution of (2.40) is easy since these are just the likelihood equations for an Exponential model with hazard $\exp\{\mathbf{x}'\gamma\}$ and data $\{\bar{z}_i\}$ that we considered in chapter 8, section 2.

Table 9.1.   Example of the EM
Algorithm

M step	Iterations	$\hat{\gamma}$	L_P
0	—	.000	−4.094
1	9	.493	−2.827
2	6	.712	−2.522
3	5	.848	−2.394
4	5	.944	−2.329
..	.	....	....
44	1	1.326	−2.227

Example 10

As a numerical example we give the results of applying the EM algorithm
to the data of example 7 where by inspection of figure 9.1 the maximum
of L_P is at about 1.2. In the table below each M step is an iterative
solution of (2.40) and these alternate with E steps in which the $\bar{z}_i$ were
recomputed using this solution in (2.38).

By contrast, a direct application of the Newton–Raphson iteration to
L_P converged to $\hat{\gamma} = 1.327$ from zero in 4 iterations though each iteration
was somewhat longer than that for an M step of the EM algorithm. The
latter is not computationally efficient for partial likelihood maximisation,
and we have explained it for its theoretical interest alone.   ∎

2.7   Partial Likelihood in General

If we now write the hazard for person i as $\theta_i(t) = \mu_i(t)\theta_0(t)$ in which
$\theta_0(.)$ is a function common to all N observations while μ_i is a person-
specific function we have a model which subsumes all the cases we have
considered so far. If μ_i is independent of time we have a proportional
hazard model and if, in addition, θ_0 is also independent of time we
have an Exponential model. The form of the partial likelihood for this
rather general model is easily written down by following the argument
of section 2.5 up to the point at which the expression simplified because
of the PH assumption. Thus the first term in $\mathcal{L}_P$ is

$$\frac{P(i_1 \text{leaves at } t_{(1)} \mid \text{the censorings before } t_{(1)})}{P(\text{first exit at } t_{(1)} \mid \text{the censorings before } t_{(1)})} = \frac{\theta_{i_1}(t_{(1)})dt_{(1)}}{\sum_{j \in \mathcal{R}_1} \theta_j(t_{(1)})dt_{(1)}}$$

$$= \frac{\mu_{i_1}(t_{(1)})}{\sum_{j \in \mathcal{R}_1} \mu_j(t_{(1)})}.$$

Note that the common function $\theta_0(.)$ cancels so an investigator is not required to supply the information provided by a functional form for $\theta_0(t)$. The second term in $\mathcal{L}_P$ is

$P(i_2 \mid$ second exit at $t_{(2)}$, first exit at $t_{(1)}$

and the censorings before $t_{(2)})$,

which reduces to

$$\frac{\mu_{i_2}(t_{(2)})}{\sum_{j \in \mathcal{R}_2} \mu_j(t_{(2)})}.$$

Similar reasoning establishes the general term and we can state

Theorem 11   *When the hazard function is $\theta_i(t) = \mu_i(t)\theta_0(t)$ the partial likelihood is*

$$\mathcal{L}_P = \prod_{j=1}^{M} \left[\mu_{i_j}(t_{(j)}) / \sum_{k \in \mathcal{R}_j} \mu_k(t_{(j)}) \right]. \tag{2.41}$$

An important feature of this expression is that the j'th term in the product is calculated at time $t_{(j)}$, the j'th observed exit time. Where there are time-varying regressors whose path to time t for person i is $\mathbf{X}_i(t)$ we require to know each person's covariate path up to and including the time at which he leaves or is censored in order to calculate (2.41).

Example 11
Suppose the function $x_i(t)$ gives the level of unemployment benefits payable to person i at time t and that $\theta_i(t) = \exp\{\beta x_i(t)\} = \theta_0(t)$ gives the hazard conditional on the covariate path to t. Then if we observe exits at uncensored times $t_1 = 6$, $t_2 = 15$, $t_3 = 10$ the partial likelihood is

$$\mathcal{L}_P = \frac{e^{\beta x_1(6)}}{e^{\beta x_1(6)} + e^{\beta x_2(6)} + e^{\beta x_3(6)}} \times \frac{e^{\beta x_3(10)}}{e^{\beta x_2(10)} + e^{\beta x_3(10)}}. \qquad \blacksquare$$

2.8   Partial Likelihood with Multiple Destinations

We now consider the extension of the partial likelihood approach to models with M destination states and transition intensities to destination m for person i of the form

$$\theta_i^m = \mu_i^m(t)\theta_0^m(t), \qquad m = 1, 2 \ldots, M, \quad i = 1, 2 \ldots, N. \tag{2.42}$$

We include 'censored' as one of the destinations, with a transition intensity that would usually not be modelled. The person- *and* destination-specific component of the transition intensity, μ, is assumed specified parametrically, for example as $\mu_i^m = \exp\{\beta_m' \mathbf{x}_{im}(t)\}$. Any components of $\theta_i^m(t)$ common to all people, but possibly destination-specific, are included in the unspecified functions $\theta_0^m(t)$.

Suppose now that we have one cycle of information – a duration and a destination – for each of N people and that the cycles are stochastically independent. Then conditionally on the origin state the likelihood contribution of person i is

$$\mathcal{L}^i = \exp\left\{\sum_{m=1}^{M}\left[\delta_i^m \log \theta_i^m(t_i) - \int_0^{t_i} \theta_i^m(s)ds\right]\right\} \qquad (2.43)$$

from chapter 8, section 2, where $\delta_i^m = 1$ if destination m is entered, zero otherwise. But this factors into the product of M terms of the form

$$\mathcal{L}^{im} = \exp\left\{\delta_i^m \log \theta_i^m(t_i) - \int_0^{t_i} \theta_i^m(s)ds\right\} \qquad (2.44)$$

and consequently full likelihood, the product of N terms like (2.43), itself factors into the product of M terms as

$$\mathcal{L} = \prod_{m=1}^{M}\left(\prod_{i=1}^{N}\exp\left\{\delta_i^m \log \theta_i^m(t_i) - \int_0^{t_i} \theta_i^m(s)ds\right\}\right)$$

$$= \prod_{m=1}^{M} \mathcal{L}^m. \qquad (2.45)$$

Inspection of $\mathcal{L}^m$ reveals it to be the likelihood for a model in which an observation is regarded as uncensored if destination m is entered and censored otherwise. Entry to any destination other than m is treated as a censoring event. Thus the discussion of the last section applies immediately to each of the M components in (2.45) for which μ^m is specified and up to M partial likelihoods can be formed. If the parameters of the $\{\mu^m\}$, the $\{\beta^m\}$, are functionally independent, separate partial likelihood maximisations can be performed. If there is functional dependence among the parameters of the transition intensities joint maximisation will be appropriate.

Theorem 12   *With M destinations, transition intensities of the form given in (2.42), and N independent cycles, M partial likelihoods can be constructed. These take the form*

$$\mathcal{L}_P^m = \prod_{j=1}^{N_m}\left[\mu_{i_j}^m(t_{(j)}) \Big/ \sum_{k \in \mathcal{R}_j} \mu_k^m(t_{(j)})\right], \qquad m = 1, 2 \ldots, M. \qquad (2.46)$$

In this expression N_m is the number of cases in which destination m was entered, that is, the number of 'uncensored' exits, the $t_{(j)}$ are the ordered times at which these exits occurred, i_j is the label of the person entering m at $t_{(j)}$, and $\mathcal{R}_j$ is the set of people who had not exited the instant before $t_{(j)}$.

It is instructive to note that theorem 12 could have been obtained by the following direct application of the likelihood factoring described in section 2.2. Let s contain the labels of all N people in the order in which they leave, regardless of destination, and let x contain both the ordered exit times and the destination indicators so that, for example, x_j gives the time of the j'th exit and the destination to which it occurred. Now examine the partial likelihood (2.8), $\mathcal{L}_P = \prod_{j=1}^{N} f(s_j \mid \mathbf{x}^{(j)}, \mathbf{s}^{(j-1)})$. The typical term in this product is

$P(i_j$was the j'th to leave | the j'th exit was at $t_{(j)}$and was to m_j

$\qquad \cap$ the labels, exit times, and destinations of all previous leavers)

$$= \frac{P(i_j\text{leaves for } m_j\text{at } t_{(j)} \mid \text{the risk set at } t_{(j)})}{P(\text{someone leaves for } m_j\text{at } t_{(j)} \mid \text{the risk set at } t_{(j)})}$$

$$= \frac{\theta_{i_j}^{m_j}(t_{(j)})}{\sum_{k \in \mathcal{R}_j} \theta_k^{m_j}(t_{(j)})}. \qquad\qquad (2.47)$$

The product of all terms of this form involving exit to destination m is, after cancellation of terms in θ_0, precisely $\mathcal{L}_P^m$ of theorem 12. This gives a proof of theorem 12 which is less mechanical and more in the spirit of the partial likelihood approach.

We remind the reader that the transition intensities used in this section are conditional on the identity of the origin state and also on the state history of each person. If these are thought relevant they can be represented by dummy or real regressors entering into the parametric specification of the $\{\mu_i\}$.

2.9   Partial Likelihood with Multiple Destinations and Cycles

We now consider the extension of the partial likelihood approach to the case in which we observe N people moving among M states over an interval of time. This is an extension which has been little studied and less applied, so our results here must be regarded as tentative. The building blocks of the argument are now the transition intensities from state l to state m at time t and we extend (2.42) to

$$\theta_i^{lm} = \mu_i^{lm}(t)\theta_0^{lm}(t); \qquad l, m = 1, 2, \ldots, M, \quad l \neq m, \quad i = 1, 2 \ldots, N.$$
(2.48)

The person-specific component is specified parametrically, as

$$\mu_i^{lm} = \exp\{\beta'_{lm}\mathbf{x}_{lm}(t)\},$$

for example, and the unspecified baseline hazard θ_0 can depend upon both origin and destination state. Time, t, is clock time measured from an origin at the start of the sampling interval, and the probability $\theta_i^{lm}(t)\,dt$ is conditional on the state history of person i, that is, upon the sequence of transitions he has made to t and the times at which he made them, including his initial or origin state, and upon survival in state l to t.

The data consist of the times and types of transitions made by the N people over the sampling interval, where by the type of a transition we mean both the origin and the destination. We can identify a partial likelihood factoring by observing that these data are equivalent to two vectors $\mathbf{s}$ and $\mathbf{x}$, where

1. $\mathbf{s}$ contains the person identifiers of the *ordered* transitions so that s_j gives the label of the person moving at the j'th transition to occur; and

2. $\mathbf{x}$ contains the times and types of these transitions so that x_j gives the information that the j'th transition occurred at time $t_{(j)}$ and was from state l_j to state m_j.

Now let us deduce the partial likelihood for $\mathbf{s}$, which is

$$\mathcal{L}_P = \prod_{j=1}^{N^*} f(s_j \mid \mathbf{x}^{(j)}, \mathbf{s}^{(j-1)}),$$

where N^* is the total number of transitions observed. The typical term in this product is

$P(i_j\text{moved at the } j\text{'th transition} \mid \text{the } j\text{'th transition}$

$\qquad \text{occurred at } t_{(j)} \text{ and was from } l_j \text{ to } m_j$

$\qquad \cap \text{ the times and types of all previous transitions})$

$$= \frac{P(i_j\text{moved from } l_j \text{ to } m_j \text{ at } t_{(j)} \mid \mathcal{H}(t_{(j)}))}{P(\text{someone moved from } l_j \text{ to } m_j \text{ at } t_{(j)} \mid \mathcal{H}(t_{(j)}))}, \quad (2.49)$$

where $\mathcal{H}(t_{(j)})$ contains the times and types of all transitions prior to $t_{(j)}$. Now, $\mathcal{H}(t_{(j)})$ includes the state history of person i_j. If this person was not in state l_j the instant before $t_{(j)}$ he could not have moved from there to m_j so the numerator is zero. If he was in l_j the instant before $t_{(j)}$

the numerator is $\theta_{ij}^{l_j m_j}(t_{(j)}) \, dt_{(j)}$ given by (2.48). Similarly, the people not in l_j the instant before $t_{(j)}$ contribute nothing to the denominator, whereas those who were in l_j contribute their transition intensities to m_j. The set of people in state l_j the instant before $t_{(j)}$ is the risk set denoted by $\mathcal{R}_j$ as usual. Notice that this is not the set of all people who could have been observed to move to m_j at $t_{(j)}$, as in the last section, but the set of people who could have been observed to move *from* l_j to m_j at $t_{(j)}$. After cancelling the baseline hazard, (2.49) reduces to

$$f(s_j \mid \mathbf{x}^{(j)}, \mathbf{s}^{(j-1)}) = \frac{\mu_{ij}^{l_j m_j}(t_{(j)})}{\sum_{k \in \mathcal{R}_j} \mu_k^{l_j m_j}(t_{(j)})}, \qquad (2.50)$$

and the product of N^* such terms is the proposed partial likelihood for this type of data. This product is itself the product of $M(M-1)$ terms each of which refers to a specific pair of origin and destination states. If the $\{\mu_i^{lm}\}$ contain functionally independent sets of parameters it will be appropriate to conduct $M(M-1)$ separate partial likelihood maximisations and the resulting estimators will be asymptotically independent. Otherwise joint maximisation will be required.

2.10 Partial Likelihood and Heterogeneous Models

We shall now go in a rather different direction by reverting to a theme of earlier chapters, the problem of inference when there is unobserved person-specific heterogeneity in the transition intensities. The partial likelihoods we have discussed so far have the merit that they allow the investigator to avoid specifying parametrically the function θ_0 which is common to all people. But from the point of view of the econometrician this is precisely the wrong virtue. He has usually been willing to specify the common time dependence in the hazard but has wished to avoid specifying unmeasured *person-specific* effects. This is probably the reason why, although the partial likelihood approach has been available since Cox's seminal 1972 paper, it has rarely been used by econometricians. It appears that this attitude is now changing and it is partly because of this change that we have given a relatively detailed account of partial likelihood methods.

One reason for this change is that recent work suggests the possibility of combining the partial likelihood approach with an allowance for unmeasured person-specific heterogeneity. A second reason is the increased interest among econometricians in semi-parametric methods of inference which allow the investigator to avoid making unwarranted functional form assumptions. A further reason for paying attention to partial likelihood methods is that it seems to the author probable that econometricians have yet to exploit fully the possibilities of the type of factoring described in section 2.2. This is particularly the case when the econometrician has available multiple-cycles of information for each person.

We shall consider models in which there exists a multiplicative person-specific term v in the hazards or transition intensities. The hazard for person i, conditional on v_i, is

$$\theta_i(t) = v_i \mu_i(t) \theta_0(t). \tag{2.51}$$

Let $\mathbf{v}$ denote the vector $v_1, \ldots, v_N$. The typical term in the partial likelihoods of the form we have been describing, *conditional on* $\mathbf{v}$, is

$$v_{i_j} \mu_{i_j}(t_{(j)}) / \sum_{k \in \mathcal{R}_j} v_k \mu_k(t_{(j)}), \tag{2.52}$$

which still depends upon the v's, although, of course, θ_0 has been eliminated. This just makes the point that these partial likelihoods do *not* eliminate unmeasured person-specific heterogeneity. We can now proceed in two possible directions. One is to find groups of observations dependent on *the same* v and study the partial likelihood for such data. The other is to assume a functional form for the joint density of the $\{V_i\}$ and integrate them out of the partial likelihood. We shall give an account of these approaches in this section.

2.10.1 Integration of the $\{v_i\}$

In the case in which the hazards are proportional so that μ does not depend upon t it is possible to proceed in a way analogous to the fully parametric case and integrate the $\{v_i\}$ out of the partial likelihood if the investigator is willing to assume a functional form for the density of the v's. Let the joint density function of the $\{V_i\}$ be denoted by $h(\mathbf{v}; \eta)$. Then the partial likelihood given $\mathbf{v}$ is

$$\mathcal{L}_{P|\mathbf{v}} = \prod_{j=1}^{M} v_{i_j} \mu_{i_j} / \Psi_j, \tag{2.53}$$

$$\Psi_j = \sum_{k \in \mathcal{R}_j} v_k \mu_k. \tag{2.54}$$

In integral form, after the change of variables

$$z_i = \int_0^{t_i} \theta_0(s) ds, \quad i = 1, 2 \ldots, N,$$

this is,

$$\mathcal{L}_{P|\mathbf{v}} = \int_R \prod_{i=1}^N v_i \mu_i \exp\{-\mu_i v_i z_i\}\, d\mathbf{z}. \qquad (2.55)$$

Since $\mathcal{L}_{P|\mathbf{v}}$ is $P(\mathbf{z} \in R \mid \mathbf{v})$ the unconditional partial likelihood is given by $E_v[P(\mathbf{z} \in R \mid \mathbf{v})]$ or

$$\mathcal{L}_P = \int_{\mathbf{v}} \int_R \prod_{i=1}^N v_i \mu_i \exp\{-\mu_i v_i z_i\} h(\mathbf{v};\eta)\, d\mathbf{z} d\mathbf{v}. \qquad (2.56)$$

Or, equivalently,

$$\mathcal{L}_P = \int_{\mathbf{v}} \left(\prod_{j=1}^M v_{i_j} \mu_{i_j}/\Psi_j \right) h(\mathbf{v};\eta)\, d\mathbf{v}. \qquad (2.57)$$

This likelihood is very difficult to evaluate but it is nonetheless possible to maximise it by the following application of the EM algorithm.

We treat both the $\{z_i\}$ *and* the $\{v_i\}$ as missing data to apply the EM algorithm thus generalising the method of section 2.6. If we could observe the z's and the v's the full data log likelihood for N independent observations would be

$$L_F = \sum_{i=1}^N \log\{g(z_i \mid v_i; \gamma) h(v_i; \eta)\}$$

$$= \sum_{i=1}^N \log v_i + \log \mu_i(\gamma) - z_i v_i \mu_i(\gamma) + \log h(v_i; \eta).$$

The algorithm requires us to take the expectation of this with respect to the z's and v's given the rank information, R, at some assumed parameter point γ^p, η^p and maximise this expectation with respect to γ, η. We take the functional forms $\mu_i = \exp\{\mathbf{x}'\gamma\}$ and let $h(v;\eta)$ be the unit mean Gamma distribution,

$$h(v;\eta) = v^{\eta-1} e^{-\eta v} \eta^\eta / \Gamma(\eta).$$

These forms are computationally simple but the method applies in principle to other choices. With these assumptions we have

$$L_F = \sum_{i=1}^N \{\eta \log v_i + \mathbf{x}_i'\gamma - v_i(\eta + z_i\mu_i) - \log\Gamma(\eta) + \eta\log\eta\}. \qquad (2.58)$$

In order to take expectations of L_F we first eliminate the $\{v_i\}$ by taking expectations conditional on $\mathbf{z}$. This will leave us to take the expectation of functions of the Z's given $\mathbf{z} \in R$. These in turn will be approximated as the functions of the expectations of the $\{Z_i\}$ given R. Finally, we shall indicate how to estimate $E\,(Z_i \mid R)$ in this model and that will complete the E step of the algorithm. The M step is straightforward given our choice of functional forms.

Since, for any person, $Z \sim \mathcal{E}(\mu v)$ given v, and V itself is marginally unit mean Gamma, we readily find that

$$h(v \mid z) = v^\eta \exp\{-v(\mu z + \eta)\}/\Gamma(\eta + 1)(z + \eta)^{-\eta-1}$$

and from the results of appendix 1 we find that

$$\begin{aligned}
E\,(\log V \mid z) &= -\log(\mu z + \eta) + \psi(1 + \eta), \\
E\,(V \mid z) &= (\eta + 1)/(\mu z + \eta).
\end{aligned}$$

If we now use these moments in taking the expectation of (2.58) conditionally on $\mathbf{z}$ and then take expectations with respect to $\mathbf{Z}$ in which we replace the expectations of non-linear functions of the z's with those functions of the expectations we have

$$\begin{aligned}
E(L_F \mid R) \sim \sum_{i=1}^N &-\eta \log(\mu_i^p \bar{z}_i + \eta^p) + \eta\psi(1 + \eta^p) + \mathbf{x}_i'\gamma \\
&-(\eta + \bar{z}_i\mu_i)[(\eta^p + 1)/(\mu_i^p \bar{z}_i + \eta^p)] - \log\Gamma(\eta) + \eta\log\eta.
\end{aligned}$$

Here $\bar{z}_i = E\,(Z_i \mid \mathbf{z} \in R)$ with γ evaluated at γ^p. Differentiation with respect to γ and η then gives approximate likelihood equations to be solved for these parameters. The equations for γ turn out to be identical to those arising in the application of the EM algorithm to the homogeneous partial likelihood function which we described in section 2.6 except that $\bar{z}_i$ is replaced by $\bar{z}_i(1 + \eta^p)/(\mu_i^p \bar{z}_i + \eta^p)$.

The final step in the E part of the algorithm is the calculation of $E\,(Z_i \mid R)$. Now if we knew the v's we could use (2.38) to give

$$E(z_i \mid \mathbf{v}, R) = \frac{1 - \delta_i}{v_i\mu_i} + \sum_{t_{(j)} \le t_i} \Psi_j^{-1},$$

where Ψ_j is given in (2.54). Furthermore, as we have seen,

$$E\,(V_i \mid z_i, R) = \frac{1 + \eta}{\mu_i z_i + \eta},$$

the conditioning on R being superfluous here. These two equations suggest the iteration

$$\bar{z}_i = \frac{1 - \delta_i}{\bar{v}_i\mu_i} + \sum_{t_{(j)} \le t_i} \Psi_j^{-1},$$

Table 9.2.   EM in a Semi-Parametric Model

	Data Set 1		Data Set 2	
	γ	σ^2	γ	σ^2
PL estimate	.703	0	.393	0
Start point	1.00	.20	1.00	.20
5 iterations	.94	.42	.48	.15
10 iterations	1.01	.53	.42	.03
15 iterations	1.06	.60	.393	.003
20 iterations	1.10	.65		
70 iterations	1.17	.74		
75 iterations	1.17	.74		

Note: An iteration is a complete E and a complete M step as described above, and the PL estimates are ordinary (homogeneous) partial likelihood estimates.

$$\bar{v}_i = \frac{1+\eta}{\mu_i \bar{z}_i + \eta}$$

which can be solved in turn until convergence. This calculation then provides the $\{\bar{z}_i\}$ to use in solving the approximate likelihood equations.

Example 12
To exemplify the method we drew fifty observations with conditional hazards $\theta_i = v_i e^{x_i \gamma}$ for $\gamma = 1$ and v_i a realisation of a Gamma variate with mean one and variance $\sigma^2 = \eta^{-1} = 1$. We give in table 9.2 the results for two such data sets.

In both cases the ordinary partial likelihood estimate underestimated the true γ. For the first data set the heterogeneous partial likelihood estimates converged to a more accurate value for γ though the estimate of σ^2 was rather poor. For the second data set the heterogeneous partial likelihood estimates converged to the homogeneous model estimate for γ and to zero for σ^2. The reason for this behaviour is that for the second data set the score statistic for testing for unmeasured heterogeneity in proportional hazard models – see chapter 11 – was negative, pointing to a *negative* estimate for σ^2. The EM algorithm rather sensibly gives zero for σ^2 and the homogeneous model estimate for γ. ∎

This method is clearly rather complicated and moreover no rigorous study of its statistical properties has been made. It was in fact devised to be applicable mainly to the case in which there is more than one observation depending on the same value of v available. We shall offer further comment on the method in section 2.10.3, which deals with inference when such multiple observations are to hand.

2.10.2 Elimination of the $\{v_i\}$

The fact that common factors cancel from the partial likelihood can be exploited to eliminate the $\{v_i\}$ if we can obtain multiple observations for each person. Suppose that for person i we can obtain n_i observations t_{ij}, $j = 1, 2 \ldots, n_i$, which are independently distributed, given v_i, with hazard functions

$$\theta_{ij}(t) = v_i\mu_{ij}(t)\theta_{i0}(t), \quad j = 1, 2 \ldots, n_i, \quad i = 1, 2 \ldots, N. \quad (2.59)$$

The factor v_i is person-specific and, like the functions $\theta_{i0}(t)$, does not vary between observations (spells) for the same person. The factors $\mu_{ij}(t)$ vary, as the notation suggests, between persons and between spells for the same person. Given the specification (2.59) we can then write down the partial likelihood for the n_i spells for person i which will be

$$\mathcal{L}_P^i = \prod_{k=1}^{m_i} \mu_{ij_k}(t_{i(k)})/\Psi_{ik}, \quad (2.60)$$

where there are m_i uncensored spells for person i, j_k is the label (spell serial number) of the k'th in magnitude, $t_{i(k)}$, and Ψ_{ik} is the sum of the μ_{ij} over the risk set at $t_{i(k)}$. Note that both v_i and θ_{i0} vanish by cancellation. The proposed likelihood is then

$$\mathcal{L}_P = \prod_{i=1}^{N} \mathcal{L}_P^i. \quad (2.61)$$

Estimators of the parameters of the μ's obtained by maximising (2.61) will, subject to regularity conditions, have the standard asymptotic properties as $N \to \infty$.

Example 13
Suppose that we observe exactly two uncensored spells for each person and that μ_{ij} is specified as $\exp\{\mathbf{x}_{ij}'\beta\}$. Then

$$\mathcal{L}_P^i = \frac{\mu_{i1}^{\delta_i}\mu_{i2}^{1-\delta_i}}{\mu_{i1} + \mu_{i2}},$$

where $\delta_i = 1$ if the first spell is the shorter, zero otherwise. This can be written

$$\mathcal{L}_P^i = \pi_i^{\delta_i}(1 - \pi_i)^{1-\delta_i},$$

$$\pi_i = \frac{1}{1 + e^{\beta'(\mathbf{x}_{i2} - \mathbf{x}_{i1})}}. \tag{2.62}$$

$\mathcal{L}_P$ can be recognised as the likelihood corresponding to a binary regression model with logit form for the event probability and with regressor vector given by $\mathbf{x}_{i2} - \mathbf{x}_{i1}$ for person i. Thus a familiar econometric model emerges as a special case of the partial likelihood approach with pairs of observations for each person. Note that the existence of a solution for β depends upon there being variation in $\mathbf{x}$ over spells.   ∎

There is obviously a close connection between this application of the partial likelihood methodology to eliminate unmeasured individual effects and classical methods for the elimination of such effects in linear models for panel data. Consider for example, the linear model

$$y_{ij} = \alpha_i + \beta' \mathbf{x}_{ij} + u_{ij}, \quad j = 1, 2; \quad i = 1, 2 \ldots, N. \tag{2.63}$$

The individual-specific parameters α_i can be eliminated either by the cross-sectional regression of $y_{i2} - y_{i1}$ on $\mathbf{x}_{i2} - \mathbf{x}_{i1}$, since

$$y_{i2} - y_{i1} = \beta'(\mathbf{x}_{i2} - \mathbf{x}_{i1}) + (u_{i2} - u_{i1}), \tag{2.64}$$

or by the binary dependent variable model with event probability

$$\pi_i = P(y_{i2} > y_{i1}) = P[u_{i2} - u_{i1} > -\beta'(\mathbf{x}_{i2} - \mathbf{x}_{i1})]. \tag{2.65}$$

The former method uses the numerical value of $y_{i2} - y_{i1}$, whereas the latter method uses only its sign. If $u_{i2} - u_{i1}$ has a Logistic distribution (2.65) is identical to the model (2.62).

This correspondence suggests that there is a linear model underlying the partial likelihood methodology, at least in the absence of censoring and when hazards are proportional. This is indeed the case. The integrated hazard for person i and observation j is $v_i \mu_{ij} \int_0^{t_{ij}} \theta_{i0}(s) ds$. As usual we denote the integral part of this expression by $z(t_{ij})$ and note that since integrated hazards are unit Exponential variates we can write the equation

$$\log v_i + \beta' \mathbf{x}_{ij} + \log z(t_{ij}) = u_{ij}, \quad j = 1, 2; \quad i = 1, 2 \ldots, N, \tag{2.66}$$

where u_{i1} and u_{i2} are independently distributed as the logarithms of $\mathcal{E}(1)$ variates given v_i. If we knew the z's we could regress the difference of their logarithms on the difference of the x's in an equation, such as (2.64), free of the person-specific $\{v_i\}$. But we don't know the z's because, by assumption, we have no hypothesis about the arbitrary functions $\theta_{i0}(t)$. But, knowing the t's, which are monotonic functions of the z's, we can deduce the rank ordering of the z's. We have ordinal, not cardinal, information about them in this semi-parametric approach. With two observations this rank information leads immediately to a method based on the *sign* of the difference of the t's, as in (2.65). And indeed since the difference of the logarithms of two independent unit Exponential variates has a Logistic distribution this linear model formulation leads back to (2.62).

Though it is interesting to see that there is a close connection between this application of partial likelihood methodology and standard linear model procedures when hazards are proportional and there is no censoring it should be emphasised that neither of these conditions is necessary for the validity of (2.61)

This 'within person' partial likelihood procedure does successfully eliminate person-specific effects, though a price of this is that it also eliminates the effect of measured regressors that do not vary between spells for the same person. These too cancel from the partial likelihood as they are eliminated by differencing in the linear model. The method does have the further disadvantage that it requires that spells be independent conditional on v_i and on the measured regressors. This rules out lagged duration dependence, for example, in which t_1 is an element of $\mathbf{x}_2$. It also rules out the case in which the spells are contiguous in time and sampled over a fixed interval since in this case, given the number of spells observed for person i, the lengths of the spells must necessarily be dependent.

There is a related within person partial likelihood procedure for the case of multiple destinations and cycles discussed earlier in section 2.9. Consider once again observing N people moving among M states with transition intensities of the form

$$\theta_i^{lm} = v_i^l \mu_i^{lm}(t)\theta_0^{lm}(t); \qquad l, m = 1, 2, \ldots, M, \quad l \neq m, \quad i = 1, 2 \ldots, N,$$
$$(2.67)$$

where we have extended 2.48 to allow for a multiplicative person-specific component in the transition intensity which may depend upon the origin state but not upon the destination. In effect we have omitted a 'regressor' which affects when you leave state l but not where you go to. Now the full likelihood contribution of person i is built up as the product of the joint densities of the state occupied after each transition and the times at which these transitions occur, conditional on the state history. Given the initial state m_0, the probability that a transition to state m_1 occurs at time t_1 is

$$f_i(m_1, t_1 \mid m_0) = f_i(m_1 \mid t_1, m_0)f_i(t_1 \mid m_0)$$
$$= \frac{\theta_i^{m_0 m_1}(t_1)}{\sum_{l=1}^{M} \theta_i^{m_0 l}(t_1)} f_i(t_1 \mid m_0)$$

$$= \frac{\mu_i^{m_0 m_1}(t_1)\theta_0^{m_0 m_1}(t_1)}{\sum_{l=1}^{M} \mu_i^{m_0 l}(t_1)\theta_0^{m_0 l}(t_1)} f_i(t_1 \mid m_0),$$

where the sums are subject to the condition $l \neq m_0$. Note that v_i has cancelled from the first factor – the baseline hazard would also cancel if it depended only on the origin state. Similarly, the joint density of the state occupied after the second transition and the time – measured from entry to the state – at which it occurs, given the state history is

$$f_i(m_2, t_2 \mid m_0, m_1, t_1) = f_i(m_2 \mid t_2, m_0, m_1, t_1) f_i(t_2 \mid m_0, m_1, t_1)$$

$$= \frac{\mu_i^{m_1 m_2}(t_2)\theta_0^{m_1 m_2}(t_2)}{\sum_{l=1}^{M} \mu_i^{m_1 l}(t_2)\theta_0^{m_1 l}(t_2)} f_i(t_2 \mid m_0, m_1, t_1),$$

where the sum is subject to the condition $l \neq m_1$. Again the unobserved v_i has been eliminated from the first factor. Clearly this is true for every cycle and if we take $\mathcal{L}_P^i$ as the product of the first factors for all transitions made by person i then $\mathcal{L}_P = \prod_{i=1}^{N} \mathcal{L}_P^i$ is a partial likelihood, based on the sequences of transition types, that is free of the person-specific heterogeneity. It corresponds to the factoring in which the vector $\mathbf{s}$ gives the destination states and $\mathbf{x}$ contains the times of transitions. The partial likelihood term $f(s_j \mid \mathbf{x}^{(j)}, \mathbf{s}^{(j-1)})$ is the probability distribution of the state occupied at the end of the j'th cycle given the time of the transition, x_j, and the state history, $(\mathbf{x}^{(j-1)}, \mathbf{s}^{(j-1)})$.

Unfortunately this model appears to lack plausibility in economic applications. Suppose, for example, that the origin state is unemployment and the possible destinations are employment and out of the labour force. The model requires us to assume that any omitted variable has the same effect on the probability of getting a job as it does on dropping out of the labour force. This seems unreasonable.

2.10.3 Integration of the $\{v_i\}$ Again

In section 2.10.1 we described a procedure for integrating a set of person-specific terms out of the partial likelihood. This procedure was in fact originally designed for the case in which there are multiple observations dependent on the same unknown v_i; that is, there are multiple spells for the same 'person'. We shall briefly indicate this generalisation with the case of exactly two spells per person with hazard functions of the form (2.59) except that the $\{\mu_{ij}\}$ do not depend upon t. Thus we have proportional hazards and independence of all spells conditional on $\mathbf{v}$. After the transformations $z_{ij} = \int_0^{t_{ij}} \theta_{i0}(s)ds$ the partial likelihood, given

v, can be written in integral form

$$\mathcal{L}_{P|\mathbf{v}} = \int_{R_1} \int_{R_2} \prod_{i=1}^{N} v_i^2 \mu_{i1}\mu_{i2} \exp\{-v_i(\mu_{i1}z_{i1} + \mu_{i2}z_{i2})\} d\mathbf{z}_1 d\mathbf{z}_2, \quad (2.68)$$

where, as before, R_j is the region in which each element of the vector $\mathbf{z}_j = (z_{1j}, z_{2j}, \dots, z_{Nj})$ is integrated from the immediately preceding uncensored z, zero if there was none. Introducing the parametrically specified mixing distribution $h(\mathbf{v}; \eta)$ the proposed partial likelihood is

$$\mathcal{L}_P = \int_{\mathbf{v}} \mathcal{L}_{P|\mathbf{v}} \, h(\mathbf{v}; \eta) \, d\mathbf{v}. \quad (2.69)$$

The likelihood equations for η and the parameters of the μ's can be solved using a generalisation of the procedure sketched in section 2.10.1. We shall not give details.

This method again requires that the only dependence between spells for the same person be that due to their dependence on the common unobserved v_i. It requires the investigator to choose a parametric form for the mixing distribution. The obvious choice, that of a unit mean Gamma distribution with variance σ^2, has been criticised for the following reason. The dependence between the two spells for the same person is solely induced by v_i, and the one parameter, σ^2, of its distribution can be determined from observations on a single spell for each person as we saw in 2.10.1. Hence we can determine the correlation between two spells from observations on only one of them, which is absurd. If one is to proceed by integrating out common person-specific effects from multiple spell data it is clearly necessary to choose a different mixing distribution. Hougaard (1986) has made this point and proposed the use of stable mixing distributions which avoid this difficulty and which we discussed in chapter 4.

Taking account also of the remarks made at the end of section 2.10.1 it seems reasonable to conclude that the literature on multiple spell mixtures is not yet mature enough to warrant empirical application of the methods described so far without some caution.

2.11   Time-Varying Covariates and Fully Parametric Hazard Models

In section 3 of chapter 2 we examined models with time-varying covariates by considering the joint probability of exit at time t_j and the covariate path to that point, $\mathbf{X}(t_j)$. We deduced that this joint probability could be written as the product of two factors,

$$P\left(T=t_j, \mathbf{X}(t_j)\right) = \theta(t_j; \mathbf{X}(t_j)) \prod_{k=1}^{j-1} [1 - \theta(t_k; \mathbf{X}(t_k))]$$

$$\times \prod_{k=1}^{j} P\left(\mathbf{X}(t_{k-1}, t_k) \mid T \geq t_k, \mathbf{X}(t_k)\right), \quad (2.70)$$

where $\mathbf{X}(t_{k-1}, t_k)$ is the increment in the covariate vector over $t_{k-1} < t \leq t_k$ and $\theta(t; \mathbf{X}(t))$ is the hazard at t conditional on the covariate path to t. We pointed out that the first factor – the first line of (2.70) – could only be interpreted as the conditional probability of exit at t_j given the path $\mathbf{X}(t_j)$ if the covariate vector satisfied the exogeneity condition of definition 1 of that chapter. And it was certainly never interpretable as the value of a probability density function of T conditional on the covariate path. We also remarked that it was nevertheless still possible to treat the product of those first factors for a random flow sample of N individuals as a likelihood and to make inferences about the parameters of a fully parametrically specified hazard model, that is, about $\theta(t; \mathbf{X}(t))$. Such a likelihood is a partial likelihood and we can use the notation and algebra of this chapter to make this point precise.

Let us adapt the general notation developed in section 2.2 of this chapter to the present case. We shall concentrate on a single individual and not, as in most of this chapter, on a sample of N people. We define

$$s_k \equiv \begin{cases} 1 & \text{for } T > t_k, \\ 0 & \text{otherwise.} \end{cases}$$

and $x_k \equiv \mathbf{X}(t_{k-1}, t_k)$. Then, in the notation of this chapter, we can write the probability of exit at t_j and the covariate path to that time, for some particular person, as

$$f(s_1, s_2, \ldots, s_j, x_1, x_2, \ldots, x_j) = f(\mathbf{s}, \mathbf{x}),$$

where the particular values of the s terms are $s_1 = 1$, $s_2 = 1$, $\ldots$, $s_{j-1} = 1$, $s_j = 0$. By the construction used in equation 2.6 we can write this as

$$f(\mathbf{s}, \mathbf{x}) = \prod_{k=1}^{j} f(s_k \mid \mathbf{x}^{(k)}, \mathbf{s}^{(k-1)}) \prod_{k=1}^{j} f(x_k \mid \mathbf{x}^{(k-1)}, \mathbf{s}^{(k-1)}). \quad (2.71)$$

But the first factor in (2.71) is

$$f(s_j \mid \mathbf{x}^{(j)}, \mathbf{s}^{(j-1)}) \prod_{k=1}^{j-1} f(s_k \mid \mathbf{x}^{(k)}, \mathbf{s}^{(k-1)}),$$

which is the first factor in (2.70). Similarly, the second factor is the second factor in (2.70). Thus we see that the first factor in (2.70) is a 'within person' person partial likelihood based on $\mathbf{s}$, the survival information. It is interpretable as a conditional likelihood only if the terms in the second factor do not depend upon $\mathbf{s}^{(k-1)}$, which is the exogeneity condition of chapter 2.

This is a most important conclusion because it shows that econometric inferences in models with time-varying covariates must generally be partial likelihood inferences, even when the hazard is specified fully parametrically. This point has not previously been made in the econometric literature. Of course, if the hazard model involves an unspecified function common to all observations then inferences would be based on the partial likelihood (2.41), as we have previously pointed out.

3   Other Limited Information Likelihoods

Although we have focused so far on partial likelihoods there are other ways of using less than all the information required by a full likelihood that are useful in eliminating components of the model specification about which an investigator is uncertain. In particular it is sometimes helpful to use likelihoods based upon marginal or conditional distributions of the data. We shall describe some of these methods in this section. They all require multiple observations for each of N individuals.

3.1   Marginal Likelihoods for Weibull Models

Let us return to the formulation (2.66)

$$\log v_i + \beta' \mathbf{x}_{ij} + \log z(t_{ij}) = u_{ij}, \quad j = 1, 2; \quad i = 1, 2 \ldots, N, \quad (2.66)$$

in which $z(t_{ij}) = \int_0^{t_{ij}} \theta_{i0}(s)ds$ and u_{i1} and u_{i2} are independently distributed as the logarithms of $\mathcal{E}(1)$ variates given v_i. If one is willing to assume that the observations have Weibull distributions conditional on v_i then this implies that $z(t) = t^\alpha$ and (2.66) reduces to a linear model for $\log t$. First-differencing then gives

$$(\log t_{i2} - \log t_{i1}) = (\beta'/\alpha)(\mathbf{x}_{i1} - \mathbf{x}_{i2}) + \alpha^{-1}(u_{i2} - u_{i1}). \quad (3.1)$$

Since, as we have seen, the difference of the u's has a Logistic distribution it is straightforward to deduce that the density function of the dependent variable in (3.1) is

$$\mathcal{L}^i = \alpha^{-1} \frac{B}{(1 + B)^2}, \quad B = \exp\{\alpha(\log t_{i2} - \log t_{i1}) + \beta'(\mathbf{x}_{i2} - \mathbf{x}_{i1})\}. \quad (3.2)$$

The product of N such terms then gives a marginal likelihood from which α and the coefficients of those x's which vary between spells can be determined. The method generalises to $n_i > 2$ spells per person, the differences of successive u's for the same person having a multivariate Logistic distribution.

It is worth noting that the result just given provides the basis of a test for neglected heterogeneity. We know that such heterogeneity renders the fully parametric estimator of the Weibull α inconsistent, and in fact biases it towards zero. Hence a comparison of the estimate of α computed by maximising the Weibull likelihood, using as data the two vectors $\mathbf{t}_1$ and $\mathbf{t}_2$, with that computed by maximising the likelihood based on (3.2) provides a test – a Hausmann test – for neglected heterogeneity. It is straightforward to work out the variance of this statistic on the null hypothesis – we leave the details to the interested reader.

It may be possible to generalise the method of this section by choosing more general forms for the function $z(t)$, for example, $\log z(t) = \alpha(t^\lambda - 1)/\lambda$, which includes the Weibull as the special case $\lambda \to 0$. This approach has not been studied, nor has the extension to handle right censored data.

3.2 A Conditional Likelihood for the Time-Dependent Poisson Process

The marginal and partial likelihoods for eliminating unobserved person-specific effects require two or more conditionally independent observations per person and they work if the regressors vary between spells. The sampling scheme which produces such conditionally independent spells has been left unspecified, which ought to leave the reader feeling uneasy. In this section we shall give another method of estimating the effects of time-varying regressors free of person-specific effects. This method makes totally explicit the sampling scheme but at the cost of specifying a specific stochastic process for the way in which repeat spells are generated.

Suppose that we are observing a time-dependent Poisson process in which events are both endings and starts of spells. A practical example might be a sequence of 'jobs', each event being the end of one job and the start of another. The probability of an event for person i in the short interval from t to $t + dt$ is specified as

$$P(\text{an event in } (t, t + dt)) = v_i \lambda_i(t) dt + \circ(dt), \tag{3.3}$$

where $\lambda_i(t) = \lambda(\mathbf{x}_i(t); \beta)$, $\mathbf{x}_i(t)$ being a vector of time-varying regressors for person i and β is a vector of parameters. The effect of any time-constant regressors can be thought of as absorbed in the person-specific parameter v_i. Note that the time variation is calendar time measured from some fixed origin, not duration time measured from the occurrence of each event. Now we know that we can change such a time-dependent Poisson process into a time-homogeneous one by a transformation of the time scale. Specifically, let us define a new, person-specific, clock by

$$z_i(t) = \int_0^t \lambda_i(s)ds, \tag{3.4}$$

with $dz_i(t) = \lambda_i(t)dt$. Then the probability of an event in the interval from z to $z + dz$ is

$$P(\text{an event in } (z, z+dz)) = v_i\lambda_i(t)dt + \circ(dt)$$
$$= v_i dz_i + \circ(dz_i)$$

and in z time events occur in an ordinary Poisson process at the constant rate v_i.

Now let us introduce the sampling scheme. Assume we observe continuously from times $t = a$ to $t = b$, chosen independently of any of the N processes so that, in general, there is no event at either a or b. Note that this is a sampling scheme which induces dependence between spell durations given the number that occur so that the differencing methods of the previous section are inapplicable. The interval from a to b on the t clock is the interval from $z_i(a)$ to $z_i(b)$ on person i's z clock, and we know from chapter 5 that, given that n_i events occur in the interval, the times at which they occur are uniformly distributed over the interval. Specifically, given that n events occur in $z_i(a) - z_i(b)$ the probability that they occur at the successive times $z_i(t_1)$, $z_i(t_2)$, ..., $z_i(t_n)$ is

$$P(z_i(t_1), z_i(t_2), \ldots, z_i(t_n)) = \frac{n!}{[z_i(b) - z_i(a)]^n}.$$

Hence if we define

$$\mathcal{L}_C^i = \frac{n_i!}{[\int_0^b \lambda_i(s)ds - \int_0^a \lambda_i(s)ds]^{n_i}}$$
$$= \frac{n_i!}{[\int_a^b \lambda_i(s)ds]^{n_i}} \tag{3.5}$$

we have, in $\mathcal{L}_C = \prod_{i=1}^N \mathcal{L}_C^i$, a likelihood free of the $\{v_i\}$ but involving the parameter vector β. This is a conditional likelihood because it conditions on the numbers of events – jobs begun – by each person. The conditioning eliminates the $\{v_i\}$ because in the Poisson process of rate v_i the number of events occurring in a fixed interval is a sufficient statistic for v_i.

4   Some Non-Parametric Estimators

4.1   Non-Parametric Estimation of the Survivor Function

In this section we shall describe the estimation of the survivor function from a set of possibly right censored exit times. These times are to be thought of as independent realisations of a random variable T with survivor function $\overline{F}(t)$. Thus we are assuming the data are homogeneous – there are no regressors to make observations on different persons' drawings from different distributions. Since economic data are rarely homogeneous this section is not of direct relevance to econometric work. It is, however, indirectly very important because the technique we describe plays a key role in testing of model specification, as we shall explain in chapter 11.

If we have a parametric model for the hazard function, and thus for the survivor function, then one would naturally estimate $\overline{F}(t)$ by replacing unknown parameters by maximum likelihood estimates. This section, however, deals with the case where there is no such model – the method is to be *non-parametric*.

To begin with, suppose we have N uncensored times and let there be $M \leq N$ distinct exit times arranged in order of magnitude as $t_{(1)}$, $t_{(2)}$, $\ldots$, $t_{(M)}$. Thus we are allowing multiple exits at the same time. Let n_j be the number of people leaving at $t_{(j)}$, where $n_1 + n_2 + \cdots + n_M = N$. Now defining $\overline{F}(t) = P(T \geq t)$, $t \geq 0$, we would naturally estimate a probability by a relative frequency and so estimate $\overline{F}(t)$ by the proportion of the N people observed to leave at or after t, which is

$$\hat{\overline{F}}(t) = 1 - \frac{(\text{number leaving before t})}{N}$$

$$= 1 - \frac{(n_1 + n_2 + \cdots + n_k)}{N}, \tag{4.1}$$

where k is the largest j such that $t_{(j)} < t$. If there is no such k then $\overline{F}(t) = 1$. Let us rearrange this expression in the following way.

$$\hat{\overline{F}}(t) = 1 - \frac{(n_1 + n_2 + \cdots + n_k)}{N} = \frac{(N - n_1 - n_2 - \cdots - n_k)}{N}$$

$$= \left(\frac{N - n_1}{N} \right) \left(\frac{N - n_1 - n_2}{N - n_1} \right) \left(\frac{N - n_1 - n_2 - n_3}{N - n_1 - n_2} \right) \cdots$$

$$\times \left(\frac{N - n_1 - n_2 - \cdots - n_k}{N - n_1 - n_2 - \cdots - n_{k-1}} \right)$$

$$= \left(1 - \frac{n_1}{N} \right) \left(1 - \frac{n_2}{N - n_1} \right) \left(1 - \frac{n_3}{N - n_1 - n_2} \right) \cdots$$

$$\times \left(1 - \frac{n_k}{N - n_1 - n_2 - \cdots - n_{k-1}}\right)$$

$$= \prod_{t_{(j)} < t} (1 - \hat{\theta}_j) \qquad\qquad 4.2$$

for

$$\hat{\theta}_j = \frac{n_j}{N - n_1 - n_2 - \cdots - n_{j-1}}. \qquad\qquad (4.3)$$

Now $\hat{\theta}_j$ is the ratio of the number of people who left at $t_{(j)}$ to the total number of people who *could* have left then – the people who had not left earlier. This latter number is the size of the risk set at $t_{(j)}$ in the language of partial likelihood. Thus $\hat{\theta}_j$ estimates the probability of leaving at $t_{(j)}$ given survival to that date; that is, it estimates the hazard at that date. This observation immediately indicates how to generalise the estimator (4.3) to handle right censored data since if r_j denotes the number of people in the risk set at $t_{(j)}$ we must surely estimate the hazard at $t_{(j)}$ by n_j/r_j, and this gives us

Theorem 13   *For homogeneous right censored data the survivor function at t can be estimated by*

$$\hat{\bar{F}}(t) = \prod_{t_{(j)} < t} (1 - \hat{\theta}_j), \qquad t \geq 0, \qquad\qquad (4.4)$$

for $\hat{\theta}_j = n_j/r_j$, where n_j is the number of people – possibly only one – observed to leave at $t_{(j)}$ and r_j is the number of people in the risk set the instant before $t_{(j)}$. The subscript j runs over the M distinct times at which exits are observed.

The estimator (4.4) is called the Kaplan–Meier survivor function estimator after the two people who first studied it.[1] It is also called the product limit estimator. It is a step function with steps at each observed (uncensored) exit time. It can be shown to be a maximum likelihood estimator in a generalisation of the usual likelihood problem in which the object is to estimate not a parameter but a function.[2] In the next section we shall describe another example of such a problem.

The estimator (4.4) can also be obtained by the following simple argument. $\bar{F}(t) = \exp\{-\int_0^t \theta(s)ds\} = \exp\{-z(t)\}$, so to estimate this we

---

[1] Kaplan and Meier (1958).

[2] Kalbfleisch and Prentice (1980) give a neat heuristic proof of this.

could estimate $z(t)$ and solve for $\overline{F}$. To estimate $z(t)$ we could estimate $\theta(s)$ at each s in $0 \leq s < t$ and add them up. At time points where no one left, the natural estimate of θ would be zero. At other points it would be $n_j/r_j = \hat{\theta}_j$. This leads to an estimate of $z(t)$ as

$$\hat{z}(t) = \sum_{t_{(j)}<t} \hat{\theta}_j, \qquad (4.5)$$

and an estimate of $\overline{F}(t)$ as

$$\hat{\overline{F}}(t) = \exp\left\{ -\sum_{t_{(j)}<t} \hat{\theta}_j \right\}. \qquad (4.6)$$

But the Kaplan–Meier estimator can be written

$$\hat{\overline{F}}(t) = \exp\left\{ \sum_{t_{(j)}<t} \log(1-\hat{\theta}_j) \right\}$$

$$\sim \exp\left\{ -\sum_{t_{(j)}<t} \hat{\theta}_j \right\}, \qquad (4.7)$$

where we have used the approximation, valid for small x, $\log(1-x) \sim -x$. Since the $\hat{\theta}_j$ usually *will* be small (4.7) will usually be numerically close to the Kaplan–Meier estimate. Alternatively, we could have used the unbiased estimator of $z(t)$ given by (2.38) at each uncensored exit time when there are no multiple exits. Setting all the $\{\mu_i\}$ equal to one, since here the data are homogeneous, we must have $\Psi_j = r_j$, which again leads to (4.6).

The $\hat{\theta}_j$ may be shown to be approximately independent with variances given by the binomial expression $\text{var}(\hat{\theta}_j) = \theta_j(1-\theta_j)/r_j$ as the r_j become large. Using the first expression in (4.7), expanding $\log(1-\hat{\theta}_j)$ about θ_j up to the linear term and taking variances gives

$$\text{var}(\log\hat{\overline{F}}(t)) \sim \sum_{t_{(j)}<t} \frac{\theta_j}{(1-\theta_j)r_j}. \qquad (4.8)$$

Since $\text{var}(x) \sim x^2\,\text{var}(\log x)$ when x is a function of variates with variances of $O(N^{-1})$ (4.8) gives

$$\text{var}(\hat{\overline{F}}(t)) = \left(\hat{\overline{F}}(t)\right)^2 \sum_{t_{(j)}<t} \frac{\hat{\theta}_j}{(1-\hat{\theta}_j)r_j} \qquad (4.9)$$

as an estimate of the variance of the estimated survivor function at t.

Table 9.3.   The Kaplan–Meier
Survivor Function Estimator

t	r	$1 - \hat{\theta}$	$\hat{\overline{F}}(t)$
0.10	40	.9750	.975
0.26	39	.9744	.950
0.40*			
0.42	37	.9730	.924
0.47	36	.9722	.899
0.58	35	.9428	.847
0.61*			
0.67	32	.9687	.821

*Note: $N = 40$ of which six were censored; two exits occurred at $t = 0.58$.

Example 14
To illustrate the calculation of the Kaplan–Meier survivor function estimate we drew forty randomly right censored observations from an Exponential distribution of mean 5 and ordered them in magnitude marking the six censored observations with an asterisk. In table 9.3 we show the calculation of the survivor function estimate at points up to $t_{(7)}$.

Had we known that the data were Exponentially distributed we would have estimated the survivor function parametrically as $\hat{\overline{F}}(t) = e^{-\hat{\lambda}t}$ where $\hat{\lambda} = 0.217$ for these data compared to a true value of $\lambda = 0.200$. Figure 9.2 compares the Kaplan–Meier and parametric estimates of $\overline{F}$.   ∎

4.2   Non-Parametric Estimation of the Mixing Distribution

Let us consider again the model in which the hazard involves an unobserved person-specific scalar v_i so that, given v_i, the hazard is $v_i \theta(t, \mathbf{x}_i)$. In this chapter we have been studying methods of inference which do not require a full parametric specification of the hazard function. We have considered the following cases:

1. v_i was absent and theta factored as $\theta(t, \mathbf{x}_i) = \mu(\mathbf{x}_i(t))\theta_0(t)$;

2. v_i was present but multiple observations on t_i allowed the elimination of v_i from partial, marginal, or conditional likelihoods; and

3. v_i was a realisation from a parametrically specified distribution and theta was a proportional hazard so that v_i could be integrated out of a partial likelihood.

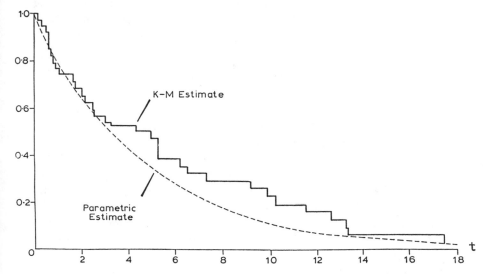

Figure 9.2. Kaplan–Meier (—) and parametric (−−) estimates of a survivor function – 40 observations of which 6 censored.

In this final section we shall consider a fourth case in which

4. v_i is a realisation from a parametrically *unspecified* mixing distribution, $H(v)$, but the remainder of the hazard is specified up to an unknown parameter vector γ. Thus we have non-parametric estimation of the mixing distribution together with fully parametric estimation of $\theta(t, \mathbf{x})$.

The density function of t given v, which we have been calling *the* conditional distribution in earlier work, is $f(t \mid v) = v\theta e^{-vz(t)}$; the data density function is

$$f(t) = \int_0^\infty v\theta e^{-vz(t)} \, dH(v), \qquad (4.10)$$

where H is the mixing distribution and we have written the mixture in the general form $\int dH(v)$ to allow for H to be *any* distribution, discrete, continuous, or mixed. We now want to focus on estimation of H so we shall, for the moment, assume that γ is known, which implies that $\theta(t)$ and $z(t)$ are known and we can transform in the usual way from t to $z(t)$ with density function

$$f_H(z) = \int_0^\infty v e^{-vz} \, dH(v), \qquad (4.11)$$

where we have subscripted f to indicate that it was derived using mixing distribution H. For an uncensored random sample of size N from (4.11) the joint density function is

$$\mathcal{L}(H) = \prod_{i=1}^{N} f_H(z_i). \qquad (4.12)$$

This is the likelihood function for H (for known γ) over $H \in \mathcal{M}$, where $\mathcal{M}$ is the set of all possible probability distributions for v. Note that the argument of the likelihood function is not a finite dimensional parameter vector but a probability distribution. This fact makes the standard distribution theory for maximum likelihood estimators inapplicable, and proofs of the properties of maximum likelihood estimators have to be derived anew. We are in a non-regular case.

In this section we shall give an account of what is known about the problem of finding an H to maximise $\mathcal{L}$ in (4.12). Though we shall give the main theorems we shall concentrate on explanation rather than proofs which sometimes require a level of mathematics beyond that at which this book is written. The exposition is based on the remarkable papers by Lindsay (1983).

The first requirement for estimation is that γ and H be identifiable. Identifiability has been proved for a number of special classes of conditional distribution of which the most relevant for the purposes of this book is the class of proportional hazard models. We gave an account of some of these identifiability results in chapter 7. The next step is to prove the *existence* of a consistent maximum likelihood estimator. Kiefer and Wolfowitz (1956) gave conditions on the joint density function of t and the regressor vector $\mathbf{x}$ for such existence and these must be verified for any proposed model. Verification of these conditions is not particularly easy and we refer the reader to the paper by Heckman and Singer (1984), who gave a detailed verification of the Kiefer and Wolfowitz conditions for the case in which the conditional density function was a proportional hazards Weibull model. We shall assume the existence of a consistent maximum likelihood estimator and concentrate our exposition on explaining the form taken by that estimator and how it might be computed.

Let us first establish some notation. We assume that we have N distinct observations $z_1, \ldots, z_N$.

Definition 4   *Consider a finite discrete mixing distribution in which probability π_j is attached to the point v_j for $j = 1, 2 \ldots, M$. The set $\{v_1, v_2, \ldots, v_M\}$ contains the points of support of the distribution and M*

is the support size. *(In the sociometric literature the $\{v_j\}$ are sometimes called mass points.)*

Definition 5   *The N vector $\mathbf{f}_V = (f_v(z_1), f_v(z_2), \ldots f_v(z_N))$ which contains the conditional density functions evaluated at the N observations is called the* atomic likelihood vector. *It is called this because $f_v(z_j)$ corresponds to a degenerate mixing distribution which puts all the probability in H on a single point or atom. A degenerate mixing distribution has only one point of support.*

Definition 6   *The N vector $\mathbf{f}_H = (f_H(z_1), f_H(z_2), \ldots f_H(z_N))$ is called the* mixture likelihood vector. *Note that if H puts all the mass at a single point $\bar{v}$ then $\mathbf{f}_H = \mathbf{f}_{\bar{v}}$.*

Example 15
For the $N = 2$ observations $z_1 = 1$, $z_2 = 2$ then

$$\mathbf{f}_V = (ve^{-v}, ve^{-2v}),$$

$$\mathbf{f}_H = \left(\int_0^\infty ve^{-v}\, dH(v), \int_0^\infty ve^{-2v}\, dH(v) \right). \quad \blacksquare$$

Definition 7   *The* likelihood curve *is the function from the non-negative real axis to R^N defined by $v \to \mathbf{f}_V$. The trace of this curve is $\Gamma = \{\mathbf{f}_V : v \in \Omega\}$ and it represents all possible atomic likelihood vectors corresponding to different values of v in Ω, the non-negative real axis.*

Example 15 (continued)
Figure 9.3 gives the curve Γ for the data of example 15. The vertical axis measures $f_v(z_1) = ve^{-v}$ and the horizontal axis measures $f_v(z_2) = ve^{-2v}$. $\quad \blacksquare$

Definition 8   *The* convex hull *of the set Γ, denoted $conv(\Gamma)$, is the intersection of all convex sets containing Γ. It is the smallest convex set in R^N containing Γ.*

Example 16
In figure 9.3, since Γ traces out a convex set, that set, shaded, is $conv(\Gamma)$. But take the case $N = 2$, $z_1 = 1$, $z_2 = 7$, for which Γ is given in figure 9.4. In this case Γ does not trace out the boundary of a convex set and the shaded area here, which gives $conv(\Gamma)$, does not coincide with the boundary and interior of Γ. $\quad \blacksquare$

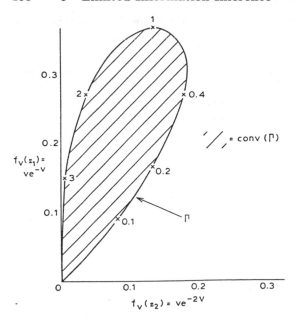

Figure 9.3.   Gamma and its convex hull for $N = 2$, $z_1 = 1$, $z_2 = 2$.

We can now give the main theorem characterising maximum likelihood estimators of the mixing distribution, H.

Theorem 14   *If Γ is closed and bounded, that is, it is compact, there exists a unique vector $\hat{\mathbf{f}}$, on the boundary of $conv(\Gamma)$, which maximises the likelihood, (4.12), on that set. The point $\hat{\mathbf{f}}$ can be expressed as $\mathbf{f}_H$, where H is a discrete distribution with at most N points of support.*

Let us take the final sentence of the theorem first. Any point in $conv(\Gamma)$ can, by the definition of a convex set, be expressed as a convex combination of points in Γ. That is, any vector $\mathbf{f}$ in $conv(\Gamma)$ can be written

$$\mathbf{f} = \sum_{j=1}^{M} \pi_j \mathbf{f}_j, \qquad (4.13)$$

where the $\{\mathbf{f}_j\}$ lie in Γ and the $\{\pi_j\}$ form a probability distribution. A theorem in convex analysis, Carathéodory's theorem, says that points on the boundary of $conv(\Gamma)$ can be expressed in this way *with M at*

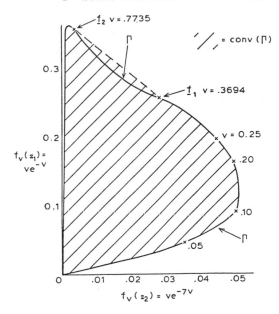

Figure 9.4.   Gamma and its convex hull for $N = 2$, $z_1 = 1$, $z_2 = 7$.

most equal to N. Any vector on the boundary of $conv(\Gamma)$ can be written as a convex combination of at most N points in Γ.

Example 16 (continued)
In figure 9.4, points on the solid portion of the boundary can be written in the form (4.13) with $M = 1$, while points on the dashed portion can be written this way with $M = N = 2$.   ■

We can now ask why we are interested in $conv(\Gamma)$ anyway when our object is to find an $H \in \mathcal{M}$ to maximise $\mathcal{L}$. The answer to this question is the key to the argument. It is that, from a theorem in convex geometry, $conv(\Gamma)$ is the set of all vectors $\mathbf{f}_H$ produced by mixing distributions $H \in \mathcal{M}$: $conv(\Gamma) = \{\mathbf{f}_H : H \in \mathcal{M}\}$. Thus instead of looking among the members of $\mathcal{M}$ to find an H that maximises $\mathcal{L}$ we can look among the set $conv(\Gamma)$ to find a vector $\mathbf{f}_H$ that maximises $\mathcal{L}$. The first part of the theorem tells us that such a maximising vector $\mathbf{f}$ does exist, is unique, and lies on the boundary of $conv(\Gamma)$. The argument underlying this proposition is as follows; $\log \mathcal{L} = \sum_{i=1}^{N} \log f_H(z_i)$, which, regarded as a function of the N arguments $f_H(z_i)$, is increasing and concave. Such a function achieves a unique maximum over a compact set on the boundary of that set. Thus $\mathcal{L}$ is maximised by a point on the boundary of $conv(\Gamma)$. But, as we have seen, any such point may be represented as a convex combination of at most N points in Γ. Thus the maximising H is a discrete mixture with at most N points of support.

One further point that may have occurred to the reader is that even though we can find an $\hat{\mathbf{f}}$ in $conv(\Gamma)$ that maximises $\mathcal{L}$ and that can be represented as a mixture with no more than N components, how do we know that such a representation is unique? It may be that $\hat{\mathbf{f}}$ can be represented as a mixture in more than one way so the maximising mixing distribution is not unique. The answer is that one can prove, for certain classes of conditional (atomic) distributions, that the mixture representation of $\hat{\mathbf{f}}$ is unique. In particular uniqueness can be proved for the conditional distribution ve^{-vz} that concerns us here.

Example 17
The case where γ is known and $N = 2$ can be solved 'by hand' in the following way. Take the data of figure 9.4 in which $z_1 = 1$, $z_2 = 7$. If the solution lies on the solid line it is in Γ and a one point or degenerate mixture. The optimal one-point mixture is found by maximising the likelihood $\mathcal{L} = \prod_{i=1}^{2} ve^{-vz_i} = v^2 e^{-8v}$ with solution $\hat{v} = 0.25$ with probability one. At this point the value of the log likelihood is 0.2381. Any possibly superior two-point mixture lies on the dashed portion of the boundary of $conv(\Gamma)$ and all such points are a convex combination of the two vectors $\mathbf{f}_1, \mathbf{f}_2$ which provide its end points. If we can calculate $\mathbf{f}_1$ and $\mathbf{f}_2$ we can easily find that weighted average of these two-points that maximises $\log \mathcal{L}$ and see if the maximum exceeds 0.2381. How do we find these end points? The answer is that they are the points at which the curvature of trace Γ changes sign. In figure 9.3 the curve is always bending to the left as we move – anticlockwise – through larger and larger values of v. In figure 9.4 by contrast the curve starts to bend to the right at $\mathbf{f}_1$ and to the left again at $\mathbf{f}_2$. The curvature of a function such as trace Γ defined parametrically, with parameter v, at a point is

$$k = \frac{f_1' f_2'' - f_2' f_1''}{(f_1'^2 + f_2'^2)^{3/2}},$$

where we have written f_i for $f_v(z_i)$ and where the primes indicate differentiation with respect to v. If we carry out the differentiation we find that k has the same sign as the quadratic in v, $M(v) = v^2(z_1 z_2) - v(z_1 + z_2) + 2$, which for the data of our example is $7v^2 - 8v + 2$. This has the two roots $v_2 = 0.7735, v_1 = 0.3694$, corresponding to the two changes in curvature, and these suffice to determine $\mathbf{f}_1$ and $\mathbf{f}_2$. The final step is to maximise the likelihood for a two-point mixture with probabilities π and $1 - \pi$

attached to v_1 and v_2. If we do this we find that the likelihood is a monotonic function of π indicating that it can be increased by reverting to a one-point mixture. Hence we conclude that the overall optimal mixture has just one point of support, $v = 0.25$. ∎

We can summarise our discussion so far as follows. For any given vector γ of parameters of $\theta(t, \mathbf{x})$ we can transform the problem to that of estimating the mixing distribution H for the distribution $\int v e^{-vz}\, dH(v)$. The maximum likelihood estimator of H exists, is unique, and is a finite discrete mixture with no more than N points of support. In practice it seems invariably to be the case that the number of points of support accorded positive probability in the maximum likelihood estimate of the mixing distribution is much smaller than the number of observations. The explanation for this fact is not known.

We can now go on from this to solve the full problem of finding the maximum likelihood estimator of both H and γ, assuming the Kiefer–Wolfowitz conditions are satisfied, by maximising the full likelihood

$$\mathcal{L} = \prod_{i=1}^{N} \int_0^{\infty} v\theta(t_i; \mathbf{x}_i, \gamma) \exp\{-vz(t_i; \mathbf{x}_i, \gamma)\}\, dH(v) \qquad (4.14)$$

with respect to γ given $H = \hat{H}$. The resulting estimate of γ can then be used to recalculate the $\{z_i\}$ and a new estimate of H is made. This in turn can be substituted into (4.14) and the iteration continued until an overall maximum is found. Some details of the computation are given in section 4.2.1.

It is possible to extend this procedure to the case of multiple observations for each individual in which the hazard for the j'th spell for person i is $v_i\theta(t_{ij}; \mathbf{x}_{ij}, \gamma)$. If the spells are stochastically independent, given v_i, the likelihood contribution for person i, for whom there were n spells, is

$$f(\mathbf{t}) = \int_0^{\infty} \prod_{j=1}^{n} v\theta(t_{ij}) \exp\{-vz(t_{ij})\}\, dH(v).$$

For a given vector γ we can transform to $z_{ij} = \int_0^{t_{ij}} \theta(s; \mathbf{x}_{ij}, \gamma)\, ds$ to get the likelihood contribution of person i as $\int_0^{\infty} v^n \exp\{-vz_{i.}\}\, dH(v)$ for $z_{i.} = \sum_{j=1}^{n} z_{ij}$. The argument then proceeds as before except that the conditional or atomic density function is not ve^{-vz_i} but $v^n e^{-vz_{i.}}$.

Although we can establish the existence and character of the non-parametric maximum likelihood estimators of the mixing distribution no asymptotic distribution theory for the estimator, apart from consistency, has been derived and, in particular, asymptotic Normality for $\hat{\gamma}$

has not been established. This procedure is also open to the criticism that it lays excessive emphasis upon the estimation of 'the error distribution', $H(v)$, which is not of economic interest. Since the calculations are long and error prone – multiple local maxima appear to be common – it is arguable that simpler approximate solutions, perhaps involving a reasonably flexible *parametric* form for H, are preferable. Practical econometric experience with this procedure has so far been very limited, so firm conclusions as to its value are not yet warranted.

4.2.1   Computational Details

This non-parametric method poses a computational problem of a type that will be unfamiliar to econometricians and we shall therefore devote some space to explaining how the maximisation of the likelihood function can actually be done.

The EM Algorithm for a Finite Mixture

Since the non-parametric maximum likelihood estimator of the mixing distribution is a finite mixture it is inevitable that part of the computations will involve fitting such a mixture. This can be done by a rather elegant application of the EM algorithm in the following way. Suppose we have to fit a mixture with known, given, number of support points, M. The points of support are the M unknown values $v_1, \ldots, v_M$ to which the M unknown probabilities $\pi_1, \ldots, \pi_M$ are attached. If we let $\delta_i = \{\delta_{ij}\}$ be a random M vector whose j'th element is unity if the value of v for person i is v_j and zero otherwise the density function of $\mathbf{d}_i$ is

$$f(\mathbf{d}_i) = \prod_{j=1}^{M} \pi_j^{\delta_{ij}}. \tag{4.15}$$

Similarly the density function of $z_i = z(t_i)$ given v_i can be written

$$f(z_i \mid \mathbf{d}_i) = \prod_{j=1}^{M} (v_j e^{-v_j z_i})^{\delta_{ij}}. \tag{4.16}$$

Their product gives the joint density of z_i and $\mathbf{d}_i$, and multiplying N of these together gives the full information likelihood for π and $\mathbf{v}$,

$$\mathcal{L}(\pi, \mathbf{v}) = \prod_{i=1}^{N} \prod_{j=1}^{M} (\pi_j v_j e^{-v_j z_{ij}})^{\delta_{ij}}. \tag{4.17}$$

To apply the EM algorithm we regard the $\{\delta_{ij}\}$ as missing data and consider the expected value of $\log \mathcal{L}$ given the observations, the $\{z_i\}$.

This is

$$Q = \sum_{i=1}^{N}\sum_{j=1}^{M} d_{ij}\log(\pi_j v_j e^{-v_j z_{ij}}), \qquad \text{where } d_{ij} = \mathrm{E}\left(\delta_{ij} \mid \mathbf{z}\right), \ (4.18)$$

$$= \mathrm{P}\left(V_i = v_j \mid \mathbf{z}\right)$$

$$= \mathrm{P}\left(V_i = v_j \mid z_i\right)$$

$$= \frac{f(z_i \mid V_i = v_j)\mathrm{P}\left(V_i = v_j\right)}{\sum_{m=1}^{M} f(z_i \mid V_i = v_m)\mathrm{P}\left(V_i = v_m\right)}, \qquad \text{by Bayes' theorem,}$$

$$= \frac{\pi_j v_j e^{-v_j z_i}}{\sum_{m=1}^{M} \pi_m v_m e^{-v_m z_i}}. \tag{4.19}$$

Let the $\{d_{ij}\}$ be calculated at the point π^p, $\mathbf{v}^p$ so that $Q = Q(\pi, \mathbf{v}; \pi^p, \mathbf{v}^p)$. The M step is to find the maximum of Q with respect to $\pi, \mathbf{v}$. The solutions $\hat{\pi}, \hat{\mathbf{v}}$ are then taken as $\pi^p, \mathbf{v}^p$ in calculating new values of the $\{d_{ij}\}$ by the E step, (4.19), and the maximisation is repeated, and so on.

The equations to determine $\hat{\pi}, \hat{\mathbf{v}}$ are

$$\partial Q/\partial v_j = \sum_{i=1}^{N} d_{ij}\left(\frac{1}{v_j} - z_i\right) = 0, \quad j = 1,2\ldots,M,$$

$$\partial Q/\partial \pi_j = \sum_{i=1}^{N}\left(\frac{d_{ij}}{\pi_j} - \frac{d_{iM}}{\pi_M}\right) = 0, \quad j = 1,2\ldots,M-1,$$

with $\pi_M = 1-\pi_1-\pi_2-\cdots-\pi_{M-1}$. These may be solved explicitly to give

$$\hat{v}_j = \frac{\sum_{i=1}^{N} d_{ij}}{\sum_{i=1}^{N} d_{ij}z_i}, \quad j = 1,2\ldots,M, \tag{4.20}$$

$$\hat{\pi}_j = \frac{\sum_{i=1}^{N} d_{ij}}{\sum_{i=1}^{N}\sum_{j=1}^{M} d_{ij}}$$

$$= \sum_{i=1}^{N} d_{ij}/N, \qquad j = 1,2\ldots,M.$$

Thus both the expectation step (4.19) and the maximisation step (4.20) of the algorithm are easy and involve no non-linear equations. There are, however, two problems. The first is the usual one that a large number of iterations may be required. It may be sensible to switch to a Newton–Raphson iteration after a number of iterations of the EM algorithm in order to speed convergence. The second is that multiple maxima can occur. It will usually be necessary to experiment with alternative initial values for the π's and v's.

Derivatives with Respect to a Mixing Distribution

It must be emphasised that the probem of non-parametric estimation of the mixing distribution and the problem of fitting a finite mixture that we have just described are not the same, even though the maximum likelihood estimator of the mixing distribution is in fact finite and discrete. The crucial difference is that in the former problem the support size, M, is an unknown parameter. A second difference is the presence of the unknown parameters γ in the former problem. Leaving aside this second difference for the moment, it is clear that a possible computational strategy is to repeat the calculations described in the last section for different values of M, which immediately suggests the desirability of having some criterion which tells us when the optimal mixing distribution has been found. In the usual parametric case one can test whether any parameter point provides a maximum of the likelihood function by examining the first and second derivatives. What we require here is some analogue of this procedure when we are maximising not with respect to a finite parameter vector but with respect to a probability distribution. The answer is provided by the Gâteaux derivative, which we shall now explain and then use to give a criterion for checking whether any claimed optimal mixing distribution is indeed so.

Using the notation of definition 6 consider two vectors $\mathbf{f}_{H_0}$ and $\mathbf{f}_{H_1}$ corresponding to the mixing distributions H_0 and H_1. The log likelihood is $\log \mathcal{L}(H) = \sum_{i=1}^{N} f_H(z_i) = L(H)$. The derivative of $L(H)$ at H_0, in the direction of H_1, the Gâteaux derivative, is

$$F_L(H_0, H_1) = \lim_{\epsilon \to 0} \epsilon^{-1}[L\{(1-\epsilon)H_0 + \epsilon H_1\} - L(H_0)].$$

Finding the limit, using l'Hôpital's rule and the definition of $L(H)$, we find

$$F_L(H_0, H_1) = \sum_{i=1}^{N} \frac{[f_{H_1}(z_i) - f_{H_0}(z_i)]}{f_{H_0}(z_i)}$$

$$= \sum_{i=1}^{N} \left[\frac{f_{H_1}(z_i)}{f_{H_0}(z_i)} - 1 \right].$$

Now let H_0 be some mixing distribution which is claimed to be optimal and let H_1 be the degenerate, one-point mixing distribution with all its probability at some point v. We denote the derivative in this special case by

$$D(v, H) = \sum_{i=1}^{N} \left[\frac{f_v(z_i)}{f_H(z_i)} - 1 \right].$$

This derivative provides the criterion for testing any claimed optimal mixing distribution.

Theorem 15

   1. *If $\hat{H}$ maximises the likelihood then $\hat{H}$ can be equivalently characterised by (a) $\hat{H}$ maximises $\mathcal{L}(H)$; (b) $\hat{H}$ minimises $\sup_v D(v, H)$; (c) $\sup_v D(v, \hat{H}) = 0$.*
   2. *The point $\mathbf{f}_{\hat{H}}, \mathbf{f}_{\hat{H}}$ is a saddle point of F_L in the sense that*

$$F_L(\mathbf{f}_{H_0}, \mathbf{f}_{\hat{H}}) \le 0 = F_L(\mathbf{f}_{\hat{H}}, \mathbf{f}_{\hat{H}}) \le F_L(\mathbf{f}_{\hat{H}}, \mathbf{f}_{H_1}),$$

for all $H_0, H_1 \in \mathcal{M}$.
   3. *The support of $\hat{H}$ is contained in the set of v for which $D(v, \hat{H}) = 0$.*

The theorem tells us that in order to tell if some H is optimal we can inspect the derivative of L from H in the direction of $\mathbf{f}_v$ regarded as a function of v and see whether its supremum is zero. Part 3 tells us that this derivative will actually be zero, if H is optimal, at values of v which are points of support for H. Notice in particular that one only needs to look at the derivative from $\mathbf{f}_{\hat{H}}$ to $\mathbf{f}_v$. If $\hat{H}$ is optimal, part 2 tells us that the derivative towards *any* other mixture, and not merely the one-point mixture $\mathbf{f}_v$, will automatically be non-positive. This is analogous to the case of maximisation of a parametric function where one only needs to check the derivatives in directions parallel to the axes in order to establish that a maximum has been reached. If $D(v, \hat{H})$ is differentiable in v, as it is when $f_v(z) = ve^{-vz}$, the theorem carries the implication that if $\hat{H}$ is optimal then at all points of support, v^*, we must have

$$D(v^*, \hat{H}) = 0, \quad D'(v^*, \hat{H}) = 0, \quad D''(v^*, \hat{H}) \le 0,$$

where primes denote differentiation with respect to v.

Example 18
For the problem of example 17 we claimed that a one-point mixture with all the probability at $v = 0.25$ was optimal. To check this we calculate

$$D(v, \hat{H}) = \sum_{i=1}^{2} \left[\frac{ve^{-vz_i}}{0.25e^{-0.25z_i}} - 1 \right].$$

It is readily verified that this function has a single maximum at $v = 0.25$ at which $D = 0$. Thus the one-point mixture is optimal and no two-point mixture could have increased the likelihood.   ■

Bounds for the Support Points

In example 17 we made use of the quadratic $M(v) = v^2(z_1 z_2) - v(z_1 + z_2) + 2$ whose roots located the changes of curvature of trace Γ. Now the best one-point 'mixture' was at $v = 1/\bar{z} = 0.25$ marked in the figure. It could, however, in principle, have been the case that the best one-point mixture lay at a value of v between the roots of $M(v)$ and if so it could not have been an optimal mixing distribution because we know optima lie on the boundary of $conv(\Gamma)$. This type of argument can be generalised to rule out certain portions of the non-negative axis, a priori, as possible locations for the support points of the optimal mixing distribution. In particular we have

Theorem 16   *Let $(z_{(1)}, z_{(2)}, \ldots, z_{(N)})$ be the order statistics of the sample and let*

$$M_{ij}(v) = v^2[z_{(i)} z_{(j)}] - v[z_{(i)} + z_{(j)}] + 2$$

be the mixture quadratic corresponding to the pair of data points $(z_{(i)}, z_{(j)})$. Then

1. There can be no more than one point of support in each interval where $M_{1N}(v) > 0$. If $M_{1N}(v) > 0$ on $[z_{(1)}, z_{(N)}]$ then $\hat{H}$ must put probability one at $v = 1/\bar{z}$;

2. The optimal mixing distribution can have no support points between the real roots of $M_{j,j+1}(v)$, $j = 1, 2 \ldots, N - 1$.

We offer some comments on the theorem rather than a proof.[3] The second part of (1) tells us that the optimal mixture will have only one point of support if $v^2(z_{(1)} z_{(N)}) - v(z_{(1)} + z_{(N)}) + 2$ is strictly positive for all non-negative v. It is readily verified that this is the case if and only if $z_{(N)}/z_{(1)} < 3 + 2\sqrt{2} = 5.828$. So if the ratio of the largest to the smallest z is no bigger than this only one point of support will be required. If this ratio exceeds 5.828 more than one point of support *may* be required. (This is why for the second numerical example the data points $z_1 = 1$, $z_2 = 7$ were chosen.) Note the reasonableness of this: if the data points are 'close' one would not believe they came from different distributions, that is, one would not believe in more than one point of support.

---

[3] See Lindsay (1983, p. 788).

In practice it seems that part 1 of the theorem is the more useful. It seems to be typically the case that the ratio of successive order statistics, $z_{(j+1)}/z_{(j)}$, is less than 5.828, so there exist no real roots to $M_{j(j+1)}(v)$ and the intervals referred to in part 2 are null.

The theorem may be generalised to the case where the atomic or conditional density functions lie in the Exponential family, $f_v(z) \propto \exp\{-vz + K(v)\}$, and hence it may be applied to the case of multiple observations discussed earlier.

NOTE

The key paper on partial likelihood is Cox (1975), which has heavily influenced our exposition. This paper clarified the basis of the methods proposed in his seminal paper of 1972. Tsiatis (1981) and Andersen and Gill (1982) provide the required asymptotic distribution theory. The paper by Oakes (1984) and accompanying discussion give a clear and insightful discussion of partial likelihood. Kalbfleisch and Prentice (1973) gave the probabilistic interpretation of partial likelihood in the class of proportional hazard models and the integral representation of $\mathcal{L}_P$ in this case. The form of exposition of partial likelihood we have adopted was partly suggested by Prentice (1978). The use of 'within person' partial likelihood to eliminate unmeasured individual effects was suggested by Chamberlain (1986) and in unpublished work by Ridder (1984a). De Stavola (1986) considered partial likelihood with multiple destinations and cycles and unmeasured individual effects in her Imperial College dissertation. Ridder and Verbakel (1983) studied the effect on maximum partial likelihood estimates of neglected unmeasured individual effects.

The discussion of marginal and conditional likelihoods for the elimination of individual effects is partly based on Chamberlain (1985). Integration of individual effects out of partial likelihoods was proposed by Clayton and Cuzick (1985). Kay (1982) has written about partial likelihood for multiple-cycle/multiple-destination data. Cox and Oakes (1984) have a lucid account of Kaplan–Meier and related estimates. Kalbfleisch and Prentice (1980) have considered partial likelihood inference in the presence of time-varying covariates, as has Petersen (1986), and section 2.11 draws, in part, on their work.

Lindsay (1983) is the key reference on non-parametric estimation of mixing distributions, and the book by Silvey (1980) on optimal experimental design is useful supplementary reading as the design and mixing problems are mathematically very similar. Heckman and Singer (1984) have studied, and advocated, Lindsay's methods in the econometric literature. Trussell and Richards (1985) have applied such non-parametric methods to real – demographic – data, as have Pickles, Davies, and Crouchley (1985). Karr (1986) is a good reference for the rigorous statistical theory of inference for point processes, including the theory of inference with partial likelihoods.

CHAPTER 10

Misspecification Analysis

1 Introduction

Fitting a model to data involves adopting hypotheses, for example, about functional forms or about independence of random quantities. These hypotheses may be wrong, in which case the model is misspecified. If the model is misspecified this may, or may not, be important for the purposes of the investigator. If a potential misspecification is likely to have serious consequences, and it is detectable in principle, then an investigator should try to detect it. These considerations apply whether the model is specified fully or only semi-parametrically.

In this chapter we shall describe the properties of estimators in certain misspecified transition models. In the next chapter we shall describe the construction of statistics and graphs to test for misspecification in such models. The emphasis will be on models with unmeasured heterogeneity.

2 Consequences of Misspecification

Let us first of all examine some maximum likelihood estimates under misspecification by applying the general theory of Cox (1961) and White (1982). Let $L(t; \gamma)$ be the log likelihood for a single observation of the variate T and let $\hat{\gamma}$ be the maximum likelihood estimator of γ based on N independent and identically distributed realisations of T. We also define

$$\mathbf{A}(\gamma) = \mathrm{E}\left(\frac{\partial^2 L(t; \gamma)}{\partial \gamma \partial \gamma'}\right), \tag{2.1}$$

$$\mathbf{B}(\gamma) = \mathrm{E}\left(\frac{\partial L(t; \gamma)}{\partial \gamma}\frac{\partial L(t; \gamma)'}{\partial \gamma}\right) \tag{2.2}$$

$$\mathbf{C}(\gamma) = \mathbf{A}^{-1}(\gamma)\mathbf{B}(\gamma)\mathbf{A}^{-1}(\gamma). \tag{2.3}$$

In (2.1) – (2.3) the expectation is taken with respect to the distribution of T actually generating the data – the true distribution. Finally we define

$$\overline{\gamma} = \arg\max \mathrm{E}\left[L(t; \gamma)\right]. \qquad (2.4)$$

The quantity $\overline{\gamma}$ is the value of γ, assumed unique, that maximises the expected log likelihood. Then, subject to regularity conditions, the maximum likelihood estimator $\hat{\gamma}$ is such that

$$p\lim_{N\to\infty} \hat{\gamma} = \overline{\gamma}, \qquad \sqrt{N}(\hat{\gamma} - \overline{\gamma}) \sim N(\mathbf{0}, \mathbf{C}(\overline{\gamma})), \quad \text{as } N \to \infty. \qquad (2.5)$$

The maximum likelihood estimator is asymptotically Normally distributed about the parameter vector that maximises the expected log likelihood. This result requires identically distributed observations but may be applied to a model with regressors by treating the regressor vectors as themselves realisations of some common multivariate distribution not involving γ.

We shall give two examples of the application of this result. Both involve single destination duration data models which are misspecified by the neglect of random multiplicative heterogeneity in the hazard function. The assumed log density function at the point $\gamma = \mathbf{c}$ is therefore

$$L(\mathbf{c}; t) = \log \theta(t; \mathbf{c}) - \overline{z}(t; \mathbf{c}), \qquad (2.6)$$

where, as usual, θ is the hazard function and $\overline{z}$ its integral. The true data distribution has conditional integrated hazard

$$z = v\overline{z}(t; \gamma), \qquad (2.7)$$

where $Z \sim \mathcal{E}(1)$ given $V = v$. The trick involved in evaluating the expectations of the terms in (2.6), which we need to do in order to calculate $\overline{\gamma}$, is to solve (2.7) for t in terms of z and write

$$\begin{aligned} \mathrm{E}\left[\overline{z}(t; \mathbf{c})\right] &= \mathrm{E}\left[\overline{z}(t(z, v; \gamma); \mathbf{c})\right], \\ \mathrm{E}\left[\log \theta(t; \mathbf{c})\right] &= \mathrm{E}\left[\log \theta(t(z, v; \gamma); \mathbf{c})\right]. \end{aligned} \qquad (2.8)$$

The expectations on the right of (2.8) are then taken first with respect to the – unit Exponential – distribution of Z given v and $\mathbf{x}$, then with respect to V given $\mathbf{x}$, and finally with respect to $\mathbf{x}$.

Example 1. The Exponential Model
Let the assumed model be

$$\theta(t; \gamma, \mathbf{x}) = \exp\{\gamma_0 + \mathbf{x}'\gamma_1\}, \qquad \overline{z}(t; \gamma, \mathbf{x}) = t\theta(\gamma). \qquad (2.9)$$

We shall redefine γ_0 so that we may take $\mathbf{x}$ to have population mean zero and also write

$$\mathrm{E}\left(\exp\{\mathbf{s}'\mathbf{x}\}\right) = M(\mathbf{s}) \qquad (2.10)$$

for the moment generating function of the regressors, with $\partial M(\mathbf{s})/\partial s_j = M^j(\mathbf{s})$. Note that $M(\mathbf{0}) = 1$ and $M^j(0) = 0$, $j = 1, 2, \ldots, K$.

The correct model has conditional integrated hazard

$$z = tv \exp\{\gamma_o + \mathbf{x}'\gamma_1\}. \tag{2.11}$$

We assume the distribution of V to be such that V^{-1} has a finite second moment and write

$$\mathrm{E}\left(V^{-1}\right) = \mu_1; \qquad \mathrm{E}\left(V^{-2}\right) = \mu_2.$$

The assumed log data density at the point $\mathbf{c} = (c_0 \; \mathbf{c}_1)$ is

$$L(\mathbf{c}; t) = c_0 + \mathbf{x}'\mathbf{c}_1 - t\exp\{c_0 + \mathbf{x}'\mathbf{c}_1\} \tag{2.12}$$

with derivatives

$$\frac{\partial L}{\partial c_0} = 1 - t\exp\{c_0 + \mathbf{x}'\mathbf{c}_1\}; \qquad \frac{\partial L}{\partial c_{1j}} = x_j(1 - t\exp\{c_0 + \mathbf{x}'\mathbf{c}_1\}); \tag{2.13}$$

$$\frac{\partial^2 L}{\partial c_0{}^2} = -t\exp\{c_0 + \mathbf{x}'\mathbf{c}_1\};$$

$$\frac{\partial^2 L}{\partial c_0 \partial c_{1j}} = -x_j t\exp\{c_0 + \mathbf{x}'\mathbf{c}_1\}; \qquad \frac{\partial^2 L}{\partial c_{1j}\partial c_{1k}} = -x_j x_k t\exp\{c_0 + \mathbf{x}'\mathbf{c}_1\} \tag{2.14}$$

From (2.11)

$$t = (z/v)\exp\{-\gamma_0 - \mathbf{x}'\gamma_1\}$$

and so

$$t\exp\{c_0 + \mathbf{x}'\mathbf{c}_1\} = (z/v)\exp\{c_0 - \gamma_0 + \mathbf{x}'(\mathbf{c}_1 - \gamma_1)\},$$

$$\mathrm{E}\left(t\exp\{c_0 + \mathbf{x}'\mathbf{c}_1\}\right) = \mathrm{E}_{v,\mathbf{x}}\mathrm{E}_{z|v,\mathbf{x}}\left[(z/v)\exp\{c_0 - \gamma_0 + \mathbf{x}'(\mathbf{c}_1 - \gamma_1)\}\right],$$

$$= \mathrm{E}_{\mathbf{x}}\mathrm{E}_{v|\mathbf{x}}\left[v^{-1}\exp\{c_0 - \gamma_0 + \mathbf{x}'(\mathbf{c}_1 - \gamma_1)\}\right],$$

$$= \mu_1 e^{c_0 - \gamma_0}\mathrm{E}_{\mathbf{x}}\left[\exp\{\mathbf{x}'(\mathbf{c}_1 - \gamma_1)\}\right],$$

$$= \mu_1 e^{c_0 - \gamma_0} M(\mathbf{c}_1 - \gamma_1). \tag{2.15}$$

Also, by similar reasoning,

$$\mathrm{E}\left[x_j t\exp\{c_0 + \mathbf{x}'\mathbf{c}_1\}\right] = \mu_1 e^{c_0 - \gamma_0} M^j(\mathbf{c}_1 - \gamma_1). \tag{2.16}$$

Thus the first-order conditions for the expected log likelihood are

$$1 - \mu_1 e^{\overline{\gamma}_0 - \gamma_0} M(\overline{\gamma}_1 - \gamma_1) = 0, \tag{2.17}$$

$$\mu_1 e^{\overline{\gamma}_0 - \gamma_0} M^j(\overline{\gamma}_1 - \gamma_1) = 0, \qquad j = 1, 2, \ldots, K \tag{2.18}$$

Equations (2.17) and (2.18) are satisfied by

$$\overline{\gamma}_1 = \gamma_1, \qquad \text{and } e^{\overline{\gamma}_0 - \gamma_0} = \mu_1^{-1}, \tag{2.19}$$

in view of $M^j(0) = 0, M(0) = 1$. A second differentiation shows this solution to be unique. Thus the maximum likelihood estimator of the slope coefficients in an Exponential regression model is consistent in the face of neglected multiplicative heterogeneity.

To work out the asymptotic covariance matrix of $\hat{\gamma}$ we need to calculate the expected Hessian, (2.14), and outer product of the gradient, (2.13), at the point $\gamma = \overline{\gamma}$. The first is straightforward using the algebra that leads to (2.15) and (2.16) and we find

$$\mathbf{A}(\overline{\gamma}) = -\begin{pmatrix} 1 & 0 \\ 0 & \Omega \end{pmatrix}, \tag{2.20}$$

where $\Omega = \mathrm{E}(\mathbf{xx'})$.

For $\mathbf{B}(\overline{\gamma})$ we need

$$\mathrm{E}\left(t^2 \exp\{2(\overline{\gamma}_0 + \mathbf{x'}\overline{\gamma}_1)\}\right) = \mathrm{E}\left((z/v)^2 \exp\{2[\overline{\gamma}_0 - \gamma_0 + \mathbf{x'}(\overline{\gamma}_1 - \gamma_1)]\}\right)$$

$$= 2\mu_2 e^{2(\overline{\gamma}_0 - \gamma_0)} M(2(\overline{\gamma}_1 - \gamma_1))$$

$$= 2\mu_2/\mu_1^2$$

$$= 2(1 + \eta^2), \tag{2.21}$$

where η is the coefficient of variation of V^{-1}. We then find that, for example,

$$\mathrm{E}\left(\frac{\partial L}{\partial \overline{\gamma}_0}\right)^2 = 1 - 2 + 2(1 + \eta^2) = 1 + 2\eta^2.$$

The complete matrix is found to be

$$\mathbf{B}(\overline{\gamma}) = (1 + 2\eta^2)\begin{pmatrix} 1 & 0 \\ 0 & \Omega \end{pmatrix}.$$

Thus

$$\mathbf{C}(\overline{\gamma}) = (1 + 2\eta^2)\begin{pmatrix} 1 & 0 \\ 0 & \Omega^{-1} \end{pmatrix}. \tag{2.22}$$

So the effect on the asymptotic covariance matrix of the maximum likelihood estimator of neglecting heterogeneity is to inflate all elements by the factor $1 + 2\eta^2$. This is natural enough since the effect of the heterogeneity is to introduce additional variation into the data. Notice the resemblance between (2.22) and the covariance matrix of the Least Squares coefficient estimator a linear model, $\sigma^2(\mathbf{X'X})^{-1}$. This resemblance suggests that the scalar factor in (2.22) is interpretable as an error variance, and we shall point out in the next chapter the sense in which this is true.

None of the usual estimators of the asymptotic covariance matrix of $\hat{\gamma}$ are consistent under this misspecification but (2.22) is consistently estimated by the matrix $\mathbf{C}_N(\hat{\gamma})$ constructed by replacing expectations in the definitions of $\mathbf{A}$ and $\mathbf{B}$ by averages over the sample and replacing γ by $\hat{\gamma}$.

It should be noted that the above derivations do not work when the data are subject to censoring since Z will not have a conditional unit Exponential distribution when T is the minimum of a duration and a censoring time.   ■

It is interesting to compare these results on the maximum likelihood estimator with the properties of the Least Squares estimator. We made this comparison for correctly specified models in chapter 8, section 8, where we saw that LS was only 71 percent efficient in the Exponential model.

Example 2. Least Squares in the Exponential Regression Model
From (2.11)

$$\log t = -\gamma_0 - \mathbf{x}'\gamma_1 + (\log z - \log v),\qquad(2.23)$$

where the error term in (2.23) has mean and variance

$$\mathrm{E}\left(\log Z - \log V\right) = \psi(1) - \mathrm{E}\left(\log V\right),\qquad(2.24)$$
$$\mathrm{var}(\log Z - \log V) = \psi'(1) + \mathrm{var}(\log V).\qquad(2.25)$$

Here we have used the fact that $Z \sim \mathcal{E}(1)$ given v. Thus, by a standard argument, the LS estimator will have mean and asymptotic variance

$$\mathrm{E}\begin{pmatrix}\tilde{\gamma}_0\\\tilde{\gamma}_1\end{pmatrix} = \begin{pmatrix}\gamma_0 - \psi(1) + \mathrm{E}\left(\log V\right)\\\gamma_1\end{pmatrix}\qquad(2.26)$$

$$\mathrm{var}\begin{pmatrix}\tilde{\gamma}_0\\\tilde{\gamma}_1\end{pmatrix} = (\psi'(1) + \mathrm{var}(\log V))\begin{pmatrix}1 & \mathbf{0}\\\mathbf{0} & \mathbf{\Omega}^{-1}\end{pmatrix}N^{-1}.\qquad(2.27)$$

Therefore the Least Squares estimator is also consistent for the slope coefficients and it will have smaller variance than the maximum likelihood estimator if

$$\psi'(1) + \mathrm{var}\log V < 1 + 2\eta^2.\qquad(2.28)$$

But $\mathrm{var}\,(\log V) = \mathrm{var}[\log(1/V)] \sim \eta^2$ to the first order so the inequality (2.28) is approximately

$$1.6449 + \eta^2 < 1 + 2\eta^2 \Rightarrow \eta > 0.803.$$

This is a large value for a coefficient of variation and suggests that maximum likelihood will generally provide a more efficient estimator than Least Squares even in the presence of this type of misspecification. ∎

Example 3. The Weibull Model
Some interesting new results arise if we extend the analysis of example 1 to the case where the fitted model is Weibull but the correct model is a heterogeneous Weibull. Let the assumed model be

$$\theta(t; \alpha, \gamma, \mathbf{x}) = \alpha t^{\alpha-1} \exp\{\gamma_0 + \mathbf{x}'\gamma_1\}, \qquad \bar{z}(t; \alpha, \gamma, \mathbf{x}) = t^\alpha \exp\{\gamma_0 + \mathbf{x}'\gamma_1\}. \tag{2.29}$$

The correct model has integrated conditional hazard

$$z = t^\alpha v \exp\{\gamma_0 + \mathbf{x}'\gamma_1\}, \tag{2.30}$$

whence

$$t = (z/v)^{1/\alpha} \exp\{-(\gamma_0 + \mathbf{x}'\gamma_1)/\alpha\}. \tag{2.31}$$

The assumed log data density at the point $(a, \mathbf{c})$ is

$$L(a, \mathbf{c}) = \log a + (a-1)\log t + c_0 + \mathbf{x}'\mathbf{c}_1 - t^a \exp\{c_0 + \mathbf{x}'\mathbf{c}_1\}. \tag{2.32}$$

We need to evaluate the expressions $\mathrm{E}\,(T^a \exp\{c_0 + \mathbf{x}'\mathbf{c}_1\})$ and $\mathrm{E}\,(\log T)$ using the relation (2.31). Let us adopt the notation

$$\bar{a} = \frac{a}{\alpha}, \qquad \mathcal{M}(s) = \mathrm{E}\,(V^s),$$

where $\mathcal{M}$ is the moment generating function of $\log V$. Then carrying out the steps that lead to (2.15) we find

$$\mathrm{E}\,(T^a \exp\{c_0 + \mathbf{x}'\mathbf{c}_1\}) = \Gamma(1+\bar{a})\mathcal{M}(-\bar{a})e^{c_0 - \bar{a}\gamma_0} M(\mathbf{c}_1 - \bar{a}\gamma_1),$$

$$\mathrm{E}\,(\log T) = \frac{\psi(1) - \mathrm{E}\,(\log V) - \gamma_0}{\alpha}.$$

Differentiating with respect to $c_0, \mathbf{c}_1$ we get the expected likelihood equations

$$1 - \Gamma(1+\bar{a})\mathcal{M}(-\bar{a})M(\bar{\gamma}_1 - \bar{a}\gamma_1) = 0, \tag{2.33}$$

$$\Gamma(1+\bar{a})\mathcal{M}(-\bar{a})M^j(\bar{\gamma}_1 - \bar{a}\gamma_1) = 0, \qquad j = 1, 2, \dots, K. \tag{2.34}$$

These have the unique solution

$$\bar{\gamma}_1 = (\bar{\alpha}/\alpha)\gamma_1, \tag{2.35}$$

where $\bar{\alpha}$ is the probability limit of $\hat{\alpha}$. Thus all elements of the slope coefficient estimator have the same proportionate inconsistency.

It remains to find $\bar{\alpha}$. If we differentiate the expected log likelihood with respect to $\bar{a}$ and use the solutions provided by (2.33) and (2.34) we find the equation

$$(1/\bar{a}) + \psi(1) - \psi(1 + \bar{a}) - \mathcal{K}'(-\bar{a}) = 0,$$

which simplifies to

$$\mathcal{K}'(-\bar{a}) + \psi(1) = \psi(\bar{a}) \tag{2.36}$$

using the recurrence relation for the digamma function,[1] $\psi(1 + x) = \psi(x) + 1/x$, and where $\mathcal{K} = \log\mathcal{M}$, the cumulant generating function of $\log V$. The left-hand side is decreasing in $\bar{a}$ and equal to $\psi(1)$ at the origin in view of E x = 0. The right-hand side is a concave increasing function equal to $\psi(1)$ at $\bar{a} = 1$. Thus (2.36) has a unique solution satisfying $0 \leq (\bar{\alpha}/\alpha) \leq 1$.

We conclude from this argument that the effect of neglected heterogeneity on the maximum likelihood estimators of γ_1 and α is to bias them, asymptotically, towards zero. The downwards bias of $\hat{\alpha}$ is consistent with the results in chapter 4 where we showed that mixture hazards rise slower or fall faster than the conditional hazards from which they were obtained. The ML estimator of α in effect reproduces this feature of the data (mixture) distribution.

An interesting explicit form for $\bar{\alpha}$ may be obtained if we linearise the right-hand side of (2.36) about $\bar{a} = 1$ and the left-hand side about $\bar{a} = 0$ giving

$$\mathcal{K}'(-\bar{a}) + \psi(1) \approx -\bar{a}\sigma^2,$$

$$\psi(\bar{a}) \approx \psi(1) + (\bar{a} - 1)\psi'(1),$$

where $\sigma^2 = \mathrm{var}(\log V)$. This gives the approximate solution

$$\frac{\bar{\alpha}}{\alpha} \approx \frac{\psi'(1)}{\psi'(1) + \sigma^2}. \tag{2.37}$$

To interpret this expression recall from chapter 4 that neglected multiplicative heterogeneity in a Weibull model can be thought of as arising from random multiplicative measurement error in the duration data. If S is the correct duration measure distributed as Weibull with parameter α and T is the recorded duration then $T = SV^{-1/\alpha}$, with S and V independent, by the argument of section 2.1 of chapter 4. Thus

$$\mathrm{var}(\log T) = \frac{\psi'(1)}{\alpha^2} + \frac{\sigma^2}{\alpha^2}.$$

[1] See appendix 1.

It follows that (2.37) can be written

$$\frac{\overline{\alpha}}{\alpha} \approx \frac{\text{var}(\log S)}{\text{var}(\log T)}$$

and the proportionate bias can be written as one minus the ratio of the variances of true and recorded log durations. This result is closely similar to the classical result on 'errors in the variables bias' in a linear mode yet here the errors are in the *dependent* variable. ∎

Example 4. Least Squares Estimates of the Weibull Model
We saw in chapter 8, example 25, that the (conditional) Weibull model implies the homoscedastic linear model

$$\log T = \beta_0 + \mathbf{x}'\beta_1 + U,$$

where

$$\beta_0 = \frac{\psi(1) - \gamma_0 - \text{E}(\log V)}{\alpha}, \quad \beta_1 = -\frac{\gamma_1}{\alpha},$$

$$\text{E}(U) = 0, \quad \text{var}(U) = \frac{\psi'(1) + \sigma^2}{\alpha^2},$$

where $\sigma^2 = \text{var}(\log V)$. Under standard regularity conditions the Least Squares residual variance from this model, s^2, will converge stochastically to

$$s^2 \to \frac{\psi'(1) + \sigma^2}{\alpha^2}, \tag{2.38}$$

and the slope coefficient, say, $\tilde{\beta}_1$, will converge to

$$\tilde{\beta}_1 \to -\frac{\gamma_1}{\alpha}.$$

An investigator unaware of the heterogeneity represented by V, and therefore taking $\sigma^2 = 0$, would estimate from the residual standard deviation by

$$\tilde{\alpha} = \frac{\sqrt{\psi'(1)}}{s},$$

and he would estimate γ_1 by

$$\tilde{\gamma}_1 = \tilde{\alpha}\,\tilde{\beta}_1.$$

But in view of (2.38)

$$\tilde{\alpha} \to \alpha \left[\frac{\psi'(1)}{\psi'(1) + \sigma^2}\right]^{1/2}. \tag{2.39}$$

Comparing (2.39) and (2.37) we see a strikingly simple relation between the probability limits of the LS and ML estimators of α and it immediately follows that the least squares estimator is always less inconsistent, both for γ_1 and for α, than the maximum likelihood estimator in the presence of this type of misspecification. In this sense it is the more robust estimator.   ∎

A comparison of properties of estimators does, of course, require an answer to the question 'estimators of what?' We have so far taken it for granted that in the Weibull model interest lies in the parameters γ_1 and α. It is, however, possible that an investigator is only interested in the response of the mean duration due to variation in a regressor. Now in the Weibull model

$$\frac{\partial \mathrm{E}\,(\log T)}{\partial x_j} = -\frac{\gamma_j}{\alpha} = \beta_j = \frac{\partial \log \mathrm{E}\,(T)}{\partial x_j}.$$

If these 'reduced form' elasticities are the only objects of interest then one would want to compare alternative estimators of them. It will be obvious that the Least Squares estimators of the $\{\beta_j\}$ are consistent but in view of (2.35) so are the Maximum Likelihood estimators. That is, the ML estimators of γ_1 and α are inconsistent but the estimators of β_1 are not. If interest is only in these elasticities there is nothing to choose between least-squares and maximum likelihood so far as bias is concerned.

3   Local Misspecification

The previous examples show that, with some persistence, explicit results can be obtained on the effects of misspecification. But in more complicated models such results will be very difficult to obtain so we need to develop approximate methods. In this section we shall give a method of obtaining the effects of neglecting heterogeneity in the hazard when the variance of the mixing distribution, σ^2, is small. Our results will be correct to $O(\sigma^2)$ as $\sigma^2 \to 0$.

We take as the correct model the local mixture of chapter 4, section 4, with density function

$$g(t; \gamma, \sigma^2) = \theta(t; \gamma)e^{-z(t; \gamma)}\{1 + \eta(z^2 - 2z)\}, \tag{3.1}$$

where

$$z = z(t; \gamma) = \int_0^t \theta(s; \gamma)\,ds, \qquad \eta = \frac{\sigma^2}{2}.$$

The assumed model at the parameter point $\mathbf{c}$ is

$$f(t;\mathbf{c}) = g(t;\mathbf{c},0) = \theta(t;\mathbf{c})e^{-z(t;\mathbf{c})}.$$

For this section only we shall write

$$F = \log f, \qquad F_1 = \frac{\partial F}{\partial \gamma}, \qquad F_2 = \frac{\partial^2 F}{\partial \gamma^2}$$

and similarly for $G = \log g$.

The expected log likelihood equations – the general form of which (2.17) and (2.18) are a particular example – are

$$\int_0^\infty F_1(t;\overline{\gamma}) \exp\{G(t;\gamma,\sigma^2\} \, dt = 0. \tag{3.2}$$

Regarding the solution of (3.2) for $\overline{\gamma}$ as a function of σ^2 let us differentiate those equations with respect to σ^2 at $\sigma^2 = 0$ to find $\partial\overline{\gamma}/\partial\sigma^2$ at that point. This gives

$$\int_0^\infty F_2(t;\overline{\gamma}) \exp\{F(t;\gamma)\} \, dt \, \frac{d\overline{\gamma}}{d\sigma^2}$$
$$+ \int_0^\infty F_1(t;\overline{\gamma}) \frac{\partial G(t;\gamma,0)}{\partial\sigma^2} \exp\{F(t;\gamma)\} \, dt = 0, \tag{3.3}$$

since $G(t;\gamma,0) = F(t;\gamma)$. Now from (3.1) we see that

$$\frac{\partial G(t;\gamma,0)}{\partial\sigma^2} = (z^2 - 2z)/2$$

and also $\mathrm{E}\,(F_2) = -\mathcal{I}$, where $\mathcal{I}$ is the information matrix for γ on the null hypothesis $\sigma^2 = 0$. Solving (3.3), we find that at $\sigma^2 = 0$,

$$\frac{\partial\overline{\gamma}}{\partial\sigma^2} = \mathcal{I}^{-1}\mathrm{E}\,(\{F_1(z^2 - 2z)/2\}).$$

Noting that $\overline{\gamma}(\sigma^2)_{\sigma^2=0} = \gamma$ we then deduce that

$$\overline{\gamma} = \gamma + \sigma^2\mathcal{I}^{-1}\mathrm{E}\,(\{F_1(z^2 - 2z)\}) + o(\sigma^2) \tag{3.4}$$

gives the effect of neglected heterogeneity on maximum likelihood estimates. Note that the expectation in (3.4) is taken on the hypothesis that $\sigma^2 = 0$.

The reader may verify that (3.4) gives the results of example 3 to $O(\sigma^2)$

4   Some Other Misspecification Results

A limited amount of evidence is available on the effect of model mis-specification in other contexts, and we shall describe the results of two investigations.

4.1   Misspecification in Partial Likelihood Analysis

Ridder and Verbakel (1983) have carried out a Monte Carlo study of the effects of neglected heterogeneity on partial likelihood estimates. The assumed model has hazard function

$$\theta(t;\gamma) = e^{x'\gamma}\psi_2(t),$$

where ψ_2 is an unknown function common to all people. The correct model had hazard function $v\theta(t;\gamma)$. The data were generated by assuming alternative functional forms for the baseline-hazard function ψ_2 and for the mixing distribution (of v) and for each data set the Cox partial likelihood estimate of γ was calculated together with a piecewise-constant estimate of the function $\psi_2(t)$.

Their results indicate that the partial likelihood estimates of γ are biased towards zero, just as with the Weibull model of example 3. The estimated standard errors, though, are approximately correct. The estimates of the time-dependence function are also biased and give an estimate of the baseline hazard which is less increasing or more decreasing than the conditional hazard. This again is exactly as in the Weibull model. It seems a fair conjecture that attenuation of regression coefficients and distortion of the baseline-hazard function in the way just described is a rather general consequence of neglected heterogeneity in the hazard function.

4.2   Misspecification of Mixture Models

Ridder and Verbakel have also carried out a Monte Carlo investigation of misspecification in a parametrically specified mixture model in which the data distribution is

$$g_m(t;\gamma_1,\gamma_2) = \int_0^\infty \theta(t;\gamma_1)e^{-v\bar{z}(t;\gamma_1)}\,dH(v;\gamma_2). \tag{4.1}$$

This model may be misspecified in two ways: the conditional hazard θ may be incorrect, or the mixing distribution H may be wrong. The authors investigated both types of misspecification but separately rather than simultaneously. Their conclusions are that 'misspecification of the time dependence function (of the conditional hazard) biases the estimates of all parameters. A flexible specification of the time dependence function solves this problem. It is difficult to distinguish between the time dependence function (especially its tail) and the unobserved heterogeneity. Misspecification of the distribution of unobserved heterogeneity has no serious consequences.'

This last conclusion is interesting because it has been widely argued in the econometric literature that misspecification of the mixing distribution has serious consequences for maximum likelihood estimates of parameters of the conditional hazard. The evidence for this position is the observation that different choices of mixing distribution when applied to a real data set gave radically varying estimates of the parameters of the conditional hazard function; see Heckman and Singer (1984). This observation could be reconciled with that of Ridder and Verbakel if in fact the form assumed for the conditional hazard function in these calculations was seriously wrong. This seems a reasonable conjecture.

The implication of the Ridder and Verbakel study is that it may, in fact, not be necessary in practice to use the computationally rather difficult methods of chapter 9 in which the mixing distribution is estimated non-parametrically. It may suffice to use a tractable parametric mixing distribution as long as the time dependence of the conditional hazard permits a variety of shapes. It should be noted that the Monte Carlo work of Ridder and Verbakel was of limited extent and that no analytical results on the question are available. This would seem to be a potentially fruitful research area.

NOTE

he general theory of maximum likelihood estimators in misspecified models used here draws very much on White (1982). The results for the Exponential model, Examples 2.1 and 2.2, were given in Lancaster (1983) and for the Weibull model, Examples 2.3 and 2.4, in Lancaster (1985c). The results of section 3 draw on Lancaster (1985). Section 4 is based on Ridder and Verbakel (1983).

CHAPTER 11

Residual Analysis

1   Introduction

Misspecification of the model may result in inconsistency of maximum likelihood estimates and of estimators of their standard errors. We have seen examples of this in the last chapter. In this chapter we shall discuss some numerical and graphical methods for detecting such misspecification, whose implementation ought to be a routine part of the econometric analysis of transition data. Of course, the main way in which an econometrician detects whether his model is wrong is when the estimates do not make economic sense. But the purely statistical tests we describe in this chapter are important supplements to the economist's judgment and are particularly valuable when economics does not provide a clear guide to what are sensible results.

When an econometrician proposes to fit a model $f(t \mid \mathbf{x})$ to data drawn from N people with regressor vectors $\mathbf{x}$ he is tentatively asserting that the data distribution, conditional on $\mathbf{x}$, is in the family f – which may be specified fully or semi-parametrically – and that this is true for all people. There is both an assumption about functional forms and an assumption about homogeneity conditional on $\mathbf{x}$. Much of this book has been about data that are not homogeneous and this is a natural preoccupation of a social scientist. The diversity of people is surely greater than can be accounted for by the values of five or ten regressor variables. The emphasis in this chapter will therefore again be on the problem of heterogeneity. But we shall also point out the form taken by some tests for incorrect functional form.

2   Errors and Residuals

Let the assumed model lie in the family $f(t; \mathbf{x})^1$ and let the log density for someone with regressor vector $\mathbf{x}_i$ be

$$L_i = \log f(t; \mathbf{x}_i). \tag{2.1}$$

A reasonable way of allowing for the possibility that the data are more heterogeneous than is represented by the variation in the regressors is to introduce person-specific parameters into the model by writing

$$L_i = \log f(t; \mathbf{x}_i, \alpha_i). \tag{2.2}$$

We normalise by supposing that (2.2) reduces to (2.1) when $\alpha_i = 0$. A way of testing whether the $\{\alpha_i\}$ are not zero is by examining the variation in the log likelihood when these parameters are allowed to depart from zero, in either direction. This suggests that a test for heterogeneity could be based on $\partial L_i / \partial \alpha_i$ at $\alpha_i = 0$, that is, upon the scores for the $\{\alpha_i\}$. Let us examine these quantities when f is a single destination, flow data, duration model with hazard function θ. We introduce α linearly into the log hazard, thus getting a fixed effect version of the heterogeneous model of earlier chapters, and write

$$\log \theta(t; \mathbf{x}_i) = \alpha_i + \log \overline{\theta}(t; \mathbf{x}_i), \tag{2.3}$$

$$z(t; \mathbf{x}_i) = \int_0^t \theta(s; \mathbf{x}_i)\, ds = e^{\alpha_i} \overline{z}(t; \mathbf{x}_i). \tag{2.4}$$

Then the log likelihood and the score for α_i at $\alpha_i = 0$ are

$$L_i = \alpha_i + \log \overline{\theta}(t; \mathbf{x}_i) - e^{\alpha_i} \overline{z}(t; \mathbf{x}_i), \tag{2.5}$$

$$\frac{\partial L}{\partial \alpha_i} = 1 - \overline{z}(t; \mathbf{x}_i)$$

$$= 1 - \int_0^t \theta(s; \mathbf{x}_i)\, ds$$

$$= \epsilon_i. \tag{2.6}$$

We refer to the quantities $\{\epsilon_i\}$ as *errors* by analogy with linear model errors. The analogy arises, first, because the errors have mean zero and constant variance when the model is correct and, second, because the error terms in a Normal linear model are precisely these scores for person-specific intercept terms, apart from a factor of proportionality. The mean

---

[1] The regressors could also be time-varying but exogenous. The results given in this chapter do not, however, apply in the presence of endogenous covariates.

zero property of the errors follows from the fact that they are scores, and their variance is that of the unit Exponential integrated hazard, that is, unity. Thus, when $\alpha_i = 0$,

$$E(\epsilon_i) = 0; \qquad \text{var}(\epsilon_i) = 1. \tag{2.7}$$

Since the observations for different people are independent, the errors and the properties of the whole N vector of errors are

$$E(\epsilon) = 0; \qquad V(\epsilon) = I_N. \tag{2.8}$$

If, as would normally be the case, there are unknown parameters entering into the hazard so that $\theta = \theta(t; \mathbf{x}, \gamma)$ the errors cannot be calculated. We define the *residuals* as the errors with unknown parameters replaced by maximum likelihood estimates on the (null) hypothesis that the data are (conditionally) homogeneous and the functional form f is correct. We denote them by

$$e_i = 1 - z(t; \mathbf{x}_i, \hat{\gamma}). \tag{2.9}$$

The $\{e_i\}$, or without the centering to mean zero, the $\{\hat{z}_i\}$, are often called generalised residuals; the $\{\epsilon_i\}$ would be generalised errors.

In practical situations we would often have models with multiple destinations, including right censoring; we might have multiple-cycles; we might have models specified semi-parametrically, involving unknown functions as well as unknown parameters; and we might have stock samples or other more complex sampling schemes. In later parts of this chapter we shall consider the definition and uses of residuals in such situations. For the moment we shall stay with the simplest situation in which we have N independent realisations from a parametrically specified flow sample and consider how to use the residual information.

2.1   Residual Plots

On the null hypothesis of homogeneity the $\{z(t_i; \mathbf{x}_i \gamma)\}$ are N independent realisations of a unit Exponential variate with survivor function e^{-z} when the covariates are exogenous. The natural graphical check on this property would be to see if the sample survivor function looks unit Exponential, and this is most simply done by plotting minus the logarithm of the sample survivor function at the point $z_i = z(t_i; \mathbf{x}_i, \gamma)$ against z_i. The points should lie approximately on a 45 degree line since $-\log e^{-x} = x$. If γ is unknown we plot the minus log survivor function of the $\hat{z}_i = z(t_i; \mathbf{x}_i \hat{\gamma})$ aginst $\hat{z}_i$. Figure 11.1 exemplifies this plot for a correctly specified model with one estimated parameter. It can be seen that the rightmost points are rather erratic, which reflects the

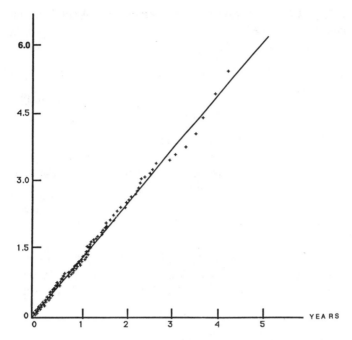

Figure 11.1.   Minus log residual survivor function: correct model; no censoring.

large variance of the sample maximum and nearby order statistics for the unit Exponential.

An alternative graphical test of the unit Exponential is to plot the ordered $\{\hat{z}_i\}$ against the expected order statistics for the unit Exponential given in chapter 9, section 2.3. In practice the order statistic plot does not appear to add anything to the information contained in the minus log survivor function plot, at least in the present writer's experience.

An interesting question is what these plots might be expected to look like when the data are not homogeneous. This is hard to answer in general but we can give the answer when the fitted model is the Exponential regression model last discussed in chapter 10, example 1, and the correct model is the heterogeneous Exponential. Consider the integrated hazards in a large sample when the maximum likelihood estimates are close to their probability limits, $\overline{\gamma}$ given in (2.19) of chapter 10.

$$\overline{z}(T; \overline{\gamma}) = T \exp\{\hat{\gamma}_0 + \mathbf{x}'\gamma\},$$
$$= (z/v) \exp\{\overline{\gamma}_0 - \gamma_0\},$$

where $\exp\{\overline{\gamma}_0 - \gamma_0\} = \mu_1^{-1}$, and we have used (2.11) of the last chapter. The survivor function of $\overline{z}$ is

$$
\begin{aligned}
\overline{G}(w) &= P(\overline{z} > w) \\
&= \mathrm{E}_v(P(z > wv\mu_1 \mid v)) \\
&= \mathrm{E}_v(\exp\{-wv\mu_1\}) \\
&= M(-w\mu_1), \tag{2.10}
\end{aligned}
$$

where M is the moment generating function of the mixing distribution. As long as this distribution is not degenerate, two differentiations establish that $-\log \overline{G}(w)$ is an increasing *concave* function of w. For example, with the unit mean Gamma mixing distribution

$$
\overline{G}(w) = \left(1 + \frac{w\sigma^2}{1 - \sigma^2}\right)^{-1/\sigma^2}, \qquad \sigma^2 < 1.
$$

Thus the minus log survivor function plot of the estimated integrated hazards from an Exponential regression model should be concave when there is neglected heterogeneity. This result unfortunately does not generalise.

2.2   Numerical Tests

The natural quantities to plot are the sample survivor functions of the integrated hazards, or one minus the residuals. Numerical tests most naturally involve the residuals themselves. To detect heterogeneity we would want to see if the errors, or their estimates, are significantly large. A possible statistic to look at might be the mean residual, although since either positive or negative α's are consistent with heterogeneity in the sample this is not really a sensible choice. And, anyway, it is not (usually) possible since the mean residual is identically zero from the likelihood equations when the log hazard has a constant term, just as it is in a linear model. To see the identities satisfied by the residuals as a consequence of the likelihood equations consider the particular case of the general expression (2.7) of chapter 8 when there is a single destination, no censoring, and we are concerned with those parameters that enter the log hazard in the form $\gamma_0 + \mathbf{x}'\gamma_1$. For such parameters, (2.7) gives

$$
\begin{aligned}
\frac{\partial L}{\partial \gamma_j} &= \sum_{i=1}^{N} x_{ij}(1 - \hat{z}_i) \\
&= \sum_{i=1}^{N} x_{ij} e_i = 0, \tag{2.11}
\end{aligned}
$$

where $x_{ij} \equiv 1$ for the constant term. Thus residuals sum exactly to zero and are orthogonal to regressors that enter the log hazard linearly. No test can be based either on the residual mean or on their covariances with such regressors.

The next natural choice is to consider the residual mean square or variance. Since the error variance is unity one might consider $s^2 - 1$, where s^2 is the residual variance. A test which asks whether s^2 is significantly greater than one is asking, in effect, whether the $\{\alpha_i\}$ are, taken together, large in absolute value, which is a reasonable way of asking whether the data are (conditionally) homogeneous. The distribution theory of $s^2 - 1$ turns out to be easy because, in fact, it is a score statistic. To see this consider the locally heterogeneous model of chapter 4, with log density

$$L = \log f(t; \gamma, \sigma^2) = \log \theta(t; \gamma) - z(t; \gamma) + \log[1 + \eta(z^2 - 2z)], \quad (2.12)$$

where $\eta = \sigma^2/2$. The score for η at $\eta = 0$ and $\gamma = \hat{\gamma}$ is

$$\frac{\partial L}{\partial \eta} = z^2(t; \hat{\gamma}) - 2z(t; \hat{\gamma}) = e^2 - 1,$$

and adding up over the N observations and dividing by N gives the total score statistic as $s^2 - 1$.

The asymptotic distribution of this statistic follows from standard score theory. Let

$$I = \begin{pmatrix} I_{\eta\eta} & I_{\eta\gamma} \\ I_{\gamma\eta} & I_{\gamma\gamma} \end{pmatrix}$$

be the whole sample information matrix corresponding to (2.12) in partitioned form and set

$$V = I_{\eta\eta} - I_{\eta\gamma} I_{\gamma\gamma}^{-1} I_{\gamma\eta}. \quad (2.13)$$

Then

$$\sqrt{N}(s^2 - 1) \sim N(0, V/N) \qquad \text{as } N \to \infty. \quad (2.14)$$

The information matrix I can be estimated by the negative Hessian at the point $\hat{\gamma}$ or by the outer product of the gradient. The rejection region in favour of the hypothesis of heterogeneity would be the right tail area under the distribution (2.14).

The statistic $s^2 - 1$ is also an example of an Information Matrix – IM – test statistic. Information Matrix tests compare the Hessian of the log likelihood with the outer product of the gradient, the sample analogues of the matrices **A** and **B** of chapter 10. The two matrices should sum to zero in expectation at the true parameter vector when the model is correctly specified but not, in general, otherwise. This test statistic has up to $K(K+1)/2$ distinct elements corresponding to the number of distinct elements in the Hessian. Consider that component of the IM test statistic which corresponds to the intercept in the log hazard. Putting all the α's equal to a common α in (2.5) we see that

$$\frac{\partial L}{\partial \alpha} = 1 - z, \qquad \frac{\partial^2 L}{\partial \alpha^2} = -z.$$

Thus

$$\frac{\partial^2 L}{\partial \alpha^2} + \left(\frac{\partial L}{\partial \alpha}\right)^2 = e^2 - z.$$

Summing over the sample and using $N^{-1}\sum z(t_i; \hat{\gamma}) = 1$ gives the statistic $s^2 - 1$ again.[2]

In the previous chapter we showed that the covariance matrix of the maximum likelihood estimator in an Exponential regression model took the form

$$\mathbf{C}(\overline{\gamma}) = (1 + 2\eta^2)\begin{pmatrix} 1 & 0 \\ 0 & \Omega^{-1} \end{pmatrix}$$

asymptotically, and remarked that the scalar factor in this expression could be interpreted as an error variance. It is in fact the variance of the generalised errors as defined above. To see this note that in large samples the error will be close to

$$\epsilon = 1 - t\exp\{\overline{\gamma}_0 + \mathbf{x}'\overline{\gamma}_1\}$$
$$= 1 - (z/v)\exp\{\overline{\gamma}_0 - \gamma_0 + \mathbf{x}'(\overline{\gamma}_1 - \gamma_1)\},$$

where the $\overline{\gamma}$'s are the probability limits of the ML estimators in the misspecified model and we have used the algebra leading to (2.15) of the last chapter. Using (2.15), (2.17), and (2.21) of chapter 10, this has mean zero and variance equal to $1 + 2\eta^2$. Thus the correct asymptotic covariance matrix of the ML estimators in the heterogeneous Exponential regression model can be consistently estimated by

$$\mathbf{V}(\hat{\gamma}) = s^2\begin{pmatrix} 1 & 0 \\ 0 & (\mathbf{X}'\mathbf{X})^{-1} \end{pmatrix},$$

---

[2] Recent work indicates that in some cases critical values calculated by using the χ^2 asymptotic distribution of Information Matrix test statistics can be seriously inaccurate unless the sample size is very large. Such tests should be used with caution. See Kennan and Neumann (1987); Chesher and Spady (1988); Orme (1987).

where s^2 is the (generalised) residual variance. This provides a neat analogy with standard linear model results.

3   Multiple Destinations

To extend the residual idea to multiple destinations we introduce person-specific intercepts $\{\alpha_{im}\}$ into each log transition intensity. Thus the log density function for the duration, t, and the destination indicators, $\{d_m\}$, $m = 1, 2, \ldots M$, become, using (2.2) of chapter 8,

$$L_i = \sum_{m=1}^{M} [d_{im}(\alpha_{im} + \log \overline{\theta}_m(t; \gamma_m)) - e^{\alpha_{im}} \overline{z}_m(t; \gamma_m)]. \qquad (3.1)$$

The score for α_{im} at $\alpha_{im} = 0$ is

$$\frac{\partial L_i}{\partial \alpha_{im}} = d_{im} - z_m(t; \gamma_m)$$

$$= d_{im} - \int_0^t \theta_m(s; \gamma_m)\, ds$$

$$= \epsilon_{im}. \qquad (3.2)$$

The $\{\epsilon_{im}\}$ are person- and destination-specific errors and the residuals are defined correspondingly. Residuals corresponding to destinations whose transition intensities are not modelled, for example, a censoring destination, cannot be calculated because θ_m is not specified.

The errors, being scores, have mean zero on the hypothesis of homogeneity, which implies that

$$E\,(z_m(t; \gamma_m)) = E\,(d_{im})$$
$$= P(\text{person } i \text{ enters destination } m) = \pi_{im}. \quad (3.3)$$

Their variances on the null hypothesis are got from the fact that the mean square score is equal to the expected negative second derivative of the log likelihood function, which implies that

$$\mathrm{var}(\epsilon_{im}) = E\,(z_m(t; \gamma_m)) = E\,(d_{im}) = \pi_{im}. \qquad (3.4)$$

Plots are a little trickier with multiple destinations because z_m is not unit Exponential on the null hypothesis. However, we know that the transition intensities θ_m can always be regarded as the hazard functions corresponding to M independent latent durations, $\{T_m\}$, of which our observation, t, is the least. If destination m is entered we observe T_m, otherwise T_m is right censored. Thus the $\{z_m\}$ are a right censored sample of unit Exponential variates and their survivor function can be

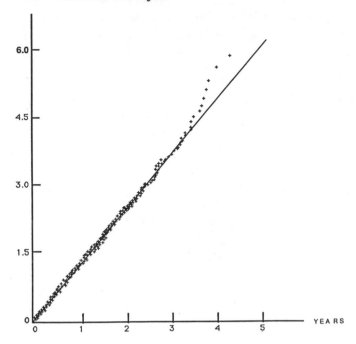

Figure 11.2.   Minus log residual survivor function: correct model; 26 percent censoring; Kaplan–Meier plot.

estimated by the Kaplan-Meier method. The appropriate plot is to re-place the γ_m by their maximum likelihood estimates on the hypothesis of homogeneity; calculate $z_m(t; \hat{\gamma}_m)$; construct the Kaplan–Meier estimate of the survivor function at each uncensored time, that is, each observation for which destination m was entered; and finally plot the minus log estimated survivor function against its argument. The points should lie about a 45 degree line under homogeneity. Figure 11.2 gives an example of such a plot from a correctly specified model with two destinations.

Numerical tests again centre on the residual variances or mean squares – the residual means being again identically zero when the log transition intensities have intercepts. The natural procedure is to compare the variances of the residuals with estimates of their expectations on the null. The natural estimate of the expectation of the variance of the $\{\epsilon_{im}\}$ over the sample is an estimate of the average value of the $\{\pi_{im}\}$ over the sample and this is

$$p_m = \text{Proportion of the sample entering destination } m.$$

Thus the test statistics would be proportional to

$$s_m^2 - p_m, \qquad m = 1, 2, \ldots M, \qquad (3.5)$$

where s_m^2 is the sample variance of the $\{e_{im}\}$.

If we differentiate (3.1) a second time we get

$$\frac{\partial L_i}{\partial \alpha_{im} \partial \alpha_{il}} = \begin{cases} -z_m(t; \gamma_m), & l = m, \\ 0, & l \neq m, \end{cases} \qquad (3.6)$$

so that cov $(\epsilon_{il} \epsilon_{im}) = 0$, $l \neq m$ and the errors corresponding to different destinations are uncorrelated. Suppose, therefore that we take a subset, M^*, of destinations the probability of entry to which is, say, π, and add the errors over this subset to get

$$\epsilon_i = \sum_{m \in M^*} \epsilon_{im}.$$

Then the variance of ϵ_i is equal to the sum of the variances of the ϵ_{im}, which is π. Thus a test can be based on the variances of (partial) sums of the residuals as well as on the residual variances taken separately. It should be noted that the sum of the errors over all destinations is

$$\epsilon_i = \sum_{m=1}^{M} \epsilon_{im}$$

$$= 1 - \int_0^t \sum_{m=1}^{M} \theta_m(s; \gamma_m) \, ds$$

$$= 1 - \int_0^t \theta(s; \gamma) \, ds,$$

which is the ordinary single destination error of section 2. So the uncorrelatedness of the ϵ_{im} provides an orthogonal decomposition of the total error into components associated with distinct destinations.

The asymptotic distribution theory of these statistics is again provided by score theory since the $s_m^2 - p_m$ are score statistics. To see this consider the multiple-destinations version of the locally heterogeneous model in which we introduce M random variables $v_1, v_2, \ldots v_M$ into the M transition intensities. The $\{v_m\}$ are jointly distributed with distribution function H, unit means, and covariance matrix Σ. The data distribution is the mixture

$$g_m(t, \mathbf{d}) = \int \exp \left\{ \sum_{m=1}^{M} [d_m (\log v_m + \log \overline{\theta}_m) - v_m \overline{z}_m] \right\} dH(\mathbf{v}). \quad (3.7)$$

Expanding this expectation about the mean of the v's up to the quadratic term we get the local mixture approximate density function whose logarithm is

$$L = \sum_{m=1}^{M} [d_m \log \overline{\theta}_m(t; \gamma_m) - \overline{I}_m(t; \gamma_m)] + \log[1 + \operatorname{tr} \mathbf{\Sigma H}/2]. \qquad (3.8)$$

By differentiation of the total log likelihood for all N observations with respect to the distinct elements of $\mathbf{\Sigma}$ at $\mathbf{\Sigma} = 0$ we find the score statistics corresponding to the diagonal elements of $\mathbf{\Sigma}$ to be proportional to $s^2 - p_m$, while those for the off-diagonal elements are the sample residual covariances. The variances of these statistics can be found by applying the general formula (2.13) where now $I_{\eta\eta}$ is a matrix of order up to $M(M+1)/2$ depending upon how many elements, if any, of $\mathbf{\Sigma}$ are set equal to zero a priori. It will be of order M, and diagonal in view of (3.6), if the off-diagonal elements of $\mathbf{\Sigma}$ are assumed to be zero.

As with the single destination case these statistics based on the residual variances and covariances are Information Matrix test statistics. They are the $M(M+1)/2$ components of that test which relate to the M intercepts in the log transition intensities.

The new possibility that arises with multiple destinations is that of using as specification test statistics the covariances of the residuals corresponding to different destinations. These statistics do not measure the size of the log density derivatives with respect to person-specific parameters α_{im} and they do not therefore test for person-specific heterogeneity. They appear instead to provide a basis for a test that the underlying model is one of *dependent* competing risks, since when the $\{v_m\}$ are independent the errors will be uncorrelated and the correct model will be one with M independent, possibly heterogeneous, latent survival times. There is, however, a danger in using the residual covariances as a basis for a specification test as is shown by the following example.

Example 1. Singularity of the IM Test Statistic
Suppose we have two destinations whose transition intensities and their integrals are proportional in the sense of chapter 5 so that

$$\theta_{i2}(t) = \lambda\theta_{i1}(t), \qquad z_{i2}(t) = \lambda z_{i1}(t). \qquad (3.9)$$

In addition to proportionality (3.9) asserts that the factor of proportionality is the same for all people. Assume further that λ is known and that there are no unknown parameters in the transition intensities so that we can compute, and base our specification test upon, the errors rather than the residuals. The three test statistics using the two error variances and the error covariance are

$$T_1 = \sum_{i=1}^{N} [(z_{i1}(t_i) - d_i)^2 - d_i],$$

$$T_2 = \sum_{i=1}^{N} [(z_{i2}(t_i) - (1 - d_i))^2 - (1 - d_i)],$$

$$T_3 = \sum_{i=1}^{N} (z_{i1}(t_i) - d_i)(z_{i2}(t_i) - (1 - d_i)),$$

where $d_i = 1$ if destination 1 is entered, 0 otherwise. Using (3.9) in these definitions and a little algebra shows that

$$T_3 = \frac{\lambda T_1}{2} + \frac{T_2}{2\lambda}$$

so that T_1, T_2, T_3 have a singular joint distribution. One of the three statistics is redundant and it would not be correct to attempt to base a test of specification on all three residual moments.   ■

The circumstances in which it is sensible to test for model misspecification using residual covariances are not well understood. The model (3.9) is very restrictive and the example would not go through, even though the transition intensities are proportional, if there are regressors in the model causing the factor λ to vary between people. Presumably there is a connection between the phenomenon illustrated in the example and the identifiability of the dependent competing risks model that would arise when the $\{v_m\}$ are correlated.

4   Limited Information Residuals

The argument so far has assumed that those transition intensities that are modelled are specified up to a finite set of unknown parameters. To calculate residuals we merely replace these unknown parameters appearing in the error definition by their maximum likelihood estimates. In this section we examine how to proceed when the hazard function involves an unknown function as in the proportional hazard model of chapter 9.

As before we introduce person-specific intercepts, $\{\alpha_i\}$, into the log hazard and find the derivatives of the log likelihood with respect to these parameters when they are zero. We consider the proportional hazards model and the partial likelihood in the integral form (2.34) or (2.35).

The log partial likelihood is

$$L_P = \log \int_R \left(\prod_{i=1}^N \mu_i \right) \exp \left\{ -\sum_{i=1}^N \mu_i z_i \right\} d\mathbf{z}$$

$$= \int_R \exp \left\{ \sum_{i=1}^N (\log \mu_i - \mu_i z_i) \right\} d\mathbf{z}$$

$$= \int_R \exp\{L\} \, d\mathbf{z}, \tag{4.1}$$

where L is the full information log likelihood (based on $\mathbf{z}$) and R is the region in z space defined by the generalised rank information. We shall also use the symbol R to stand for the generalised rank information itself. Differentiating, we find

$$\frac{\partial L_P}{\partial \alpha_i} = \frac{\int_R (\partial L/\partial \alpha_i) e^L \, d\mathbf{z}}{\int_R e^L \, d\mathbf{z}}$$

$$= \mathrm{E} \left(\frac{\partial L}{\partial \alpha_i} \mid R \right)_{\alpha=0}$$

$$= \mathrm{E}\left(\epsilon_i \mid R \right) = \bar{\epsilon}_i. \tag{4.2}$$

This expression is the expected value of the generalised (full information) error, given the (generalised) rank information, and it defines the generalised error for a proportional hazard model with unspecified baseline hazard. Without a model for the baseline hazard we cannot calculate ϵ_i, but we can estimate it – and this estimate is the error definition suggested by the general approach of this chapter. The corresponding residual is defined by replacing unknown parameters in $\bar{\epsilon}$ by their maximum partial likelihood estimates. The residual is denoted by $\bar{e}_i$.

To calculate $\bar{\epsilon}$ note that

$$\bar{\epsilon}_i = 1 - I(t_i) = 1 - \mu_i \int_0^{t_i} \theta_0(s) \, ds = 1 - \mu_i \bar{z}_i. \tag{4.3}$$

Thus,

$$\bar{\epsilon}_i = 1 - \mu_i \mathrm{E}\left(\bar{z}_i \mid R \right)$$

$$= 1 - \mu_i \left[\frac{1 - d_i}{\mu_i} + \sum_{t_{(j)} \le t_i} \Psi_j^{-1} \right], \qquad \text{from (2.38) of chapter 9,}$$

$$= d_i - \mu_i \sum_{t_{(j)} \le t_i} \Psi_j^{-1}, \tag{4.4}$$

which can be compared with (3.2). The corresponding residual is

$$\bar{e}_i = d_i - \hat{\mu}_i \sum_{t_{(j)} \leq t_i} \hat{\Psi}_j^{-1}. \tag{4.5}$$

Proceeding as in the last section we would construct a test of neglected heterogeneity by comparing the variance of the residuals with an estimate of the expectation of the error variance. By examination of the second derivative of the log partial likelihood – extending the argument leading to theorem 10 of chapter 9 – we may show that

$$\text{var}\,\bar{e}_i = \text{E}\left(d_i - \mu_i^2 \sum_{t_{(j)} \leq t_i} \Psi_j^{-2}\right). \tag{4.6}$$

The first term on the right is the same as for the full information case, (3.4). When these terms are summed over the sample the first term is $O(N)$ and the second of $O(\log N)$ so that the average variance of the $\{\bar{\epsilon}_i\}$ in large samples is the mean probability that an observation is uncensored, exactly as in the full information case.

The suggested test statistic is proportional to

$$S = \sum_{i=1}^{N}\left[\left(d_i - \hat{\mu}_i \sum_{t_{(j)} \leq t_i} \hat{\Psi}_j^{-1}\right)^2 - \left(d_i - \hat{\mu}_i^2 \sum_{t_{(j)} \leq t_i} \hat{\Psi}_j^{-2}\right)\right]. \tag{4.7}$$

The simplest way to deduce the asymptotic distribution of this statistic is to show that it is a score statistic and then apply standard results. To do this we replace the expression under the integral sign in (4.1) by the joint density function corresponding to the locally heterogeneous model (2.12). This gives

$$L_P = \int_R \left(\prod_{i=1}^{N}\mu_i\right) \exp\left\{-\sum_{i=1}^{N}\mu_i z_i\right\} \left(\prod_{i=1}^{N}[1 + \eta h_i]\right) d\mathbf{z}, \tag{4.8}$$

where

$$h_i = z^2(t_i) - 2z(t_i)$$
$$= \mu_i^2 \bar{z}_i^2 - 2\mu_i \bar{z}_i,$$

and $\eta = \sigma^2/2$. The score for η at $\eta = 0$ is

$$\frac{\partial L_P}{\partial \eta} = \text{E}\left\{\sum_{i=1}^{N}[(\mu_i \bar{z}_i)^2 - 2\mu_i \bar{z}_i] \mid R\right\}.$$

Now

$$\mu_i^2 \mathrm{E}\left(\bar{z}_i^2 \mid R\right) = \mu_i^2 \sum_{t_{(j)} \leq t_i} \Psi_j^{-2} + 2(1 - d_i) + 2\mu_i(1 - d_i) \sum_{t_{(j)} \leq t_i} \Psi_j^{-1}$$

$$+ \mu_i^2 \left(\sum_{t_{(j)} \leq t_i} \Psi_j^{-1}\right)^2,$$

and, by the partial likelihood equation for the constant term in the log hazard,

$$\sum_{i=1}^N \left(d_i - \hat{\mu}_i \sum_{t_{(j)} \leq t_i} \hat{\Psi}_j^{-1}\right) = 0.$$

Using these relations we find that the calculated score test statistic will be proportional to

$$S = \sum_{i=1}^N \left[\hat{\mu}_i^2 \sum_{t_{(j)} \leq t_i} \hat{\Psi}_j^{-2} - 2d_i\hat{\mu}_i \sum_{t_{(j)} \leq t_i} \hat{\Psi}_j^{-1} + \hat{\mu}_i^2 \left(\sum_{t_{(j)} \leq t_i} \hat{\Psi}_j^{-1}\right)^2\right],$$

which is identical to (4.7). The variance of the test statistic can be obtained from the general formula (2.13) with information matrices replaced by negative Hessians of the log partial likelihood.

Plotting procedures for semi-parametric residuals are more difficult than in the fully parametric case since $\bar{\epsilon}_i$ estimates the expected value of the ϵ_i rather than ϵ_i itself, which will cause the distribution of the $\bar{e}_i$ to depart from that of a right censored unit Exponential. The reader is referred to Lagakos (1981) for examples and further discussion.

5   Multiple Cycles

The extension to the case in which we observe multiple-cycles of information is straightforward except that there exists the additional feature that one can calculate errors and residuals for each cycle as well as for each origin/destination state pair. Consider, for example, a model with a single state repeatedly re-entered and suppose that we observe the process from calendar time t_1, at which an entry occurs, until time c. The probability that k stays in the state (spells) are completed and that the j'th lasts for s_j days is

$$p(k, s_1, s_2, \ldots, s_k) = \exp\{-\sum_{j=1}^k [z_j(s_j) - \log \theta_j(s_j)]$$

$$-z_{k+1}(s_{k+1}) \left(c - t_1 - \sum_{j=1}^{k} s_j \right) \}, \qquad (5.1)$$

$$k = 0, 1, \ldots, \quad \sum_{j=1}^{k} s_j \leq c - t_1, \quad s_j \geq 0, \qquad j = 1, 2, \ldots, k.$$

The first sum is taken as zero if $k = 0$. Here $z_j(t)$ is the hazard for the j'th cycle integrated to elapsed duration t measured from zero when the cycle began. This hazard may have the calendar date of entry as one of its arguments giving calendar time dependence to the process.

To define errors and residuals introduce a cycle-specific intercept into the log hazard and differentiate the log density with respect to it. This gives

$$\epsilon_j = d_{j-1}[d_j - z_j(y_j)], \quad d_j = \begin{cases} 1, & k \geq j, \\ 0, & \text{otherwise,} \end{cases}, \quad d_0 = 1, \ j = 1, 2, \ldots,$$

and,

$$y_j = \min \left(s_j, c - t_1 - \sum_{i=1}^{j-1} s_i \right), \quad j = 1, 2, \ldots.$$

The multiplication by d_{j-1} ensures that no residual for spell j is defined if we observe neither a complete nor an incomplete j'th spell. For a person observed to complete k spells $k + 1$ residuals are defined. The moments of the errors follow by differentiation under the integral of the density function over the sample and are

$$E(\epsilon_j) = 0;$$
$$E(\epsilon_j^2) = E(d_{j-1} z_j(y_j)) = E(d_{j-1} d_j) = P(k \geq j);$$
$$E(\epsilon_i \epsilon_j) = 0, \quad i \neq j.$$

Thus the errors for a multiple-cycle model are uncorrelated between cycles and have variances which can be estimated by the fraction of times, over all people, that j complete cycles are observed. The specification tests which compare residual variances with their expectations are tests for neglected person-specific heterogeneity. A test based on the between-cycle correlation of residuals is a test for residual autocorrelation. We shall not give details here. The extension to models with multiple-cycles and multiple destinations can also be done.

6   Miscellaneous Tests

We conclude with some miscellaneous remarks about residual definitions and other tests of specification.

When the sampling scheme is not an observation of the flow, as, for example, when the appropriate data density is the length biased sampling density $\overline{G}(t)/\mu$, the method of deriving residuals that we have adopted above does not give useful results. In particular, tests for neglected heterogeneity with such distributions have not been studied. It is, of course, possible to apply standard graphical and numerical tests of goodness of fit with such distributions, but since these do not exploit the special character of duration distributions we shall not discuss them.

Tests to detect other types of misspecification, particularly misspecification of the conditional hazard function, are useful, and generally follow from standard arguments. We shall mention three.

6.1   Test for Non-Monotone Hazard

In the context of a Weibull model a test for non-monotonicity of the hazard function can be done by writing the log hazard as

$$\log \theta(t) = \log \mu(\mathbf{x}_i'\gamma) + \alpha_1 \log t + \alpha_2 (\log t)^2,$$

and score testing the null hypothesis $\alpha_2 = 0$. If the hazard is in fact non-monotone then, in general, $\alpha_2 \neq 0$. The score test procedure is useful here because ML estimates on the null hypothesis are the readily computed Weibull estimates, whereas when $\alpha_2 \neq 0$ the hazard must be integrated numerically and ML estimates are much harder to calculate. With censoring, the log data density is

$$d \log \theta(t) - \int_0^t \theta(s) \, ds,$$

and differentiation with respect to α_2 at the origin gives the score statistic

$$
\begin{aligned}
S &= \sum_{i=1}^{N} \left[(d_i - \hat{z}(t_i))(\log t_i)^2 + 2 \frac{d_i \log t_i}{\hat{\alpha}} \right], \\
&= \sum_{i=1}^{N} e_i (\log t_i)^2 + 2 \frac{\sum_{i=1}^{N} d_i \log t_i}{\hat{\alpha}}.
\end{aligned}
\tag{6.1}
$$

Integration by parts was used to get the explicit form (6.1) together with the likelihood equations on the null. The test compares the covariance of the residuals and the squared log duration with an estimate of its expectation on the null. The asymptotic distribution of S follows from standard score theory.

6.2   Test for Non-Proportional Hazard

Consider the hazard model

$$\theta_i(t) = \mu(\mathbf{x}_i'\gamma)e^{\beta w_i(t)}\theta_0(t). \tag{6.2}$$

Here $\mathbf{x}$ is a vector of time-independent regressors and θ_0 is the baseline hazard. The expression $w_i(t)$ represents a suitably constructed time-varying regressor. A possible choice would be the product of a time-constant regressor and a function of time which takes the value zero up to some time t_0 and is one thereafter. This model reduces to a proportional hazard model if $\beta = 0$. A score test for this reduction can be constructed by writing down the partial likelihood of chapter 9, section 2.7, and differentiating its logarithm with respect to β at $\beta = 0$. This gives a statistic proportional to

$$S = \sum_{i=1}^{N} w_i(t_i)\bar{e}_i, \tag{6.3}$$

where $\bar{e}_i$ is the i'th partial likelihood residual. The test amounts to seeing if the covariance of the residual with the time-dependent regressor is large in modulus.

6.3   An Information Matrix Test

The Inverse Gaussian provides both an important duration model and an interesting example of the Information Matrix (IM) test of model specification. We gave the density and survivor functions in chapter 5, section 7, as

$$f(t) = \frac{\alpha}{\sigma t^{3/2}}\phi\left(\frac{\alpha - \mu t}{\sigma\sqrt{t}}\right),$$

$$\overline{F}(t) = \Phi\left(\frac{\alpha - \mu t}{\sigma\sqrt{t}}\right) - \exp\left\{\frac{2\mu\alpha}{\sigma^2}\right\}\Phi\left(\frac{-\alpha - \mu t}{\sigma\sqrt{t}}\right).$$

As usual, ϕ and Φ are the standard Normal density and distribution functions. We normalise by setting $\sigma = 1$. To test this model specification we could examine the IM statistics corresponding to α and μ, and if we do this the result is interesting and cautionary.

The log density for the i'th observation is

$$L_i = d_i \log f(t_i) + (1 - d_i) \log \overline{F}(t_i),$$

where d is the censoring indicator. The score contributions are

$$\frac{\partial L_i}{\partial \alpha} = \frac{d_i}{\alpha} - \frac{d_i c_i}{\sqrt{t_i}} + (1 - d_i)\frac{\overline{F}_\alpha}{\overline{F}},$$

$$\frac{\partial L_i}{\partial \mu} = d_i c_i \sqrt{t_i} + (1 - d_i)\frac{\overline{F}_\mu}{\overline{F}}, \tag{6.4}$$

where $\overline{F}_\alpha = \partial \overline{F}/\partial \alpha$ and so on, and $c_i = (\alpha - \mu t_i)/\sqrt{t_i}$. The Hessian is

$$\frac{\partial^2 L_i}{\partial \alpha^2} = -\frac{d_i}{\alpha^2} - \frac{d_i}{t_i} + (1 - d_i)\left[\frac{\overline{F}_{\alpha\alpha}}{\overline{F}} - \left(\frac{\overline{F}_\alpha}{\overline{F}}\right)^2\right]$$

$$\frac{\partial^2 L_i}{\partial \mu^2} = -d_i t_i + (1 - d_i)\left[\frac{\overline{F}_{\mu\mu}}{\overline{F}} - \left(\frac{\overline{F}_\mu}{\overline{F}}\right)^2\right] \tag{6.5}$$

$$\frac{\partial^2 L_i}{\partial \alpha \partial \mu} = d_i + (1 - d_i)\left[\frac{\overline{F}_{\alpha\mu}}{\overline{F}} - \frac{\overline{F}_\alpha \overline{F}_\mu}{\overline{F}^2}\right].$$

The squares and products of the score contributions are

$$\left(\frac{\partial L_i}{\partial \alpha}\right)^2 = \frac{d_i}{\alpha^2} - \frac{2 d_i c_i}{\alpha \sqrt{t_i}} + \frac{d_i c_i^2}{t_i} + (1 - d_i)\left(\frac{\overline{F}_\alpha}{\overline{F}}\right)^2,$$

$$\left(\frac{\partial L_i}{\partial \alpha}\right)^2 = d_i c_i^2 t_i + (1 - d_i)\left(\frac{\overline{F}_\mu}{\overline{F}}\right)^2, \tag{6.6}$$

$$\left(\frac{\partial L_i}{\partial \alpha}\frac{\partial l_i}{\partial \mu}\right) = \frac{d_i c_i \sqrt{t_i}}{\alpha} - d_i c_i^2 + (1 - d_i)\left(\frac{\overline{F}_\alpha \overline{F}_\mu}{\overline{F}^2}\right).$$

The Information Matrix test compares the sums of the matrices (6.5) and (6.6) at the ML estimates of α and μ. The three distinct components of the statistic are

$$\alpha, \alpha; \quad \sum_{i=1}^{N}\left[-\frac{d_i}{t_i} - \frac{2 d_i c_i}{\alpha \sqrt{t_i}} + \frac{d_i c_i^2}{t_i} + (1 - d_i)\frac{\overline{F}_{\alpha\alpha}}{\overline{F}}\right];$$

$$\mu, \mu; \quad \sum_{i=1}^{N}\left[-d_i t_i + d_i c_i^2 t_i + (1 - d_i)\frac{\overline{F}_{\mu\mu}}{\overline{F}}\right]; \tag{6.7}$$

$$\alpha, \mu; \quad \sum_{i=1}^{N}\left[d_i + \frac{d_i c_i \sqrt{t_i}}{\alpha} - d_i c_i^2 + (1 - d_i)\frac{\overline{F}_{\alpha\mu}}{\overline{F}}\right].$$

Now if we differentiate $\overline{F}$ with respect to α and μ using the observation that

$$e^{2\alpha\mu}\phi\left(\frac{-\alpha - \mu t}{\sigma\sqrt{t}}\right) = \phi\left(\frac{\alpha - \mu t}{\sigma\sqrt{t}}\right), \tag{6.8}$$

we find that

$$\overline{F}_{\alpha\mu} = \left(\frac{1}{\alpha} + \mu\right)\overline{F}_{\mu} + \alpha\overline{F}_{\alpha}. \tag{6.9}$$

But from the likelihood equations we find that

$$\sum_{i=1}^{N}(1 - d_i)\frac{\overline{F}_{\mu}}{\overline{F}} = \sum_{i-1}^{N} d_i c_i \sqrt{t_i},$$

$$\sum_{i=1}^{N}(1 - d_i)\frac{\overline{F}_{\alpha}}{\overline{F}} = \sum_{i=1}^{N}\left[\frac{d_i}{\alpha} - \frac{d_i c_i}{\sqrt{t_i}}\right]. \tag{6.10}$$

Using these relations we can then deduce that the α, μ component of the IM statistic in (6.7) is identically zero. This might have been expected in view of the fact that there are only two distinct components of the IM statistic for the Normal distribution and the known close analogy between the two distributions. The point of this example is that the algebra required to reveal this identity is not trivial, and numerical work may fail to reveal it clearly as the following numbers show.

Example 2

The Inverse Gaussian model without regressors was fitted to the first job tenures of 3423 British university graduates, of which 1083 observations were right censored. The maximum likelihood estimates of α and μ were

$$\hat{\alpha} = 5.134(0.048), \qquad \hat{\mu} = 0.050(0.003).$$

The unit time period was a month. The matrices to be compared in the IM test are

$$\begin{pmatrix} 0.0854 & -0.9357 \\ -0.9357 & 32.9280 \end{pmatrix} \text{ and } \begin{pmatrix} 0.1525 & -0.9356 \\ -0.9356 & 31.8260 \end{pmatrix},$$

where the left matrix is the negative Hessian divided by N and the right matrix is the outer product of the scores also divided by the sample size. The off-diagonal elements of these matrices which should be identical are in fact equal only to three decimal places. If one had not known that these elements should be identical and had assumed that there were in fact three linearly independent elements to the test statistic one would have computed a quadratic form whose matrix would be nearly, but not exactly, singular. This would have resulted in absurd values for a statistic whose null distribution is supposedly $\chi^2(3)$. The correct statistic is in fact a quadratic form in the differences only of the diagonal elements, that is, in

$$D = \begin{pmatrix} 0.1525 - 0.0854 \\ 31.8260 - 32.9280 \end{pmatrix} = \begin{pmatrix} 0.0671 \\ -1.1020 \end{pmatrix}.$$

The estimated asymptotic covariance matrix of this vector is

$$V = \frac{1}{3423} \begin{pmatrix} 0.4199 & -6.992 \\ -6.992 & 395.90 \end{pmatrix}.$$

This gives two $\chi^2(1)$ test statistics of

$$\alpha, \alpha: \quad 36.70; \qquad \mu, \mu: \quad 4.50,$$

which may be compared to the 1 percent significance level of 6.63. For a combined test one calculates $D'V^{-1}D = 27.23$ compared to the 1 percent significance level for a $\chi^2(2)$ variate of 9.21. These statistics indicate that the model is misspecified, which is scarcely surprising. Two-parameters could not hope to describe a sample of over 3000. ∎

NOTE

his chapter draws on the work of Cox and Snell, (1968, 1971), which introduced the idea of generalised residuals. There are specific applications to duration data in Cox and Oakes (1984). The main references in the statistics literature are Crowley and Hu (1977) and Lagakos (1981). The chapter also draws on Lancaster (1983, 1985c) and Lancaster and Chesher (1985)[3] and unpublished work by the present author on residuals with multiple destinations and cycles. The work on score tests for heterogeneity draws on Chesher (1984), Cox (1983), Lancaster (1984), and Clayton and Cuzick (1985).

---

[3] The printers of this paper randomly rematched figures and their titles.

Appendix 1

The Gamma Function and Distribution The Gamma function is the integral

$$\int_0^\infty x^{\alpha-1} e^{-x}\, dx, \qquad \alpha > 0, \tag{1}$$

denoted by $\Gamma(\alpha)$. The value of the function is positive for every positive α and $\Gamma(1) = 1$. Its derivative is negative for $0 < \alpha < 1.4616$ and positive for greater values of α. If we consider

$$\Gamma(\alpha + 1) = \int_0^\infty x^\alpha e^{-x}\, dx$$

and integrate by parts we get

$$\Gamma(\alpha + 1) = [-x^\alpha e^{-x}]_0^\infty + \alpha \int_0^\infty x^{\alpha-1} e^{-x}\, dx = 0 + \alpha\Gamma(\alpha),$$

so $\quad \Gamma(\alpha + 1) = \alpha\Gamma(\alpha). \tag{2}$

If α is an integer, repeated application of (2) implies

$$\Gamma(\alpha + 1) = \alpha!. \tag{3}$$

For $\alpha = 1/2$ it may be shown that

$$\Gamma(1/2) = \sqrt{\pi}. \tag{4}$$

The derivative of the logarithm of the Gamma function – the digamma function – is denoted by

$$\frac{d \log \Gamma(\alpha)}{d\alpha} = \psi(\alpha), \tag{5}$$

which is strictly increasing and negative for $0 < \alpha < 1.4616$, and positive thereafter. Taking logs of both sides of (2) and differentiating gives the recurrence relation

$$\psi(\alpha + 1) = (1/\alpha) + \psi(\alpha). \tag{6}$$

327

Some particular values of the function are

$$\psi(1) = -0.5772,$$
$$\psi(2) = 0.4228.$$

The second derivative of $\log \Gamma(\alpha)$ is denoted by $\psi'(\alpha)$ and is positive for every $\alpha > 0$. Differentiating (6) gives the recurrence relation

$$\psi'(\alpha + 1) = -(1/\alpha^2) + \psi'(\alpha). \tag{7}$$

A useful particular value of the function is

$$\psi'(1) = 1.6449. \tag{8}$$

In general, the $(j + 1)$'th derivative of $\log \Gamma(\alpha)$ is denoted by $\psi^{(j)}(\alpha)$ and it satisfies the recurrence relation

$$\psi^{(j)}(\alpha + 1) = (-1)^j \, j! \, \alpha^{-j-1} + \psi^{(j)}(\alpha). \tag{9}$$

If we change the variable of integration in (1) from x to $y = x/\beta$, $\beta > 0$, with $dx = \beta \, dy$ we see that

$$\Gamma(\alpha) = \beta^\alpha \int_0^\infty y^{\alpha-1} e^{-\beta y} \, dy. \tag{10}$$

Since the integrand is non-negative the function

$$f(y) = \frac{\beta^\alpha y^{\alpha-1} e^{-\beta y}}{\Gamma(\alpha)}, \qquad y \geq 0, \tag{11}$$

is non-negative and integrates to one over the positive axis. It is therefore a probability density function and is the family of Gamma distributions. By use of (10) the moment generating function of Y is found to be

$$M_Y(s) = E(e^{sY}) = (1 - s/\beta)^{-\alpha}, \qquad s < \beta, \tag{12}$$

with cumulant generating function,

$$K_Y(s) = -\alpha \log(1 - s/\beta), \tag{13}$$

from which we deduce

$$E(Y) = \alpha/\beta, \qquad \text{var}(Y) = \alpha/\beta^2. \tag{14}$$

Similarly the moment generating function of $\log Y$ is

$$M_{\log Y}(s) = E(Y^s) = \left[\frac{\Gamma(\alpha + s)}{\Gamma(\alpha)} \right] \beta^{-s},$$

with cumulant generating function

$$K_{\log Y}(s) = -s \log \beta + \log \Gamma(\alpha + s) - \log \Gamma(\alpha), \tag{15}$$

and first two moments

$$\mathrm{E}\,(\log Y) = -\log \beta + \psi(\alpha), \qquad \mathrm{var}(\log Y) = \psi'(\alpha). \qquad (16)$$

The *standard* Gamma distribution has $\beta = 1$ and is denoted by $\mathcal{G}(\alpha)$. Its mean and variance both equal α, from (14), and the cumulants of $\log Y$ are equal to the successive derivatives of $\log \Gamma(\alpha)$, from (15).

The Gamma distribution of unit mean has $\alpha = \beta$ and $\mathrm{var}(Y) = 1/\beta = \sigma^2$. It is denoted in the text by $\mathcal{G}(1, \eta)$, where $\eta = \beta = 1/\sigma^2$, since it is more convenient there to use β to denote a regression coefficient.

The Gamma distribution with $\beta = 1/2, \alpha = k/2$ for each positive integer k is the $\chi^2(k)$ distribution. It has density function

$$f(y) = \frac{y^{k/2-1} e^{-y/2}}{2^{k/2} \Gamma(k/2)},$$

moment generating function

$$M_Y(s) = (1 - 2s)^{-k/2},$$

and cumulant generating function

$$K_Y(s) = -\frac{k}{2} \log(1 - 2s).$$

The j'th cumulant is $k2^{j-1}(j-1)!$ so the mean is k and the variance $2k$.

The standard reference on the Gamma function is Abramowitz and Segun (1964).

Appendix 2

Some Properties of the Laplace Transform In this appendix we shall outline the main properties of the Laplace transforms of probability distributions of random variables whose sample space is the non-negative axis. We emphasise the properties that we have used in this book.

Let $F(x)$ be the distribution of a random variable X whose sample space is the non-negative axis. The Laplace transform of F, with non-negative argument s, is

$$L(s) = \int_0^\infty e^{-sx}\, dF(x) = \mathrm{E}\,(e^{-sX}), \qquad s \geq 0. \tag{1}$$

We note the properties of the transform used in chapter 7: $L(0) = 1; \lim_{s\to\infty} L(s) = 0$. Also, since $L'(s) < 0$ there is an inverse function, L^{-1}, where $L^{-1}(1) = 0; L^{-1}(0) = \infty$. In addition, if $X = (Z_1 + Z_2 + \cdots + Z_n)$ where the $\{Z_j\}$ are distributed independently with Laplace transforms $L_j(s)$, then the transform of X is

$$
\begin{aligned}
L(s) &= \mathrm{E}\,(\exp\{-sX)\}) \\
&= \mathrm{E}\,(\exp\{-s(Z_1 + Z_2 + \cdots + Z_n)\}) \\
&= \prod_{j=1}^n \mathrm{E}\,(\exp\{-sZ_j\}) \\
&= \prod_{j=1}^n L_j(s).
\end{aligned}
$$

The first point, used extensively in chapter 7, is that Laplace transforms are unique – to any Laplace transform there corresponds a unique probability distribution.

Lemma *A probability distribution concentrated on a finite interval is completely determined by its moments.*

Proof: See Feller (1966, chapter VII). ∎

Theorem 1   *Laplace transforms are unique.*

Proof: Change the variable in (1) to $y = e^{-x}$ where Y has distribution function $G(y) = 1 - F(x)$. Then

$$L(s) = \int_0^1 y^s \, dG(y).$$

But $L(1)$, $L(2)$, ... are the moments of G and, by the lemma, determine it, and consequently $F(x)$, uniquely.   ■

In our discussion of mixture models we used the fact that mixture distributions can appear as the Laplace transform of the mixing distribution. Of interest is the question of when a function can be a Laplace transform, of the form (1).

Definition 1   *A function $\phi(s)$ is completely monotone iff it possesses derivatives of all orders and*

$$(-1)^n \phi^{(n)}(s) \geq 0, \qquad s > 0. \tag{2}$$

Theorem 2 (Bernstein)   *A function $\phi(s)$ is the Laplace transform of a probability distribution F iff it is completely monotone and $\phi(0) = 1$.*

Proof: Necessity is clear from (1). Sufficiency is given in Feller (1966, chapter XIII).   ■

In chapter 4 we used the Laplace transform of the non-negative stable distributions.

Definition 2   *A non-negative random variable X has a stable distribution of index α, $G_\alpha(x)$, $0 < \alpha < 1$, iff*

$$Y = n^{-1/\alpha}(X_1 + X_2 + \cdots + X_n)$$

has distribution function G_α whenever the $\{X_j\}$ are independently distributed with distribution function G_α, for $n = 1, 2, \ldots$.

Lemma   *If $\phi(s)$ is completely monotone and $\psi(s) > 0$ with $\psi'(s)$ completely monotone, then $\phi(\psi(s))$ is completely monotone.*

Proof: See Feller (1966, chapter XIII).   ■

Theorem 3 $L(s) = \exp\{-s^\alpha\}$ *is the Laplace transform of the family of non-negative stable distributions.*

Proof: First, $L(s)$ is completely monotone because it is of the form taken in the preceding lemma with $\phi(\psi) = e^{-\psi}, \psi(s) = s^\alpha$. Also, $L(0) = 1$. Thus $L(s)$ is the Laplace transform of a probability distribution. Second, the Laplace transform of Y given in the definition above is

$$\begin{aligned} \mathrm{E}\left(\exp\{-sY\}\right) &= \mathrm{E}\,\exp(\{-s(X_1 + X_2 + \cdots + X_n)/n^{1/\alpha}\}) \\ &= L^n(sn^{-1/\alpha}) \\ &= \exp\{-s^\alpha\}, \end{aligned}$$

which proves stability. ∎

The first passage time distribution of chapter 5, section 7, and other places in the book, is stable with index $\alpha = 1/2$ when $\mu = 0$, by inspection of (7.11) of chapter 5 interpreted as the Laplace transform with argument sign reversed.

Bibliography

Aalen, O., 1978. Nonparametric inference for a family of counting processes. *The Annals of Statistics* 6, 4: 701–726.

Aalen, O., 1987(a). Mixing distributions on a Markov chain. *Scandinavian Journal of Statistics* 14: 281–289.

Aalen, O., 1987(b). Two examples of modelling heterogeneity in survival analysis. *Scandinavian Journal of Statistics* 14: 19–25.

Aalen, O., O. Borgan, N. Keiding, & J. Thormann, 1980. Interaction between life history events. Nonparametric analysis for prospective and retrospective data in the presence of censoring. *Scandinavian Journal of Statistics* 7: 161–171.

Abramowitz, M., & I. A. Segun, 1964. *Handbook of Mathematical Functions.* New York: Dover.

Aitchison, J., & J. A. C. Brown, 1957. *The Lognormal Distribution.* Cambridge: Cambridge University Press.

Akerlof, G. A., & B. G. M. Main, 1981. Pitfalls in Markov modeling of labor market stocks and flows. *The Journal of Human Resources* 16: 1, 141–151.

Alaouze, C. M., 1984. The hazard rate from unemployment when the search environment is characterised by a decreasing probability of offer. *Economics Letters.*

Amemiya, T., 1985. Advanced Econometrics. Oxford: Blackwell.

Andersen, P. K., & O. Borgan, 1985. Counting process models for life history data: A review. *Scandinavian Journal of Statistics* 12: 97–158.

Andersen, P. K., O. Borgan, R. Gill, & N. Keiding, 1982. Linear nonparametric tests for comparison of counting processes, with applications to censored survival data. *International Statistical Review* 50: 512–549.

Andersen, P. K., & R. D. Gill, 1982. Cox's regression model for counting processes: A large sample study. *The Annals of Statistics* 10: 1100–1120.

Andersen, P. K., & A. Green, 1985. Evaluation of estimation bias in an illness–death–emigration Model. *Scandinavian Journal of Statistics* 12: 63–68.

333

Andrews, M., & S. Nickell, 1982. Unemployment in the United Kingdom since the war. *Review of Economic Studies* 49, 5: 731–759.

Arbous, A. G., & J. E. Kerrich, 1951. Accident statistics. *Biometrics* 7, 4: 340–432.

Arley, N., 1943. On the theory of stochastic processes and their application to the theory of cosmic radiation. Copenhagen: GEC Gads Forlag.

Arnold, B. C., & P. L. Brockett, 1983. Identifiability for dependent multiple decrement/competing risks models. *Scandinavian Actuarial Journal* 31: 117–127.

Ashenfelter, O., 1980. Discrete choice in labor supply: The determinants of participation in the Seattle and Denver income maintenance experiments. Working Paper No. 136, Princeton University.

Atkinson, A. B., & Flemming, J. S., 1978. Unemployment, social security and incentives. *Midland Bank Review* 5: 6–16.

Atkinson, A. B., & J. Micklewright, 1985. Unemployment Benefits and Unemployment Duration. London: Suntory–Toyota International Centre for Economics and Related Disciplines, London School of Economics.

Baker, G. M., & P. K. Trivedi, 1985. Estimation of unemployment duration from grouped data. *Journal of Labor Economics* 3, 2: 153–174.

Banerjee, A. K., & G. K. Bhattacharyya, 1979. Bayesian results for the inverse gaussian distribution with an application. *Technometrics* 21, 2: 247–251.

Barlow, R. E., & A. W. Marshall, 1954. Bounds on interval probabilities for restricted families of distributions. Fifth Berkeley Symposium, III.

Barndorff-Nielsen, O., P. Blaesild, & C. Halgreen, 1978. First hitting time models for the generalised inverse Gaussian distribution. *Stochastic Processes and their Applications* 7: 49–54.

Barndorff-Neilsen, O., J. Kent, & M. Sorensen, 1982. Normal variance–mean mixtures and z distributions. *International Statistical Review* 50: 145–159.

Barnes, W. F., 1975. Job search models, the duration of unemployment, and the asking wage: Some empirical evidence. *The Journal of Human Resources* 10, 2: 230–240.

Barron, J. M., & O. W. Gilley, 1979. The effect of unemployment insurance on the search process. *Industrial and Labor Relations Review* 32, 3: 363–366.

Bartlett, M. S., 1953. Approximate confidence intervals. *Biometrika* 40, 13–19, 306–317, 201–204.

Basu, A. P., 1981. Identifiability problems in the theory of competing and complementary risks – a survey. In *Statistical Distributions in Scientific Work*, vol. 5, ed. C. Taillie, G. P. Patil, & B. A. Baldaressi. Dordrecht: D. Reidel.

Bates, G. E., & J. Neyman, 1952. Contributions to the theory of accident proneness. *University of California Publications in Statistics* 1, 9: 215–254; 1, 10: 255–276.

Beach, C. M., & S. F. Kaliski, 1983. Measuring the duration of unemployment from gross flow data. *Canadian Journal of Economics* 16, 2: 258–263.

Bjorklund, A., & R. Moffitt, 1983. The estimation of wage gains and welfare gains from self-selection models.

Blumen, I., M. Kogan, & P. J. McCarthy, 1955. The Industrial Mobility of Labor as a Probability Process. Ithaca, New York: Cornell University Press.

Brannas, K., 1983. Measuring the duration of unemployment: A note. *Scottish Journal of Political Economy* 30, 2: 175–180.

Breslow, N., 1974. Covariance analysis of censored survival data. *Biometrics* 30: 89–99.

Broom, D., 1982. A two-stage model of shopping behaviour calibrated on diary data. Paper presented at the annual conference, Regional Science Association (British Section), September 1–3.

Buckley, J., & I. James, 1979. Linear regression with censored data. *Biometrika* 66, 3: 429–436.

Burdett, K., 1978. A theory of employee job search and quit rates. *The American Economic Review* 68, 1: 212–220.

Burdett, K., & D. T. Mortensen, 1978. Labor supply under uncertainty. In Research in Labor Economics, vol. 2, ed. R. G. Ehrenberg. Greenwich, Conn.: JAI Press.

Burdett, K., & J. Ondrich, 1985. How changes in labor demand affect unemployed workers. *Journal of Labor Economics* 3, 1: 1–10.

Burdett, K., N. M. Kiefer, D. T. Mortensen, & G. R. Neumann, 1984. Earnings, unemployment, and the allocation of time over time. *Review of Economic Studies* 51, 4: 559–578.

Burdett, K., & B. Hool, 1983. Layoffs, wages and unemployment insurance. *Journal of Public Economics* 21, 3: 325–357.

Carlson, J. A., & M. W. Horrigan, 1983. Measures of unemployment duration as guides to research and policy: Comment. *The American Economic Review* 73, 5: 1143–1150.

Chamberlain, G., 1980. Comment on Lancaster and Nickell. *Journal of the Royal Statistical Society* A, 144: 160.

Chamberlain, G., 1985. Heterogeneity, omitted variable bias, and duration dependence. in *Longitudinal Analysis of Labor Market Data*, ed. J. J. Heckman & B. Singer. Cambridge: Cambridge University Press.

Chesher, A. D., 1984. Testing for neglected heterogeneity. *Econometrica* 52, 4: 865–872.

Chesher, A. D., & T. Lancaster, 1983. The estimation of models of labour market behaviour. *Review of Economic Studies* 50: 609–624.

Chesher, A. D., T. Lancaster, & M. Irish, 1985. On detecting the failure of distributional assumptions. *Annales de l'INSEE* 59/60: 7–45.

Chesher, A. D., & R. Spady, 1988. Asymptotic expansions of the information matrix test statistic. Discussion Paper 88/206, University of Bristol.

Clark, K. B., & L. H. Summers, 1978. Labor force transitions and unemployment. NBER Working Paper Series No. 277.

Clark, K. B., & L. H. Summers, 1979. Labor market dynamics and unemployment: A reconsideration. *Brookings Papers on Economic Activity* 1: 13–72.

Clark, K. B., & L. H. Summers, 1981. Unemployment insurance and labor market transitions. In *Workers, Jobs and Inflation*, ed. M. N. Bailey. Chicago: University of Chicago Press.

Clayton, D. G., 1983. Fitting a general family of failure time distributions using GLIM. *Applied Statistics* 32, 2: 102–109.

Clayton, D. G., & J. Cuzick, 1985. Multivariate generalisations of the proportional hazards model (with discussion). *Journal of the Royal Statistical Society* A: 82–108.

Cline, H., 1980. To quit or not to quit: Reservation values, job offers, and the costs of mobility. Chapter of Ph.D. dissertation, University of Rochester.

Coppock, D. S., 1981. Multiple spell data and the duration of unemployment: What can we learn? University of Chicago.

Cox, D. R., 1961. Tests of separate families of hypotheses. *Proceedings of the 4th Berkeley Symposium on Probability and Statistics* 1, 105–123.

Cox, D. R., 1962. *Renewal Theory*. London: Methuen.

Cox, D. R., 1972. Regression models and life tables (with discussion). *Journal of the Royal Statistical Society* B, 34: 187–220.

Cox, D. R., 1975. Partial likelihood. *Biometrika* 62, 2: 269–276.

Cox, D. R., 1983. Some remarks on overdispersion. *Biometrika* 70, 1: 269–274.

Cox, D. R., & D. V. Hinkley, 1974. *Theoretical Statistics*. London: Chapman & Hall.

Cox, D. R., & H. D. Miller, 1965. *The Theory of Stochastic Processes*. London: Methuen.

Cox, D. R., & D. Oakes, 1984. *Analysis of Survival Data*. London: Chapman & Hall.

Cox, D. R., & E. J. Snell, 1968. A general definition of residuals (with discussion). *Journal of the Royal Statistical Society* B, 30: 248–275.

Cox, D. R., & E. J. Snell, 1971. On test statistics calculated from residuals. *Biometrika* 58, 3: 589–594.

Creedy, J., 1981. *The Economics of Unemployment in Britain.* London: Butterworths.

Crowley, J., & M. Hu, 1977. Covariance analysis of heart transplant survival data. *Journal of the American Statistical Association* 72: 27–36.

Dagsvik, J. K., & R. Aaberge, 1985. An econometric framework for analyzing the effect of changes in observable and unobservable characteristics on the flows into and out of employment. Oslo: Central Bureau of Statistics.

Daniel, W. W., 1974. *A National Survey of the Unemployed*. London: PEP.

Davies, R., & R. Crouchley, 1985. Gender effects in voting behaviour. In *Sequence Analysis, Surrey Conferences on Sociological Theory and Method 2*. ed. M. Proctor & P. Abell. Brookfield, Vt.: Gower.

David, H. A., & M. L. Moeschberger, 1978. *The Theory of Competing Risks* London: Griffin.

David, H. A., 1970. *Order Statistics*. New York: Wiley.

Dempster, A. P., N. M. Laird, & D. B. Rubin, 1977. Maximum likelihood from incomplete data via the EM algorithm (with discussion). *Journal of the Royal Statistical Society* B, 39: 1–38.

De Stavola, B. L., 1985. Multi-state Markov processes with incomplete information. Ph.D. dissertation, Imperial College, London.

De Stavola, B. L., 1986. Sampling designs for short panel data. *Econometrica* 54: 415–424.

Devine, T. J., & N. M. Kiefer, 1989. Empirical labor economics in the search framework. Cornell University.

Diamond, P. A., & J. A. Hausman, 1982. Individual retirement and savings behavior. NBER–SSRC Conference on Microdata and Public Economics, Oxford.

Dubey, S. D., 1965. A compound Weibull distribution. Presented to the Central Regional Meeting of the Institute of Mathematical Statistics, Lincoln, Nebraska.

Efron, B., 1979. Bootstrap methods: Another look at the jackknife. The 1977 Rietz Lecture. *The Annals of Statistics* 7: 1–26.

Elbers, C., & G. Ridder, 1982. True and spurious duration dependence: The identifiability of the proportional hazard model. *Review of Economic Studies* 49, 3: 403–410.

Engle, R. F., D. F. Hendry, & J-F. Richard, 1983. Exogeneity. *Econometrica* 51: 277–304.

Espenshade, T. J., 1986. Markov chain models of marital event histories. In *Current Perspectives on Aging and the Life Cycle*, vol. 2, ed. Z. Blau. Greenwich, Conn.: JAI Press, 73–106.

Farber, H. S., 1980. Are quits and firings actually different events? A competing risk model of job duration. Massachusetts Institute of Technology.

Farewell, V. T., & D. R. Cox, 1979. A note on multiple time scales in life testing. *Applied Statistics* 28, 1: 73–75.

Feldstein, M., & J. Poterba, 1982. Unemployment insurance and reservation wages. NBER–SSRC Conference on Microdata and Public Economics, Oxford.

Feller, W., 1966. *An Introduction to Probability Theory*, vol. II. New York: Wiley.

Fenn, P., 1981. Sickness duration, residual disability, and income replacement: An empirical analysis. *The Economic Journal* 91: 158–173.

Fishe, R. P. H., 1982. Unemployment insurance and the reservation wage of the unemployed. *The Review of Economics and Statistics* 64, 1: 12–17.

Flinn, C. J., & J. J. Heckman, 1982(a). New methods for analyzing structural models of labor force dynamics. *Journal of Econometrics* 18: 115–168.

Flinn, C. J., & J. J. Heckman, 1982(b). Models for the analysis of labor force dynamics. In *Advances in Econometrics*, vol. 1, ed. R. Bassmann & G. Rhodes. Greenwich, Conn.: JAI Press, 35–95.

Flinn, C. J., & J. J. Heckman, 1983. The likelihood function for the multi-state multiepisode model. In Models for the Analysis of Labor Force Dynamics, *Advances in Econometrics*, vol. 3, ed. R. Bassmann & G. Rhodes. Greenwich, Conn.: JAI Press.

Galambos, J., 1978. *The Asymptotic Theory of Extreme Order Statistics*. New York: Wiley.

Gill, R. D., 1980(a). Nonparametric estimation based on censored observations of a Markov renewal process. *Z. Wahrscheinlichkeitstheorie verw* Gebiete, 53: 97–116.

Gill, R. D., 1980(b). *Censoring and Stochastic Integrals*. Mathematical Centre Tracts 124, Amsterdam: Mathematical Centre.

Gill, R. D., 1981. Testing with replacement and the product limit estimator. *The Annals of Statistics* 9, 4: 853–860.

Gill, R. D., 1984. Understanding Cox's regression model: A martingale approach. *Journal of the American Statistical Association* 79: 441–447.

Ginsberg, R. B., 1971. Semi-Markov processes and mobility. *Journal of Mathematical Sociology* 1: 233–262.

Ginsberg, R. B., 1972. Critique of probabilistic models: Application of the semi-Markov model to migration. *Journal of Mathematical Sociology* 2: 63–82.

Gotz, G. A., & J. J. McCall, 1980. Estimation in sequential decisionmaking models. *Economics Letters* 6: 131–136.

Gotz, G. A., & J. J. McCall, 1983. Sequential analysis of the stay/leave decision: U. S. Air Force officers. *Management Science* 29, 3: 335–351.

Granger, C. W. J., 1969. Investigating causal relations by econometric models and cross spectral methods. *Econometrica* 37: 424.

Hasan, A., & S. Gera, 1979. Reservation wages, duration of job search and labour markets. Economic Council of Canada, Discussion Paper No. 138.

Hasan, A., & P. de Broucker, 1982. Duration and concentration of unemployment. *Canadian Journal of Economics* 15, 4: 735–756.

Hausman, J. A., & W. E. Taylor, 1981. Panel data and unobservable individual effects. *Econometrica* 49, 6: 1377–1398.

Hazelrig, J. B., M. E. Turner, & E. H. Blackstone, 1982. Parametric survival analysis combining longitudinal and cross sectional censored and interval censored data with concomitant information. *Biometrics* 38: 1–15.

Heckman, J. J., 1981. Heterogeneity and state dependence. In *Studies in Labor Markets*, ed. S. Rosen, Chicago: University of Chicago Press, 91–139.

Heckman, J. J., 1982. The structural analysis of longitudinal data. In *Advances in Econometrics*, ed. Werner Hildenbrand. Cambridge: Cambridge University Press.

Heckman, J. J., & G. J. Borjas, 1980. Does unemployment cause future unemployment? Definitions, questions and answers from a continuous time model of heterogeneity and state dependence. *Economica* 47: 247–283.

Heckman, J. J., & T. E. Macurdy, 1981. New methods for estimating labor supply functions: A survey. *Research in Labor Economics* 4: 65–102.

Heckman, J. J., & B. Singer, 1982(a). Population heterogeneity in demographic models. In *Multidimensional Mathematical Demography*, ed. K. C. Land & A. Rogers. New York: Academic Press, 567–599.

Heckman, J. J., & B. Singer, 1982(b). The identification problem in econometric models for duration data. In *Advances in Econometrics*, ed. W. Hildenbrand. Cambridge: Cambridge University Press, 39–77.

Heckman, J. J., & B. Singer, 1984(a). Econometric duration analysis. *Journal of Econometrics* 24: 63–132.

Heckman, J. J., & B. Singer, 1984(b). The identifiability of the proportional hazard model. *Review of Economic Studies* 51: 231–241.

Heckman, J. J., & B. Singer, 1984(c). A method for minimising the impact of distributional assumptions in econometric models for duration data. *Econometrica* 52, 2: 271–320.

Heckman, J. J., & B. Singer, 1985. Longitudinal analysis of labor market data. In *Econometric Society Monograph 10*. Cambridge: Cambridge University Press.

Heckman, J. J., & B. E. Honoré, 1989. The identifiability of the competing risks model. *Biometrika* 76, 2: 325–330.

Hoem, J. M., 1969. Purged and partial Markov chains. *Skandinaviska Aktuariet Tidskrift*, 147–155.

Hoem, J. M., 1972. Inhomogeneous semi-Markov processes, select actuarial tables, and duration dependence in demography. In *Population Dynamics*, ed. T. N. E. Greville. New York: Academic Press, 251–296.

Hoem, J. M., & U. Funck Jensen, 1982. Multistate life table methodology: A probabilistic critique. In K. Land & A. Rogers, *Multidimensional Mathematical Demography*. New York: Academic Press, 155–264.

Holzer, H. J., 1986. Reservation Wages and their labor market effects for black and white male youth. *Journal of Human Resources* 21: 157–177.

Horowitz J. L., 1987. Semiparametric *M* estimation of censored linear regression models. Mimeo, University of Iowa.

Hougaard, P., 1984. Life table methods for heterogeneous populations: Distributions describing the heterogeneity. *Biometrika* 71, 1: 75–83.

Hougaard, P., 1985. Contribution to the discussion of D. Clayton and J. Cuzick: Multivariate generalizations of the proportional hazards model. *Journal of the Royal Statistical Society*, A, 148.

Hougaard, P., 1986(a). A class of multivariate failure time distributions. *Biometrika* 73, 3: 671–8.

Hougaard, P., 1986(b). Survival models for heterogeneous populations derived from stable distributions. *Biometrika* 73: 387–396.

Hougaard, P., 1987. Modelling multivariate survival. *Scandinavian Statistical Journal* 14: 291–304.

Hui, W. T., & P. K. Trivedi, 1986. Duration dependence, targeted employment subsidies and unemployment benefits. *Journal of Public Economics* 31: 105–129.

Johansen, S., 1978. The product limit estimator as maximum likelihood estimator. *Scandinavian Journal of Statistics* 5: 195–199.

Johnson, W. R., 1978. A theory of job shopping. *Quarterly Journal of Economics* 92: 261–277.

Jones, S. R. G., 1988. The relationship between unemployment spells and reservation wages as a test of search theory. *Quarterly Journal of Economics* 103: 741–765.

Jones, S. R. G., 1989. Reservation wages and the cost of unemployment. *Economica* 56: 401–421.

Jorgensen, B., 1982. *Statistical properties of the generalised inverse gaussian distribution.* Berlin: Springer-Verlag.

Jovanovic, B., 1979. Job matching and the theory of turnover. *Journal of Political Economy* 87, 5: 972–990.

Jovanovic, B., 1984. Wages and turnover: A parametrization of the job matching model. In *Studies in Labor Market Dynamics*, ed. G. R. Neumann & N. C. Westergaard-Nielsen. Berlin: Springer-Verlag.

Kalbfleisch, J. D., & R. L. Prentice, 1980. *The Statistical Analysis of Failure Time Data.* New York: Wiley.

Kalbfleisch, J. D., & R. L. Prentice, 1973. Marginal likelihoods based on Cox's regression and life model. *Biometrika* 60, 2: 267–278.

Kaplan, E. L., & P. Meier, 1958. Nonparametric estimation from incomplete observations. *Journal of the American Statistical Association* 53: 457–481.

Karlin, S., 1962. Stochastic models and optimal policy for selling an asset. In *Studies in Applied Probability and Management Sciences*, ed. K. J. Arrow, S. Karlin, & H. Scarf. Stanford, Calif.: Stanford University Press, 148–158.

Karlin, S., & H. Taylor, 1975. *A First Course in Stochastic Processes*, 2nd ed. New York: Academic Press.

Karr, A. F., 1986. *Point Processes and their Statistical Inference.* New York: Marcel Dekker.

Kasper, H., 1967. The asking price of labor and the duration of unemployment. *The Review of Economics and Statistics* 49: 165–172.

Katz, A., & J. Ochs, 1982. Is the observed relation between length of unemployment and unemployment benefits consistent with search theories? University of Pittsburgh, Pa.

Kay, J. A., C. N. Morris, & N. A. Warren, 1980. Tax, benefits and the incentive to seek work. *Fiscal Studies* 1: 8–25.

Kay, R., 1982. The analysis of transition times in multistate stochastic processes using proportional hazard regression models. *Communications in Statistical Theory & Methods* 11, 15: 1743–1756.

Kay, R., 1983. Multistate survival analysis: An application in breast cancer. Meth. Inform. Med.

Kay, R., 1986. A Markov model for analysing cancer markers and disease states in survival studies. *Biometrics* 42: 855–865.

Kennan, J., & G. R. Neumann, 1987. Why does the information matrix test reject too often? Mimeo, University of Iowa.

Kiefer, J., & J. Wolfowitz, 1956. Consistency of the maximum likelihood estimator in the presence of infinitely many incidental parameters. *Annals of Mathematical Statistics* 27: 887–906.

Kiefer, N. M., 1985. Specification diagnostics based on Laguerre alternatives in econometric models of duration. *Journal of Econometrics* 28: 135–154.

Kiefer, N. M., & G. R. Neumann, 1979. An empirical job search model with a test of the constant reservation wage hypothesis. *Journal of Political Economy* 87: 89–107.

Kiefer, N. M., & G. R. Neumann, 1981. Individual effects in a nonlinear model: Explicit treatment of heterogeneity in the empirical job-search model. *Econometrica* 49: 965–980.

Kiefer, N. M., & G. Skoog, 1984. Local asymptotic specification error analysis. *Econometrica* 52, 4: 873–885.

Kooreman, P., & G. Ridder, 1983. The effects of age and unemployment percentage on the duration of unemployment. *European Economic Review* 20: 41–57.

Koul, H., V. Susarla, & J. Van Ryzin, 1981. Regression analysis with randomly right censored data. *The Annals of Statistics* 9: 1276–1288.

Lagakos, S. W., 1979. General right censoring and its impact on the analysis of survival data. *Biometrics* 35: 139–156.

Lagakos, S. W., 1981. The graphical evaluation of explanatory variables in proportional hazard regression models. *Biometrika* 68: 93–8.

Laird, N., 1978. Nonparametric maximum likelihood estimation of a mixing distribution. *Journal of the American Statistical Association* 73: 805–811.

Laird, N., N. Lange, & D. Stram, 1987. Maximum likelihood computation with repeated measures: Application of the EM algorithm. *Journal of the American Statistical Association* 82: 97–105.

Lancaster, T., 1972. A stochastic model for the duration of a strike. *Journal of the Royal Statistical Society* A 135, 2: 257–271.

Lancaster, T., 1973. An approach to the construction of stochastic models

342   Bibliography

for the duration of disputes. In *Stochastic Models in Sociology*, A Sociological Review Monograph, 97–102.

Lancaster, T., 1976. Redundancy, unemployment and manpower policy: A comment. *The Economic Journal* 86: 335–338.

Lancaster, T., 1978. Contribution to discussion. *Journal of the Royal Statistical Society* B, 40, 3.

Lancaster, T., 1979. Econometric methods for the duration of unemployment. *Econometrica* 47, 4: 939–956.

Lancaster, T., 1983. Generalised residuals and heterogeneous duration models: The exponential case. *Bulletin of Economic Research* 35, 2: 71–85.

Lancaster, T., 1984. The covariance matrix of the information matrix test. *Econometrica* 52, 4: 1051–1053.

Lancaster, T., 1985(a). Simultaneous equations models in applied search theory. *Journal of Econometrics* 28: 155–169.

Lancaster, T., 1985(b). Some remarks on wage and duration econometrics. In *Unemployment, Search and Labour Supply*, ed. R. Blundell & I. Walker. Cambridge: Cambridge University Press.

Lancaster, T., 1985(c). Generalised residuals and heterogeneous duration models – with applications to the Weibull model. *Journal of Econometrics* 28: 113–126.

Lancaster, T., & A. D. Chesher, 1980. Computation of search duration probabilities and the integral of the normal distribution function. *Economics Letters* 4: 319–321.

Lancaster, T., & A. D. Chesher, 1981. Stock and flow sampling. *Economics Letters* 8: 63–65.

Lancaster, T., & A. D. Chesher, 1984. Simultaneous equations with endogenous hazards. In *Studies in Labour Market Dynamics*, ed. G. R. Neumann & N. Westergaard-Nielsen. Berlin: Springer-Verlag.

Lancaster, T., & A. D. Chesher, 1983. An econometric analysis of reservation wages. *Econometrica* 51, 6: 1661–1676.

Lancaster, T., & A. D. Chesher, 1985(a). Residual analysis for censored duration data. *Economics Letters*, 12: 723–725.

Lancaster, T., & A. D. Chesher, 1985(b). Residuals, tests and plots with a job matching application. *Annales de L'INSEE* 59/60: 47–70.

Lancaster, T., & G. W. Imbens, 1986. Log-linear transition intensities, Hull University.

Lancaster, T., G. W. Imbens, & P. Dolton, 1987. Job matching and job tenure. In *The Practice of Econometrics: Studies on Demand, Forecasting, Money and Income*. ed. R. D. H. Heijmans & H. Neudecker. Dordrecht: Martinus Nijhoff.

Lancaster, T., & S. Nickell, 1980. The analysis of reemployment probabilities for the unemployed. *Journal of the Royal Statistical Society* A, 143, 2: 141–165.

Lindsay, B. G., 1981. Properties of the maximum likelihood estimator of a mixing distribution. In *Statistical Distributions in Scientific Work*, vol. 5, ed. G. Taillie et al. Hiungham, Mass.: Kluwer Academic Publishers, 95–109.

Lindsay, B. G., 1983(a). The geometry of mixture likelihoods: A general theory. *Annals of Statistics* 11, 1: 86–94.

Lindsay, B. G., 1983(b). The geometry of mixture likelihoods, part II: The exponential family. *Annals of Statistics* 11, 3: 783–792.

Lindsay, B. G., 1986. Moment matrices: Applications in mixtures. The Pennsylvania State University, Department of Statistics.

Lippman, S. A., & J. J. McCall, 1976. The economics of job search: A survey. *Economic Inquiry* 14: 155–367.

Lippman, S. A., & J. J. McCall, 1980. Search unemployment: Mismatches, layoffs, and unemployment insurance. *Scandinavian Journal of Economics* 88: 253–272.

Luckett, J. P., 1979. A communication: Estimating unemployment duration. *Brookings Papers on Economic Activity* 2: 477–479.

Lynch, L. M., 1983. Job search and youth unemployment. *Oxford Economic Papers* 35, 2: 271–282.

Lynch, L. M., 1985. State dependence in youth unemployment: A lost generation? *Journal of Econometrics* 28: 71–84.

Lynch, L. M., 1986. The youth labor market in the 80's: Determinants of re-employment probabilities for young men and women. National Bureau of Economic Research Working Paper No. 2021.

MacKay, D. I., & G. L. Reid, 1972. Redundancy, unemployment and manpower policy. *The Economic Journal* 82: 1256–1272.

McElroy, M. B., 1980. Unemployment, employment and temporary layoff: A three-state job search model. University of Chicago Economics Research Center/NORC Discussion Paper No. 80–7.

Manski, C. F., & S. K. Lerman, 1977. The estimation of choice probabilities from choice based samples. *Econometrica* 45: 1997–1988.

Mayer, T. F., 1968. Birth and death process models of social mobility. Working Paper, University of Michigan Mathematical Sociology Program.

Mayer, T. F., 1968. Multi-class Markov models and the rank criterion. University of Michigan Working Paper.

Meyer, B. D., 1986. Semi-parametric estimation of hazard models. Department of Economics, MIT.

Miller, R. G., Jr., 1981. *Survival Analysis*. New York: Wiley.

Miller, R. G., & J. Halpern, 1982. Regression with censored data. *Biometrika* 69: 521–531.

Moffitt, R., 1985. Unemployment insurance and the distribution of unemployment spells. *Journal of Econometrics* 28: 85–101.

Montgomery, M. R., 1988. A dynamic model of contraceptive choice. Mimeo, Department of Economics, Princeton University.

Moore, E. H., & R. Pyke, 1968. Estimation of the transition distributions of a Markov renewal process. *Annals of the Institute of Statistics and Mathematics* 20: 411–428.

Mortensen, D. T., 1976. Job search, the duration of unemployment, and the Phillips Curve. *The American Economic Review* 66: 847–862.

Mortensen, D. T., 1978. Specific capital and labor turnover. *The Bell Journal of Economics* 9: 572–586.

Mortensen, D. T., 1984. Job search and labor market analysis. The Center for Mathematical Studies in Economics and Management Science, Northwestern University, Discussion Paper No. 594.

Mortensen, D. T., & G. R. Neumann, 1984. Choice or chance? A structural interpretation of individual labor market histories. In *Studies in Labor Market Dynamics*, ed. G. R. Neumann & N. C. Westergaard-Nielsen. Berlin: Springer-Verlag.

Narendranathan, W., S. Nickell, & J. Stern, 1985. Unemployment benefits revisited. *Economic Journal* 95: 307–329.

Narendranathan, W., & S. Nickell, 1985. Modelling the process of job search. *Journal of Econometrics* 28: 29–49.

Neumann, G. R., & N. C. Westergaard-Nielsen, 1984. *Studies in Labor Market Dynamics*. Berlin: Springer-Verlag.

Newman, J. L., & C. E. McCulloch, 1985. A hazard rate approach to the timing of births. *Econometrica* 52, 4: 939–961.

Nickell, S., 1979. Estimating the probability of leaving unemployment. *Econometrica* 47: 1249–1266.

Oakes, D., 1981. Survival times: Aspects of partial likelihood. *International Statistical Review* 49: 235–264.

Olsen, J., & K. I. Wolpin, 1983. The impact of exogenous child mortality on fertility: A waiting time regression model with dynamic regressors. *Econometrica* 51, 3: 731–750.

Ondrich, J. I., 1985. The initial conditions problem in work history data. *The Review of Economics and Statistics* 67, 3: 411–421.

Orme, C., 1987. The small sample performance of the information matrix test statistic. Mimeo, Department of Economics, University of Nottingham.

Pakes, A., 1986. Patents as options: Some estimates of the value of holding European patent stocks. *Econometrica* 54, 4: 755–784.

Parsons, D. O., 1972. Specific human capital: An application to quit rates and layoff rates. *Journal of Political Economy* 80, 6: 1121–1143.

Parsons, D. O., 1973. Quit rates over time: A search and information approach. *The American Economic Review* 63, 3: 390–401.

Pedersen, P. J., & N. C. Westergaard-Nielsen, 1984. A longitudinal study of unemployment: History dependence and insurance effects. Studies in Labor Market Dynamics, Aarhus, Working Paper 84-4.

Peterson, T., 1986. Simultaneous equations models for analysis of duration data. Mimeo, Department of Sociology, Harvard University.

Pickles, A. R., 1983. The analysis of residence histories and other longitudinal panel data. *Regional Science and Urban Economics* 13: 271–285.

Pickles, A. R., R. Davies, & R. Crouchley, 1985. Understanding life histories and recurrent choice: A framework for analysis. In *Sequence Analysis, Surrey Conferences on Sociological Theory and Method 2*, ed. M. Proctor & P. Abell. Brookfield, Vt.: Gower.

Pierce, D. A., 1982. The asymptotic effect of substituting estimators for parameters in certain types of statistics. *The Annals of Statistics* 10, 2: 475–478.

Prentice, R. L., 1975. Discrimination among some parametric models. *Biometrika* 62, 3: 607–614.

Prentice, R. L., 1978. Linear rank tests and right censored data. *Biometrika* 65, 1: 167–179.

Prentice, R. L., 1979. Hazard rate models with covariates. *Biometrics* 35: 25–39.

Prentice, R. L., & N. E. Breslow, 1978. Retrospective studies and failure time models. *Biometrika* 65, 1: 153–158.

Prentice, R. L., & L. A. Gloeckler, 1978. Regression analysis of grouped survival data with application to breast cancer data. *Biometrics* 34: 57–67.

Pyke, R., 1961. Markov renewal processes: Definitions and preliminary properties. *Annals of Mathematical Statistics* 32: 1231–1242.

Pyke, R., 1961. Markov renewal processes with finitely many states. *Annals of Mathematical Statistics* 32: 1243–1259.

Rao, M. M., 1966. Inference in stochastic processes, II. *Z. Wahrscheinlichkeitstheorie verw. Geb.* 5: 317–335.

Ridder, G., 1987. Life cycle patterns in labor market experience. Ph.D. dissertation, University of Amsterdam.

Ridder, G., & J. W. Velthuijsen, 1982. The analysis of transitions and durations, with an application to a sample of Dutch schoolleavers. University of Amsterdam, Faculty of Actuarial Science and Econometrics A & E Note N1/82.

Ridder, G., 1984. An event history approach to the evaluation of training, recruitment and employment programs. University of Amsterdam, Faculty of Actuarial Science and Econometrics A & E Report 14/84.

Ridder, G., 1984. The distribution of single spell duration data. In *Studies in Labor Market Dynamics*, ed. G. R. Neumann & N. C. Westergaard-Nielsen. Berlin: Springer-Verlag.

Ridder, G., 1986. Empirical Markov models for labor market transitions. University of Amsterdam.

Ridder, G., & W. Verbakel, 1983. On the estimation of the proportional hazard model in the presence of heterogeneity. University of Amsterdam, Faculty of Actuarial Science and Econometrics, A & E Report 22/83.

Ridder, G., 1988. On generalized accelerated failure time models. Center for Analytic Economics Working Paper CAE 88–26, Cornell University. (Forthcoming in the Review of Economic Studies, 1990.)

Ross, S. M., 1983. *Stochastic Processes*. New York: Wiley.

Rothschild, M., 1974. Searching for the lowest price when the distribution of prices is unknown. *Journal of Political Economy* 82, 4: 689–709.

Rust, J., 1987. Optimal replacement of GMC bus engines: An empirical model of Harold Zurcher. *Econometrica* 55: 999–1033.

Salant, S. W., 1977. Search theory and duration data: A theory of sorts. *Quarterly Journal of Economics* 91: 39–57.

Sattinger, M., 1983. Distribution of the time spent in one state of a two-state continuous time Markov process. University of Aarhus.

Sheps, M., & J. Menken, 1973. *Mathematical Models of Conception and Birth*. Chicago: University of Chicago Press.

Silvey, S. D., 1980. *Optimal Design*. London: Chapman & Hall.

Simar, L., 1976. Maximum likelihood estimation of a compound Poisson process. *The Annals of Statistics* 4, 6: 1200–1209.

Singer, B., & S. Spilerman, 1976. Some methodological issues in the analysis of longitudinal surveys. *Annals of Economic and Social Measurement* 5/4: 447–473.

Spilerman, S., 1972. Extensions of the Mover–Stayer model. *American Journal of Sociology* 78, 3: 599–626.

Titterington, D. M., A. F. M. Smith, & V. E. Makov, 1986. *Statistical Analysis of Finite Mixture Distributions*. New York: Wiley.

Tooze, M. J., & P. G. Chapman, 1982. The displacement effect: The impact of redundancies on unemployment duration. University of Dundee.

Trivedi, P. K., & G. M. Baker, 1982. Estimation of the average length of an unemployment spell from labour force experience data. Australian National University.

Trivedi, P. K., & G. M. Baker, 1983. Unemployment in Australia: Duration and recurrent spells. *The Economic Record* 59: 132–147.

Trivedi, P. K., & J. N. Alexander, 1989. Reemployment probability and multiple unemployment spells: A partial likelihood approach. *Journal of Business and Economic Statistics* 7, 3: 395–402.

Trivedi, P. K., & W. T. Hui, 1987. An empirical study of long-term unemployment in Australia. *Journal of Labor Economics* 5, 1: 20–42.

Trussell, J., & T. Richards, 1985. Correcting for unmeasured heterogeneity in hazard models: An application of the Heckman–Singer strategy to demographic data. *Sociological Methodology* 242–276.

Tsiatis, A., 1978. A nonidentifiability aspect of the problem of competing risks. *Proceedings of the National Academy of Sciences* 72: 20–22.

Tsiatis, A., 1981. A large sample study of Cox's regression model. *Annals of Statistics* 9: 93–108.

Tuma, N. B., 1976. Rewards, resources, and the rate of mobility: A nonstationary multivariate stochastic model. *American Sociological Review* 41: 338–360.

Tuma, N. B., M. T. Hannan, & L. P. Groeneveld, 1979. Dynamic analysis of event histories. *American Journal of Sociology* 84, 4: 820–853.

van der Berg, G., 1987. Nonstationarity in job search theory. Tilburg University Discussion Paper 241.

Vaupel, J. W., K. G. Manton, & E. Stallard, 1979. The impact of heterogeneity in individual frailty on the dynamics of mortality. *Demography* 16: 439–454.

Warner, J. T., J. C. Poindexter, Jr., & R. M. Fearn, 1980. Employer-employee interaction and the duration of unemployment. *The Quarterly Journal of Economics* 94, 2: 211–233.

Weiner, S. E., 1984. A survival analysis of adult male black/white labor market flows. In *Studies in Labor Market Dynamics*, ed. G. R. Neumann & N. C. Westergaard-Nielsen. Berlin: Springer-Verlag.

Westergaard-Nielsen, N. C., 1981. Pre and post graduation search, Universitets Okonomiske Institut, Kobenhavn, Cykelafdelingen Memo No. 82.

Westergaard-Nielsen, N. C. 1983. Estimation of the reservation wage. Studies in Labor Market Dynamics Working Paper 81–4. University of Aarhus.

Westergaard-Nielsen, N. C. 1983. A study of a professional labor market – introduction and data. Studies in Labor Market Dynamics Working Paper 81–2. University of Aarhus.

White, H., 1982. Maximum likelihood estimation of misspecified models. *Econometrica* 50, 1: 1–24.

Whitmore, G. A., 1983. A regression method for censored inverse-Gaussian data. *The Canadian Journal of Statistics* 11, 4: 305–315.

Whitmore, G. A., 1985. First-passage-time models for duration data – regression structures and competing risks, McGill University, Montreal.

Wolpin, K. I., 1984. An estimable dynamic stochastic model of fertility and child mortality. *Journal of Political Economy* 92: 852–874.

Wolpin, K. I., 1987. Estimating a structural search model: The transition from school to work. *Econometrica* 95: 801–817.

Wu, C. F. J., 1983. On the convergence properties of the EM algorithm. *The Annals of Statistics* 11, 1: 95–103.

Yoon, B. J., 1983. Search theory and the hazard function of leaving unemployment. State University of New York at Binghamton.

Index

absorbing barrier, 120, 125
accepted wage, 126
alternating renewal process, 97
alternating Poisson process, 112, 215
approximate linear regression model, 227
arrival of wage offers, 126
asymptotic distribution theory, 210, 216
asymptotic relative efficiency, 216
atomic likelihood vectors, 283

backward recurrence time, 91, 98, 185
baseline hazard, 149, 304
binary regression model, 269
birth interval, 212
bivariate Normal, 155
Box–Cox hazards, 171
Burr distribution, 68

Carathéodory's theorem, 284
case-control method, 191
censoring, 106
choice based sampling likelihood, 190
competing risks model, 106, 154
completely monotone function, 148, 331
concentrated log likelihood, 175, 223

conditional hazard, 58, 147
conditional likelihood, 238, 276
constant hazard, 14
continuous-time Markov chain, 109, 131
convex hull, 283
cost of search, 124, 132
covariate, 21
cumulant generating function, 20, 328

defective distribution, 9, 139
degenerate limiting distribution, 224
degenerate mixing distribution, 283
digamma function, 327
discount rate, 128
discrete choice, 122, 233
discrete-time hazard, 12
discrete-time model, 127
discrete-time sampling, 215
distribution of the minimum, 79
distribution of the rank and order statistic vectors, 236
doubly stochastic model, 6
duration distribution function, 7
duration of first jobs, 14
duration of search, 127
duration of unemployment, 83, 126
dynamic programming, 123, 128

349